Greenhill Books

1805
Austerlitz

1805
Austerlitz

Napoleon and the
Destruction of the Third Coalition

Robert Goetz

Greenhill Books, London
Stackpole Books, Pennsylvania

1805: Austerlitz

First published in 2005 by
Greenhill Books, Lionel Leventhal Limited, Park House,
1 Russell Gardens, London NW11 9NN
and
Stackpole Books, 5067 Ritter Road,
Mechanicsburg PA 17055, USA

ISBN 1-85367-644-6

Typeset and edited by Donald Sommerville

Original maps by Max Sewell

Printed and bound in the USA by
R. R. Donnelley & Sons

Contents

Illustrations

The following abbreviations are used in the picture credits which appear with the illustrations:

RMN: Réunion des Musées Nationaux, France
T&JB: Tony & James F. Broughton

Maps

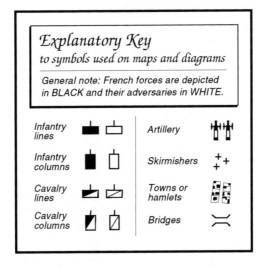

Explanatory Key
to symbols used on maps and diagrams

General note: French forces are depicted
in BLACK and their adversaries in WHITE.

Infantry lines		Artillery	
Infantry columns		Skirmishers	
Cavalry lines		Towns or hamlets	
Cavalry columns		Bridges	

Tables

Introduction

The shadow of the Emperor Napoleon I looms large over the history of the nineteenth century. His influence was so profound that it directly altered the course of European history for the first fifteen years of the century and exercised considerable influence for many decades after his exile. Millions of people fought and died for him—or opposing him. In conquering a continent, he redrew the map of Europe in ways that are, in places, still recognizable today. So great is Napoleon's influence and so great is the romantic appeal of his meteoric rise and equally dramatic fall that it is difficult to view Napoleon in the context of 1801—as simply a gifted general who had seized control of the government of France in a *coup d'état*. At the time some had seen in Napoleon a potential parallel to the British General Monk who might return the Bourbons to the throne of France. Others had seen in him the heir to the French Revolution, a strong leader who embodied the ideals of the Enlightenment, a ruler who had risen by his abilities, not by an accident of birth. But regardless of political views (and dreams), in 1801 Napoleon Bonaparte was the First Consul of France, ruler of the dominant power in Western Europe. Over the next several years, he brought peace and stability to a nation rocked by a decade of political and social turmoil and nearly continual warfare. In doing so he earned the respect and devotion of millions and in 1804 he secured his position in what he intended to be a permanent fashion by placing an imperial crown upon his own head.

The story of the 1805 Campaign and the stunning victory of Austerlitz is the story of the beginning of the Napoleon of history and the Grande Armée of legend. Our view of that period today is distorted by what would come after. The series of wildly successful campaigns in which French armies soundly defeated every army in Europe and marched through Vienna, Berlin and Moscow make it difficult to imagine a time during this period when the preeminence of the French Army was seriously questioned.

From the perspective of 1803, Second Zurich, Marengo and Hohenlinden were the great French victories of recent memory, and only one of those—the narrowest of the three—belonged to Napoleon. French armies had been everywhere victorious by the end of the last war, but they had been challenged and defeated by both Austrians and Russians, most notably at Stockach, First Zurich, Trebbia and Novi, while the talented General Bonaparte had been stopped short at Acre. These French defeats were sufficiently noteworthy that, in 1805, Napoleon would address the questions they had raised in a proclamation to his troops following the Austrian capitulation at Ulm, declaring that the next campaign would determine whether Russian or French infantry was better. The reputation earned by Suvorov's Russians in 1799 was so great that *The Times* of London refused to believe they could have been beaten by the French for several weeks after the first news of Austerlitz arrived.

The campaign of 1805 is rightly viewed as the beginning of "the glory years" of the French Empire, but it is far more helpful for understanding the era to view the campaign as its first great test. In the preceding decade, France had twice emerged victorious from wars but only after the coalitions arrayed against it had fragmented as a result of conflict among the members, leaving Austria alone among the continental powers to face a much larger France. Now France faced a powerful new coalition, one that included what one French officer described as "these famous Russians" as well as the ever-persistent Austrians. The Battle of Austerlitz itself, so often viewed with the benefit of hindsight as a foregone conclusion, in fact represented the ultimate trial for the army that Napoleon had assembled and trained on the shores of the English Channel. Through the course of the campaign and in the decisive French victory at Austerlitz, the forces of Napoleon's new empire humiliated an overconfident coalition, answering with absolute certainty all questions concerning the position of the French in any ranking of the armies of Europe.

My focus throughout this study has been less on the French, who have been dissected, studied and analyzed many times over in the past 200 years, and more on the Russians and Austrians who have received only cursory attention in past accounts of the battle. With this focus, I am certain that there will be some feeling that I have produced "the allied version" of events, and in a sense this is true—and long overdue. But in the process I have made a very conscious effort to examine both sides with equal emphasis, and I am convinced that any perception that this account neglects the French is a reflection of the fact that nearly all histories of this period focus almost exclusively on them, making any more balanced account appear slanted in the opposite direction. In the final analysis, this account remains more French than allied due to the preponderance of accessible material available on the French side—ironically even in some of the German and Russian language sources. It can only be hoped that over the next hundred years more of the mass of archival material in the Kriegsarchiv (Vienna) and the RGVIA (Moscow) relating to the Austerlitz campaign will be studied by other researchers who will be able to expand, clarify and even correct my interpretation of the dramatic events of 2 December 1805.

Notes on Names, Spellings and Ranks

One difficulty in researching events in east central Europe lies in the several names associated with most locations. For events in Moravia, every town and river has a Czech name as well as a German name dating from the days of the Habsburg Empire. Austerlitz is now Slavkov, Brünn is Brno and Olmütz is Olmucz, to name just a few examples. Compounding the challenge is the existence of a wide variety of spellings of each name. In addition, while French and German names are mostly familiar to the English-speaker (and are written in a familiar alphabet), the Austrian Army included Hungarians and Slavs and the Russian Army contributed Russians, Poles and Baltic individuals as well as many officers with German or French names (sometimes recent immigrants, other times Livonians or individuals tracing their line for several generations in Russia). I have tried to be consistent throughout in my spellings of the many people and places, but will admit to being somewhat arbitrary in my selection of the spelling to use at times. For example, I have gone with the translations of the Emperor Francis and Archduke Charles rather than sticking with Kaiser Franz and Erzherzog Carl while with lesser known figures I have retained their German names. In the orders of battle presented in the appendices, I have been more careful to provide correct transliterations of the names of Russian officers, even where the direct transliteration from the Cyrillic deviates from the proper German spelling—as with General Vitgenshtein (Wittgenstein). The Russian and Austrian emperors appear in the Order of Battle as Aleksandr and Franz but are rendered differently in the text, where I have used the more common spellings, which I hope will not cause undue confusion.

It is also worth mentioning that a somewhat peculiar practice in the Russian Army of the time was the numbering of officers with the same last name by seniority. This provided a convenient shorthand used in all official correspondence, and allowed easy differentiation between generals with the same surname—for example, between General-Major Sergei Mikhailovich Kamensky (Kamensky-1) and General-Major Nikolai Mikhailovich Kamensky (Kamensky-2). While the two Kamenskys were brothers, the numbered generals were not always related. While it is probably more common to see the names shown with Roman numerals, I have taken the liberty to switch to Arabic numerals for clarity.

I have not always identified the full ranks of general officers, sometimes simply referring to General So-and-so, and in addition in places have used the abbreviations listed in the table below.

Abbreviations used in the text and approximate equivalent ranks:

French	*Austrian*	*Russian*
Maréchal (Marshal)	Feldmarschall	Field Marshal
—	Feldzeugmeister (FZM)/ General der Kavallerie	General of Infantry (GOI)/ General of Cavalry (GKAV)
Général de Division (GdD)	Feldmarschalleutnant (FML)	General-Lieutenant (GL)
Général de Brigade (GdB)	General-Feldwachmeister (GM)	General-Major (GM)
Colonel	Oberst	Polkovnik (PK)
Lieutenant-Colonel	Oberstleutnant	Podpolkovnik (PPK)
Chef de Bataillon	Major	Maior

Acknowledgments

My personal road to Austerlitz has been a twenty-five-year journey from my first explorations of the French Revolution and Napoleonic era. I am also deeply indebted to many remarkably knowledgeable individuals who have assisted me along the way. Foremost among these are Alexander Mikaberidze, David Hollins and Ian Castle, each of whom contributed materials I otherwise could not access. Steven Smith, Mark Conrad, Geert van Uythoven, Alex Stavropoulos, Digby Smith and Peter Hofschröer have provided invaluable assistance in identifying sources and also provided me with obscure materials from their own collections or other libraries. I am also indebted to the Interlibrary Loan staff of Virginia Tech's Newman Library who have been wonderfully resourceful in fulfilling my requests for obscure texts from libraries across the country.

Beyond the research, I must offer hearty thanks to Max Sewell, who has produced the wonderful maps to accompany the text. In addition, I would like to thank Jonathan North for suggesting this project to me in the first place and encouraging me to accept the challenge, Robert Ouvrard for the excellent battlefield photographs, and James Arnold, Tony and James Broughton and Alexander Mikaberidze for sharing portraits from their personal collections. In addition, I would like to thank Dave Watkins of Greenhill Books who has seen it through to publication and Donald Sommerville for his outstanding editing. I would also like to extend my gratitude to my former professor of French Revolution and Napoleonic studies, the late Thomas Adriance, whose untimely death nearly a decade ago corresponded with a resurgence of my lifelong interest in the Napoleonic period.

The Napoleon Series Discussion Forums (both the original and its offspring) have been instrumental in introducing me to nearly all of the individuals to whom I am indebted and have also provided a place to ask research questions and to gain a broader knowledge of the period from enthusiasts around the world. I also owe thanks to four gentlemen whom I have never met, but who are responsible for sparking my interest in this particular period of history and providing the essential background I needed to delve deeper—Christopher Duffy, most influential of all, and also David Chandler, John Elting, and Gunther Rothenberg. Two of these gentlemen have sadly passed away in just this past year and a third only recently.

Without their talents and efforts, the present work would never have come to be written.

Most of all, I am especially indebted to Helene Shine Goetz who has tirelessly assisted in everything from translation to editing and without whom none of this would be possible. She has encouraged me, pushed me, nagged me and otherwise kept me on-task when my enthusiasm lagged, and picked up the slack at home to give me time to write. I must also thank my children, Stephanie and Bobby, whose patience with dad's time spent writing and buoyant enthusiasm for the project have helped carry me through.

1805
Austerlitz

Napoleon and the
Destruction of the Third Coalition

Chapter 1

Formation of the Third Coalition and the Opening Phase of the War

Soldiers, the war of the third coalition has started. The Austrian Army has crossed the Inn, violated the treaties, attacked and chased our ally from its capital . . . Even you had to rush in forced marches to the defence of our frontiers.

But already you have crossed the Rhine: we will not stop until we have ensured the independence of the Germanic corps, assisted our allies, and confounded the pride of the unjust aggressors.

We will never make peace without guarantee: our generosity will never again deceive our politics.

Soldiers, your Emperor is in your midst. You are only the advance guard of the great People; if it is necessary, all of it will rise up on hearing my voice to confound and dissolve this new league woven by the hatred and the gold of England.

But, soldiers, we have forced marches to do, some fatigues and privations of all kinds to endure; no matter what obstacles oppose us, we will vanquish them, and we will not rest until we have planted our eagles on the territory of the enemy.[*]

With these stirring words, Napoleon announced the start of a new war to the newly formed Grande Armée, the largest single army that had ever been fielded by France. Only six weeks earlier the Grande Armée had not even existed. From separate camps, stretching from Brest to Hanover, nearly 200,000 men had been brought together under Napoleon's personal command. Over 165,000 of them had already crossed the Rhine on their way to engage the Austrian Army in Bavaria by the time Napoleon issued his proclamation from his headquarters at Strasbourg on 1 October. The War of the Third Coalition, as Napoleon named it, would last barely three months during which time the Grande Armée would astonish the world with an unprecedented string of victories culminating in the Battle of Austerlitz.

[*] J. David Markham, *Imperial Glory: The Bulletins of Napoleon's Grande Armée, 1805–1814* (London: Greenhill Books, 2003), pp. 9–10.

The Failure of the Peace of Amiens

The outbreak of war in 1805 was the culmination of three years of escalating tensions between France and the other European powers since the signing of the Treaty of Amiens (25 March 1802) had brought peace to Europe. France and Great Britain had been at war continuously for nearly a decade from February 1793 until the signing of the Treaty of Amiens. While the various continental powers had made peace with France at various times, either willingly or unwillingly, the conclusion of the treaty meant that all of Europe was finally at peace. The terms of the treaty were remarkably generous for France. France would retain all of its continental gains, including the former Austrian Netherlands (Belgium), the Rhineland, Nice and Savoy. France's only concessions would be to withdraw its forces from the three satellite republics (the Batavian, Helvetic and Italian republics) and the Neapolitan ports, effectively a withdrawal of French troops from foreign soil. Britain, on the other hand, would relinquish nearly all of its territorial gains, including Malta, Minorca, Elba, and the French Antilles and withdraw all forces from Egypt, which had just been retaken from the French. Only Trinidad (formerly Spanish) and Ceylon (formerly Dutch) would be retained. While Britain stopped short of meeting Napoleon's demand for recognition of the three French satellite republics, the British also failed to demand any indemnities for the deposed Prince of Orange or compensation for the King of Sardinia, dispossessed of his mainland possessions. In short, Napoleon had secured full acceptance of the expansion of France to the Rhine and of France's dominant position in northern Italy and had regained French colonial territories, while the British had fully relinquished their enhanced influence in the Mediterranean in exchange for Trinidad and Ceylon.

In both Britain and France, a war-weary public joyously welcomed the Treaty of Amiens. Beyond the obvious relief from military obligations, peace promised to be good for business on both sides of the Channel. While at war with Britain, France had closed its own ports, as well as the ports of its satellite states and occupied territories, to British goods. With peace restored, French merchant shipping could resume overseas trade while in Britain there was a general expectation that peace would open new markets in France, Italy and the Low Countries to British merchants. British trade had profited from British domination of the seas during the wars of the previous decade, but it was hoped that the restoration of continental trade would more than compensate for some loss of Atlantic and Mediterranean business to French shipping. Over the next twelve months, however, the illusion of peace would be shattered as both sides sought to turn the treaty to their own advantage.

In the end, Britain quickly became frustrated at Napoleon's refusal to open French-controlled ports to British trade and in the autumn of 1802 grew concerned over the strengthening of French control over Italy with the French annexation of Elba (August), Piedmont (September) and Parma (October). In addition, reports of the intelligence activities of Colonel Sebastiani, travelling to Egypt, Syria and Corfu, produced concerns of renewed French designs for conquest in the eastern Mediterranean. These concerns reached a peak when excerpts from Sebastiani's report were published in the French newspaper *Le Moniteur*, including the statement that "six thousand men would suffice to reconquer Egypt."* News that General Decaen had been sent to India in March 1803 raised fears that Napoleon intended to stir up opposition to Britain there. Another French agent was reported to be making contacts in Muscat. In the north, Napoleon refused to withdraw French forces from the Batavian Republic until the British withdrew from Malta, despite repeated demands of the Dutch leader Rutger Schimmelpenninck that Napoleon do so immediately. With serious concerns over French intentions, along with misgivings at having given away too much at Amiens, the British government felt justified in delaying its own withdrawal from Malta indefinitely, even though Napoleon had done nothing to violate the terms of the treaty explicitly.

Napoleon was justifiably outraged over British refusal to relinquish Malta according to the terms of the treaty, though he steadfastly refused to recognize the role his own actions had played in generating suspicion as to his motives. By the end of March 1803 Napoleon had resolved upon a show of force designed to intimidate Britain into handing over Malta in compliance with the terms of Amiens. He ordered the formation of an army at Nijmegen that would be poised to invade Hanover, the hereditary territory of the British king. On 15 April, General Mortier was placed in command of this army. Plainly Napoleon would have preferred Britain to back down and relinquish Malta. However, he looked upon war as an opportunity. "A first consul," he stated, "cannot be likened to these kings-by-the-grace-of-God, who look upon their States as a heritage . . . His actions must be dramatic, and for this war is indispensable."†

With the mobilization of Mortier's Army of Hanover, the gauntlet had been hurled down and the British were quick to pick it up. On 16 May, Parliament declared an embargo of France and French-controlled ports. Two days later, a British frigate seized a French vessel after a brief exchange of fire under the terms of the blockade, the first overtly hostile act of the new war. On 20 May

* Georges Lefebvre, *Napoleon from 18 Brumaire to Tilsit, 1799–1807* (New York: Columbia University Press, 1969), p. 176.

† Ibid., p. 169.

Napoleon declared that Britain had broken the peace, on the 22nd he ordered the arrest of all British citizens in France, and on the 23rd General Mortier marched into Hanover at the head of 12,000 men.

At the time that Anglo-French hostilities resumed in May 1803, the British had little support on the continent. Austria, still recovering militarily and economically from two losing wars with France, had little interest in renewing the struggle. Prussia expressed more concern over the closing of Hanoverian ports to British commerce, which produced serious economic repercussions across northern Germany, than over the French occupation of Hanover itself. In Russia, Tsar Alexander fancied himself as the logical mediator between the two traditional enemies, a position that Napoleon had previously encouraged, and in the summer of 1803 he instructed his ambassador in Paris to present a proposal for Russian occupation of Malta as a compromise position. At the same time, Alexander sent several frigates to Corfu, where Russia maintained a small garrison (with the full approval of Napoleon) to discourage any French seizure of Corfu and to be prepared for the occupation of Malta should Napoleon accept his proposal. By the summer of 1803, despite what one eminent French historian termed "smoldering hostility" against France, continental Europe remained unwilling to become involved in the latest Anglo-French conflict. The events of the next twenty-four months, however, would generate determined opposition to France and enable the formation of the Third Coalition.

The Formation of the Third Coalition

Following the resumption of war between France and Britain, Russia and Prussia first sought to reach agreements with France. Alexander's offer of mediation, presented to Napoleon in July 1803, fell on deaf ears. The Russian ambassador in Paris, Markov, was known to be pro-British and Napoleon thought he perceived an Anglo-Russian plot designed to entrap him, but in fact Alexander's attempts at mediation had strained relations with the British, who had expected Russian support. Nevertheless, in August Napoleon demanded the recall of Markov and in the summer of 1803 he ordered the re-occupation of the Neapolitan ports. These actions triggered an immediate response in St Petersburg in the form of assurances of support for the Bourbon rulers of Naples and orders for additional land and naval forces to bolster the defense of the Ionian Islands. At the same time, the Francophiles in the Russian court had been discredited and Anglophile ministers gained influence with Alexander, leading to tentative discussions of an alliance with Britain on the one hand, and renewed British offers of subsidies for Russian land forces committed to the struggle against France on the other.

Prussia had opened negotiations with Napoleon in June 1803, offering a guarantee of Prussian neutrality if France agreed to reopen Hanoverian ports. Napoleon refused this offer and instead demanded that Prussia become an active ally of France in exchange for reopening the ports. Negotiations continued in a desultory fashion until finally being abandoned in April 1804. Immediately following the abandonment of negotiations with France, Prussia began working out a defensive alliance with Russia.

For Austria, it seemed that no amount of persuasion could budge the country from its determined position of neutrality. Between September 1803 and January 1804, the Austrians snubbed Russian offers of a defensive alliance guaranteeing the support of 100,000 Russians in the event of war with France. Francis II,* Holy Roman Emperor and hereditary ruler of Austria and the sprawling Habsburg dominions, even went so far as to declare that "France has done nothing to me." In March 1804, however, an event would occur that would fan the smoldering hostility of the continental powers into flames of open opposition.

Throughout 1803 and into 1804, various conspirators had plotted against Napoleon. Their conspiracies drew in royalists and disaffected republican generals who wanted to see Bonaparte removed from power, either through a coup or by assassination. Napoleon's secret police learned of several of the plots and arrested suspects for questioning, collecting enough information to locate and arrest a former leader of a royalist rebellion in the 1790s, Georges Cadoudal, and a former hero of the revolutionary armies, General Pichegru. Other prisoners, after being subjected to torture, implicated General Moreau and revealed that a prince would soon arrive in France to head the plot to overthrow Napoleon. Soon after, an informant passed on information indicating that a Bourbon prince, the Duc d'Enghien, was living at Ettenheim in Baden, a short distance from Strasbourg. In addition, the informant claimed that other émigrés had assembled at Offenburg.

Although the evidence against the Duc d'Enghien relied on vague information extracted from prisoners under torture, Napoleon resolved to take decisive action against the forces conspiring against him. On 14 March 1804, a party of French cavalry launched a raid into Baden, scouring Offenburg and seizing the Duc d'Enghien at Ettenheim. Although no émigrés were found at Offenburg, calling into question the reliability of the informant, papers were found at Ettenheim that proved that the Duc d'Enghien was in the pay of Britain. In legal terms, this could not be considered a crime outside of the borders of France, but Enghien had served in an émigré army against the

---

* Francis II would later assume the title of Emperor (Kaiser) of Austria as Francis I. Lefebvre, p. 207.

French republic in the past wars, and a law passed during the Terror had required that all such individuals be brought to trial no matter where they lived. The evidence was sufficient to convince the French officers conducting the raid to bring him back to France for trial. After spending five days in prison, the duke was brought before a tribunal and shot three hours later, despite the fact that the tribunal had not felt the case against him to be very strong. Over the next several months, additional conspirators were arrested. Some were tried and executed, while General Pichegru mysteriously died in his cell before trial, reportedly by his own hand.

News of the execution of the Duc d'Enghien reverberated throughout Europe. The King of Sweden, the unstable Gustav IV Adolf, immediately severed ties with France. The other powers expressed their outrage at the French raid into a neutral country, the arrest (or kidnapping) based on scanty evidence, and the execution based on the mockery of a trial. The duke's possible complicity in the plot to assassinate Napoleon notwithstanding, the methods used in his seizure and execution outraged the rest of Europe and belied French claims of the moral superiority of their republican institutions over the corruption of monarchical Europe. Even Napoleon's disdainful references to the hypocrisy of Russian regicides, aimed directly at Alexander who had rewarded a number of his father's assassins with high positions, could not deflect the public outcry at the seizure and rapid nocturnal execution of the last surviving member of one of the oldest families of the French aristocracy.

From the spring of 1803 to the spring of 1804, Anglo-Russian cooperation had been limited to pursuing a common policy of containment of any French attempts to expand in the Mediterranean. This cooperation formed the nucleus around which the Third Coalition would form. Prime Minister Addington, his popularity plummeting due to what was perceived as his weak handling of the war effort, resigned in April 1804 and was replaced by William Pitt the Younger. Pitt, the architect of the prior coalitions against France, immediately began working toward uniting the divided continental powers. However, despite the fresh hostility whipped up by the execution of the Duc d'Enghien, no amount of British gold could at first woo Prussia and Austria from their positions of neutrality but Pitt's persistence and fresh provocative actions by Napoleon soon changed matters, most significantly in Austria.

In May 1804, a new constitution was presented and approved by the French Senate declaring that the government would be entrusted to a hereditary emperor. In Vienna, the news was perceived as a direct challenge to the authority of Francis as the Holy Roman Emperor, particularly in light of French diplomatic efforts among the various German states. This prompted Francis to assume the title of Emperor of Austria in August. In November, goaded by fears of French imperial ambitions, Austria agreed to a defensive alliance with Russia. The following month, Sweden signed a defensive pact with Britain. By the time Napoleon crowned himself emperor in a glittering ceremony at Notre Dame Cathedral with the Pope himself in attendance, all of the major powers of Europe save Spain had entered into formal defensive agreements out of concern over the threat of renewed French expansion.

Over the next few months these fears would be realized. In March 1805, Napoleon granted the Principality of Piombino, formerly a fiefdom of the Holy Roman Emperor, to his sister Elisa. In May, Napoleon was crowned King of Italy in Milan in direct violation of the Treaty of Lunéville which had guaranteed separation of the Cisalpine Republic from France. Finally, on 6 June the Ligurian Republic (Genoa) was formally annexed to France. Napoleon's new activities in Italy proved to be the last straw for Francis, who clearly now felt that Napoleon had indeed done something that directly affected him. Eleven days later Austria opened negotiations with Russia and Britain to join in a new coalition against France. Britain responded with an immediate commitment to subsidize Austria's military effort.

Throughout 1804 and into 1805, Napoleon's actions had increased hostility against France, accomplishing what British gold and persuasion had been unable to accomplish alone. Rather than seeking to keep the continental powers divided, from the summer of 1803 through the summer of 1805 Napoleon pursued programs designed to oppose Britain's "economic interests and policy of maritime imperialism" by expanding French power with complete disregard for the opposition these policies might produce. The seizure of Hanover, a possession of the British king, could be accepted as an act of war between the two belligerents. Continued military occupation of the Batavian Republic and northern Italy could be accepted as a part of the *status quo*. But renewed French expansion into Italy and the assumption of an imperial crown caused alarm in both Vienna and St Petersburg. "Napoleon, as if daring the Powers, had inflamed this smouldering hostility, had alarmed them all and driven even the feeble Austrian monarchy to desperation."*

War Plans of the Third Coalition and the Allied Armies

As a result of the alarm generated by French activities in Italy and the Mediterranean, Britain had gained two powerful continental allies along with the strategically positioned, but militarily insignificant, Sweden and Naples. In addition, Pitt had hopes of convincing Prussia to join as well. The armies of the coalition members, though collectively formidable, were scattered across Europe and were not in a position to concentrate rapidly against France.

* Lefebvre, p. 212.

Prussian participation, however, would place allied forces in a position to oppose France immediately across the breadth of Europe. Prussia resisted Pitt's efforts, though, preferring to stick to the policy of neutrality it had pursued since making its separate peace with France in 1795. The coalition had to plan the campaign without Prussia.

Allied plans for the campaign of 1805 were strongly influenced by the success of the opening operations of the previous war, constituting what amounted to a replay of the strategy adopted by the Second Coalition in 1799. The opening moves of the War of the Second Coalition had involved the seizure of almost the whole of northern Italy by the Austro-Russian army of the Russian Field Marshal Suvorov, while in Germany Archduke Charles had deflected a French offensive and then driven the French armies back to the Rhine. On the periphery, small amphibious landings in southern Italy (successful) and in Holland (unsuccessful) had supported the efforts of the main armies.

Between 1801 and 1805, Archduke Charles had produced the outline for Austrian strategy in the event of renewed war with France based on the experiences of 1799. Because French and Austrian troops faced each other directly in northern Italy, where the French-controlled Cisalpine Republic (later Kingdom of Italy) bordered Austrian Venetia, Charles proposed massing the greater portion of the Austrian Army in northern Italy with the intention of first defeating the French there. On the Danube, the southern German states constituteded a buffer between Austrian territory and the Rhine, which the French forces would have to cross before coming to grips with the Austrians. This buffer would provide more time for the assembling of reserves and the arrival of Russian allies to allow the smaller Austrian Army of Germany to meet the advancing French on something approaching equal terms.

Allied leaders in 1805 adopted Charles's plan for deploying the greater part of the Austrian Army in Italy with a smaller army assembling in Germany to be expanded over time by the arrival of additional regiments that would have to march from the eastern parts of the Habsburg Empire. In addition, the main Russian Army would advance by forced marches to support the Austrian Army in Germany. On the periphery, British and Russian troops would join with the Neapolitan Army to drive the French out of central Italy, while in the north Swedish participation would allow allied forces to operate from Swedish Pomerania against the lower Rhine. Russian and Swedish troops would be transported to Swedish Pomerania and would advance overland, while a British force would be landed near Bremen to join them. Additional Russian forces would be massed on the Prussian frontier and would march across Prussian territory once Prussia could be convinced to join the coalition.

In all, allied war planners calculated that, even without Prussian support, they would be able to oppose France with over 250,000 men by the end of October with the number growing to 350,000 by the end of November. In northern Italy, the allies would field an army of about 94,000 Austrians under the Archduke Charles. In Germany, the Archduke Ferdinand, seconded by FML Baron Mack, would command 72,000 Austrians and would be joined by 38,000 Russians under Kutuzov. In the north, 20,000 Russians and 12,000 Swedes would advance from Swedish Pomerania to be joined by about 10,000 British and Hanoverian troops, the entire force under the command of the Swedish King Gustav IV Adolf. In the south, 25,000 Russians and British, under the overall command of the Russian GL Lacy, would join the Neapolitan Army for a sweep up the peninsula. Finally, an additional 100,000 Russians would follow Kutuzov's Advance Guard as soon as they could be assembled on the frontier. If Prussia could be convinced to join the coalition, over 100,000 additional troops could be brought to bear against the French. While the allied war plans were not entirely unrealistic, they failed to take into consideration the situation of the various allied armies, particularly in comparison to the French Army, which stood fully mobilized on the Channel coast.

The Austrian Army of 1805

In Austria, the army had been undergoing a period of reorganization and reform since 1801. This was spearheaded by Francis's younger brother, the Archduke Charles, who served as Minister of War and was arguably the best of the Austrian generals of his era. Charles, however, felt that the army was not yet ready for a renewal of the decade-old conflict against France. In addition, he distrusted the Russians and considered the British to be opportunistic, manipulative and unwilling to risk their own troops on the continent. The coalition, he concluded, would rely on Austrian troops to bear the brunt of the fighting. Despite Charles's influence as one of the leaders of the Austrian peace party, alarm over developments in Italy and France had strengthened the war party. In April 1805, FML Mack, a proponent of war, submitted a glowing report describing the war readiness of the Austrian Army. Although Charles dismissed the report as fiction and Mack as a madman, the war party seized upon the report as a means to discredit the gloomy pessimism of the Minister of War. By the end of April, Mack had been appointed Chief of Staff for the Austrian Army and Charles's powers as War Minister had been severely limited.

With the rise of the war party and its victory over the Archduke Charles, Mack assumed control over policy. With war planning already underway, Mack unwisely chose to push through a series of reforms that addressed what

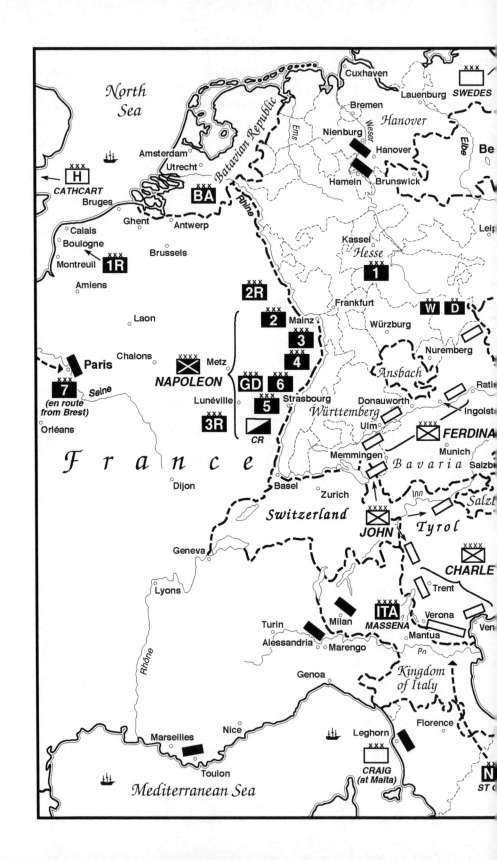

Stettin

TOLSTOI
(at Reval & Riga)

BENNIGSEN
(forming to
the north)

ESSEN-1
(forming)

Thorn

Vistula

Russia

P r u s s i a

Posen

Warsaw

Brest-Litovsk

Oder

Bug

BUXHÖWDEN
(forming)

Saxony

Dresden

Silesia

Breslau

Ustiluge

Prague

B o h e m i a

Teschen

Cracow

Vistula

Radzivilov

Iglau

Olmütz

M o r a v i a

Brünn

Austerlitz

March

KUTUZOV

udweis

ssau

Dürrenstein

Danube

Hollabrunn

Linz

nau

Vienna

Pressburg

Steyr

AUERSPERG

Komorn

Buda Pest

Leoben

H u n g a r y

Graz

u

s

t

r

i

a

Laibach

Danube

Trieste

Zagreb

tria

Rijeka

Sava

Danube

*riatic
Sea*

Belgrade

Split

Ottoman Empire

Ancona

NAPLES

LACY
(in Ionians)

War Preparations: 25 September 1805 N

0 20 40 60 80 100 120 140 160km

0 10 20 30 40 50 60 70 80 90 100miles

he felt were fundamental flaws in the tactical structure of the Austrian Army. Austrian regimental organization had long been based on regiments of twenty companies, each organized into three six-company battalions with two additional grenadier companies that were united with the grenadier companies of other regiments to form combined grenadier battalions. Mack, however, believed the three-rank tactical formation in use up to this time to be outdated and replaced it with a two-rank formation. Because this required only two-thirds of the men for the same unit frontage, Mack reduced the battalion size by a third, placing the Austrian battalions at four companies each instead of six. This allowed the even division of the twenty companies in each regiment into five battalions of equal strength. One of these battalions would be designated a grenadier battalion by re-designating two fusilier companies as grenadier companies. In the regimental depots, the traditional two reserve companies were expanded to four, thereby constituting a full reserve battalion for each regiment.

The Mack reforms of 1805 reflected careful consideration of the recent experience of the Austrian armies in the wars against France but, while sound enough on their own, their implementation in June 1805 as Austria lurched toward war with France demonstrated a complete departure from reality. Carrying out the reforms meant that the number of field battalions increased from 192 to 318 while the changes also resulted in the creation of 122 new reserve companies. For the cavalry, additional squadrons were formed to bring all regiments up to eight squadrons. While the overall numbers of men required remained constant (except for the need for nearly 20,000 recruits for the new reserve companies) the new companies and battalions required additional officers. Moreover, the Army had only about twelve weeks to accomplish its reorganization before Mack led the Army of Germany into Bavaria.

In addition the general tactical implications of the reduction in battalion size had not been taken into consideration. No training had been conducted and it is doubtful if all of the officers were even up to speed before being thrust into a combat situation. As late as 1 October 1805, many new recruits had still not received any musketry training.[*] These considerations never even entered into Mack's thoughts as he prepared the Austrian Army for war and Mack thus squandered four years of careful preparation and rebuilding sponsored by Charles through hurried adjustments to the fundamental structure of the army. Whatever the long-term merits of these reforms may have been, their timing placed the Austrian Army at a serious handicap at the outbreak of hostilities.

[*]   Christopher Duffy, *Austerlitz 1805* (London: Seeley Service, 1977), p. 27.

At the higher level of organization, the Austrian Army of 1805 was characterized by a two-tier structure. Like the French, the Austrians had realized a need for higher level formations to manage larger armies effectively. Through the second half of the 1790s, the Austrians, like the French, had experimented with different methods of achieving this. While the French devised a three-tier organization based on formally-established corps and divisions with fluid brigade organization, the Austrians developed a different model. Rather than grouping regiments into permanent larger units, the Austrians retained the concept of mission-oriented larger formations with the assignment of battalions and squadrons made according to need. Once established for a particular mission, this assignment or Order of Battle would remain constant and operate in much the same way as the French structure. The groups of regiments would typically be termed columns rather than divisions, but would be broken into brigades and collected together into wings under a senior commander in a manner parallel to the French corps structure. However, it was expected that these formations would be regrouped and individual regiments or battalions reassigned between operations. The root difference between the two models is that for the French the division and corps existed as an administrative and operational entity to which the commander was assigned. For the Austrians, the commander and his staff were the administrative and operational entity to which regiments were assigned. The primary flaw in the Austrian higher organization was the administrative overhead involved in making on-the-fly adjustments to the various formations and the resulting lack of cohesion and familiarity of officers with their commands—and vice versa.

The Austrian infantry had long had the reputation of being solid and reliable, and had fought the French to a standstill on a number of occasions since 1792. At the beginning of the campaign of 1805, Austria fielded sixty-one line infantry regiments raised from the various lands of the empire, along with two garrison regiments. Each regiment was numbered and also took the name of its *Inhaber* or proprietor (not the commander as was the practice in the Prussian Army). Each regiment was composed of twenty companies organized into five battalions, one of which was designated a grenadier battalion, each with four companies after the Mack reforms. Each company consisted of 160 men in peacetime (180 in the Hungarian regiments), to be raised to 200 men in wartime with additional recruits. In reality, however, most companies were understrength to begin with and delays in mobilization and the hurried advance into Bavaria at the outset of the 1805 campaign meant that in the Army of Germany the four-company battalions more typically numbered 500 men (about 125 per company) instead of the wartime establishment of 800.* Each line regiment would also raise a sixth (reserve) battalion in wartime but, at the outbreak of war in 1805, formation of these battalions had just begun.

In addition to the line infantry, in 1805 Austria converted the fifteen Jäger battalions that had been raised for the previous war into one Jäger regiment. Raised in mountainous Tyrolia, the regiment assumed the structure of the infantry regiments at the time of its formation, with three battalions of six companies each (there was no equivalent to the grenadier companies). The Tyrolean Jäger Regiment retained this structure after the reorganization of the line infantry, most likely because in practice the Jäger typically operated in two-company divisions rather than as a regiment.

Austria also maintained seventeen Grenz (Border) infantry regiments plus the Tschaikisten battalion, an independent pontonier unit also on the military border. The institution of the Grenz or military border was unique to Austria. The Grenz had been established as a solution to repopulating and defending the territories taken from the Turks during the 18th century, and for this purpose special privileges, including land ownership and tax-exempt status, were granted to settlers on the border. In exchange, the settlers were subject to military service in wartime. The Grenzers had emerged in European warfare as the original light infantry, specializing in open-order fighting and raids during the wars against Prussia in the middle of the 18th century. By 1805, the Grenz regiments were receiving the same training as line regiments and served more or less in the same capacity as the French light infantry and Russian or Prussian Jäger. Because the Grenz regiments retained a border defense mission, regardless of where a war might be fought, four companies of each regiment were always left behind to defend the border while the remaining twelve companies went off to war. In 1805, these twelve companies formed three battalions of four companies each like the regular infantry battalions, the exception being the two Székler and two Wallachian regiments from Transylvania which fielded only two battalions.

After the outbreak of war in 1805, a number of irregular units were raised, most notably a numerous Tyrolean militia twelve battalions strong. These irregulars, sometimes designated Jäger and sometimes as "free battalions" or "free corps," were constituted in various regions and served little military purpose except for garrison duty or, in the case of the Tyrolean militia, in tying down French or Bavarian troops.

The Austrian cavalry had been reduced in numbers between the wars as an economy measure. In 1805, there were eight cuirassier regiments, six of

---

* Gunther E. Rothenberg, *Napoleon's Great Adversary: Archduke Charles and the Austrian Army, 1792–1814* (New York: Sarpedon Publishers, 1995), p. 112.

dragoons, six of chevauxleger, twelve of hussars (including one Grenz hussar regiment) and three of Uhlans. The cavalry had in part a regional character with the hussars being raised exclusively in Hungary and the Uhlans in Galicia. All cavalry regiments were composed of eight squadrons, which typically operated in pairs (termed divisions) except for the Székler Grenz Hussars, which fielded six squadrons. The cuirassier and dragoon squadrons numbered 112 while the light cavalry squadrons numbered 166. In addition, each regiment maintained a depot squadron which could be called upon in wartime. Like the infantry, at the outset of the 1805 campaign the cavalry, particularly in the Army of Germany, stood well below the wartime establishment.

In all, the Austrian Army totaled 305 line battalions, 3 Jäger battalions and 51 Grenz battalions, with an additional 10 garrison battalions and 61 reserve battalions. Irregular units included 12 battalions of Tyrolean militia and 12 volunteer Jäger or free battalions. The cavalry included 64 cuirassier squadrons, 48 dragoon squadrons, 48 chevauxleger squadrons, 94 hussar squadrons and 24 Uhlan squadrons. The majority of these forces (171 battalions and 96 squadrons) were allocated to the Army of Italy, under the Archduke Charles. The Army of Germany (88 battalions and 148 squadrons) would be commanded by the Archduke Ferdinand with Mack as his chief of staff and would be reinforced by the arrival of the Russians. Between the two, the Archduke John would command an Army of Tyrol consisting of 65 battalions and 16 squadrons. John's army, pushed out far to the west, would cover the flank of the Army of Germany and stand poised to descend through the passes into northern Italy in support of Charles. A total of 44 battalions and half of the cavalry formed in two divisions were positioned facing Italy around Trent and in the Valtelline. The remainder faced Bavaria in the north. The rest of the Austrian Army, largely composed of units from the eastern reaches of the sprawling Habsburg dominions, would form a reserve or would be retained in garrisons.

In the end, at Charles's urging, substantial portions of both his Army of Italy and the Army of Tyrol were detached to strengthen the army in the north in early October. The Army of Tyrol diverted about two-thirds of its strength into Bavaria, with the northern Tyrol division of 21 battalions advancing to cover the right of the Army of Germany and an additional 24 battalions being reassigned to the Army of Germany outright. Charles detached 31 battalions to the southern Tyrol to join the 11 battalions remaining there and sent 24 more battalions to reinforce the Army of Germany. About half of the units en route to the Army of Germany arrived too late to effect the outcome of the campaign in Bavaria. The Army of Germany also received 10 battalions from the interior while 5 battalions from Dalmatia were transferred to Italy.

Table 1:

Initial Disposition of Austrian Forces, 1805

Original Dispositions	*Battalions*	*Squadrons*
Army of Germany – Archduke Ferdinand	88	148
Army of Tyrolia – Archduke John	65	16
Army of Italy – Archduke Charles	171	96
Garrison/Interior*	45	18
Total	369	278
Adjusted Dispositions		
Army of Germany – Archduke Ferdinand[†]	167	156
Army of Tyrolia – Archduke John	51	24
Army of Italy – Archduke Charles	121	80
Garrison/Interior	30	18
Total	369	278

Overall, the Austrian Army of 1805 was not what it had been in the previous war. The bitter disappointment of Marengo, followed by the humiliation of Hohenlinden, had left the army seeking to explain what had gone wrong after a string of nearly unbroken successes against the French in 1799. After a period of reform and rebuilding under the one general the army trusted fully, political intrigue had ushered in new leadership and a host of new reforms on the eve of war. The deep divisions between the peace and war parties had divided the officer corps. Charles, the most prominent leader of the peace party, commanded in Italy. Mack, the architect of the war party, served as *de facto* commander in Germany. The cavalry was perhaps the least affected and had always enjoyed a fine reputation on the battlefield, but was still hampered by the practice of dispersing squadrons in small bodies for close support of the infantry. The regular infantry, always solid and reliable, was forced to adapt to the new structure immediately upon mobilization, without adequate retraining, and then was forced to learn how to forage, cutting into what little time was available for drill. Even the Grenzers, who had been enthusiastic in prior wars, were becoming tired of conflicts in the west that tore them away from their homesteads in violation of what they perceived their role on the military border to be—receiving land in exchange for defending it from the Turks. Finally, while in 1799 the Army had mobilized in August with hostilities commencing the following March, Mack had

---

* Includes two garrison regiments, designated Infantry Regiment (IR) 5 and IR 6, each of five battalions, and battalions left in garrisons on the frontiers or in reserve in Vienna.

† Nearly a third of the official strength of the reinforced Army of Germany was still en route by mid-October and was prevented from reaching the main body by the rapid French advance.

conceived a plan to speed up the commencement of operations by marching immediately into Bavaria prior to complete mobilization. This meant that the units of the Army of Germany would theoretically be at or near peacetime establishment (though in reality they did not even reach this level) and the recruits needed to bring the regiments to a wartime footing would be sent to join them later, picking up whatever training they could along the way. This, coupled with the internal reorganization of the regiments and the shift to French-style foraging to reduce the supply train, meant that the Austrian Army as a whole, and the Austrian Army of Germany in particular, would be understrength, disorganized and ill-supplied, which in turn resulted in extremely poor morale from the outset.

The Russian Army of 1805

Like the Austrian Army, the Russian Army of 1805 was just emerging from a difficult period. Under Tsar Paul, between 1796 and 1800 the army had been buffeted by a series of dramatic reforms, some sensible and others arbitrary, ranging from administrative reforms designed to reduce corruption to ill-conceived uniform changes implemented for appearances' sake to the detriment of the soldiers' comfort. Paul's mercurial temperament had led to the dismissal of a number of experienced and popular officers. As a result, the army was plunged into considerable confusion. Regimental names that had been established under Peter the Great were abolished and the regiments instead named after their commanders. Uniforms and drill were Prussianized in emulation of the army of Frederick the Great without regard to the many changes occurring in the forty years since the glory days of Frederick's army. In a typically arbitrary fashion, in December 1796 Paul ordered the reduction of the Jäger corps to twenty battalions, only to double the number of battalions six months later, ordering each battalion to be split into two battalions and gradually brought up to regimental strength.* With Paul's assassination in March 1801, the Russian Army began reversing many of Paul's reforms. While the administrative reforms that had been implemented to reduce corruption were retained, the traditional regimental names were restored, the uncomfortable and impractical uniforms replaced with more sensible designs, and the internal organization of the regiments adjusted. One legacy of Paul's reforms was the position of *shef*, a general officer assigned to each regiment to curb the corruption of regimental commanders.

---

* Although these changes, resulting in a reduction of the Jäger of the Russian Army by nearly two-thirds, have been viewed by some as evidence that Paul dramatically reduced the army's light infantry, the almost immediate rebuilding suggests that this may have been part of a reorganization of severely understrength Jäger corps on a regimental basis more consistent with the line infantry.

The Russian infantry, when well led, could be formidable opponents. The soldiers had earned a reputation for being almost fanatical fighters. The Russian officer corps, however, suffered from considerable inconsistency. While there were a number of outstanding officers, most notably among the Jäger regiments, there were also many officers who had been enlisted in Guard regiments as children and reached high rank without gaining much experience. In 1805, the Russian infantry was organized into 13 grenadier regiments and 77 musketeer regiments, each composed of three battalions, each battalion with four companies of 154 men. In addition, there were 20 Jäger regiments, also organized into three battalions of four smaller companies composed of 104 men. In August 1805, Alexander ordered the formation of seven additional musketeer and two new Jäger regiments, but these new regiments would not be fully formed until 1806.

Russian regular cavalry had never earned the reputation of their Austrian counterparts, but managed to perform reasonably well in the field, with the inconsistencies in the Russian officer corps resulting in highly variable combat performance in the cavalry as in the infantry. The army cavalry consisted of 6 regiments of cuirassiers, 26 of dragoons, 9 of hussars and 4 of light horse (Uhlans/lancers). Each of the heavy cavalry regiments was composed of 5 squadrons and maintained a half-squadron as a depot. The light cavalry regiments were composed of 10 squadrons (two battalions of 5 squadrons each) and maintained one depot squadron.

In addition to the regular infantry and cavalry, Russia could draw on the Cossacks, rugged frontiersmen who populated the open plains of the Ukraine, for an almost unlimited supply of irregular cavalry. The Cossacks were organised into regiments composed of five *sotnias* (literally "hundreds") that were equivalent to squadrons in the regular cavalry. Although the Cossacks were generally regarded as useless in combat, they specialized in scouting, raids and harassing the enemy. Unfortunately, their illiteracy limited their value for reconnaissance and their wild character terrorized the local population, even where friendly. Non-Russian generals, even those in Russian service, often did not know how to employ the Cossacks attached to the army productively.

Finally, the Russian Life Guard constituted the elite of the Russian Army. The Guard was composed of soldiers selected for their physical size and officered by members of the most powerful and influential families in Russia. In 1805 it was composed of three regiments of grenadiers, the senior regiment (Preobrazhensky) composed of four battalions, and the other two regiments (Semenovsky and Ismailovsky) composed of three battalions each. In addition, the Life Guard included a Life Guard Jäger battalion. (Note that the Life Grenadiers, which formed part of the 2nd Guard Column at Austerlitz, was a line regiment.) The Guard cavalry consisted of two regiments of cuirassiers (the Life Guard Horse and the Cavalier Guard), along with a regiment of Life Guard Hussars and two squadrons of Life Guard Cossacks. In all, the Life Guard included eleven battalions and seventeen squadrons, bringing the total establishment of the regular forces of the Russian Army to 341 battalions and 302 squadrons, supported by numerous garrison regiments and the seemingly innumerable Cossacks.

While the Russian Army was one of the largest in Europe, the vast size of Russia made it impossible for forces to be shifted from front to front, the way France, Austria and Prussia were able to do. Forces stationed in Siberia, on the central Asian frontier, or in the Caucasus could not be used for a war in the west. In addition, centuries-old tensions with the Turks required a permanent presence on the Black Sea coast and in Moldavia to counter any Turkish move against the sparsely populated territory along the Dnieper and in the Crimea. In the north, the surprise attack by the Swedes in 1789 was still a recent memory and some forces had to be retained in the region as a precaution. In all, 212 battalions (including 2 of marines) and 207 squadrons out of a total 343 battalions and 297 squadrons were committed to the war against France.

Table 2:
Initial Disposition of Russian Forces, 1805

	Battalions	Squadrons	Sotnias
Army of Podolia – Kutuzov	54	40	30
Army of Volhynia – Buxhöwden*	39	55	20
Army of Lithuania – Essen-1†	30	42	80
Army of the North – Bennigsen	39	50	35
Descent Force – Tolstoi‡	23	15	8
Ionians – Anrep§	27	5	10
Reserve Army – Rimsky-Korsakov	12	5	15
Army of Moldavia – Tormasov	25	40	55
Finland and St Petersburg¶	13	0	0
Kherson and Crimea	30	5	Unknown
Caucasus	27	25	Unknown
Orenburg and Siberia	24	15	Unknown
Total	343	297	

* The Izyum Hussars, originally assigned to Buxhöwden's Army of Volhynia, joined Tolstoi's descent force in September and are included in the totals for Tolstoi's force.

† Includes seven battalions and seventeen squadrons of the Guard.

‡ Including two battalions of the 3rd Marine Regiment.

§ Of the forces designated, five battalions, five squadrons and ten sotnias remained in Russia due to a lack of transports.

¶ Includes four Guard battalions.

Mobilization of large armies in the sparsely populated frontier areas of Russia had always been problematic due to a deficiency of supplies. As had been the case in 1799, the plan in 1805 was for the Russian regiments closest to the frontier to assemble first and march into Austrian Galicia at the same time as the regiments stationed further east marched to points of concentration on the frontier. In this way, an advance guard for the Russian Army, termed the Army of Podolia, would march westward roughly a month sooner than the remainder of the army. Behind this advance guard, three armies would assemble. The Army of the North, under General Bennigsen, would assemble on the Prussian frontier around Taurogen, the Army of Lithuania under General Essen-1 would assemble between Grodno and Brest-Litovsk and the Army of Volhynia under General Buxhöwden would assemble between Brest-Litovsk and Ustiluge.

The Russian Army of 1805 had enjoyed four years of rebuilding after the turbulence of Tsar Paul's reign and was as well prepared for war as a Russian Army could be expected to be. Its inherent liabilities, however, worked against it. The very considerable distances over which the army was unavoidably spread during peacetime made assembling for large-scale maneuvers difficult or impossible and, as for the Austrian forces, insufficient funding resulted in a lack of musketry training with live rounds. Despite its iron discipline, extreme fortitude and a smattering of exceptional commanders, the army as a whole had not developed as much experience as the French and Austrians over the preceding decade. Suvorov's small army that had been so influential in driving the French from Italy in 1799 had lost severely in its march into Switzerland and among the rank and file there were not many remaining veterans of Suvorov's last campaign. The brief and disastrous experience of Rimsky-Korsakov's army, crushed ignominiously at the Second Battle of Zurich, may have provided some valuable lessons for those inclined to heed them but provided little in the way of practical experience in fighting the French.

Beyond this limited experience, the Russian Army's recent campaigns included only the brief action against Polish irregulars in 1795 and a short war against the Swedes in 1788–90. While the Russian Army was confident that it would repeat Suvorov's successes of 1799 as it marched westward, in reality it was no better prepared that the Russian Army of 1799 had been and it was marching to meet a foe that was considerably more formidable than the army that Suvorov and Charles had defeated six years earlier.

Other Allied Contingents

While Austria and Russia provided the vast majority of the coalition land forces, commitments by Great Britain, Sweden and Naples provided significant bodies of troops for use on the periphery of the main theater of operations. The coalition planned two amphibious operations, one a landing in Hanover and the other in Naples. For these, the British committed a sizeable portion of the forces available in England, strengthening forces in the Mediterranean and assembling forces in the southeast of England for a landing in Hanover. The British troops committed to the amphibious operations were generally quite good. Among the regiments destined for Hanover were the 2nd (Coldstream) and 3rd Guards regiments. The forces designated for the Naples landing would distinguish themselves by defeating the French at Maida in 1806. Despite British dominance of the seas, the French naval threat remained very real and the British did not attempt to land these forces until after Trafalgar had destroyed the ability of the French to intervene. By that time, however, the British forces were too late to be of much use.

In addition, on the fringes of the main theater of operations, Sweden and Naples contributed forces to the coalition. Sweden, like Russia, retained a significant force in Finland, emphasizing the degree to which the allies distrusted each other. Suffering from financial problems and under the rule of an unstable king, the Swedish Army was not the formidable force it had been a hundred years before. With some difficulty, Sweden brought the first battalions of twelve regiments up to wartime strength and sent them to Swedish Pomerania along with some supporting cavalry. The regiments stationed in Stralsund were also weak and remained as its garrison, never joining the field army. Naples placed nearly its entire army, such as it was, at the disposal of the coalition. Naples, lacking even Sweden's glorious military tradition, contributed about forty battalions and fourteen squadrons, all seriously understrength and of dubious military value to the allied cause. Nearly a third of the Neapolitan battalions were retained in various garrisons, leaving about thirty battalions available for the war effort.

Neither the Swedish nor Neapolitan forces would contribute anything of substance to the war effort aside from providing a secure base for British and Russian forces to land.

Table 3:

Disposition of British, Swedish and Neapolitan Forces, 1805

	Battalions	Squadrons
Britain		
Hanover Force – Cathcart*	24	8
Naples Force – Craig	10	2
Mediterranean (excluding Craig)	12	0
England†	68	109
Ireland	24	38
Americas	35	0
India, Far East, Africa	30	25
Total	203	182
Sweden		
Pomerania‡	16	14
Sweden	30	39
Finland	22	12
Total	68	65
Naples		
Mainland	40	24
Sicily	12	8
Total	52	32

The remaining force potentially available to the coalition was the substantial army of Prussia. Prussia had resisted all efforts to draw it into the coalition against France, and, on the outbreak of hostilities, Prussia mobilized its own troops with the intention of protecting its neutrality. Roughly 40 percent of the Prussian forces were positioned in East Prussia and Poland facing the Russians. A small force occupied Upper Silesia to watch the Austrians while the remainder, roughly 50 percent of the Prussian Army, stood in the west facing France. In all, Prussia had 168 battalions and 245 squadrons to contribute to the war effort if it would commit to joining the coalition.

Once a new coalition began forming against him, Napoleon made continuous efforts to buy off the Prussians by granting them Hanover. When they failed to take the bait, Napoleon tried threats. In the end, Napoleon ignored Prussia and ordered French troops to march through the Prussian

* Includes six King's German Legion (Hanoverian) battalions, and sixteen KGL squadrons. Three additional KGL battalions and the cadre of a fourth, along with eight squadrons, were raised in Hanover after landing.

† Includes 35 new battalions raised in 1804.

‡ Four battalions formed the Stralsund Garrison.

territory of Ansbach during their advance into Bavaria. This gave Alexander sufficient leverage finally to convince Frederick William of Prussia to join the coalition, but Frederick William insisted on delivering an ultimatum to Napoleon. The Prussian king took three weeks to draft and send the ultimatum and allowed three additional weeks for Napoleon's reply. The delay in sending the ultimatum proved critical in keeping Prussia out of the war. Nevertheless, throughout the war Napoleon had continually to be aware of the strong Prussian forces mobilized facing France and to plan for the possibility that they might march against him.

Taken as a whole, the allied forces assembled against France appeared more formidable on paper than they were in reality. The Austrians were disorganized and demoralized from the outset and the Russians were over-confident and lacking in training or relevant experience. The Swedish and Neapolitan contingents must be regarded as second-rate troops that are not likely to have fared well against the French, while the British forces had to be transported and landed on the continent, which in the age of sail made them the victims of wind and tide. In addition to the individual liabilities of the various armies, all of the allies were keeping a wary eye on the opportunistic Prussians. Despite the fact that the British were the paymasters of the coalition, all of the coalition members were suspicious of British motives in fanning the flames of conflict on the continent to distract the French while refusing to commit their own forces, reflecting the strong feelings of anti-British sentiment generated during the last war.

The French Army and Its Preparations for War

The French Army of 1805 had benefited considerably from the four years of peace on the continent since the Treaty of Lunéville had ended the War of the Second Coalition. The track record of the French Army in the previous war had been inconsistent. The regime of the Directory in France had been extremely unpopular, inefficient and by many accounts thoroughly corrupt, though this may in fact have been a symptom of its inefficiency. French armies had lost a significant number of battles in 1799 and it was only General Massena's victory at the Second Battle of Zurich that had salvaged French pride and quite possibly saved France from invasion by the allies. After a *coup d'état* brought Napoleon Bonaparte to power in November 1799, the French Army of 1800 provided better results. Minor victories on the Rhine and the stunning but narrow defeat of the Austrians at Marengo in June 1800 announced a change in French fortunes. After an armistice lasting from June to November the hostilities were renewed and the French Army of General Moreau delivered a crushing defeat to the main Austrian Army in Germany at

Hohenlinden, forcing the Austrians to agree to a peace that restored the *status quo* of 1797.

Despite the turnaround in French fortunes, due in large part to Napoleon's more effective administration, the army still suffered the effects of the preceding years of neglect and two years of hard-fought battles. Many regiments were severely understrength. The regular regiments amounted to 110 line demi-brigades (regiments) and 30 light, ranging from two battalions to four battalions in strength. In addition, a large number of provisional demi-brigades, legions and other regional units still existed. By 1803, Napoleon had dissolved the provisional demi-brigades and irregular units and reallocated their men to the line regiments. Taking advantage of his popularity following the successful conclusion of the war with Austria, Napoleon also set to work on a broad range of civil and military reforms.

To create greater consistency among regiments, Napoleon merged the regiments of two battalions to form regiments of four battalions, placing all regiments on an establishment of three or four battalions and dropping the term demi-brigade in the process. As a result, the number of line regiments was reduced from 110 to 89 and the number of light regiments from 30 to 27, even though the number of regular battalions remained essentially the same. In the cavalry, a similar reduction occurred. In 1800 the French cavalry consisted of 2 carabinier, 25 heavy cavalry, 20 dragoon, 23 chasseur and 12 hussar regiments, the heavy regiments of three squadrons and the light regiments of four squadrons. Between 1800 and 1803, these forces were reorganized on a consistent establishment of four squadrons for all regiments. While the number of regiments was reduced substantially, the number of men under arms remained roughly the same. However, while the reduction in the number of units did not effect the number of men under arms, it did effect the number of officers required. This allowed the politically suspect and less capable officers to be weeded out, improving the skill of the officer corps while minimizing political dissent.

Following the breakdown of the Peace of Amiens, Napoleon took the opportunity to assemble an Army of the Ocean Coasts along the English Channel in preparation for an invasion of England. While forces were assembled from Holland to Brest, the main forces intended for the invasion were collected around Boulogne. The full mobilization of the army and the maintenance of that army in a training camp for approximately eighteen months provided an unprecedented period of intense training for the assembled troops. The generals selected to command at Boulogne included many of the most illustrious commanders of the wars of the republic and represented an extraordinary collection of talent. In some cases, generals who had exercised independent command in prior wars, like Suchet, commanded only a division in the new army. The Camp of Boulogne would be instrumental in forging the enthusiastic and disciplined Grande Armée that Napoleon would lead against the allies.

In 1805, the French Army was the largest in Europe. The French infantry numbered 19 line and 4 light regiments with 4 battalions and 70 line and 23 light regiments with three battalions, a total of 371 battalions of regular infantry. Each infantry battalion was composed of nine companies: in line infantry battalions one grenadier company of 99 officers and men and eight additional companies (one voltigeur and seven fusilier) with 123 officers and men each. (Light battalions had the same organization but had carabiniers and chasseurs rather than grenadiers and fusiliers.) French battalions were therefore larger than their four-company Austrian or Russian counterparts, numbering over 1,000 men while the Austrian battalion had a theoretical strength of about 800 and the Russian battalion just over 600.

In addition to the permanently established regiments, Napoleon had ordered the formation of grenadier battalions from companies drawn from the regiments stationed on the Rhine and on the coasts. Each of these regiments contributed the first three companies of its battalions to produce seventeen provisional grenadier battalions, which were placed under the command of General Oudinot.

The French infantry was quite good overall, but in particular the regiments that had enjoyed the months of training at the Camp of Boulogne stood out from the rest. At Austerlitz, a number of observers in the allied army noted that the units maneuvered calmly and with precision "as if on a parade ground," while the French musketry proved far more effective due to the considerable musketry practice with live ammunition that the French soldiers had received. Coupled with experienced and capable officers who had worked with the units at Boulogne, the French infantry was indisputably the finest in Europe in 1805, and perhaps even the finest infantry fielded throughout the wars of 1792–1815.

In addition to the regular French infantry regiments, there were a number of other units that had been raised. These included four battalions of Paris Municipal Guard, the Chasseurs d'Orient, five battalions of Corsican light infantry, two battalions raised in Elba, and the Legion du Midi, the last of the legions raised during the revolution—a total of 16 additional battalions—along with 10 colonial battalions. In addition to these, there were 13 foreign regiments in French service, including 4 Swiss, 3 Polish, 2 Irish and 2 Hanoverian. Of these the Swiss and Polish troops were of sufficiently good quality to be employed with the French in Italy. The remaining forces were used for coastal defense or in colonial service. In all, excluding a battalion of deserters and depots for the colonial battalions, there were 410 battalions of infantry in the French Army.

French cavalry in 1805 included 2 regiments of carabiniers, 12 of cuirassiers, 30 of dragoons, 24 of chasseurs à cheval and 10 of hussars. Each regiment was composed of four squadrons, providing a total of 312 squadrons of regular cavalry. In addition, two regiments of foreign cavalry (four squadrons of Poles and three of Hanoverians) also served France in 1805, bringing the total cavalry in the service of France to 319 squadrons. Each squadron had an establishment of 180 men, though shortages of horses meant that a number of the cavalrymen remained dismounted. For the projected amphibious operation against England, Napoleon formed provisional regiments of dismounted dragoons which were to locate mounts after landing in England. When Napoleon wheeled his troops eastward, these provisional regiments formed an additional division of dismounted dragoons that was employed on the line of communications and in observation of Prussian forces and Austrian forces in Bohemia.

The French Army also included the famous Imperial Guard, which had been formed to be an elite unit, composed of veterans and commanded by officers who had distinguished themselves for their loyalty and ability. The Imperial Guard had its own infantry, cavalry and artillery. The infantry of the guard consisted of two battalions of grenadiers à pied, two battalions of chasseurs à pied, and one battalion of marines of the guard. The Imperial Guard cavalry consisted of four squadrons of grenadiers à cheval, four squadrons of chasseurs à cheval, a company of mamelukes and two squadrons of elite gendarmes. While the French Imperial Guard occasionally comes under criticism as a pampered and overrated unit, in 1805 it was still a relatively small force and its veterans all had recent combat experience in the previous war. By contrast, the Russian Guard lacked a comparable level of experience. Much more so than its predecessor, the Consular Guard, the French Imperial Guard of 1805 gives every indication of having been a truly elite unit, as the performance of the guard cavalry at Austerlitz would attest.

Beyond the forces of France, Napoleon had at his disposal the forces of the French satellite states. The Army of the Batavian Republic included 2 grenadier battalions, 30 line battalions and 9 light battalions in the infantry, along with 8 squadrons of dragoons and 4 of hussars plus assorted colonial troops. Of these, 12 battalions and 4 squadrons served with the 2nd Corps of the Grand Armée while 8 battalions were stationed overseas in the colonies (three at the Cape, four in the West Indies, and one in Java). The remainder were retained on the Dutch coast to defend against the threat of invasion. In general, the Dutch battalions were understrength, some with a high proportion of recruits. None of the Dutch troops fought any significant actions during the course of the campaign, although in 1807 they would perform quite well alongside French troops.

The Kingdom of Italy provided 5 guard battalions, 13 line battalions and 5 light battalions, supported by 8 squadrons of dragoons and 4 of chasseurs. The forces of the Kingdom of Italy served in many different places. Two battalions of the Royal Guard served with the French Imperial Guard (Napoleon being King of Italy as well as Emperor of France), six battalions joined the Camp of Boulogne, and eight battalions and the chasseurs served under St Cyr with the French Army of Naples. The remainder garrisoned the Kingdom of Italy and Elba. The Italian troops seem to have been reliable and served effectively alongside the French throughout Italy.

In addition to the satellite states, Napoleon would gain three allies almost immediately after the outbreak of hostilities in September 1805. Of these, the Bavarians had a substantial army with 24 line and 6 light battalions, 8 squadrons of dragoons and 16 squadrons of chevauxleger. Württemberg provided 11 battalions and 4 squadrons while Baden contributed 10 battalions and 6 squadrons. Most of the German forces were used in garrisons and in protecting the line of communications of the Grande Armée as it marched eastward, but two Bavarian divisions served with the Grande Armée.

The huge number of troops available to Napoleon of course included a substantial number required for the defense of the colonies, the islands and coasts of France, and the Rhine frontier. In addition, three bodies of troops were retained for internal security, one in Paris, one in the historically rebellious Vendée, and one in the recently annexed Piedmont. The remainder formed four separate armies: the Army of the Ocean Coasts (by far the largest), the Army of Italy, the Army of Hanover and the Army of Naples. On 16 August, Napoleon had instructed his foreign minister, Talleyrand, to assure the Elector of Bavaria that, if Austria did not call off its mobilization, he would abandon the Channel coast and Hanover and march with 200,000 men against Austria. On 26 August, the French emperor dictated orders detailing the formation of a new army for the war against the allied forces mobilizing against him. Three days later, he gave the new army a name that would soon become famous—the Grande Armée.

Napoleon intended to strike quickly at the Austrians, and the formation of the Grande Armée reflected careful consideration and inspired deviation from standard practice. The forces assembled from Hanover to Brest included full regiments of three or four battalions each. In order to march with units as close to establishment as possible, Napoleon ordered the first two or three battalions to draw men from the last battalion(s) to bring them up to full strength. The 3rd or 4th battalions would then be left behind to form three Reserve Corps for the defense of Boulogne and the Rhine frontier. Similarly, the 4th squadrons of the cavalry regiments would also be left behind. The 4th squadrons of the light cavalry regiments would be collected into brigades for the reserve corps on the Rhine while the 4th squadrons of the heavy cavalry regiments formed a cavalry reserve. These reserve corps would serve a dual purpose, acting as a depot for training recruits and sending columns of replacements to replenish losses of the regiments in the main army and also observing Prussia and forming a ready defense for France in the event of an amphibious landing on the coasts.

Table 4:
Disposition of French, Batavian and Italian Forces, 1805

	Battalions	*Squadrons*
La Grande Armée – Napoleon	190 *	213 †
Army of Italy – Massena	71	68
Army of Reserve – Joseph Bonaparte	67	12
Army of Naples – St Cyr	22	24
Interior/Coasts ‡	124	36
Colonies	25	1
Total	499	354

In forming the Grande Armée, Napoleon employed the organizational system that had been developed in the armies of the French republic. The forces from each of the main camps along the coast would form a semi-autonomous corps d'armée, composed of infantry, cavalry and artillery in sufficient strength to fight independently until reinforcements could arrive. Each corps would be commanded by the marshal or general commanding the camp from which it was drawn. In addition, the Army of Hanover would form the 1st Corps of the Grande Armée in its entirety, leaving only a regiment behind to garrison the fortress of Hameln.

The reorganization of the Army of the Ocean Coasts occurred quickly, and within days the various corps were on the march via parallel routes to the Rhine. Marshal Berthier, Napoleon's long-time chief of staff, worked through a mountain of minutiae to plan each day's march for the army, ordering the

---

* Includes seventeen grenadier battalions formed by detaching companies from the regiments stationed on the coasts and interior of France.

† Includes twenty-four squadrons of dismounted dragoons formed into a division of foot dragoons.

‡ Includes forces left in Hanover, Holland, France and the Kingdom of Italy.

collection of supplies at the termination point of each march and addressing the myriad of logistical details required in moving 200,000 men across France. While Marshal Bernadotte (who had replaced Mortier in May 1804) concentrated his Army of Hanover near Hesse-Kassel, the other corps set out across France and the Low Countries: General Marmont marched from Holland with one Dutch and two French divisions to form the 2nd Corps, Marshal Davout marched from Bruges with three divisions to form the 3rd Corps. At Boulogne itself, Marshal Soult formed the 4th Corps with his four divisions while Marshal Lannes formed the 5th Corps from the Advance Guard of the Army of the Ocean Coasts, the two divisions which had been intended as the spearhead for the cross-Channel landing. Marshal Ney's three divisions at Montreuil formed the 6th Corps, while the forces around Brest constituted the 7th Corps under Marshal Augereau. While the seven corps moved into position to strike at Austria, the heavy cavalry was assembled into a large Cavalry Reserve under the command of Marshal Joachim Murat. The Imperial Guard marched from Paris in the wake of the vast body of troops executing their rapid descent on the Rhine.

With the departure of the majority of the forces from the Channel coast, Napoleon designated the forces remaining in France to be the Army of the Reserve and left it under the command of his brother, Joseph Bonaparte. The forces remaining at Boulogne, including the Italian contingent, a handful of complete regiments and a number of 3rd and 4th battalions from the regiments of the Grande Armée, formed three divisions and were designated the 1st Corps of the Army of the Reserve under Marshal Brune. The remaining 3rd and 4th battalions would march to Mayence (Mainz) and Strasbourg to form two additional corps. The 3rd and 4th battalions of the 3rd and 6th Corps would form two divisions at Mayence, designated the 2nd Corps of the Army of the Reserve under Marshal Lefebvre. The 3rd and 4th battalions of the 4th, 5th and 7th Corps marched to Strasbourg to form two divisions designated as the 3rd Corps of the Army of the Reserve under Marshal Kellermann. Each of the reserve corps on the Rhine would have an attached light cavalry brigade formed from the 4th squadrons of the light cavalry regiments of the Grande Armée.

Overall, the French Army constituted a well-led and well-trained force, particularly the forces that had composed the Camp of Boulogne. In addition, the Grande Armée was led by the foremost general in Europe, who also served as Emperor. This combination of ultimate civil and military authority in one person conferred advantages that other armies did not enjoy. Conflict between political agendas and military necessity did not exist with the Grande Armée, nor was there any higher authority to issue orders to the commander of the army that would compromise operations. No head of state since Frederick the Great had been a professional soldier who led his army into the field. Like the Prussian Army of Frederick the Great, Napoleon's Grande Armée would prove itself to be a devastatingly effective weapon when wielded by its Emperor.

The 1805 Campaign in Bavaria

The allied planners had not anticipated Napoleon's complete abandonment of his plans to invade England, one of many mistaken assumptions on the part of the allies. General Mack had urged that mobilization be delayed until the last possible moment in order to avoid alarming the French prematurely, but had not considered the fact that the French Army was already mobilized and could march as soon as the French received word that Austrian mobilization had begun. Mack also believed that the Elector of Bavaria would join the coalition against France, though in fact he had been negotiating an alliance with France. As early as 6 August, Mack had received the news that Kutuzov's forces would not arrive on schedule and would be fewer than originally anticipated. While Archduke Charles proposed refraining from any aggressive movement until after the Russian forces actually arrived, Mack persisted in proceeding with his original plans. Calculating that Kutuzov's Russians could arrive at Braunau within 64 days of leaving their assembly point in Russia (a reasonably accurate estimate), Mack determined that there was no chance that Napoleon could strike at an Austrian Army in Bavaria in less than 68 days.* While his method for arriving at this figure is unclear and plainly counter-intuitive given the distances involved and the quality of the roads over which the French and Russian armies would have to pass, Mack managed to convince the Emperor Francis of the validity of his calculations.† Little did Mack realize that, by the time he ordered his army forward into Bavaria, the French had already been on the march for a week.

On 5 September 1805 Mack ordered his forces to advance from their camp at Wels and on 8 September the first Austrian troops crossed the River Inn en route to establishing a fortified camp around Ulm, squarely on the direct route between France and Austria. Bavarian troops offered no resistance to the Austrian advance and instead withdrew to the northwest. As the Austrian Army of Germany advanced in several echelons, Mack's plan to emulate the

---

* Wilhelm Rüstow, *Der krieg von 1805 in Deutschland und Italien* (Frauenfeld: Verlags-Comptoir, 1853), p. 56.

† French agents are known to have supplied misinformation to Mack, which might explain Mack's failure to discover what would appear to be obviously faulty figures by simply looking at the distances on a map. While some authors have suggested that the 12-day difference between the Julian Calendar used by Russia and the Western Gregorian Calendar provides an explanation, there is no evidence that this was the case and no record of any difficulties in coordinating calendars in this campaign or in the 1799 campaign.

French and have the troops forage for subsistence quickly gave way to chaos. Unlike the French, the Austrian troops were unaccustomed to foraging for food and moreover were even expected to obtain their own pack horses.* As a result, the Austrian troops became scattered as they ineffectually attempted to provide for themselves. In the end, discipline suffered, the men went hungry and little time remained for drill.

Compounding the confusion of the Austrian Army of Germany, the nominal commander, the Archduke Ferdinand, had serious reservations about the advance into Bavaria, and had suggested that the French might strike in force at any time before the Russian forces could possibly arrive. Mack, who inexplicably had earned the confidence of Francis, emphasized the value of securing the position of Ulm in order to protect the passes into Tyrolia, join forces with the Bavarian Army, and to be within striking distance of the Black Forest defiles through which, he assumed, the French must pass. Ferdinand's efforts to slow the advance prompted Francis to issue direct orders to the commander of the Army of Germany instructing him to obey his chief of staff, Mack, in all things. Mack had already received secret orders entrusting him with the ultimate authority in the army, making Ferdinand no more than a figurehead.

Austria viewed the move into Bavaria as no more than a routine military preparation. In all of the wars with France of the prior decade, Austrian troops had enjoyed the right of free passage through Bavaria. The ruler of Austria, Francis, was Holy Roman Emperor after all, and in prior wars Bavaria and other states of the empire had contributed troops to fight alongside the Austrians against France. In 1799, both the Austrians and the French had marched into southern Germany prior to the outbreak of hostilities. In some towns, officers and men of both armies had openly fraternized, even knowing that in a few days they might be called upon to kill each other. Neither side had considered this movement into and through the Grand Duchies of Bavaria and Württemberg and the Duchy of Baden an act of war. Six years later the situation had changed dramatically. Bavarian hostility came as a surprise to the Austrians and Napoleon successfully used the Austrian movement to justify a preemptive strike before the allied armies were ready to strike at France.

While Mack ordered his Austrians forward into Bavaria, Kutuzov was marching his Russian army through Austrian Galicia. Unlike the situation in France, Italy and western Germany, in Eastern Europe there were few parallel routes to follow and road quality was poor. As a result, Kutuzov's forces were strung out along a single route and progress was far slower than would have

---

* Duffy, *Austerlitz*, p. 28.

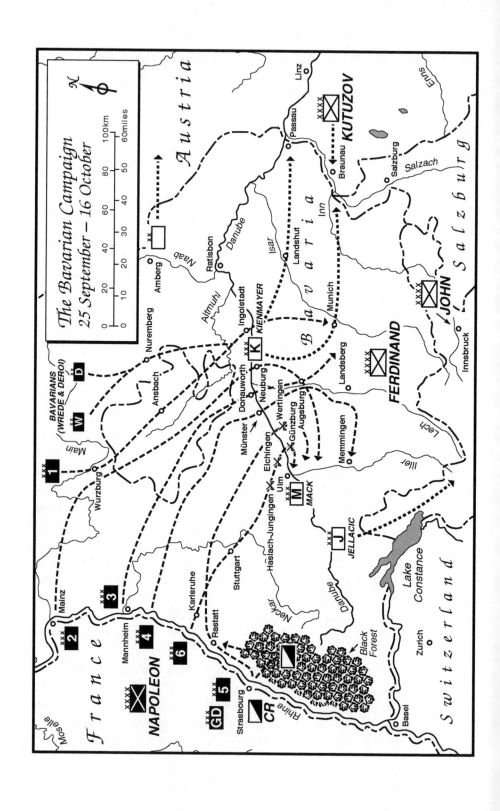

The Bavarian Campaign
25 September – 16 October

100km
60miles

France
Mosalle
Mainz
Mannheim
Karlsruhe
Rastatt
Strasbourg
Stuttgart
Basel
Switzerland
Zurich
Lake Constance
Black Forest
Rhine
Neckar
Danube

NAPOLEON
GD 5
CR
6
4
3
2
1

Würzburg
Main
BAVARIANS
(WREDE & DEROI)
W
D
Nuremberg
Ansbach
Amberg
Naab
Ratisbon
Nuremberg

JELLACIC
J
Ulm
MACK
M
Haslach-Jungingen
Elchingen
Münster
Günzburg
Wertingen
Augsburg
Memmingen
Iller
Lech
Donauworth
Neuburg
Ingolstadt
KIENMAYER
K
Altmuhl
Danube

Bavaria
FERDINAND
Landsberg
Munich
Isar
Landshut
Inn

JOHN
Innsbruck
Salzburg
Salzach
Salzburg

Austria
Linz
Passau
Braunau
KUTUZOV
Enns

been possible on the better road network of western Europe. By the end of September, while Mack's army had assumed its position around Ulm, the head of Kutuzov's column had only reached Teschen and Kutuzov had been forced to divert the tail of his army toward Moldavia in response to threatened hostilities with the Turks. At Teschen, the Austrians provided a large number of carts to help transport the foot-sore Russians, which accelerated the rate of advance through Moravia and into the Danube valley. Nevertheless, the anticipated date of 20 October for Kutuzov's arrival in Bavaria soon became obviously unrealistic.

The leading elements of Napoleon's Grande Armée, which had left the Channel coast on 27 August, arrived on the Rhine on 25 September. With five corps in position on the Rhine from Mayence to Strasbourg and Bernadotte's 1st Corps (the majority of the Army of Hanover) in position east of the Rhine near Hesse-Kassel, Napoleon planned to turn Mack's right flank and descend on his rear, cutting him off from the advancing Russians and reinforcements from Austria. With a cavalry screen pushed out into the Black Forest to fix the attention of the Austrians to the west, French troops began crossing the Rhine immediately on the 25th, the six corps marching along parallel routes to converge on the Danube between Ulm and Ingolstadt. While the armies were en route, Napoleon concluded alliances with Baden and Württemberg, which promised troops, while Bavaria revealed its prior decision to throw in its lot with the French, placing two additional divisions at the disposal of Napoleon.

The march from the Rhine to the Danube was conducted quickly and efficiently, though the troops suffered from shortages and some artillery and munitions had to be left behind because there were too few horses Nevertheless, the French corps covered between 190 and 320 kilometers in about 12 days, reaching the Danube by 7 October with Bernadotte and the Bavarians on the far left near Ingolstadt and the remaining corps distributed along the Danube to Günzburg.

Bernadotte's 1st Corps, which formed the extreme left of the French Army, had marched directly through the Prussian enclave of Ansbach during its march to avoid delays that would have been incurred by going around Prussian territory. As with the Austrian movement into Bavaria a month earlier, the movement of troops through Ansbach had been accepted without comment in previous wars. Now, however, members of the Prussian war party seized upon the encroachment as a violation of Prussian neutrality. Ultimately the action was profoundly embarrassing for Prussia. Prussian mobilization had positioned 40 percent of its forces in the east facing Russia and the Prussians had refused to allow Russian armies assembled on the Prussian frontier to cross their territory. With French troops marching freely through Ansbach, appearances of Prussian neutrality were compromised. This had the effect of causing Tsar Alexander briefly to toy with the idea of ordering his troops to force a passage through Prussia, even if they had to fight their way through.

Upon reaching the Danube, Napoleon immediately ordered his forces across. On 8 October, Murat's cavalry encountered an isolated detachment of Austrians under General Auffenberg at Wertingen and mauled it badly. In the process, he learned from prisoners taken that the bulk of Mack's army remained to the west and had not yet begun to retire. On 9 October the French corps poured across the Danube, Ney's 6th Corps forcing a passage in the face of Austrian resistance at Günzburg, the other corps crossing largely unopposed. Once across, Napoleon ordered the 1st Corps (with the Bavarians) and the 3rd Corps to march to the east to block the advance of any reinforcements. The remaining corps maneuvered to encircle Ulm. Soult's 4th Corps marched south to Landsberg and then turned west, reaching Memmingen (due south of Ulm) on 13 October. Marmont's 2nd Corps marched in a narrower arc to Soult's right while the 5th and 6th Corps, along with most of Murat's Cavalry Reserve, marched due west on Ulm.

With the French noose tightening, many of the generals surrounding Mack urged him to take decisive action to break out of the trap. Mack finally agreed, and ordered a probe down the north bank of the Danube in preparation for retreat. On 11 October, this force of roughly 23,000 met the lone French division remaining north of the Danube, General Dupont's division from the 6th Corps, between Haslach and Jungingen. The outnumbered French put up fierce resistance against the half-hearted attacks by the confused and demoralized Austrians. In the end, the French were forced to withdraw after inflicting heavy losses on the Austrian force, but the Austrian force also withdrew to Ulm. Mack now insisted that the westward movement of the French indicated not an encirclement of his position but rather a desperate attempt to return to France where he imagined that a British landing or fresh uprising had created a grave crisis. For two days Mack did nothing, allowing the French to concentrate for the *coup de grâce*.

Finally, on 14 October, in a "muddle of orders and counterorders," Mack resolved once again to attempt a breakout to the north. Two Austrian corps under Generals Werneck and Riesch set out in parallel columns along the north bank of the Danube. Riesch's corps, marching closest to the Danube, was intercepted by Ney's 6th Corps at Elchingen. After several hours of desperate fighting, Riesch's corps was badly mauled and driven back to Ulm while Werneck's corps was separated and escaped to the north pursued by Murat's cavalry. The failure of the attempt plunged Mack into a fit of despondency while his generals urged him to take action. Finally, despairing of any positive action from Mack, on the night of 14/15 October, Ferdinand and Schwarzenberg led a small body of 6,000 cavalry out of Ulm in hopes of joining forces with Werneck's corps, abandoning Mack and the bulk of the army to its fate. By 15 October, the encirclement of Ulm was completed as Ney's 6th Corps moved into position west of the city. Ney immediately stormed the outer redoubts of the defenses of Ulm, occupying advance positions from which he could begin a bombardment of the city itself.

By the end of the next day, the French forces encircling Ulm were ready to begin the bombardment of the city and Napoleon sent his staff officer, Segur, in search of Mack to seek a capitulation. Segur met with Mack around 3:00 A.M. on the 17th. After several hours of negotiation in which Mack sought the best terms possible, the Austrian commander, architect of his own misfortune, agreed to capitulation if reinforcements did not arrive by 25 October. It seems clear that Mack still expected the Russians to arrive by 20 October or soon after, and he seems to have had some expectation that Kutuzov's 35,000 or so men would join with the 18,000 Austrians remaining off to the east and Werneck's corps of 9,000 to drive off the nearly 200,000 French and Bavarian troops that stood between them and Ulm.

In the aftermath of Mack's negotiations, circumstances kept getting worse for his army. On 18 October Murat caught up with Werneck's corps at Trochtelfingen and forced it to surrender. One of Werneck's columns that was marching along a parallel route refused to surrender despite being included in Werneck's capitulation and continued on to Bohemia, eventually linking with the remnants led by Ferdinand and Schwarzenberg. The next day, Napoleon notified Mack of the capitulation of Trochtelfingen.

Meanwhile the forces within Ulm were rapidly disintegrating. The departure of Ferdinand and Schwarzenberg had inflicted a devastating blow to the already low morale of the army, which now felt abandoned by its general (figurehead though he may have been). The damage to morale rendered by their commander's departure was compounded when word of Mack's terms spread and the troops learned that they were to become prisoners of the French while their officers would be released on parole. In light of the rapidly deteriorating situation, what little will to resist that Mack still possessed evaporated. On 19 October Mack agreed to surrender his forces the next day, the only condition being that Ney's single corps remain at Ulm until 25 October. On 20 October, the Austrians marched out of Ulm. In all 51 battalions, 18¼ squadrons, and 60 guns were surrendered to the French.

The rapidity with which Napoleon abandoned his plans for the invasion of England and flung an army of overwhelming force against Austria stunned the allies and shattered their plans for the campaign. This had devastating repercussions for the allied armies. The Austrian Army of Germany had ceased to exist except for scattered detachments that were being hunted down by the French. To the south, General Jellacic's division which had been detached from the Army of Tyrol had been cut off and forced to beat a hasty retreat back into the mountains where it joined the other forces arriving from the southern Tyrol and Italy. To the north a small corps of about 18,000 under General Kienmayer that had been positioned on Mack's right flank (later placed under the command of General Merveldt) pulled back behind the Inn where it joined Kutuzov's Russians, which had begun arriving at Braunau on 9 October. By 26 October Kutuzov had assembled roughly 27,000 Russians around Braunau, with another 11,000 strung out behind him from straggling, detachments, illness and exhaustion.* Napoleon, having destroyed the first allied army he had encountered, now looked to destroy this Russian force and bring the war to a swift conclusion.

---

* Punin, L. *Feldmarshal Kutuzov: voenno-biograficheskii ocherk* (Moscow: Voennoe izdatelstvo Ministrstva Oboroni Souza SSR, 1957), p. 61.

Chapter 2

The Campaign of Austria: 25 October – 20 November

On 21 October 1805, Napoleon issued a proclamation of victory from his headquarters at Elchingen:

> Soldiers of the Grande Armée, in 15 days we have made a campaign. What we proposed is accomplished. We have chased the troops of the House of Austria from Bavaria, and re-established our ally in the sovereignty of his states. That army, which with equal ostentation and impudence came to place itself on our frontiers, is annihilated . . . But we shall not stop here: you are impatient to commence a second campaign. We shall make the Russian Army, which the gold of England has transported from the ends of the universe, undergo the same fate. To this combat is more especially attached the honour of the infantry; it is there that is to be decided, for the second time, that question which has already been decided in Switzerland and Holland [in 1799]: if the French infantry is the second or the first in Europe. There are among them no generals against whom I can have any glory to acquire: all my care shall be to obtain victory with the least possible bloodshed: my soldiers are my children. *

With these words Napoleon announced the beginning of a new campaign to follow on the heels of the decisively successful engagements in Bavaria.

The Allied Armies in the Aftermath of Ulm

The situation of the allies had changed radically by the end of October. Several Austrian battalions had surrendered at Haslach-Jungingen (11 October), Memmingen (13 October), and Elchingen (14 October). But the capitulation at Trochtelfingen (18 October), where Murat's cavalry had caught up to the fleeing remnants of Mack's army, followed by the capitulation of Ulm (20 October) had eliminated practically the entire Austrian Army of Germany. In all, ninety-six Austrian battalions and twenty-six squadrons had surrendered to the French in the course of a week, the majority at Ulm. Many had hardly fired a shot. The French advance had cut off detachments that

---

* Markham, pp. 22–3.

Mack had sent to the south and southwest. Some troops had managed to escape to the south, joining forces with the Archduke John in the Tyrol, while others were trapped by the French at Dornbirn or were captured defending the Tyrolean passes against the French. By 13 November, an additional ten battalions had surrendered.

This unprecedented complete destruction of an entire army derailed all of the allies' war planning. While the advancing Russians had been intended to be a supporting force comprising less than half of the allied Army of Germany, they now constituted the main body. Supporting them was an Austrian corps commanded by Kienmayer, composed mainly of Grenz troops and a few regiments that had peacetime garrisons further to the east and had not yet arrived in Bavaria. Added to these were the handful of scattered detachments that had not fallen into the French net. To the north, approximately 1,900 out of the 6,000 cavalry that had escaped from Ulm with Ferdinand and Schwarzenberg arrived exhausted at Eger in Bohemia on 23 October.

Immediately orders were issued to assemble all available forces. Battalions that had been left as garrisons in various parts of the empire were called in, their places in the garrisons being taken by their regimental reserve battalions. The reserve battalions of the remaining regiments accelerated recruitment and were hurried into service while the cavalry depots contributed partial squadrons, sometimes with as few as forty mounted troopers each. Even the Grenz battalions that were permanently retained on the Turkish frontier contributed to the effort, each providing a company to be assembled into a provisional regiment at Agram (Zagreb). As the French Army advanced inexorably eastward down the Danube valley, these battalions trickled in from every corner of the Habsburg lands, assembling at Vienna, Prague, Laibach and Ofen (Buda) in the month following the capitulation of Ulm. Even in the face of disaster, however, the deep traditional divisions of the Habsburg Empire were apparent. The reserve battalions of the fifteen Hungarian regiments and all of the mounted hussars from the regimental depots were assembled at Ofen, Raab, and Ödenburg where they would remain for the defense of the Hungarian lands. In an attempt to secure its own territory further, the Hungarian Diet had agreed to raise the *Insurrectio*, a sort of traditional feudal militia, promising 20,000 additional men within six to eight weeks, but like the reserve battalions these were to be used for the defense of Hungary.

The capitulation of Ulm also forced Russia to make adjustments. On 20 October, apparently in response to Prussian actions, Alexander issued orders reorganizing the Russian armies still gathering on the frontier. Prussia remained uncommitted and in fact still maintained a substantial body of troops in Poland facing east. This mobilization, designed to protect Prussian neutrality from any hostile act by the Russians, reflected the tensions that had existed between Berlin and St Petersburg since the Second and Third Partitions of Poland a decade before. At that time, Prussia and Russia had been poised to wage war against each other until the weight of Austria's alliance with Russia forced Prussia to back down. Now Alexander faced a Prussia that he hoped to win over as an ally, but that he feared would take advantage of any opportunity that presented itself for gains at Russia's expense.

The three Russian field armies that were mobilizing on the frontier were arrayed from the Baltic coast to Volhynia in the south. Bennigsen's Army of the North stood with its right at Taurogen and its left at Grodno. Buxhöwden's Army of Volhynia and Essen-1's Army of Lithuania assembled in roughly the same area, the Army of Volhynia between Ustiluge and Brest-Litovsk and the Army of Lithuania extending slightly further north from Ustiluge to Jalovka (near Bialystok). To the rear of these armies, a small Reserve Corps under GL Rimsky-Korsakov was assembling, composed of a few full regiments and most of the assembled depot squadrons and half squadrons of the cavalry of the other armies.

While the original allied planning had been based on the assumption of Prussian cooperation, with the northernmost armies marching in parallel across Prussian territory, circumstances now required a different approach. Alexander briefly considered the idea of ordering his army to force a passage through Prussian territory, but hesitated to make an enemy of Prussia at a time when all available manpower was needed to oppose France. Instead, Alexander ordered the reorganization of the three armies and Reserve Corps to form two new armies to march westward while a much larger Reserve Army would remain on the frontier to observe Prussia. The Reserve Army, to be commanded by Rimsky-Korsakov, would be composed of fifty-six battalions and seventy squadrons distributed between Taurogen in the north and Ustiluge in the south, organized in four main divisions positioned at key points on the Prussian frontier. The remaining forces were divided into two armies, the Army of Volhynia under the command of Buxhöwden, and the Army of Lithuania under the command of Bennigsen. Essen-1's army (formerly the Army of Lithuania) would be split between the two, the Russian Life Guard at Brest-Litovsk joining Buxhöwden's army and the remainder (less the regiments assigned to the Reserve Army) assigned to Bennigsen. Buxhöwden's reorganized army was ordered to march as soon as possible, and set off five days later (25 October), skirting the edge of Prussian territory and passing through Austrian Galicia. The forces from Buxhöwden's original army from Ustiluge and Brest-Litovsk set off first, formed into five columns. The Life Guard, along with the Life Grenadier regiment, formed in two columns and brought up the rear after a short delay, presumably to amass supplies for the march and to prevent the columns from bunching up en route.

With roughly 38,000 troops marching to reinforce Kutuzov, Alexander set off for Berlin to try to persuade Frederick William to join the coalition or, at a minimum, to allow the passage of Bennigsen's army of about 38,000 (assembled at Taurogen, Grodno and Brest-Litovsk) by the most direct route across Poland and Silesia. Alexander met with Frederick William at Potsdam on the night of 2 November, and finally persuaded the reluctant king to allow the passage of Russian troops and to join the coalition against France. However, Frederick William, still concerned about the possible outcome of Napoleon's devastatingly effective campaign in the Danube valley that was drawing nearer and nearer to Vienna, insisted on drafting an ultimatum to issue to Napoleon, demanding French withdrawal from Austrian territory and giving Napoleon time to comply before actively joining the coalition. Nevertheless, by 11 November, Bennigsen's army was on the march across Prussian territory, the two southernmost columns under the command of Essen-1 angling south to reinforce Kutuzov while the remainder marched directly from Taurogen and Grodno toward Bohemia.

While the Austrians and Russians were doing everything possible to bring additional forces to bear against the French, their prospects on the Danube remained bleak. At the time of the capitulation of Ulm, the Russian Army was hardly in a position to take on the victorious Grande Armée in its entirety. Having left the camp of Radzivilov with roughly 46,000 men, impending war with the Turks had forced Kutuzov to send the rearmost column of his Army of Podolia, that of GL Rosen, marching off toward Moldavia, drawing off about 7,000 men or 15 percent of his command. In addition, detachments, stragglers and illness during the long and (for Russian troops) rapid march had reduced the remainder of Kutuzov's corps by an additional 11,000 men by the time it had reached Braunau. Prussia's vacillation had already delayed the march of the additional supporting armies, which could not be expected in the Danube valley for at least another month.

Kutuzov was well aware of the tremendous disparity in strength between his depleted army, even considering Austrian detachments that were now his auxiliaries, and the powerful French forces. In assessing the situation, Kutuzov arrived at the only possible course of action—to withdraw eastward, taking whatever opportunities might present themselves for slowing the French advance. This strategy, celebrated by Russian historians as a glorious "march-maneuver," was no more than a retreat upon the army's line of communications. Nonetheless, it was based on sound military reasoning. The detachments, stragglers and convalescents left on the line of march would be collected as the army retreated, allowing the recovery of most of the 11,000 men who had faded away as the army had marched from Radzivilov to Braunau. Further, retreat would draw Kutuzov's army closer to the Russian forces advancing from the east while the series of rivers running from the mountains in the south to the Danube presented a series of defensive lines that could be used to slow the French pursuit. Finally, while Kutuzov could expect his own numbers to increase the further he retreated, the French would inevitably grow weaker as they detached forces to cover their southern flank and occupy the Tyrol, watch Austrian forces assembling in Bohemia, and secure their long line of communications. The Campaign of Austria, which Napoleon hoped to bring to a conclusion in a great battle west of Vienna, would instead take on the character of a game of cat and mouse.

From the Isar to the Enns: 25 October – 8 November

Following the capitulation of Ulm on 20 October, the French Army stood in an excellent position to capitalize on its astonishing success. Under the terms of the capitulation, the French 6th Corps had to remain in position at Ulm until 25 October—the amount of time that the forces at Ulm could conceivably have held out in expectation of relief. Beyond this, Napoleon was free to operate against Kutuzov with the rest of his forces. Accordingly, Napoleon ordered his corps to assemble on the Isar in preparation for launching his campaign against Kutuzov. On the right, the 1st and 2nd Corps assembled near Munich with Marmont detaching Dumonceau's (Dutch) division from the 2nd Corps at Augsburg where Napoleon established his headquarters. Davout's 3rd Corps marched from Dachau (near Munich) to take position at Freising further north. Lannes's 5th Corps, which had pursued Ferdinand's fugitive force as far as Nordlingen, recrossed the Danube and assembled at Landshut. The Cavalry Reserve, spread out in the encirclement of Ulm, assembled at these three main points on the Isar with Klein's dragoon division taking position on the far left along the Danube. Soult's 4th Corps, which had circled to the south of Ulm, had further to march, and reached Landsberg on the 23rd and proceeded toward Munich. Further west, Marshal Augereau's 7th Corps, which had reached the Rhine at Huningen on 23 October, was ordered to march south into the Vorarlberg where General Jellacic's division had been cut off by the French forces around Ulm. Finally, to Augereau's left stood Ney's 6th Corps on the left bank of the Danube opposite Ulm.

As the French maneuvered into position for a fresh offensive, the Bavarian troops that had withdrawn to the northwest as the Austrians advanced also placed themselves at Napoleon's disposal. Napoleon joined two Bavarian divisions to the 1st Corps. The remaining Bavarian forces, along with several

the Austrian rearguard on three sides, driving them from the position. Although the French netted 400 Austrian prisoners at the cost of 54 of their own wounded, Schustek's force had held the position long enough that nightfall prevented any significant French pursuit of the remainder.[*]

On the next day, Davout ordered the 1st Chasseurs à Cheval and 17th Line to advance at the head of the column, followed by the remainder of GdB Demont's brigade. Beaumont's dragoons and the remainder of Bisson's division followed four kilometers to the rear with Walther's dragoon division and d'Hautpoul's cuirassiers trailing behind. Schustek had halted at Lambach, where he was reinforced by an additional battalion sent by Merveldt. The leading French forces, though outnumbered, engaged the Austrians, keeping them busy until the remainder of Bisson's infantry and Beaumont's dragoons arrived. At this point, Schustek sent an urgent plea for reinforcements to Bagration, who stood with his rearguard a short distance to the north near Wels. Bagration detached GM Ulanius with two battalions of Jäger and a squadron of Pavlograd Hussars, and the Russian force arrived in time to prevent a flanking maneuver on the Austrian right. To the south, however, the French extended their line and eventually drove the Austrians back after having been engaged for about five hours. In all, the French claimed 500 Austrian prisoners and one Russian gun. Bagration reported 100 killed and 44 wounded from the small Russian contingent.[†]

The actions at Ried and Lambach were minor delaying actions by the allied rearguards, but successfully slowed the French forces leading the advance. While the 3rd Corps had advanced due east from Braunau, Lannes's 5th Corps had marched northeast to Schärding from Braunau before turning east and marching on Linz. To the south, the 1st and 2nd Corps swept the countryside, skirting the edge of the mountains and driving small Austrian detachments before them. Marmont marched due east to the Traun before marching downstream (northeast) to cross the Traun behind Davout and Soult at Lambach. On the far right, Bernadotte occupied Salzburg on the morning of the 30th and the next day sent Deroi's 1st Bavarian Division in pursuit of Austrian detachments falling back to the south into the Alpine passes to safeguard the flank of the retreating Army of Tyrol.[‡] Bernadotte then led the

---

[*] Ibid., pp. 51–2.

[†] GdD Bisson was wounded the next day (1 November) near the bridge at Lambach, which was burnt by the Austrian rearguard, and replaced by GdD Caffarelli. The *shef* of the Russian 8th Jäger, Colonel Golovkin, was killed and Colonel Laptev would later replace him in command of the regiment. Alombert and Colin, IV, p. 61.

[‡] Deroi would later fall under the orders of Ney whose 6th Corps was operating in the Tyrol further to the west. The Austrian forces were composed of 6½ battalions and 2 squadrons under the command of General Szenassy. They fell back to defend the Lueg Pass, the main route south from Salzburg, and also the more rugged Potschenhohe Pass.

remainder of his divisions down the Traun behind Marmont toward Lambach.

By 3 November, the leading French corps stood on the Traun, with Lannes's 5th Corps at Linz and Ebelsburg and Davout's 3rd Corps just east of Lambach. Soult's 4th Corps approached Lambach from the west and Marmont's 2nd Corps from the southwest, strengthening the French center. Further to the rear, Bernadotte's 1st Corps followed in Marmont's wake. Two additional divisions, Dupont's (detached from the 6th Corps at Ulm on 25 October) and Dumonceau's Dutch division (detached from 2nd Corps at Augsburg), along with Klein's dragoon division, converged on Passau.

Except for the rearguard left at Ried and Lambach and scattered Austrian detachments, the French had met with little resistance on their march from the Isar to the Traun. Faced with pressure from the Austrians, however, Kutuzov finally determined to make a stand behind the Enns River. The French had paused for two days on the line of the Traun to assemble their forces, and Kutuzov took advantage of this respite to take position behind the Enns while the allied rearguards of Bagration and Nostitz remained west of the river to slow the French advance. Kutuzov had no intention of fighting a pitched battle, still being severely outnumbered by the five French corps pursuing him. Nevertheless, he considered the position strong enough to be able to delay the French advance for a couple of days before being forced to retire.

As the French forces worked to repair the burnt bridges over the Traun and sought alternative crossings, Kutuzov drew his main body through Linz and across the River Enns at the town of Enns and set them to work preparing the defenses of the river line. On Kutuzov's left, Merveldt assembled his corps of Austrians behind the Enns near Steyr. It was not until 4 November that the French forces finally crossed the Traun in force and drove the Russian rearguard back on the Enns, with Bagration's forces crossing the river just minutes before the pursuing French cavalry arrived. A party of hussars from Bagration's rearguard burned the bridge behind them under enemy fire. With the Russians assuming a strong position near Enns, Napoleon intended to outflank the main Russian force by directing Gazan's division (from 5th Corps) to cross to the left bank of the Danube to outflank the position to the north. Davout would march with his three divisions on Steyr where he would engage Merveldt's forces, which were considered an easier opponent.

Davout's forces arrived at Steyr at 8:00 A.M. on 5 November where they found four Austrian battalions defending the crossing. Davout deployed his forces and stormed the bridge, Eppler's brigade of Caffarelli's division (formerly Bisson's) seizing the bridge with difficulty. Once the bridge was in

French hands, they quickly occupied the town, capturing the better part of one Austrian company in the process. Unlike the action at Lambach, however, no reinforcements were forthcoming. Merveldt, operating on direct orders from Vienna, had marched off to the southeast to link up with the armies of the Archdukes John and Charles. Kutuzov was unaware of these orders and it seems that a later order instructing Merveldt to remain in position only arrived after the Austrian corps had drawn off. As a result, once the French occupied the town, the Austrian rearguard retired to rejoin Merveldt and Kutuzov's left rear was exposed.[*]

Merveldt's withdrawal from Steyr made any attempt by Kutuzov to hold the line of the Enns futile. By the evening of 5 November, Kutuzov's forces had left their defenses on the Enns to beat a hasty retreat eastward, covered by their rearguard. Murat and Lannes, eager to engage their elusive enemy, set off in hot pursuit. The weather had changed a few days earlier, and a blanket of snow covered the ground, slowing the movements of both armies. Icicles hung from the trees "like glittering chandeliers" according to one account.[†] Murat ordered his forces across the Enns and by 9:00 A.M. on 5 November they were all across and ready to set off on the trail of the fleeing Russians.[‡]

GdB Trelliard's two regiments of hussars led the French forces and soon encountered the enemy, a small party of Austrians composed of three battalions of infantry and some supporting cavalry near Strengberg. Trelliard called for reinforcements and Murat immediately sent part of Dupas's brigade of grenadiers and a regiment of chasseurs to reinforce Trelliard. The French quickly drove the Austrians from their position and pursued them into a forest where they opposed the French force for a while longer before being flanked by French chasseurs and forced to retreat again. The pursuit continued, with the Austrians making several more stands and being driven from each position in succession. By 3:00 P.M., the French pursuit had led them into a long narrow defile, the road lined on both sides by forest. There the leading regiments of French light cavalry drew up short at the edge of a clearing where, in addition to the three battalions of weary Austrians they met a line of nine battalions of Russian infantry supported by two regiments (eighteen squadrons) of Russian and Austrian hussars.

The French hussars, with Murat himself in their midst, immediately

---

[*] Napoleon's spy, Schulmeister was supplying intelligence to Napoleon at this time and it is possible that Merveldt's orders to withdraw were known to Napoleon at the time that he issued orders for the flanking maneuver. Alombert and Colin, IV, p. 68.

[†] Duffy, *Austerlitz*, p. 59.

[‡] Murat's forces consisted of Milhaud's light cavalry and Walther's dragoons, which were to cross the Enns between 5:00 and 6:00 A.M. Trelliard's light cavalry and Oudinot's grenadiers would follow between 6:00 and 7:00, with the cuirassiers of d'Hautpoul and Nansouty bringing up the rear, crossing after 7:00. Alombert and Colin, IV, pp. 89–90.

wheeled about and fled down the road pursued by the Russian hussars, who nearly overwhelmed the French. An alert young officer with two pieces of artillery, however, salvaged the situation by firing his guns and setting off an avalanche of snow and icicles from the trees, which spooked the horses sufficiently to allow the French hussars to escape, but not before they lost 300 killed or prisoners. "This was a new experience for Murat," observed Segur, "who recognised that he had no longer to do with the Austrians but with very different kind of men."[*]

Somewhat shaken, Murat ordered up additional forces, first Dupas's two battalions and then the whole of Oudinot's grenadier division, supported by additional cavalry (the light cavalry brigade of Milhaud and the dragoon brigade of Sebastiani). Soon the ten battalions of French grenadiers were advancing against Bagration's position and Bagration was requesting assistance from Kutuzov. Kutuzov responded by sending Miloradovich with twelve battalions and ten squadrons to support Bagration. With Miloradovich's arrival, the French forces were hard pressed and only with effort managed to repulse three successive counterattacks by the Russians. The fighting continued long after it had grown dark, and it was not until 9:00 P.M. that the firing ceased and the allied forces withdrew from their position.

The action at Amstettin had left an impression on the French. Segur wrote that:

> In this first encounter 2,000 Russians were killed or taken; not one of them surrendered; wounded, disarmed, and biting the dust, they not only defended themselves but even continued to attack us. After the fighting was over, in order to carry away a few hundreds of them, we were obliged to prick them up with our bayonets, like a badly broken-in flock of sheep, or to knock them down with the butt ends of our muskets.[†]

Far from pursuing a demoralized enemy who lacked the ability to oppose them, the French now realized that Kutuzov's army had teeth and could bite.

At his headquarters at Linz, Napoleon, frustrated at his failure to pin down Kutuzov's army up to this point, was laying new plans for trapping it. On 6 November, Napoleon ordered Marshal Mortier to proceed immediately to Linz to assume command of Gazan's division (from the 5th Corps), which had just been ordered to the north bank of the Danube from Linz on the day before. The forces assembled at Passau, which included the two infantry divisions of Dupont and Dumonceau along with Klein's dragoon division, were already marching toward Linz, and once there would cross to the left bank of the

---

[*] Philippe-Paul Segur, *An Aide-de-Camp of Napoleon: Memoirs of General Count Segur* (Tyne & Wear: Worley Publications, 1995), p. 215.

[†] Ibid., p. 216.

Danube as well. These forces would comprise a new 8th Corps under Mortier's command. The 8th Corps would then march down the left bank of the river, seeking to cut off Kutuzov's retreat by securing the Danube river crossings between Linz and Vienna, effectively separating him from the reinforcements marching from Russia.

The detachment of these divisions to the left bank of the Danube carried considerable risk and was based on Napoleon's erroneous assumption that Kutuzov intended to stand and fight in front of Vienna—probably near St Pölten—based on the fierceness of the Russian defense at Amstettin.* The forces north of the Danube would be largely isolated from the rest of the army, and if attacked could not be reinforced easily. Still, Napoleon considered the opportunity to trap Kutuzov south of the river to be worth the risk. To help minimize the danger, Napoleon ordered the formation of a small flotilla from fifty boats to be procured at Passau, placing Captain Lostange, a naval captain who was serving on Murat's staff, in command. Men for the flotilla would be provided by drawing fifty men from each of the divisions of Lannes and Marmont (250 men in all) plus dragoons who had lost their mounts. This flotilla would ensure communications between the forces on both banks of the Danube and facilitate the coordinated operations that Napoleon was convinced would trap Kutuzov south of the Danube and bring about a pitched battle near St Pölten within a week.

The Threat to France

Once he had taken care of his preparations for trapping Kutuzov, Napoleon paused at Linz to attend to matters further afield. Reports had been coming in from various corners of Europe, the most important news arriving from the French embassies in Berlin and Copenhagen.

On 8 and 9 October Duroc, special emissary in Berlin, and Laforest, the French ambassador to Prussia, both wrote of increasing Prussian hostility as a result of the Ansbach incident and of the growing influence of the Russian, Austrian and British ministers in the Prussian court. French agents reported on 13 October that the Prussian king had ordered full mobilization of the Prussian Army by 1 November and on the 14th several Prussian regiments had marched into Hanover with the stated purpose of occupying the territory until the cessation of hostilities. Ten days later French agents were reporting that Prussian forces in Franconia had been ordered to double march to Bayreuth and that Hessian forces were to arrive in four days.† Finally, and

---

* Paul-Claude Alombert-Goget, *Campagne de l'an 14 (1805) Le corps d'armée aux ordres du maréchal Mortier* (Paris: Berger-Levrault et cie, 1897), p. 21, quoting Mathieu Dumas. Also Segur, p. 216.

† Alombert and Colin, III, pp. 677–9; 703–4; 720–1; 1132.

perhaps most alarmingly, Napoleon received the report that Frederick William had met with Alexander at Potsdam on the night of 2 November. While the details of the meeting were not yet known, the increasing tensions with Prussia reported by Duroc and Laforest provided a good indication of the direction Prussia was heading.

In addition to Prussian mobilization, General Victor, special emissary to Copenhagen, wrote to Napoleon on 12 October informing him of the arrival of a Russian force of 20,000 men at Stralsund. Victor also noted that a portion of the Russian fleet was to continue on to reinforce the Russians at Corfu, that the Swedish forces in Pomerania now numbered 8,000 and that more Swedes were en route from Karlskrona. In addition to the more than 30,000 Russians and Swedes that were massing, Victor also reported that the Danes had mobilized their army to join the coalition, although in fact this force was only intended to occupy Schleswig-Holstein to defend Denmark's neutrality. Denmark, along with Mecklenburg, Hesse-Kassel, Brunswick and Saxony had made tentative commitments to join the coalition only if Prussia joined.* By 14 October the Russian troops had been disembarked at Stralsund in Swedish Pomerania and on 17 October the Russian force had entered Mecklenburg and was heading west. By 30 October, the Russians were poised on the frontier of Hanover awaiting the arrival of their allies.

While Napoleon had already taken measures to secure his line of communications, the massing of Russian and Swedish troops in the far north confirmed the allies' intention to move on the undefended lower Rhine. French and Batavian forces left in Holland had been deployed to defend against a seaborne invasion by the British, while Lefebvre's 2nd Reserve Corps at Mayence was integral to securing the communications of the Grande Armée. To counter the new allied threat in the north, Napoleon ordered the formation of a new Armée du Nord to be commanded by Louis Bonaparte. Forces for this army would be drawn from the interior of France, Holland and the three Reserve Corps. The Armée du Nord would then provide the defense of the lower Rhine and Batavian territory east of the Rhine while the Armée du Réserve would defend Boulogne and the middle and upper Rhine as before. The defense of the coasts would be left to a handful of regiments stationed in the major ports along with the flying camps at Poitiers and Alessandria (in Piedmont). To compensate for the withdrawal of regular troops, the National Guard would raise additional cohorts and assume greater responsibility for the defense of the coasts.

With the formation of the Armée du Nord to augment the Armée du Réserve, Napoleon created a direct obstacle to the advance of the coalition

---

* Ibid., III, p. 1132.

forces in the north. In reality, both armies were more impressive on paper than in reality. Only the first two of the six divisions of the Armée du Nord were composed of complete French battalions. The 3rd and 4th Divisions were formed from provisional battalions created from the first three companies of each of the battalions of the 2nd and 3rd Reserve Corps. These battalions, the 3rd and 4th battalions of the regiments of the Grande Armée, were already understrength and contained a high proportion of recruits. The 5th and 6th Divisions of the Armée du Nord were composed primarily of severely understrength Dutch battalions along with the handful of French battalions left on the coast of Holland.

While the military worth of the improvised Armée du Nord was therefore somewhat dubious, misinformation that was circulated regarding its strength successfully disguised its weakness. Prussian sources estimated the strength of the two armies remaining in France at 81,000 men, taking reports from France at face value. Even in early December, British reports placed the strength of French forces on the Ems River at about 30,000 men, more than the entire strength of the Armée du Nord, even though it seems that not all of the army was present on the Ems at the time of the British report. In fact, the armies amounted to about 25,000 men each, but the exaggerated reports prompted the allied forces in the north to proceed with caution.

Although Napoleon's orders issued from Linz indicated some worry over the allied forces in the north, he did not have much cause for concern. GL Tolstoi ordered his forces across the Elbe at Lauenburg on 9 November, and GM Ostermann-Tolstoi marched with the Russian advance guard on Lüneburg and then into Hanoverian territory without meeting any opposition. To the contrary, the advance resembled a triumphant march, the crowds in Mecklenburg and Hanover cheering the Russian columns as they passed.[*] When the Russian main body arrived in Hanover, Tolstoi detached GM Verderevsky with a brigade to observe Hameln where the French forces remaining in Hanover had been assembled after the departure of Bernadotte's I Corps. Tolstoi then proceeded with the remainder of his force to the Weser, placing his main body between Hameln and Cuxhaven where a British force was expected to arrive. Tolstoi established his headquarters at Nienburg with the main body in and around that town on the right bank of the Weser while Ostermann-Tolstoi established a bridgehead on the left bank of the Weser opposite Nienburg.

Despite the slow beginning to the operations, by the end of the first week of November Tolstoi had reasons to be optimistic. Swedish forces had finally

---

[*] A. Mikhailovski-Danilevski, *Relation de la Campagne de 1805* (Paris: J. Dumaine, 1846), pp. 342–3.

set out from Pomerania to join Ostermann and the British were finally en route to Hanover. The Swedish advance guard of von Cardell had crossed the frontier on 1 November, marching for Lüneburg, and King Gustav IV Adolf had arrived in Stralsund on 6 November to assume command of the combined coalition forces. The main body of the Swedish corps, in two columns, left Pomerania on the 7th and 10th, while an additional 3,600 men from Sweden arrived in Stralsund on the 8th. The British contingent had assembled at Ramsgate, embarked at the Downs on 5 November and would soon arrive at Cuxhaven. Finally, Prussia had moved firmly into alignment, if not yet active alliance, with the coalition, after the meeting between the king and the tsar at Potsdam on the night of 2–3 November. This served to secure the rear of the allied forces, though Prussian insistence on first issuing an ultimatum to Napoleon and giving him until 15 December to comply before joining the allies would delay any actual military cooperation.

The allies in Hanover quickly proved the disadvantages of coalition armies, however, being as wary of each other as they were of the French. Gustav IV Adolf, inexperienced and probably temperamentally unsuited for command of any military force (or ruling a country), almost immediately began floundering. On 12 November, while his advance guard was still moving on Lüneburg, the Swedish king became alarmed at the mobilization of Prussian forces, immediately relinquished his position as commander of the coalition forces and recalled the Swedish Army to defend the borders of Swedish Pomerania. Accordingly all but an advance guard of four battalions and two squadrons of cavalry withdrew and lined the borders of Pomerania while the advance guard maintained a tentative position straddling the Elbe at Haarburg and Lauenburg.

The withdrawal of the Swedes had caught Tolstoi, and indeed everyone else, completely by surprise. While the tsar issued a personal appeal to Gustav IV Adolf to resume active participation in the operations against the French, Tolstoi looked for Prussian leadership, but Prussia was adamant about waiting until 15 December. With Prussia on hold and Gustav Adolf stoutly defending the frontiers of his province, Tolstoi had become the *de facto* commander of the coalition forces, which at that moment included only his own troops and the newly arrived British.

The Russian and British forces, with little concrete information about the enemy they were facing, consolidated their positions in Hanover on the line of the Weser. The first of Cathcart's British force—6,000 men of the King's German Legion (KGL) under the command of General Don—had arrived at Cuxhaven on 8 November, after encountering rough weather during the crossing from England, and immediately marched up the Weser to make contact with Tolstoi. Nine days later the second contingent, nine battalions of British regulars, including two Guards battalions, arrived at Cuxhaven. In addition, Colonel von der Decken, a Hanoverian who was given the local rank of major-general for this mission, was sent ahead of the British corps to reconnoiter the area and to drum up local support in Hanover. Within a few weeks, Decken had signed up over 5,000 recruits—enough to expand the ranks of the existing KGL battalions to 1,000 men each, to form three new KGL infantry battalions also of 1,000 men, and to form two additional KGL cavalry regiments of 650 men each. While the new forces were not trained sufficiently to be used for front-line tasks, the recruits could be used for line of communications and garrison duties in the rear areas, freeing up the trained troops for front-line service.

Despite the promising situation of the allied forces in Hanover by 20 November, it was a case of too little too late. The Russian and British forces, which included some of the finest units in either army, numbered 35,000 (excluding the new Hanoverian recruits) but still lacked sufficient numbers simultaneously to screen or invest Hameln and undertake offensive operations against the French on the Rhine with any confidence of success. Reports of the strength of the French armies opposing them and lack of immediate support from either Sweden or Prussia prevented the allied forces in Hanover from having any significant effect on the course of the war aside from the small amount of administrative work forced upon Napoleon at Linz.

Operations in Italy

The situation in Italy was affected more directly by events in the Danube valley. As the Grande Armée tightened the noose around Mack's Army of Germany, Marshal Massena was preparing to assume the offensive in Italy. On 13 October, the same day that the main body of the Grande Armée was encircling Ulm and the 3rd Corps had reported clashes with Russian cavalry, Massena formally notified the Archduke Charles that hostilities in Italy would commence the following day. Then, after five days of desultory reconnaissances, Massena received the orders he had been waiting for, changing his mission from one of delay and defensive action to actively pinning the Austrian Army in Italy to prevent it from reinforcing the main army to the north.

On 18 October Massena seized a bridgehead over the Adige at Veronetta (near Verona) in preparation for engaging the Austrians. Charles, having received word of the French occupation of Munich the previous day, chose not to attempt to retake the bridgehead. Writing to Francis, Charles stated his concerns and reiterated the need to withdraw from Italy should the army in

Germany suffer defeat. His dispositions clearly show his determination to protect his line of retreat on Vienna. Charles deployed his forces on the Caldiero line where they would be in position to crush any attempted turning maneuver via Legnano, but he gave up the bridgehead at Veronetta without a contest as if to invite a frontal attack. This deployment reflected the fact that a frontal attack posed no threat to his line of retreat while retaking the bridgehead at Veronetta would invite a flanking maneuver in which his line of retreat might be compromised.

Following the French seizure of Veronetta, both sides did little, allowing events in the north to dictate their course of action. On 24 October Hiller, commanding the extreme left of the Austrian Army of Tyrol, conveyed the news of the surrender of Mack's main body at Ulm, confirming Charles's worst fears. Mack had not retreated before the French advance, had allowed his army to be surrounded by the much larger French Army, and his army had ceased to exist. Kienmayer's corps and Kutuzov's Russians were all that remained to oppose the French advance on Vienna. Detachments of the Army of Germany and Archduke John's army in the Tyrol were effectively cut off and would have to scramble to avoid meeting the same fate as Mack. Charles immediately sent a status report to Vienna and announced the news to his army the next day, indicating the need to withdraw from Italy. The French reports bearing the same news, having to travel via a more circuitous route, did not reach Massena's headquarters until the 26th.

The news of Ulm triggered activity in both camps. Massena, outnumbered by the Austrians, had moved most of his forces to the east bank of the Adige in order to attempt to meet them on equal terms, forestall their retreat and to inflict significant casualties. Charles, for his part, planned to attack the French and drive them into their bridgehead at Veronetta. Massena attacked on 30 October, and for two days fought an indecisive battle around Caldiero in which he was unable to gain any significant advantage and in the end was unable to interfere with the Austrian withdrawal. On 1 November, Charles issued orders for the withdrawal from Italy. A rearguard under General Frimont held the French cavalry at bay until nightfall while the Austrian forces made good their retreat. The French pursued, their cavalry harassing the Austrian rearguard, but this did not significantly delay the retreat nor did it accelerate its pace. By 14 November, the day after French forces entered Vienna, the Austrian Army of Italy was across the Isonzo. On the 16th Massena halted his pursuit to consolidate his forces and to link with forces of the Grande Armée, the corps of Ney and Marmont, which were advancing into the Tyrol and Styria.

The final element in the grand allied offensive plan, the landing in Naples which had been intended to drive the French from central Italy in conjunction with Charles's campaign in northern Italy, had become utterly pointless after the surrender of Ulm and Charles's withdrawal from Italy. Nevertheless, three days after the Austrian army crossed the Isonzo, leaving Italy behind, the Anglo-Russian expedition began landing in Naples, unaware of the withdrawal of the Austrians from Italy. Their timing could not have been much worse. The Naples landing force had been intended as a diversion, to distract French forces in central Italy and prevent them from reinforcing the army in the north. The landing had been delayed by several factors, though: lack of Russian transports and the corresponding shortage of British transports to make up for the Russian deficiencies; disagreement over the plan of operations between the Russian chief of staff and the British commander; and finally the bane of every amphibious expedition in the age of sail, contrary winds. Although there was little to oppose a move north, the overall strategic situation kept Lacy's force paralyzed more effectively than a French corps. Lacy's army remained fixed in position while the allied diplomats in Naples and the British and Russian officers argued whether they should remain in place, march north, or re-embark and transfer the entire force to Venice or Trieste. In the end, they remained in place until the outcome of the war had been decided.

Successes and Setbacks: 8–11 November

While Napoleon was issuing orders to secure the lower Rhine from invasion and Massena was pursuing Charles out of Italy, operations were proceeding on the Danube. After seizing Steyr on 5 November, Davout had managed to catch up with Merveldt's Austrian corps, which had marched off to the southeast. After a series of clashes with Austrian rearguards, Davout met up with Merveldt's main body near Mariazell on 8 November. Merveldt's route of march had brought his corps into the Styrian Alps and its rapid pace had left equipment scattered in its wake. By 8 November, Davout had his cavalry and light infantry nipping at Merveldt's heels, driving back detachments that had been left to slow the French pursuit. Davout's advance guard came upon the greater portion of Merveldt's corps occupying a patch of woods near Mariazell around midday. In an engagement lasting several hours, Davout deployed the 13th Light and 108th Line, the four battalions being sufficient to drive the eight Austrian battalions from their positions. The 108th Line continued the pursuit for two hours and, as the fleeing Austrian columns became increasingly disordered, the French took large numbers of prisoners, particularly from the last two battalions, which were nearly cut off from the rest of the force. In all, while incurring only minor losses, Davout's men took 2,000 prisoners and 18 guns from Merveldt's small corps, leaving the remainder fleeing to the southeast, providing an excellent example of how losses become magnified when a body of troops loses its cohesion.

To the south of Davout, Marmont had pursued another portion of Merveldt's corps into the narrow valley of the upper Enns. Marmont destroyed the rearguard of this force, six battalions and six squadrons under General Ruschovsky, at Gross Ramig and Weyer and then pursued the remnants through the Styrian Alps toward Leoben, placing his two divisions across the most direct line of retreat for the Army of Tyrol. From Leoben, Marmont moved on toward Graz while Archduke John's army was forced to divert its march to the southeast to join Archduke Charles.

To the north, Kutuzov's weary Russians were faring much better than Merveldt's tired Austrians. The action at Amstettin had forced the French to proceed with greater caution and the ferocity of the Russian resistance had convinced Napoleon that Kutuzov would make a stand in front of Vienna, most likely near St Pölten. While this seems to have been what the Austrians would have preferred, Kutuzov had no intention of offering battle at the severe numerical disadvantage he faced. Even with the 15,000 Austrians assembled at Vienna, the French forces closing in on the capital were more than double his own strength. On 9 November, Kutuzov ordered his troops to the north bank of the Danube at Krems, burning the bridge behind him. In doing so, Kutuzov abandoned the political prize of Vienna for the military prize of securing his forces and drawing nearer to the reinforcements approaching from Galicia.

Once across the Danube, Kutuzov had good cause to heave a deep sigh of relief. Even outnumbered as he was, the barrier of the Danube presented a formidable obstacle. Crossing the Danube would require the construction of bridges, and then the French would need to file across, presenting opportunities to disrupt bridge construction or to strike at the heads of the French columns as they crossed. The army's Cossacks, though not terribly useful on a battlefield, were splendidly suited for patrolling the banks of the river and even swimming it to seize an unsuspecting French picket to bring back to headquarters for interrogation. Part of the cavalry of Rosen's column, which had been sent toward the Turkish frontier during the advance, had also now arrived and the remainder of this column was nearby. In addition, Buxhöwden's corps was in Moravia, less than two weeks' march away. Any large-scale crossing would require time to prepare, time during which Buxhöwden's corps would draw nearer. Kutuzov finally had reason to be optimistic.

Temporarily relieved of any concern of being attacked by the main body of Napoleon's army, Kutuzov turned on the small body of French troops north of the Danube—Mortier's 8th Corps. By 10 November, all four divisions assigned to Mortier had crossed to the left bank of the Danube, but Gazan's division had crossed at Linz on the 5th and 6th while the other two divisions were just leaving Passau, which gave Gazan a substantial head start. Klein was patrolling with his dragoon division north from the river on independent orders from Napoleon, but had detached a regiment to catch up with Gazan's division to provide cavalry support. By the evening of 10 November Mortier stood with Gazan's division (plus the regiment of dragoons) between Dürrenstein and Loiben. Dupont's division stood at Marbach almost fifty kilometers upstream, while Dumonceau's division was at Persenbeug about seven kilometers beyond Marbach. Kutuzov learned of the positions of the French divisions on the left bank from prisoners captured from the flotilla who had landed in search of food.

Having decided to strike at Gazan's division, Kutuzov instructed his Austrian chief of staff, Schmidt, to draw up a plan to surround and crush the isolated French division with overwhelming force. Bagration's weary Advance Guard would move off to the northeast accompanying the heavy artillery. Essen-2 would remain at Krems with a small reserve of five battalions and three squadrons. The remaining twenty-nine battalions and twelve squadrons would pounce on Mortier.* The attack force would be composed of a flanking group under the overall command of GL Dokhturov. This force would be formed from the columns of Dokhturov and GL Maltitz, each with twelve battalions and five squadrons. The flanking force would march, over mountain paths led by a local guide, around to the rear of Gazan's division so as to emerge from the mountains west of the town of Dürrenstein in three columns. The westernmost, commanded by Schmidt, would face west and oppose any attempts by Dupont to reinforce Gazan's division. The easternmost, commanded by Gerhardt, would arrive north of Dürrenstein and Dokhturov's own column would reach the Danube between the other two columns to be in a position to support either. A detachment from this flanking force (five battalions) under GM Strik would hit the French directly in flank, emerging from the mountains just east of Dürrenstein. While the flanking maneuver was developing, GL Miloradovich with five battalions and two squadrons (about 2,600 men) would pin the French forces frontally. In all, something in the neighborhood of 16,000 men would encircle approximately 5,800 French. Finally, to bait the trap, word was circulated that the Russian

---

* Two battalions, one each from the Narva and Novgorod Musketeers, are not mentioned in the dispositions. They both turn up two days later with Bagration's rearguard, so it seems these battalions may have been accompanying the baggage or have been held in reserve. Mikhailovsky-Danilevsky notes that these battalions were assigned to Bagration's column. "Dispozitsiya Kolonn k Atake Nepriyatelya pri Veiskirkhene, 1805 g. [Oktyabrya 29]" [10 November 1805], in *Dokumenty shtaba M. I. Kutuzova, 1805–1806 Sbornik* (Vilnius: 1951), pp. 135–7.

army was retreating into Moravia and that only a rearguard would be left at Krems.*

The Russian forces set off during the night with the intention of completing their march through the narrow mountain passes by midday on the 11th. At Loiben, Mortier set off first thing in the morning with Gazan's division, intending to seize Stein and Krems. At about the same time, Miloradovich advanced along the river toward Dürrenstein. The two opposing forces met just east of Loiben, and both sides deployed. At first Miloradovich's forces drove back the surprised French advance posts, quickly occupying Unter-Loiben and the woods north of the town. In the woods to the north, Miloradovich deployed parties of skirmishers from his battalion of the 8th Jäger as well as some of his grenadier battalions, though the grenadiers, who had been selected for their height, made conspicuous targets. One Russian officer noted that "At Krems, our grenadiers, of great height and with large plumes, were sent to skirmish; the weak and small French shot them from behind the rocks, as they wished."†

Gazan soon reinforced the 4th Light with a battalion of the 100th Line and counterattacked but, after some initial success, the French attack stalled. Another battalion of the 100th Line and two pieces of artillery were fed into the action, finally tilting the numbers in favor of the French, but by 10:30 the fierce fighting around Unter-Loiben remained deadlocked. Seeking to end the deadlock, Mortier finally decided to commit his remaining forces to drive back Miloradovich. Leaving a single battalion of the 103rd Line to cover his northern flank, Mortier sent the other two battalions along with a battalion of the 100th Line to attack the Russian right. By 11:00, about 4,500 French opposed the 2,600 Russians, and the French were forcing back the Russian right while pressing the attack along the river. Miloradovich, outnumbered and without any information as to the whereabouts of the other Russian columns, was forced to retire, pursued by the French as far as Stein by around noon.

As Miloradovich was being pushed back to the east, GM Strik finally made his belated appearance, emerging from the mountains between Dürrenstein and Loiben. The timing of his arrival varies in different sources, but it appears

---

* The strengths of the Russian columns are typically given as six battalions with Miloradovich and twenty-one battalions for the flanking force. These figures turn up in Furse, Bowden and other secondary accounts and appear to derive from Mikhailovsky-Danilevsky's account. The original Russian dispositions give the totals given in the text above. These dispositions are confirmed in the after-action reports authored by the various generals involved. It is possible that the three missing battalions were left in the mountains to cover the line of communications or remained with the artillery that could not make it through the narrow tracks. The original dispositions and after-action reports are presented in *Dokumenty Shtaba Kutuzova*, pp. 135–61.

† Alexander and Yuri Zhmodikov, *Tactics of the Russian Army in the Napoleonic Wars* (West Chester, Ohio: The Nafziger Collection, 2003), I, p. 44.

that between noon and 1:00 the head of his column arrived. Surprised, Mortier sent the 100th Line to counter Strik's column, called off the advance toward Stein, and pulled his forces back toward Dürrenstein. Strik, with only five battalions, attacked aggressively but, as the French forces assembled, he was soon outnumbered. According to Mortier's report, by 3:00 Strik's column had been driven back into the mountains and fighting had ceased.

The final act of the Battle of Dürrenstein, occurred after 5:00 when Dokhturov's columns descended from the mountain passes and reached the banks of the Danube west of Dürrenstein, cutting off Mortier from the remainder of his corps. Dokhturov's forces, roughly 10,000 strong, substantially outnumbered Gazan's 5,800. Mortier immediately repositioned his units to meet the new threat, leaving only a rearguard to observe Miloradovich to the east. A party of French dragoons sent through Dürrenstein was quickly repulsed by GM Ulanius and the 6th Jäger, but they managed to delay the Russian advance long enough for Mortier to get his forces into position. As darkness fell, Mortier's position was critical.

General Dupont, marching eastwards with his division, had heard the sound of guns earlier in the day and had sent a detachment of cavalry to investigate. They returned around 4:00 P.M. with reports of Russian columns descending toward Dürrenstein and the river road between Dupont and Gazan's division. Dupont immediately rushed off for Dürrenstein at the head of his division, detaching some companies into the mountains to his left as he approached to take the Russian columns in flank. Attacking with his two leading regiments (the 9th Light and 32nd Line), Dupont's forces soon made some headway. Mortier took the opportunity also to launch a fresh attack, and managed to take the town of Dürrenstein. Dokhturov's forces were now the ones in a critical position, attacked in front and rear, having no artillery and being unable to take advantage of their numbers in the narrow space between the river and the mountains. Fierce fighting raged into the night until finally, around 9:00, the firing died down and Dokhturov withdrew his forces over the same mountain passes by which he had arrived.

As at Amstettin, both sides claimed victory at Dürrenstein and again both sides had some justification. The French had performed magnificently. Finding themselves in a very bad situation, they had fought well and had beaten off the disjointed Russian advances by shifting their forces to meet each successive attack. Though Gazan's division had suffered heavy losses, and the entire force retired across the Danube the next day, the battle had been a remarkable achievement of survival against steep odds. For the Russians, the results had been somewhat disappointing. Their own losses had been heavy and the lack of coordination among the Russian columns had prevented the anticipated destruction of Gazan's division. Nevertheless, after a campaign marked by a series of disastrous reverses for the allies, Dürrenstein was a substantial improvement and Francis was so pleased with the results that he awarded Kutuzov the Order of Maria Theresa for his achievement. Gazan's division had been badly mauled, and the French withdrawal to the opposite bank of the river had effectively secured Kutuzov's right flank which had been the primary objective, even if the anticipated complete destruction of Gazan's division had eluded him.

Deception and Counter-Deception: 13–20 November

On Kutuzov's left, the Russian army was secured by the corps of FML Prince Auersperg opposite Vienna. Auersperg's force, though containing a high proportion of recruits in the Austrian 6th battalions, included some of the toughest of the Grenzers, the Székler infantry and hussars from the wilds of Transylvania. In addition, several field battalions that had been left in garrisons when the Army of Germany had assembled at the beginning of the campaign had been gathered and three formidable regiments of cuirassiers completed the force. The Széklers and cuirassiers had been pushed forward to St Pölten as the French had advanced, but after Kutuzov crossed to the north bank of the Danube they had crossed the river as well over the last bridge remaining intact. With the situation apparently secure, Kutuzov looked forward to giving his troops a badly needed rest and awaiting the arrival of Buxhöwden's corps to help even the odds.

Napoleon had been furious with Murat for advancing up the right bank of the Danube in advance of Mortier but Murat soon restored himself in the emperor's good graces. With the small Austrian force in front of Vienna retiring before them, on 12 November, Murat and Lannes led their fast-marching forces into Vienna, but while this political prize was not enough to redeem Murat in Napoleon's eyes, the flamboyant cavalryman would deliver a more valuable success almost through force of will. Frustrated at Kutuzov's escape, the French were anxious to get across the Danube themselves. On arriving in Vienna, they found that a key series of bridges spanning the several channels of the Danube at Vienna, collectively called the Tabor Bridge, remained intact. Auersperg had collected his forces, some 15,000 men, on the opposite bank.

Auersperg had made preparations for destroying the bridges, and charges of gunpowder had been placed at points across the entire length. At the far end of the bridges stood an artillery battery while the Székler Hussars and infantry stood at the ready. Although the French had marched into Vienna on the 12th, Auersperg hesitated to blow the bridges. His reasons are not entirely certain, but it seems that pressure from notables in Vienna, who faced hardship if the only bridge over the Danube for some distance were destroyed, may have played a part. Auersperg may also have anticipated an armistice following the French occupation of the capital. Whatever his reasons for not destroying the bridge immediately on the 12th, at 11:00 A.M. the next day the bridge was still standing when a party of French officers led by General Bertrand arrived at the near side of the bridge.

The French officers met with Colonel Geringer of the Székler Hussars, informing him that an armistice had been signed. Geringer, somewhat suspicious, rode back to the other side for instructions, with the French officers accompanying him. While Geringer was seeking out Auersperg, a column of French grenadiers approached the bridge in the company of Marshals Murat and Lannes and Murat's chief of staff, General Belliard. The French officers approached the Grenzers on the bridge amiably:

> The two marshals dismounted, and only a small detachment entered upon the bridge. General Belliard advanced, walking with his hands behind his back, accompanied by two officers of the staff; Lannes joined him with some others; they walked about, talking together, and at length joined the Austrians. The officer commanding the post, at first directed them to stand back; but at length permitted them to advance, and they entered into conversation together. They repeated what had already been affirmed by General Bertrand, namely, that the negotiations were advancing, that the war was at an end, and that there would be no more fighting and slaughter.*

The relaxed, amicable attitude of the high-ranking French officers persuaded the officer in command that an armistice had indeed been signed. When Lannes suggested that the artillery pointing at the French represented a provocative attitude that might jeopardize the spirit of the armistice, the officer agreed to turn the guns around to face in the other direction. So convincing were Lannes's honeyed words that the Austrian troops even began laying down their arms.

In the wake of the French officers, strolling casually across the bridges, came a platoon of grenadiers, followed by sappers and gunners who cut fuses on the charges on the bridge and threw the charges in the Danube. At this, the Austrian commander finally became suspicious. As he warned the French to halt their progress across the bridges, Lannes and Belliard assured him that the troops were just exercising their legs to keep warm. The officer's gullibility, though, was insufficient to accept this last outrageous bluff and he ordered his men to retrieve their arms and fire on the French. At this point the head of the French party was three-fourths of the way across. As the artillery

---

* Jean Rapp, *Memoirs of General Count Rapp* (Cambridge: Ken Trotman Ltd., 1995), p. 58.

men wheeled their guns back around to aim them at the bridge, the French officers seized the Austrian officer and began yelling and causing a commotion, the Austrian troops holding their fire amidst the confusion. Soon Auersperg arrived with General Bertrand and rode out onto the bridge to confer with the French marshals, who told him that he would be allowed to withdraw his forces unharmed. While Auersperg was meeting with Murat and Lannes, the French troops on the bridge proceeded to destroy the charges on the remainder of the last span. By evening, parties of French cavalry were conducting reconnaissances on the other side and Auersperg's corps was retreating toward Brünn, having dispatched several officers to carry the bad news to Kutuzov and Francis. As soon as news reached Francis, Auersperg was immediately relieved of his command, court-martialed, and replaced by Prince Johann Liechtenstein.

News of the capture of the Tabor Bridge came as a shock to Kutuzov, who had considered it a simple matter to hold the line of the Danube by destroying the bridge. Now, with his left flank and rear compromised, Kutuzov was left with no choice but again to beat a hasty retreat. Kutuzov ordered Bagration's column, already positioned on his left flank, to place itself in the path of the fast-marching French and to buy sufficient time for the remainder of the army to escape. He then ordered his forces to march immediately on Brünn, setting off on the evening of the 13th. The situation was so dire that the wounded were left behind in order to accelerate the pace of the march.

With the capture of the Tabor Bridge intact, the French had an immediate bridgehead on the north bank of the Danube and Lannes and Murat immediately started moving their men across the river. Soult would follow Lannes with his 4th Corps while Davout's three divisions would be positioned around Vienna and would occupy Pressburg. At the same time, Napoleon issued orders for Bernadotte and Mortier to begin crossing to the north bank of the Danube at Melk. Once across, Bernadotte would pursue Kutuzov directly while Mortier would march to Vienna to garrison the city. Marmont would try to make contact with Massena advancing from Italy.

On the 14th, Napoleon himself entered Vienna, while his army streamed across the Tabor Bridge. Margaron's light cavalry brigade from the 4th Corps set off after the retreating Austrians while Walther's dragoon division immediately probed toward Stockerau in search of Kutuzov. On the morning of the 15th, Murat set out toward Stockerau with Trelliard's light cavalry brigade, Oudinot's grenadier division and the cuirassier divisions of d'Hautpoul and Nansouty. Murat's orders were to seize Znaym and cut the road from Krems to Brünn before Kutuzov could pass. Suchet's division and Soult's 4th Corps would follow the next day. Murat had not got very far toward

Znaym when he encountered a party of Russians and Austrians blocking the route to Znaym near the town of Ober-Hollabrunn.

Bagration had set off with his 8,000 men, Austrian and Russian, and arrived at Ober-Hollabrunn around midday on the 15th. Upon reconnoitering the area, Bagration selected a suitable defensive position a short distance to the north near the town of Schöngrabern. After deploying his force and summoning a council of war to discuss plans for battle with the French, outposts reported an enemy column approaching—the leading brigade of Walther's dragoon division. Nostitz had been left in front of Ober-Hollabrunn to provide a first line of defense and to screen the main Russian position, but French officers soon convinced him that an armistice had been signed, pointing to their own apparently unmolested passage over the Tabor bridge as proof. Nostitz withdrew from his advanced position, which the French dragoons occupied with considerable satisfaction.

As Murat arrived at the head of the French light cavalry and cuirassiers, he decided to continue the game that had been begun and maintained the deception of the armistice. Bagration, however, was not easily taken in and decided to play along and turn the game to his own advantage. The Russian commander immediately offered to begin negotiating the terms of an armistice between the French and Russians and sent word to Kutuzov, who ordered two negotiators, Winzingerode and Prince Dolgoruky, to finalize terms. While Kutuzov's troops were marching hard on Znaym, the Russian delegation met with Murat and concluded an arrangement by which the Russians would leave Austrian soil while the French would not advance past Moravia. Both parties agreed to give four hours' notice before resuming hostilities. The terms concluded, Bagration sent the articles off to Kutuzov for ratification and Murat sent them to Napoleon. While the negotiations were going on, Lannes reportedly grumbled that "[if] he had his own way, they would be fighting at the moment, and not exchanging empty compliments."*

When Napoleon received the terms of Murat's negotiated armistice he was understandably furious. He immediately sent a scathing letter to Murat ordering him to break the armistice immediately.

> It is impossible for me to find words to express my displeasure with you.
> You command only my advance guard, and have no right to conclude an
> armistice without my order. You made me lose the fruits of a campaign.
> Break the armistice at once, and march upon the enemy.[†]

* George Armand Furse, *Campaigns of 1805: Ulm, Trafalgar & Austerlitz* (Felling: Worley Publications, 1995), p. 298.

[†] "To Murat," Schönbrunn, 16 November 1805, 8:00 A.M., *Correspondance de Napoléon 1er* <www.histoire-empire.org/correspondance_de_napoleon/correspondance_de_napoleon.htm>.

Then the French emperor set off from Vienna for Schöngrabern forthwith, ordering the Imperial Guard and Caffarelli's division of the 3rd Corps to follow. Murat's actions, apparently intended to buy time for him to bring up the infantry of the 4th and 5th Corps, had backfired badly as he, in turn, was deceived. While Napoleon had perhaps exaggerated when he accused Murat of losing the fruits of what remained an astonishingly successful campaign, Murat had indeed squandered the fruits of the successful subterfuge that had resulted in the capture of the Tabor Bridge, restoring the situation somewhat for Kutuzov's army. Upon receiving Napoleon's letter around midday on the 16th, Murat immediately notified Bagration that he would be resuming hostilities in four hours. In all, Bagration had bought a full 24-hour head start for Kutuzov's forces to allow them to reach Znaym ahead of the French.

Between 4:00 and 5:00 P.M. on the 16th, Murat opened a bombardment of Bagration's position, prompting Bagration to withdraw his first line and to set fire to the town of Schöngrabern to deny the French the shelter of the wooden buildings and to help cover his own positions with smoke from the blaze.[*] Murat deployed Oudinot's grenadier division on the left and Legrand's division from 4th Corps on the right with cavalry supporting the flanks and the remaining divisions in reserve. Even with only a third of Murat's roughly 30,000 troops committed to the action, the French still outnumbered Bagration's 8,000-man rearguard.

The French forces advanced in darkness, illuminated only by the blaze of Schöngrabern, and over several hours of confused night fighting they slowly pushed back the Russian forces. It was not until 11:00 P.M. that Bagration was finally able to disengage and retire northward toward Brünn, leaving about 2,200 killed and badly wounded behind, along with eight guns that Bagration claimed had damaged carriages. French losses had amounted to about 1,200 killed and wounded. Bagration's route of retreat intersected the route of Kutuzov's march at Pohrlitz on 18 November, and the Russian commander-in-chief, surprised that Bagration's rearguard had not been utterly destroyed, embraced him heartily and declared, "I do not ask about the casualties—you are alive and that is enough for me."[†] The next day, Kutuzov's leading troops met up with the head of Buxhöwden's column at Wischau.

With Murat's failure to cut off Kutuzov's forces at Znaym, Napoleon failed in his objective of pinning and destroying Kutuzov's army before it could unite with reinforcements coming from Russia, an objective he had been pursuing since announcing it at the outset of the Danube campaign a month earlier. In

---

[*] Russian accounts state that the firing of the village was intentional. French accounts attribute this to an accidental ignition caused by Russian artillery fire, though they would have no way of knowing for certain if it had been intentional.

[†] Mikhailovski-Danilevski, p. 171.

addition to this disappointment, the news of Admiral Nelson's destruction of the French and Spanish fleets at Trafalgar reached Napoleon on the 18th, making a decisive victory against the allies even more imperative. As the French army occupied Brünn, the Danube campaign effectively ended, and the war entered a new phase, prompting Napoleon to halt his pursuit of Kutuzov's army and begin planning for a new campaign in Moravia.

Chapter 3

The Campaign of Moravia: 21 November – 1 December

The union of Kutuzov's weary forces and Buxhöwden's fresh troops quickly changed the situation of the two armies. Napoleon had counted on preventing this union and had pinned his hopes on destroying Kutuzov's forces in a decisive battle before reaching Vienna. Kutuzov's cagey withdrawal, the failure of the risky attempt to cut off Kutuzov's path of retreat north of the Danube with Mortier's corps, and Bagration's quick action (and quick thinking) had prevented Napoleon from achieving his objective. While the campaign had resulted in the occupation of upper and lower Austria, the seizure of Vienna, the capture of arsenals filled with arms, powder and shot and the capture of magazines loaded with supplies and provisions of all kinds, the impressive results failed to be decisive. The enemies that Napoleon had intended to destroy had eluded him, met with reinforcements and finally had an army of sufficient strength to hold their ground and face the French. Moreover, the Austrian Army of Italy had made its way through the Julian Alps and was approaching Laibach, converging with the remnants of Archduke John's Army of Tyrolia marching eastwards from Klagenfurt.[*] The union of these armies would place a powerful force south of Vienna in a position to act against the right of the Grande Armée while Kutuzov's army was positioned to operate on its left. As a result, the pace of Napoleon's eastward advance slowed and finally came to a halt around the Moravian capital of Brünn.

For the first time since the beginning of the war, the French did not have local numerical superiority nor could they easily achieve it against the widely separated allied armies. After uniting at Wischau on 19 November, the main coalition forces withdrew to a strong position at Olschan, just west of the fortified city of Olmütz. Buxhöwden's corps had added nearly 27,000 men to Kutuzov's army and provided Kutuzov with the opportunity to make a stand without fear of a French attack. Kutuzov left Bagration with a rearguard, mostly cavalry, at Rausnitz on the Brünn–Olmütz road just southwest of Wischau while the remainder of the army reached Olschan on 21 November. The next day Alexander formally appointed Kutuzov commander of the combined Austro-Russian armies. Kutuzov drew up an order of battle dividing

---

[*] The advance elements of the two armies made contact with each other on 26 November at Gonobitz, southeast of Marburg. The main bodies converged at Marburg. Rüstow, p. 316.

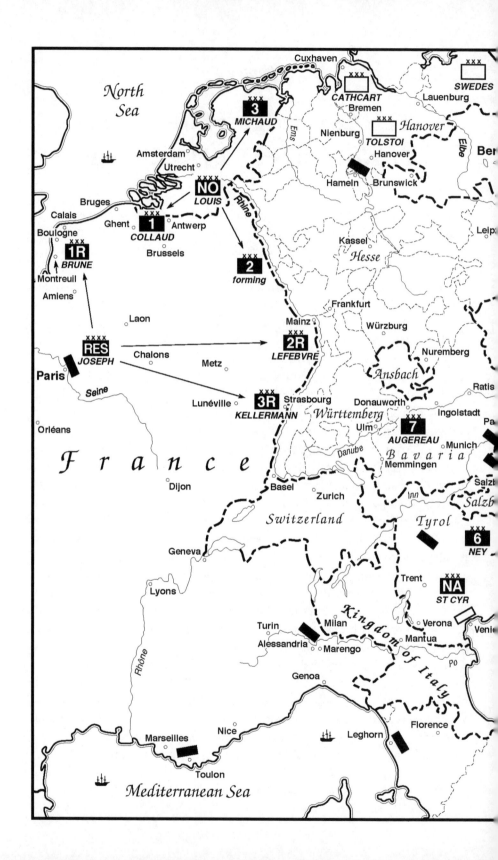

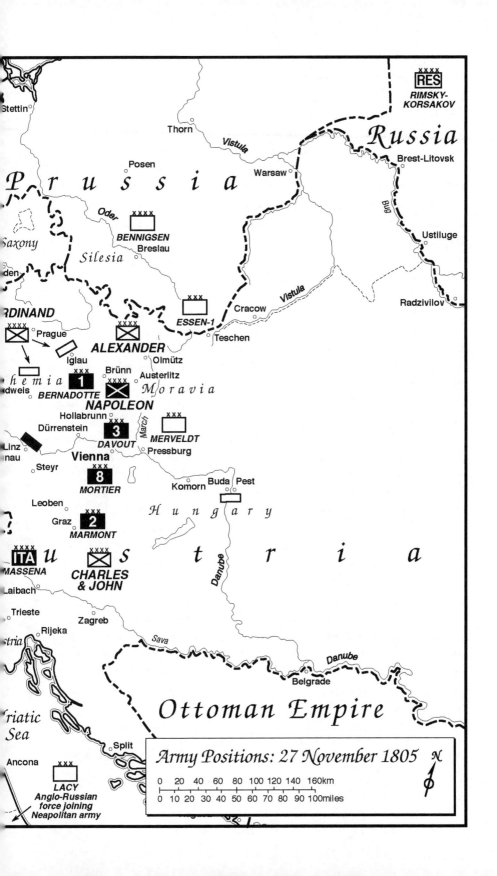

Army Positions: 27 November 1805

0 20 40 60 80 100 120 140 160km
0 10 20 30 40 50 60 70 80 90 100miles

N

his army into three columns and deployed it in a strong defensive position stretching across the heights at Olschan with its right anchored in the foothills to the north and the left anchored on the River March. The Austrian forces which had retired from Vienna, now under the overall command of FML Prince Liechtenstein, stood in reserve. In all, the combined allied forces in and in front of Olmütz numbered just over 80,000 men.* Although his army had more than doubled in strength overnight, Kutuzov resolved to wait at Olschan before resuming operations. The French pursuit had fallen off and all indications were that the tide had definitely turned. The respite from the dogged French pursuit allowed Kutuzov's weary troops an opportunity to rest and refit from the arsenals at Olmütz. Further, Constantine's column, composed of the 8,500 men of the Russian Imperial Guard along with about 2,000 line troops, was nearing Olmütz and another column of about 10,000 men under Essen-1 was about ten days' march behind the Guard.

While the Russians and remnants of the Austrian Army coalesced around Olmütz, a force of comparable size was also approaching the Danube from the south. The armies of the Archdukes Charles and John had met at Marburg on 26 November and marched together toward Körmend, but the entire force paused on the Mur River northeast of Marburg to rest, only reaching Körmend on 6 December. From their camp on the Mur, however, the combined army could threaten the French position at Vienna on the right bank of the Danube or cross to the north bank via Komorn and operate in concert with the Austro-Russian army at Olmütz. Estimates of the strength of this force vary, but with John's remaining forces from the Tyrol and the assembly of depot battalions, the strength of Charles's army approached 80,000–85,000 men.[†]

In addition to the two main armies, the remnants of the Austrian Army of Germany had formed the nucleus of two additional corps. To the west, Ferdinand had assembled the forces that had escaped with him from Ulm, and joined them with some hastily raised Freikorps and reserve battalions in Bohemia. His small army had grown to about 10,000 men and stood ready to support Bennigsen's stronger Russian corps of about 25,000 that was currently in Silesia and which would be able to join with Ferdinand in another two weeks' time. Although weak and with troops of questionable value, Ferdinand's corps was in a position to harass the rear of the Grande Armée and its communications with Vienna. In addition, between the two main

---

* There is considerable disagreement over the exact strength of the allied forces and the precise figures available in various sources do not always agree. About 8,000 men were left in the Olmütz garrison when the army advanced to Austerlitz. See Appendix A for a full discussion of the strength of the allied army.

[†] Schönhals notes Charles's force as 155 battalions and 96 squadrons with a total of about 80,000 men. Schönhals, p. 146.

allied armies stood a small corps assembled by Merveldt. Following his defeat at Mariazell, Merveldt had withdrawn into Hungary. However, Merveldt had subsequently crossed the Danube with his small force, taking position on the River March between the Danube and Göding and making contact on his right with the allied army at Olschan and on his left with the right bank of the Danube and Charles's army via Kormend.*

Opposing the allied armies were French forces extending from Brünn in the north to Graz in the south, along with the French Army of Italy that had been following Charles's army through Styria. The forces that had pursued Kutuzov's army into Moravia stood in and around Brünn, including the 4th and 5th Corps and supporting cavalry with the Imperial Guard in reserve—altogether about 50,000 men. Around Vienna were the 3rd Corps, which had chased Merveldt into Hungary, and the 8th Corps, somewhat the worse for wear after the fierce fighting at Dürrenstein, with supporting cavalry. This central force around Vienna comprised about another 45,000–50,000 men. Finally, to the south stood Marmont's 2nd Corps at Graz and Massena's Army of Italy south of Laibach with about 50,000 men. Thus, while the French were in a position to shift forces easily to meet a threat from any quarter on equal terms, they could not strike effectively at the widely separated allied armies without extending themselves into Moravia or Styria and risking disaster in the opposite direction.

Allied Plans of Campaign

During 21–27 November, the two armies that had been clawing at each other almost non-stop for the previous month rested while their commanders planned. The French, pressing up the road toward Olmütz, pushed the Russian rearguard out of Rausnitz and Wischau, capturing stragglers, but the main forces remained idle. The French army around Brünn stood at one end of the road to Vienna. To the west of Brünn stood Ferdinand's small corps, to the east the main Austro-Russian army at Olschan. Kutuzov saw no reason to rush into operations. Napoleon, he reasoned, could not strike at the army at Olschan due to the strength of the position and the difficulty of concentrating sufficient forces so far to the east. Moreover, reinforcements were at hand that would increase the coalition's advantage. Constantine was approaching with a total of 10,500 men, GL Essen-1 was en route with 10,000 additional troops and GL Bennigsen was about to enter Bohemia with a corps of 25,000 men. Further, the imminent entry of Prussia into the war would dramatically alter the military position, creating new opportunities for action as Napoleon reacted to the changing situation. By waiting a few more weeks the coalition

---

* Rüstow, p. 336.

forces would be doubled, Napoleon's communications would be threatened by the main Prussian Army, and Holland and the lower Rhine would be attacked in accordance with the plan worked out between Alexander and Frederick William of Prussia. Kutuzov concluded, with good reason, that Napoleon would have no choice but to withdraw from his positions in Moravia and around Vienna and the Russians would have their revenge by harassing the French retreat. Everything pointed to several weeks of caution before going over to the offensive, and Kutuzov clearly had no intention of tempting fate by rushing matters.

While militarily sound, Kutuzov's cautious approach had little appeal to the Russian emperor and his advisors, who were eager for action. Alexander's entourage included a number of young, arrogant and inexperienced officers, confident of victory, who were eagerly urging him to attack the French. Waiting for Prussia's entry into the war would give Prussia added prestige and influence in the defeat of the French, which was regarded as inevitable by the hawks in Alexander's retinue. Far better to act now, to seize the advantages at hand and to deal Napoleon a severe blow—perhaps a decisive blow—before Prussia entered the war, they reasoned. Alexander's headquarters, buoyed by the apparent change in momentum and its own optimism, proceeded with plans for an immediate offensive against the French, an action that their commander-in-chief opposed.

Prince Czartoryski recorded his observations of those exercising the greatest influence on Alexander:

> Colonel Weirother, who was to act as chief of the general staff, had already passed some time at Pulawy, and had obtained much influence over Alexander's mind. He was an officer of great bravery and military knowledge, but, like General Mack, he trusted too much in his combinations, which were often complicated, and did not admit that they might be foiled by the skill of the enemy. His presence at Olmütz and that of Dolgorouky, whose impetuous ardour acted on the Emperor's mind, contributed not a little to reassure and animate him.*

Czartoryski also noted in his memoirs that Count Cobenzl arrived at Alexander's headquarters at Pulawy and:

> . . . spoke some imprudent words as to its being necessary for sovereigns to place themselves at the head of armies in times of difficulty. The Emperor [Alexander] thought these words were meant as advice, perhaps as reproach . . .

---

* Adam Czartoryski, *Memoirs of Prince Adam Czartoryski and his correspondence with Alexander I* (London: Remington & Co., 1898), p. 103.

He did not pay any attention to our remonstrances, and would not believe what we continually repeated to him—that his presence would prevent General Kutusoff from exercising any real authority over the movements of the army. This was especially to be feared in view of the General's timorous character and courtier-like habits.*

Cobenzl's statement reinforced Alexander's vision of himself as the savior of Europe, the monarch who would lead his troops in the destruction of Bonaparte, and encouraged him to take the army into his own hands. Alexander wanted a battle, wanted to recover the glory of Russian arms, and to be the one finally to defeat Napoleon. On 24 November, Emperor Alexander of Russia, participating in his first military campaign, assumed direct command of the Austro-Russian army, effectively superceding Kutuzov who retained the title with none of the authority.

Alexander having decided on the offensive, operations against Napoleon's army could take any of three possible courses. The first would be to attack Napoleon head on. This would provide the quickest means for coming to grips with the French but would likely serve only to push them back to Brünn and then toward Vienna on their line of communications without a decisive outcome. This outcome was feared by Alexander's entourage who sought a decisive battle.

A second option, supported by GL Langeron, was to move through the mountains north of Brünn to join forces with Ferdinand's corps in Bohemia. This had the benefit of concentrating available forces and drawing the main army closer to Bennigsen's corps. The army's line of communications would then pass through Prague and would be further protected by Prussia once it entered the war. The army could then move on Napoleon at Brünn from the northwest and could more easily operate in conjunction with the main Prussian army in Franconia against the French communications in the Danube valley. This plan had several disadvantages, however. Beyond requiring the movement of a large army over difficult mountain roads, direct offensive operations would involve debouching from mountain passes in the face of the waiting French. Shifting the entire army fully into Bohemia would also delay contact with the enemy for several weeks while the movement was taking place.

Finally, there was the option of operating against the French right. By shifting its line of communications from Olmütz to Hungary, the army could move closer to Charles while threatening the French communications and line of retreat to Vienna. An aggressive advance on the French communications would cut Napoleon off from Vienna and leave him with his only line of

* Ibid.

retreat through Bohemia—beyond which the main Prussian army in Franconia was poised to strike once the ultimatum ran out. This plan, Alexander's advisers reasoned, offered the best potential for dramatic results. Napoleon was at the end of his tether, no longer advancing, and showing apparent signs of hesitation. The army at Olschan enjoyed local numerical superiority over the French. If the French communications could be cut and Napoleon's army beaten in battle, the only route remaining open for a French retreat would be the difficult route to Linz via Budweis. On paper, operations on the French right were clearly the best suited to the purposes of the new commander of the coalition army. They had the potential of producing decisive results and those surrounding Alexander were confident of victory once the French were engaged. A quick strike and Napoleon would be cut off and forced to retreat; and it would be a victory achieved without the Prussians who would be left with the task of blocking his retreat once the victory was won.

Given the confidence of Alexander and his entourage, the choice was obvious and the offensive was first scheduled to begin immediately on the 25th. Given the condition of the army and the inadequate supplies at Olmütz, which had never been intended as a depot for 80,000 men, it was then decided to delay the offensive for two more days in order to allow the collection and issuing of two days rations to the men. The new date set for initiating the offensive that would result in Napoleon's defeat was 27 November.

French Plans of Campaign

Napoleon's plans for operations in Moravia contrasted sharply with the Coalition plans. While the Coalition plans called for a specific maneuver against the enemy and were based on the assumption that the enemy would remain stationary and not be reinforced, Napoleon's plans were characteristically dynamic and flexible.[*] In his planning, Napoleon clearly recognized the weakness of his position. The main coalition army had been forced to withdraw continually for a full month but had not yet been pinned and defeated. It stood now to the northeast, had been reinforced with a large body of fresh troops, and occupied a strong position with a well-supplied fortress to its rear. Further pursuit of this enemy was clearly impossible. To the south, Charles's army threatened Vienna and required a substantial force to contain it. Offensive operations against this army would be difficult if Charles chose to withdraw into Hungary. To the west, Ferdinand's small corps was a

---

[*] While the plans of generals often must be deduced from dispositions and orders, Napoleon laid out his plans for the campaign in Moravia explicitly and in considerable detail in his notes on Stutterheim's account of Austerlitz (originally published in 1806). While these notes must be considered with some suspicion as being written after the fact, when matched against the actual dispositions they are entirely consistent with his deployments and there is little cause to disbelieve his account of his intentions.

minor annoyance, but one that required watching. And finally, while Napoleon had already made provisions for the defense of France and the Batavian Republic against the coalition forces in Hanover and the looming intervention of Prussia, some arrangements for protecting the line of communications of the Grande Armée along the Danube had to be made.

As he had in Italy nearly a decade earlier, Napoleon established a defensive perimeter, taking into consideration the available roads to allow for rapid shifting of forces over interior lines to meet enemy offensive operations in any direction, even the most unlikely. This time, however, the forces involved and the area covered were on a much larger scale. The main French force pursuing Kutuzov consisted of the 4th and 5th Corps along with Murat's cavalry. Murat remained in contact with the Russian Advance Guard, his cavalry positioned on the Brünn–Olmütz road. Two brigades of light cavalry were extended as far as Wischau, with a division of dragoons supporting them in the vicinity of Rausnitz and two divisions of cuirassiers even further back around Posorsitz. The 4th Corps stood behind Murat's forces, occupying the high ground to the south of the road—the soon-to-be famous Pratzen heights and vicinity—with Margaron's three regiments of light cavalry extended to patrol the area to the south as far as the River March. The 5th Corps remained in and around Brünn, Suchet's division to the east of the city, Oudinot's division to the north and in Brünn proper. The Imperial Guard remained in Brünn.

To secure his left and rear, Napoleon ordered the 1st Corps to occupy Budweis to open the Brünn–Budweis–Linz route to the Danube, and then to press Ferdinand's small force back into Bohemia. In these operations, Bernadotte was always to keep his two French divisions in reserve and to employ his Bavarian division and cavalry for offensive operations. The French divisions were to advance only as far as Iglau while the Bavarians were to press Ferdinand back on Kolin and, if possible, Prague. In the unlikely event the Russian and Prussian forces in Silesia reinforced Ferdinand in the near future, the Bavarian division could fall back on the remainder of the 1st Corps at Iglau. Otherwise, the Bavarians would be sufficient to hold Ferdinand at bay and allow Bernadotte to march with his French divisions to oppose the main allied army at Olmütz if needed.

Similar dispositions were made to the south to secure the right rear of the forces around Brünn. Caffarelli's division of the 3rd Corps was positioned at Pohrlitz, between Brünn and the Thaya River. Friant's division, reinforced by the 1st Dragoons from Klein's division, occupied a position of observation on the right bank of the March River (the Marchfeld that would be the scene of the Battle of Wagram) between the Thaya and Vienna. Gudin's division of the 3rd Corps, reinforced by a brigade of dragoons from Klein's division, was ordered to occupy Pressburg (Bratislava), while the light cavalry of the 3rd Corps patrolled the area between Pressburg and Graz. Davout's divisions were supported by a large body of cavalry. Beaumont's and Bourcier's divisions of dragoons were positioned between Caffarelli and Friant near the confluence of the March and Thaya Rivers. The remainder of Klein's dragoon division remained near Stockerau just west of Vienna. Together, these forces formed a cordon stretching from Pohrlitz to Pressburg and could concentrate in either direction to oppose an advance by either Charles or Kutuzov. The cavalry formed a screen in front of these divisions to alert the French to any enemy movements directed between Vienna and Brünn.

To the south of the Danube, Dumonceau's division of Mortier's 8th Corps was ordered to Neustadt to form a link with Marmont at Graz. Mortier's other two divisions, which had sustained serious losses at Dürrenstein, stood in Vienna proper. Marmont's 2nd Corps occupied Graz, maintaining contact between Mortier and the advancing Army of Italy. These forces could be concentrated around Vienna in the event of offensive operations by Charles.

Prussia's entry into the war constituted the least of Napoleon's worries at this point. Nevertheless, Napoleon sent instructions to Ney and Augereau, busily occupying the Tyrol and Vorarlberg and suppressing local insurrections, ordering them to be prepared to march northward to the Danube valley in the event of Prussia's entry into the war. These front-line troops were to oppose any Prussian movement in that direction while the Reserve Corps of Kellermann and Lefebvre and the Armée du Nord would defend the Rhine and the Batavian Republic from any westward advance by the Prussians or the Anglo-Russian army in Hanover.

With the general dispositions made, Napoleon went beyond to make plans based on the specific options open to the coalition forces. The most likely activity, and one which Napoleon had been hoping for since the capitulation of Ulm, was an offensive operation by the main Austro-Russian army, which could take one of three general courses. The first was a maneuver on the left of his army, through the mountains to the north of Brünn. In this event, it would be a simple matter to strike at the heads of the Russian columns as they debouched from the mountains. No special dispositions would be necessary. Given the difficulty of the roads in the mountains to the north, Napoleon considered this an unlikely option. Nevertheless, Napoleon ordered Fauconnet's cavalry brigade to probe toward Zwittau on the road north of Brünn in order to detect any allied movement to the north.[*]

The second option open to the coalition forces was a direct assault on the French position east of Brünn. This possibility concerned Napoleon the most,

---

[*] Fauconnet's brigade consisted of two regiments of chasseurs à cheval. The 21st Chasseurs was positioned at Lettowitz and the 13th Chasseurs at Czernahora.

as the attack could come quickly before his forces could be fully concentrated. This action would require a simple withdrawal through Brünn and then southward toward Znaym on the road to Vienna. A strong body of cavalry was already positioned on the road to Olmütz, as already described, and Napoleon retained this force in position to slow any allied advance and to alert the main army to any direct offensive action.

The third possibility was a flanking maneuver on the French right. This maneuver seemed more likely than a maneuver on the left as it would draw the Austro-Russian army closer to Charles's army in Hungary and would threaten the French line of communications. This eventuality, Napoleon concluded, offered the best opportunity for a decisive French victory. If this were to occur, Napoleon planned to call in Bernadotte's 1st Corps and Davout's 3rd Corps, wait for the allied maneuver to develop and then crush his enemies' right flank and drive their army into the swamps and ponds to the south of the Olmütz road. This would produce the decisive result that Napoleon had been seeking, an outcome that would force Austria to sue for peace and would forestall Prussia's entry into the war. Accordingly, Napoleon positioned cavalry to the south to detect any movement of the allies on his right. However, in this sector a single cavalry brigade, that of Margaron from the IV Corps, stretched from in front of Austerlitz to Göding on the March River. This thin string of outposts would provide ample warning of an allied movement on the right, but its weakness would not discourage any allied flanking maneuver.

Having determined his general plan of operations, Napoleon studied the ground on which it could be carried out. While Napoleon's choice of the ground along the Goldbach has been acclaimed as a bit of remarkable prescience, and detractors have identified this as an example of after-the-fact myth-making, in fact it was nothing more than careful selection of ground most suitable for his plans. If the allies were to attack head-on, Napoleon needed easily defensible terrain from which a small rearguard could delay the numerically superior allied army sufficiently to allow the French forces to withdraw toward Znaym. At the same time, the ground had to provide a commanding position from which to launch a counterattack on the allied right if the circumstances would allow it. Between Brünn and Wischau stood a strong position on the Pratzen Heights from which any turning maneuver by the allies could be effectively disputed by the French if they were to commit their full army. Closer to Brünn, however, a series of brooks running north–south, lined with swamps and with occasional ponds and woods, broke the terrain into a series of defiles around which small bodies of troops could effectively hold off stronger forces. At the north end, closest to the mountains, stood the Bosenitzberg, a hill the French dubbed "the Santon" because the chapel on the top of it resembled the little shrines called santons that they had seen in Egypt.* This hill was located east of the brooks and commanded the road and the northern edge of the plain the road passed through before coming to the brooks. A short distance to the south of the Brünn–Olmütz road stood another hill, less imposing but still able to command the ground in front of it.

With these two hills and the main road between them, Napoleon saw the ideal position to maintain a toehold to the east of the brooks from which his forces could move *en masse* against the allied right without having to negotiate narrow defiles. Sweeping to the south over the Pratzen heights they could separate the allies from the road and drive them into the swamps and rugged terrain to the southeast. At the same time the terrain would serve as a strong position to delay any direct attack by the allies, either gaining time for reinforcements to arrive or for his army to retire on Brünn or Znaym. Thus the choice of the positions the French would take at Austerlitz was not based on a prediction of what the allies would do, but rather was made to enable the range of options Napoleon wanted to retain for his own operations, regardless of the direction of the hoped-for allied attack.

While Napoleon's dispositions were flexible and anticipated all possible actions by the enemy, including inaction, the third option in which the enemy sought to turn the French right involved some considerable risk. If the Austro-Russian army succeeded in turning the French right and cutting the Brünn–Vienna road before the French forces concentrated, Napoleon's army would be left with only the difficult route to Linz through Budweis for its retreat and the French forces would be split in two parts separated by the Danube. Thus, while the third option carried with it the greatest chance for decisive victory, it also carried with it the greatest risk for defeat. With typical confidence in himself and his troops, Napoleon's planning stopped short of outlining any alternate line of communications or retreat in the event the Brünn–Vienna road was cut. Everything was to be staked on both Davout's 3rd Corps from Vienna and Bernadotte's 1st Corps from Iglau arriving in time, the Austro-Russian flanking maneuver being stopped, and the enemy right being crushed. As he had in previous campaigns, Napoleon gambled on the outcome of a single battle, confident in the strength of his forces.

The Coalition Offensive Begins:
Wischau/Rausnitz, 27–28 November

With Kutuzov pushed aside and reduced to a mouthpiece to disseminate orders, Alexander relied on his entourage for support and on his Austrian chief

---

* "Santon" was the western term for Moslem hermits or monks. This term was also extended to their shrines or chapels.

of staff, GM Weyrother, for the plan by which his offensive scheme would be implemented. Weyrother had not been a prominent figure in the earlier part of the campaign and only chance had brought him to the forefront now. His predecessor, Schmidt, had been killed at Dürrenstein and the successor nominated to replace him had not yet arrived. Weyrother had less experience than Schmidt, but on the surface seemed well suited for the position. Weyrother had joined the staff of Suvorov's Austro-Russian army in Italy in April 1799 and when Suvorov was ordered north into Switzerland Weyrother had become his chief of staff. In the end, Suvorov's army marched into the arms of the waiting French and barely extricated itself from the trap, suffering severe losses in the process. But Suvorov valued Weyrother, protecting him from other Russian officers who were lashing out at the Austrians for delays and for what they felt was the abandonment of the Russian army of General Korsakov at Zurich. Suvorov credited Weyrother with helping to extricate his army from its difficult situation. Weyrother, in turn, was loyal to his chief, despite allegations that he had been "planted" in Suvorov's headquarters by a hostile government in Vienna. While there seems to have been a positive personal relationship between Suvorov and Weyrother, the Austrian was despised by most of the Russian officers with the army. The officers who had been with Suvorov in '99, who included Generals Bagration, Miloradovich, Kamensky-2 and Miller-3, could not have been pleased with Weyrother's appointment given the disastrous result of their last collaboration and the hostile dynamics between the Austrian chief of staff and Suvorov's Russian officers.

Once the decision to take the offensive was made, Weyrother immediately began drafting plans for the operation. The approach he took followed typical Austrian methodology, grouping regiments into columns and assigning a commander to each column.* Marches would be fairly short in order to avoid wearing out the troops unnecessarily or causing confusion or disorganization. Weyrother's planning, however, relied more on theory than practical application. Troop movements assumed an almost geometric nature, with the general route of march changing directions at right angles rather than taking the shortest and most direct route. Weyrother also disregarded existing relationships between units and commanders, which may not have been well-established in the Austrian Army but were quite important to the Russians. Finally, Weyrother's planning did not seem to consider the reality of the

---

* During this period, the Austrian army used higher formations based around the officers commanding them. Each officer had administrative responsibility for the specific battalions, but their commands would be adjusted according to situational requirements, resulting in different combat assignments. Roland Kessinger, "Managing Armies in the 2nd Coalition War, 1799–1800," *First Empire*, No. 71, pp. 22–3.

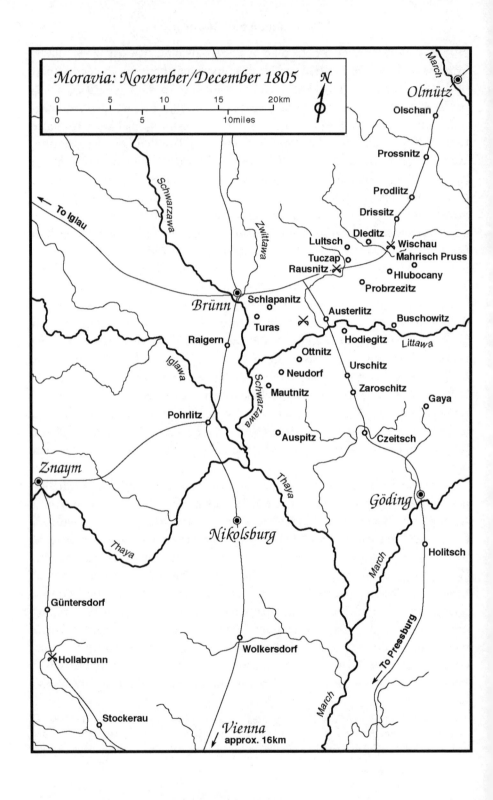

Moravia: November/December 1805

N

0   5   10   15   20km
0   5   10miles

To Iglau

Schwarzawa

Zwittawa

Olmütz

Olschan

Prossnitz

Prodlitz

Drissitz

Dleditz

Lultsch

Tuczap

Rausnitz

Wischau

Mahrisch Pruss

Hlubocany

Probrzezitz

Brünn

Schlapanitz

Turas

Raigern

Austerlitz

Buschowitz

Littawa

Hodiegitz

Ottnitz

Neudorf

Urschitz

Iglawa

Mautnitz

Zaroschitz

Gaya

Schwarzawa

Pohrlitz

Auspitz

Czeitsch

Znaym

Göding

Holitsch

Thaya

Nikolsburg

March

Thaya

Güntersdorf

Hollabrunn

Wolkersdorf

To Pressburg

March

Stockerau

Vienna
approx. 16km

terrain his forces were traversing and the advantage the French would derive by observing the army's movements from the heights left unoccupied during the course of the allied advance. Instead he seems to have considered that an advance behind the heights would screen the movement from an immobile enemy waiting for their arrival and does not seem to have believed it necessary to control the heights to prevent the maneuver from being observed. Whether stemming from Weyrother's prior reputation from 1799 or from his actual performance and lack of consideration for the practical concerns of the army he served in 1805, the Russian officers had neither respect for nor confidence in their chief of staff. Unlike Suvorov in 1799, Alexander had no experience and offered no guidance or critique of Weyrother's dispositions. Kutuzov, while certainly capable of doing so, was either disregarded or was disinclined to offer advice in his role as army figurehead.

Weyrother began operations by discarding Kutuzov's dispositions, implemented a few days before, and organizing the regiments into five new columns. General Buxhöwden would have overall command of the columns of Generals Wimpfen and Langeron and would advance to the north of the main Olmütz–Brünn road. A third column under the direct command of Kutuzov, seconded by GL Dokhturov, would advance up the road itself. The last two columns of Miloradovich and Prince Liechtenstein would advance south of the road. Despite the decision to move on the enemy right, these dispositions reflect a preconceived notion that the French would retreat in the face of an allied advance, and any maneuver to the south was to be delayed until after contact was made.

At 8:00 A.M. on 27 November the allied army began its offensive in five parallel columns as planned. The Advance Guard of Prince Bagration remained in position to screen the allied advance up the main road. GL Kienmayer, commanding the Austrian advance guard, moved forward into line with Bagration to the left of the main road. GL Stutterheim, commanding a third advance guard, screened the extreme left of the allied advance to the south of Kienmayer. The three advance guards concentrated their leading elements on a line in front of the village of Prodlitz. In conjunction with the offensive of the main army, GL Merveldt's small corps advanced up the March to apply pressure to the outlying French cavalry outpost at Göding.

During the 27th, the allied columns were to close on the advance guards and the next day to continue on to Nemojan. In the instructions issued to Bagration for the operations on the 28th, signed by Kutuzov but very likely authored by Weyrother, the Advance Guard was directed to take Wischau and advance to Rausnitz to clear the way for the allied columns advancing southeast from Olschan. Because the allied columns were to march as far as

Nemojan, about seven kilometers southwest of Wischau, it was imperative that Bagration overwhelm the French in Wischau and drive them back past Rausnitz.

Reconnaissance reports brought in during the preceding days placed the French forces at Wischau at seven squadrons, with an additional twenty squadrons a short distance to the rear at Tuczap.[*] Bagration's advance guard of twelve battalions and twenty-five squadrons, with a regiment of supporting Cossacks, was therefore plainly too small for the allocated mission. To insure success, Kutuzov (or Weyrother) assigned the cavalry divisions of Kienmayer and Essen-2 to Bagration, bringing total cavalry at Bagration's disposal to sixty-one squadrons of regular cavalry plus twenty-five squadrons of Cossacks, an ample force to overwhelm the French at Wischau.[†] During the night of 27 November, Essen-2's forces, detached from the 3rd Column, moved up the road to join Bagration's main body concentrating between Prodlitz and Drissitz. Kienmayer's force, which had bivouacked south of the main road, drew even with the left of Bagration's forces during the night.

Before dawn on 28 November, the forces of Bagration's Advance Guard assembled near Drissitz for the attack on the French positions at Wischau. As the sky began to lighten, the allied forces began their advance. To the right, a battalion of the 6th Jäger and the Old Ingermanland (Staroingermanland) Musketeer Regiment veered off toward Dieditz to advance on a route parallel to the main road and flank Wischau from the north. On the left the Austrian General Kienmayer led his sixteen squadrons of cavalry and his horse artillery, supported by ten squadrons of Cossacks, on a broad flanking maneuver covering Bagration's left. Kienmayer was to parallel the main road and then veer to his right toward the village of Podbrzezitz just east of Rausnitz to flank the position of the French heavy cavalry at Tuczap. The main Russian force, eight battalions, forty-five squadrons and supporting Cossacks, advanced directly up the road toward Wischau.

For main attack on Wischau, Bagration planned to flank the town to the south while he pinned the French with a frontal attack. Bagration allocated the cavalry of the Advance Guard, twenty-five squadrons of regulars and five squadrons of Cossacks under GM Wittgenstein, to the flanking move and ordered him off to the left. Wittgenstein directed his force to the southeast through the village of Mahrisch Pruss, following a defile formed by a small stream. On this route the Russians would remain out of sight of the French at

[*] The reports on French strength and positions were surprisingly accurate given the complete failure of the allies to collect accurate information over the next four days. Actual French strength totaled thirty squadrons with seven in Wischau and twenty-three behind Wischau at Dieditz, Tuczap and Hlubocany.

[†] See Milhaud's report in Alombert and Colin, V, pp. 103–4.

Wischau until they ascended the heights of Bründlitz from where they would sweep down onto the right rear of the French, cutting their retreat on the road to Rausnitz. The main column, consisting of eight battalions of infantry under the command of Prince Dolgoruky, moved directly on Wischau. Essen-2 with twenty squadrons of regular cavalry and two regiments of Cossacks remained in reserve.

The weak French forces in and around Wischau were intended only as a tripwire to alert the army to any Russian advance. Accordingly the forces were extended up the main road to Olmütz and scattered for their subsistence. In the event of a major Russian movement, the French forces were to sound the alarm and immediately retire toward Posorsitz, falling back on the cuirassier divisions there, while the 5th Corps advanced to support them and the 4th Corps assembled on the Pratzen heights to the south. The brigade of GdB Trelliard, consisting of the 9th Hussars, along with a dismounted squadron of 6th Dragoons, occupied the town of Wischau with the 10th Hussars bivouacked just behind the town. To their left stood the brigade of GdB Milhaud, consisting of the 16th and 22nd Chasseurs, with the 16th stationed closest to the Olmütz road and the 22nd in and behind Dieditz. These advance posts of the French army had their left anchored on the mountains to the north, but were exposed to the south. Both Milhaud and Trelliard had sent out pickets, but Trelliard had only sent patrols out on the roads to Olmütz and Kremsier, northeast of Wischau, neglecting to post any on his exposed right flank. Behind the advance posts of light cavalry stood GdD Walther's dragoon division of six regiments around Tuczap. GdB Sebastiani, with the 3rd Dragoons, was at Hlubocany, about four kilometers south of Wischau, and the two remaining squadrons of the 6th Dragoons between Wischau and Tuczap. Roget's brigade (10th and 11th Dragoons) stood in and around Tuczap while the remaining two regiments appear to have been west of Tuczap.

While the Russian forces maneuvered into position, the French were blissfully unaware that the allies had assumed the offensive. During the night of 27 November, Milhaud's outposts reported Cossack activity opposite Dieditz, immediately prompting Milhaud to place his regiments on alert. Milhaud soon judged the incursion to be a routine patrol, however, and his troops had returned to quarters by 7:00 A.M. To their right, the forces in Wischau do not appear to have had any warning of allied activity whatsoever. The sudden arrival of the Russians in force in front of Wischau came as an unpleasant surprise.

The Russian forces had set off just before dawn (around 6:45) and covered approximately ten kilometers from their bivouacs at Prodlitz and Drissitz to Wischau over the next two hours. Bagration's main body arrived in front of

Wischau around 9:00 A.M. Wittgenstein's cavalry arrived in position on the Bründlitz heights while the infantry column on the right arrived in front of Dieditz at about the same time, with French outposts being driven in on all sides. To the north, the column of Russian infantry, supported by a small party of Cossacks, was stopped in its tracks by Milhaud's cavalry but reports from Milhaud's outposts indicated Russian forces advancing on the right. Having received no word from Trelliard to the south, Milhaud rode toward the main road near Wischau. Nearing the road, Milhaud found chaos.

> I went close to the main road near the 16th [Chasseurs] . . . to examine what was happening on our right, because I had not received any notice or report on this side [which was being] attacked in lively fashion by 2,000 horse, including Cossacks as well as dragoons and hussars. At that moment, I witnessed two successive charges of Cossacks, which were initially repulsed by the hussars and a regiment of dragoons, but [the enemy then] uncovering the front of seven or eight squadrons of cavalry of the line, overflowed the flanks of the hussars and the dragoons on the right and gained much ground.*

Milhaud was witnessing Wittgenstein's cavalry, which had descended from the Bründlitz heights on the French right flank shortly after 9:00, advancing toward the road southwest of Wischau. The outposts in front of Wischau had already sounded the alarm, and the French hussars were in the process of abandoning the town. Prince Dolgoruky advanced up the main road with a battalion of Jäger and occupied Wischau as the French scrambled to leave. While the hussars managed to escape the town, the dismounted dragoons lacked their mobility, and Dolgoruky netted three officers and sixty men of the 6th Dragoons as prisoners. Meanwhile some *eclaireurs* (cavalry scouts), supported by two *peletons* (platoons) of hussars (probably 10th Hussars) hastily formed up in the marshes south of the main road in an attempt to hold back Wittgenstein's cavalry and buy time for the 9th Hussars to escape the trap.

Wittgenstein, who had initially committed only four squadrons of hussars and two squadrons of Cossacks, committed more squadrons, using his numerical superiority to good effect. He directed the Tver Dragoons, along with the Pavlograd Hussars and several squadrons of Cossacks, to the left in order to flank the small French force in front of them while Wittgenstein's own regiment, the Mariupol Hussars, formed his reserve. Seeing themselves about to be enveloped, the French began to withdraw from their position. As they pulled back, Colonel Sebastiani with the 3rd Dragoons appeared on their

---

* Ibid., pp. 104–5.

right from Hlubocany and immediately charged the Cossacks covering the Russian left. At the same time, the 11th Dragoons, arriving about the same time from Tuczap, deployed to the left of the 10th Dragoons, allowing the retreating hussars and dragoons to reform in a second line behind them. Faced with two fresh French regiments, the Russians reformed and launched two more charges against the French, both of which were repulsed, before extending their line sufficiently to outflank the French on both sides. Despite the arrival of the dragoons, Wittgenstein's thirty squadrons (including Cossacks) were simply too much for the fourteen French squadrons. Overwhelmed, the French withdrew in confusion toward Tuczap with the Russians in hot pursuit.

Milhaud, after seeing the magnitude of the Russian attack, had rushed back to his own force by 9:30, and ordered an immediate withdrawal from Dieditz to avoid being cut off by the Russian cavalry to the south. Already engaged by Cossacks from the Russian right column, the French chasseurs pulled back behind the Durnowitz ravine about three kilometers behind Dieditz. As the Russian forces extended past the left of the French cavalry on the main road, Milhaud reported that 600 or 700 "Cossacks" (who may in fact have been Russian hussars) had swept past them and toward the retreating French. Detaching a peleton to slow the Russian cavalry, Milhaud ordered a retirement by echelons, the 22nd Chasseurs covering the retreat of the 16th.

When the 16th Chasseurs arrived at Lultsch, they found the main road already occupied by the victorious Russians (about six squadrons of Pavlograd Hussars and three squadrons of Cossacks from Wittgenstein's left). The three squadrons of the 16th Chasseurs negotiated the narrow defile through the ravine and swamps around Lultsch in pairs at a gallop, formed up on the other side of the defile and wheeled to face the Russians to the south.

Holding the winded Russian cavalry at bay with the 16th, Milhaud sent an aide to request support from the 10th Dragoons, which were still in position on the heights near Tuczap and in a position to charge the right rear of the Russian force on the main road. The remainder of the French dragoons and hussars, however, were already retreating in confusion past Tuczap toward Rausnitz and the 10th Dragoons joined the retreat, refusing to support Milhaud.

With the French hussars and dragoons retiring southwest from Tuczap, the 16th Chasseurs were joined by Colonel Guyot of the 9th Hussars with one peleton of his regiment that had been separated from the rest of the unit in the confused fighting. The combined formation now faced destruction by the much larger Russian force. The Tver Dragoons soon joined the Russian hussars and Cossacks on the main road, threatening to drive back the 16th Chasseurs and block the escape of the 22nd, which was just beginning its passage through the defile of Lultsch.* Colonel Latour-Maubourg of the 22nd left an elite peleton at the entrance to the village to slow down the four squadrons of hussars and two of Cossacks pursuing his regiment. Milhaud led another charge by the 16th and Colonel Guyot's peleton of the 9th Hussars, distracting the Tver Dragoons and buying time for the 22nd to rejoin. At the same time, the Cossacks and Pavlograd Hussars from the main road fell on the 22nd Chasseurs as they cleared the defile, driving them back and entering the village from the west. The entire elite peleton left in the village, three officers and forty non-commissioned officers and chasseurs, fell into the hands of the Russian forces now surrounding the town. The remainder of Milhaud's brigade, reunited, regained the main road at Tuczap and followed the other fleeing French forces, the lot finally coming to a halt near the Posorsitz post house southwest of Rausnitz. Here they met the cuirassier divisions of Nansouty and d'Hautpoul and the 17th Light Infantry, the leading element of the 5th Corps, which were hurrying up to support the hard-pressed cavalry.

Bagration's three columns advanced with the cavalry and main body on the main road to Rausnitz and the right-hand column on a parallel route through Lultsch and Nemojan to Habrowan north of Rausnitz. Kienmayer's column, having covered the Russian left without incident, now arrived at Podbrzezitz just east of Rausnitz. Despite instructions to give ground before any serious Russian attack, some dragoons remained in Rausnitz. As General Thiébault would later observe, the forces at Rausnitz "certainly had no idea of holding [Rausnitz], and only defended for a moment in order to make the prince [Dolgoruky] pay for what we should anyhow have evacuated for nothing."[†] Bagration brought up his artillery and began bombarding the French dragoons occupying Rausnitz while he prepared to storm the town. Once again, Prince Dolgoruky was given command of the force assigned to clear the town, this time two battalions of Arkhangel Musketeers. As the Russians stormed into the town, the French quickly withdrew, presumably content at having made their enemy exert themselves for its capture.[‡]

---

* While the Russian forces opposing the 16th Chasseurs at this point in the battle appear to have included up to six squadrons of Pavlograd Hussars, three squadrons of Cossacks and five squadrons of Tver Dragoons, the hussars and Cossacks appear to have been in some disorder. This disorder may have been caused by having been involved in at least three cavalry charges in the preceding hours or may have resulted from the sudden appearance of the 16th Chasseurs from Lultsch. Effectively, the Russians opposed the five fresher squadrons of Tver Dragoons against the three squadrons of the 16th Chasseurs.

† Paul-Charles-François Thiébault, *The Memoirs of Baron Thiébault* (Tyne & Wear: Worley Publications, 1994), II, p. 148.

‡ GM Kamensky-2 was *shef* of the Arkhangel Musketeers and is noted in some accounts as having led the charge. Bagration's report noted that the town was taken by two battalions of the Arkhangel Musketeers of Kamensky-2 but did not state who was in overall command. Colonel

For the Russians, the day had been a success. They had inflicted significant losses on the extended French forces and driven them back easily. Although the French had no intention of resisting a Russian advance at Wischau, or even Rausnitz, the suddenness of the Russian attack and the inadequate positioning of pickets had resulted in a confused scramble. Only sheer tenacity and discipline had allowed the majority of the French forces to escape encirclement.

The actions at Wischau and Rausnitz, though relatively minor, had a disproportionate effect on the events that ensued. As noted, Napoleon had extended his forces toward Olmütz as a tripwire to warn of any allied offensive operation. If some sloppiness in the posting of pickets had resulted in heavier losses than should have been necessary, the warning had been delivered and there was little doubt that the allied army had left Olmütz and was acting aggressively and in force. On the allied side, the operation had been successful, inflicting significant losses on the French advance guard while incurring negligible losses themselves. This success boosted allied morale and drove the French back past Rausnitz to allow the main allied columns to advance as far as Nemojan and the Rausnitz Brook.

Of greater significance, however, was the effect the battle had at the allied headquarters. Stutterheim noted that "The allies flattered themselves that the enemy would not risk the fate of a battle in front of Brünn. After the 28th, this *hope* became the prevailing *opinion* at head quarters."* Czartoryski added:

> It was here that the Emperor Alexander and his advisers were in fault. They imagined that Napoleon was in a dangerous position, and that he was on the point of retreating. The French outposts had an appearance of hesitation and timidity which nourished these illusions, and reports came at every moment from our outposts announcing an imminent movement of the French army to the rear. Alexander forgot the extreme importance of the moment, and thought only of not allowing so good an opportunity to escape of destroying the French army, and dealing Napoleon a decisive and fatal blow.†

Ermolov, commander of a horse artillery company attached to the 5th Column, reported that Dolgoruky had been given the honor of commanding for political reasons due to his close ties to Alexander. "1805 g. Noyabrya 16—Raport P. I. Bagrationa M. I. Kutuzovu o Stolknoveniyakh c Protivnikom pod Vishau, Gabrau i Raussnitsem," [28 November 1805] in L. G. Beskrovnyi, ed., *M. I. Kutuzov: Sbornik Dokumentov* (Moscow: 1951), II, pp. 215–6; A. P. Ermolov, *Zapiski A. P. Ermolova, 1798–1826* (Moscow: 1991), pp. 51–2.

* Major-General [Karl Freiherr von] Stutterheim, *A Detailed Account of the Battle of Austerlitz* (Cambridge: Ken Trotman, 1985), p. 53.

† Czartoryski, II, pp. 104–5.

The confusion of the French and the ease of the victory had convinced many at allied headquarters that the French were ill-prepared to meet them and that the French withdrawal from Wischau—a veritable flight—indicated that they were unlikely to stand their ground in the face of the allied advance.

Once again, opinions were divided. Some, like Langeron, felt that the allies should take advantage of their positive momentum and the tight concentration of the whole of their army between Wischau and Rausnitz and immediately strike the French at Posorsitz and Austerlitz the next day. Others in the allied army viewed the success at Wischau as a great victory and imagined it sufficient to have caused a general French retreat. Prince Dolgoruky, like Langeron, favored immediate action against the French because he feared they would get away and spoil the allies' opportunity to defeat Napoleon decisively. Kutuzov, predictably, still favored the waiting game and was not anxious to rush into a situation with too many unknown variables. While Dolgoruky's mood infected the allied headquarters, Weyrother's steady determination and carefully formulated plan ultimately prevailed.

The French Reaction and the Russian Flanking Maneuver: 28–29 November

While the French were clearly surprised at Wischau, they were quick to react to the wake-up call. By the evening of the 28th the French forces had abandoned their camps and were in motion. The 4th Corps had received word of the attack on Wischau by 11:00 A.M., and Soult's three divisions concentrated toward the Brünn–Olmütz road. Legrand's division moved into position northwest of Austerlitz. Vandamme detached a brigade to Posorsitz and moved with the remainder of his division into a second line behind Legrand. St Hilaire concentrated his division around Krenowitz, forming a third line behind Vandamme. In the meantime, the light cavalry and dragoons from Wischau and Rausnitz were retreating down the road on the two divisions of cuirassiers, with the entire body of cavalry ending up in the vicinity of Posorsitz.

Reports arrived at Napoleon's headquarters in Brünn around 4:00 P.M., while Napoleon was meeting with the Prussian envoy, Haugwitz. Napoleon quickly dismissed Haugwitz, sending him to meet with Talleyrand in Vienna without accepting the sealed document he carried—the ultimatum from Frederick William. Napoleon immediately turned his mind to the reports, but at this point his enemies' intentions remained unclear. Did this activity signal a full-scale allied operation or was it simply a cavalry skirmish? Were they attacking directly up the road toward Brünn or would something else be attempted? By 7:00 P.M. Napoleon had collected enough information to believe that the enemy army was moving in force and immediately issued orders to Bernadotte, Davout, Fauconnet, Klein, Bourcier and Boyé (commanding Beaumont's division, Beaumont being ill) to concentrate in the vicinity of Brünn. During the night he ordered the cavalry to retire to Belowitz, Bosenitz and Schlapanitz and the 4th Corps to retire to the vicinity of Turas, behind the Goldbach stream and southeast of Brünn. By these dispositions, Napoleon was prepared to fight a rearguard action on the Goldbach to allow the army to withdraw toward Znaym or to concentrate for battle east of Brünn, as circumstances dictated. In either case, Napoleon expected a continuation of the action on the 29th.

The attack on the French forces at Wischau and Rausnitz signaled activity by the allied army, but before he could make any specific plans, Napoleon needed more information regarding the allies' intentions. On the night of 28 November, Napoleon issued orders to his aide-de-camp, General Savary, to ride to Alexander's headquarters at Wischau to negotiate a 24-hour suspension of hostilities. Napoleon calculated that this move would achieve positive results whether it was accepted or rejected. Acceptance would be a good indication that the allied position was weak and that there was no fear of a major battle. Rejection would reveal a determination to attack on the part of the allies while the offer itself would convey the impression of French weakness to Alexander. Alexander received Savary in the company of his staff on the morning of 29 November. Taking Napoleon's letter from Savary, Alexander withdrew for thirty minutes to compose his reply. Returning, the tsar delivered his response and, after a brief private interview, sent Savary with Prince Dolgoruky to Napoleon with a counter-proposal.

While Dolgoruky and Savary rode to deliver Alexander's ultimatum to Napoleon, the allies were busy executing the second phase of their maneuver behind the screen formed by their Advance Guard. On the right, Bagration remained in position west of Rausnitz, advancing only as far as Posorsitz, in order to screen the Russian movement. Kienmayer, on Bagration's left, moved south to the town of Austerlitz as the French 4th Corps withdrew from its positions around the town. Stutterheim, still further to the left, advanced to Buschowitz east of Austerlitz. Behind this screen the allied columns began their flank march to the left on a route perpendicular to that of the day before. Despite the successes at Wischau and Rausnitz, the French remained firmly in control of the heights with the allied advance guards occupying the low ground to the east. As a result, the allies failed to gain any firm details of the French positions or strength, despite their local numerical superiority, while the French were able to observe every move of the allied army.

Rather than wheeling entire columns around to march on a perpendicular route, Weyrother broke the columns into brigades ("lines") and reassembled each line into a new column running perpendicular to the original columns. With the 2nd Column in line behind the first, these two columns formed four lines while the 3rd and 4th Columns each formed four lines as well. Each line then marched to its left, again along parallel routes. At the end of the day, the lines again changed facing and the columns were reformed. In typical Austrian fashion, however, the nomenclature and the command structure were shifted for this single day's march, the first lines becoming the 1st Column and so forth. In this manner, every column commander received a column of a different number and with an entirely different composition (although one brigade in each column was from the commander's original command). The next day the columns returned to the composition they had previously.

While such a maneuver may have been standard operating procedure for Austrian commanders, the Russian commanders were utterly baffled.

> Each general had to spend the morning seeking the regiments in the other four columns that were to compose his [column], and sometimes were obliged to go one or two miles to arrive at them. On the 29th, I was given only one Russian battalion and all the Austrian battalions . . .

This was Langeron's claim—though according to the dispositions he commanded four Russian regiments (twelve battalions) and Jurczik's brigade of Austrians (four battalions).

> It was always 10 or 11 o'clock before one could gather. Often the columns were crossed, a fault which one would not forgive with the least and most ignorant staff officers. On arriving late, one relaxed only to go and seek food, plunder villages . . . *

Langeron, in his anger, placed the blame fully on Weyrother and the Austrian staff, but more fairly the obvious confusion during the march resulted from the complete unfamiliarity of the Russian generals with Austrian methods and a total lack of awareness of this fact on the part of Weyrother and the Austrian staff. In addition, orders had to be translated, which slowed the dissemination of the voluminous Austrian staff work.

While the allies were maneuvering to the south in order to fall on the French right flank, the French were rushing to concentrate their troops. Napoleon expected the allies to strike in force on the 29th. Marshal Berthier had written to Mortier on the evening of 28 November that "It is to be

---

* Alexandre Andrault de Langeron, *Journal Inédit de la Campagne de 1805: Austerlitz. With Karl Freiherr von Stutterheim, Mikhail Hilairionovich Golénistchev-Kutusov. Relations de la Bataille d'Austerlitz* (Paris: La Vouivre, 1998), p. 32.

presumed that, tomorrow or afterwards, we will have a great battle."* The next day the chief of staff wrote to Marmont that "There will be a bloody battle tomorrow by Brünn," and urged him to keep his troops on alert in order to react "in case of extraordinary circumstances."† But the battle was not forthcoming. The men of Bagration's advance guard consolidated their positions, but failed to attack the French cavalry showing itself in front of them, or to make any effort to take the high ground from which they would be better able to assess the French strength and positions. While there were a number of clashes between outposts, the hesitation of the allies left Napoleon puzzled, and uncertain of their plan.

During the 29th, Napoleon deployed his forces between the Goldbach stream and Brünn, with the cavalry in advance of the Goldbach. Artillery and infantry were positioned on the Santon and the Zuran Hill south of the road, soon to be famous as the site of Napoleon's headquarters during the battle, in order to command the approaches to the stream. Caffarelli's division, which had arrived the night before, stood near Latein while the three divisions of the 4th Corps stood near Latein and Turas. Boyé, commanding Beaumont's division, arrived around 7:00 P.M. after a twelve-hour march and strengthened the cavalry force occupying the heights east of the Goldbach.

Once again, the French dispositions were designed to allow a range of options. The *Relation de la Bataille d' Austerlitz* noted that Napoleon's aim in the event of any serious attack was to retreat and ". . . to place [the army] on the heights of Brünn behind the Zwittawa."‡ At the same time, six divisions were concentrated between Turas and Latein behind a powerful cavalry screen in a position which allowed them to strike across the Goldbach in keeping with Napoleon's original plan if the allies moved on the French right. During the course of the day, the French took advantage of their possession of the heights to observe the allied movements, particularly to the south where the chasseurs of Margaron's cavalry brigade (4th Corps) were operating between Austerlitz and Blaziowitz. Czartoryski noted that "On the heights that hid the French positions from us, we saw officers who appeared successively to observe our march."§ The allies did nothing to drive off these observers and by evening it

---

* "Le Major-Général au Maréchal Mortier (28 novembre 1805)," in Alombert-Goget, p. 275.

† "Le Major-Général au Général Marmont (29 novembre 1805)," in Alombert-Goget, pp. 284–5.

‡ Léger-Marie-Philippe Tranchant, comte de Laverne, "Relation de la Bataille d'Austerlitz," in *Relations et Rapports Officiels de La Bataille d'Austerlitz, 1805* (Paris: La Vouivre, 1998), p. 86; Alombert and Colin, V, p. 115. Colin identifies the position as behind the "Zwittawa," which flows southward into the Schwatzawa near Brünn. The 1998 printing of the "Relation," the official account of the battle authorized by Napoleon, renders this as the "Littawa" which makes little sense in context. The Littawa runs south of Austerlitz in a generally northeast to southwest direction and would be of little use as a defensive position.

§ Czartoryski, II, p. 105.

was becoming clear that the allies were maneuvering as Napoleon had hoped. The main French forces, in full view of the allied cavalry on the Brünn–Olmütz road, withdrew from the heights to the valley of the Goldbach, encouraging the allies in their belief in the weakness of the French army.

> The two corps [of Lannes and Soult] executed this [rearward] movement in squares, chequer-wise, reminding Morand of the marches in Egypt amid immovable swarms of Mamelouks. For my own part I was no less struck by the novelty than by the magnificence of the spectacle. Nothing could be finer or more imposing than those thirty moving masses, which after two hours' march were extended over a distance of five miles, while their arms sparkled in the sun.*

Around midnight on the 29th, Savary and Dolgoruky met Napoleon on the road near the Posorsitz Post House on their way back through the opposing lines. Dismounting, Napoleon and Dolgoruky walked some distance down the road to conduct a private interview. Savary, among those waiting at a distance, noted that the conversation became "very warm." Savary noted that "It seems that Prince Dolgoruky had been deficient in tact in the manner of delivering the message."† Segur, who had been accompanying Napoleon, described Dolgoruky's attitude as "vainglorious and haughty." Dolgoruky had been instructed to offer Napoleon terms appropriate to a defeated enemy— withdrawal from Italy and the left bank of the Rhine, including Belgium. Napoleon angrily refused this obviously excessive demand, which was followed by a somewhat more modest proposal that Napoleon would be allowed to withdraw behind the Danube if he subsequently withdrew from Austria. The offers Alexander conveyed through Dolgoruky demonstrate his conviction that Napoleon stood exposed at the end of a tenuous line of communications, vulnerable to the blow the allied army was about to deliver. Napoleon dismissed Dolgoruky after only about fifteen minutes. Although Segur claimed that Dolgoruky and some officers of his escort had "insulted [Savary] by their arrogant expressions," Savary seems to have parted with Dolgoruky on good terms and with mutual respect.‡ "On your part you are

---

* Thiébault, II, p. 147.

† M. Savary, Duke of Rovigo, *Memoirs of the Duke of Rovigo* (London: H. Colburn, 1828), I, p. 128.

‡ It is interesting to note that Segur was aware of an unconscious tendency by Russian noblemen to be "too imperious." When relating the story of his capture by the Russians in December 1806, Segur observed the attitude of General Ostermann-Tolstoi, noting that "That is their manner when restrained by no special consideration, a consequence probably of their habits as masters in the midst of slaves." But, overall, Segur was impressed by Ostermann-Tolstoi's "courteous and kind consideration." It seems perhaps that Dolgoruky's brief interview with Napoleon did not allow sufficient time for a warming of the imperious façade. Segur, pp. 233–4; 326–7.

bent for war," Dolgoruky told Savary when the two parted. "We will meet it like brave men."*

The Coalition Offensive: Advance to Austerlitz, 30 November – 1 December

During the following days, the allies continued their methodical advance. On the 30th, the columns moved only about six kilometers westward, but finally decided to seize the higher ground that had masked the French positions from them for the past two days. On the allied right, Bagration's forces seized the heights beyond Rausnitz, while to his left Kienmayer gained the Pratzen heights beyond Austerlitz and Stutterheim mounted the Pratzen further still to the left. These three bodies formed a line from the mountains in the north through Welspitz and Klein-Hostieradek to the Mönitz Pond in the south. Although each allied advance guard seized the heights immediately in front of it, making contact with the French advance posts, they failed to take the heights by Krenowitz, which allowed the French to continue to observe the allied flanking maneuver.

Colonel Geringer of the Székler Hussars (part of Stutterheim's force) led the cautious allied advance of Stutterheim's command and around 4:00 P.M. on the 30th, as the sun was setting, his party crept to the far edge of the Pratzen Heights to reconnoiter the French positions. Geringer reported French advance posts at the foot of the heights from Augezd to Girzikowitz. Campfires revealed more French in Mönitz, Tellnitz, Sokolnitz, Kobelnitz and Schlapanitz, the first concrete information the allies were able to collect on French strengths and positions.

The main body continued its shift to the left behind the screen of the advance guard, reaching the edge of the Pratzen Heights, with their movements finally screened from French observers. By the evening of the 30th, the allied columns were nearing the eastern edge of the Pratzen plateau, close to the advance guard. The allies had moved gingerly for two days in complete ignorance of the positions or strength of the enemy army in front of them. Their columns, reformed into more or less their original configurations, had adopted new numbers that morning and now stood near the town of Austerlitz.

Dolgoruky returned from his meeting with Napoleon convinced that the French emperor feared an allied attack and that the allies were sure to succeed, his certainty dispelling any lingering doubts the allied high command may have had. An anxious allied headquarters was relieved when Colonel Geringer's report arrived and revealed that the French forces remained in

* Savary, I, p. 128.

position in the low ground from Tellnitz to the main Brünn–Olmütz road. That evening the Russian advance guard tested the extremities of the French positions. Bagration's forces probed on the right toward Bosenitz, where they were repulsed by a French battery of thirty-eight guns while Stutterheim sent two divisions (four squadrons) of hussars to Augezd to secure the road to Tellnitz and Mönitz for the flanking maneuver on the left.

As the allied forces advanced, the French abandoned their outposts on the eastern edge of the Pratzen, an action that seemed to suggest that they might be planning a withdrawal. In fact, the allied shift to the south had provided Napoleon with enough evidence of a flanking maneuver to order his forces to deploy accordingly. French movements on the 30th followed the general plan outlined by Napoleon a week earlier for an allied attack that Napoleon now expected on 1 December. While occupation of the heights would have effectively prevented any allied turning maneuver, Napoleon saw more advantage in allowing this maneuver to develop and feigning weakness in the process to encourage the allies in this direction.

A key element in Napoleon's plan to give battle east of Brünn was the rapid concentration of his outlying forces. The slowness of the allied movements after the first contact at Wischau made this possible. While a rapid allied strike on the 29th would have caught the French outnumbered and forced Napoleon to execute his plans for withdrawal, the awkward right-angle flank march the allies executed on the 29th gave the French an entire day during which the allied forces moved no closer to the French. The slow pace of the allied advance the next day provided Napoleon with the remaining time he needed. While Colonel Geringer was conducting his reconnaissance of the French positions on the evening of the 30th, Bernadotte was entering Brünn with his advance guard, placing two infantry divisions and a cavalry division at Napoleon's disposal. Friant's division, after hard marching for over twenty-four hours had covered seventy kilometers. His footsore troops plodded into Nikolsburg around 10:00 P.M. while Davout and his staff forged ahead, stopping just short of Brünn around 1:00 A.M. on 1 December. While Friant's troops were just out of range of any action on 1 December, they were in position to support the extreme right of the French position by the next evening if necessary or to support the 8th Hussars, which had fallen back toward Auspitz under pressure from Merveldt's small corps. Gudin's division, with Viallanes's light cavalry brigade, which had not left Pressburg until 11:00 A.M. on the 30th, managed only twenty-five kilometers, reaching Marchegg and was the only portion of the force that Napoleon had intended to assemble that was clearly out of range.

The slowness of the allied advance and their failure to seize the heights clearly puzzled Napoleon. Colonel Francheschi of the 8th Hussars, however, reported that the Austrian force opposing him (Merveldt) was heading toward Nikolsburg and the French communications with Vienna. With clear indications of enemy activity on his extreme right directed at Nikolsburg and the shift of the allied main body to the south that had occurred on the 29th, Napoleon finally committed his forces to counter the anticipated allied flanking maneuver on his right. Napoleon ordered the French outposts deployed on the Pratzen heights back to the line of the Goldbach to occupy the ground between the stream and the high ground. At the same time, Napoleon ordered the forces stationed around Turas and Latein to advance into the positions he had conceived as a theoretical option a week earlier.

In the north, Suchet's division took position in front of the Girzikowitz brook near the Santon, a position that was intended to be the point of the French advance against the Russian right. Suchet's light infantry, the 17th Light, occupied the Santon, which Napoleon ordered the regiment to hold at all costs. Oudinot's grenadier division remained in front of Belowitz, between the Girzikowitz brook and the Goldbach and directly behind Suchet. Vandamme's division advanced to a position in front of Schlapanitz in line with the grenadiers. St Hilaire's division advanced into the position vacated by Vandamme behind Schlapanitz and detached the 10th Light to Kobelnitz, which Napoleon believed to be the point on which the allied turning maneuver would be focused. Legrand positioned his division between Turas and Kobelnitz. Most of the French cavalry massed in the north where Napoleon anticipated his decisive blow. The light cavalry of Trelliard and Milhaud stood at Bosenitz, Boyé's dragoon division stood at Girzikowitz in support of Suchet. The two cuirassier divisions and Walther's dragoons stood behind Oudinot. Further to the rear, on the main Brünn–Olmütz road, stood the reserve consisting of Caffarelli's division and the Guard. Clearly these preparations were intended to set up the projected counterstroke once the allies launched their attack on the French right flank that day. Interestingly enough, even though it was becoming apparent that the allies were shifting to the south, the presence of a strong reserve between Latein and Brünn reveals that Napoleon was still well-prepared to retreat on Brünn if his assumptions about the allies' intentions proved wrong.

During the course of 1 December it became increasingly obvious that the measures Napoleon had taken to safeguard his retreat to Brünn and the line of the Zwittawa would be unnecessary. Reports indicated that by nightfall on the 30th the allied main body was encamped in a compact area just east of the town of Austerlitz in the valley of the Littawa, apparently intending to follow the course of the river toward Tellnitz and Mönitz or to ascend the Pratzen heights to strike the French right further north. Either way, Napoleon had the information he needed. Given the proximity of the allied army and its clearly belligerent attitude, Napoleon was certain the attack would come the next day and would be directed against his right. Once again, he was to be disappointed.

The dispositions Weyrother penned for the allied army on 1 December finally brought the army into direct contact with the French. Once again the columns were renumbered to reflect the positions they were to assume at the conclusion of the day's march. As the heads of the columns moved through the town of Austerlitz and ascended the Pratzen heights, the French advance posts slowly pulled back, offering no resistance. The Székler Hussars, part of Kienmayer's Advance Guard covering the allied left, pressed the French outposts back toward Tellnitz in advance of the allied columns. By 3:00 P.M. the last remaining French forces on the Pratzen Heights (the 11th and 26th Chasseurs of Margaron's cavalry brigade) had been driven back and the allied columns took position in full view of the French, the setting sun illuminating the Russian and Austrian regiments as if they were on a stage. Though the allies had begun the day within reach of the French forces, Weyrother chose not to press them forward to attack the French positions. Instead, the allied forces assembled methodically on the high ground, showing themselves to the French as if to intimidate them.

> The enemy line offered an imposing aspect. Immobile, they crowned the heights; the Russians occupied the center; the debris of many Austrian armies formed the flanks. One never saw such beautiful lines of men ready for combat. Their front was covered by Jäger, hussars and light artillery; more than 2,000 cannon were about to thunder. Their masses of fine cavalry appeared in the second line. The front of the Russians stood in the open; groups of immobile Cossacks and regiments of white-uniformed cavalry appeared here and there along the green line of Russian infantry.*

Despite the magnificent spectacle they presented, the allied forces were experiencing difficulties. The march from Olmütz had generated considerable friction between the Russian column commanders and the Austrian chief of staff. Langeron, highly critical of Weyrother's entire scheme, later expressed his frustration with the whole operation.

> It was necessary to go by the main road right at the enemy; it should be kept in mind that probably Napoleon would have withdrawn behind Brünn. Perhaps he did not expect so prompt an attack; he did not have

---

* Baron de Comeau, *Souvenirs des Guerres d'Allemagne pendant la Révolution et l'Empire* (Paris: Plon-Nourrit et cie., 1900), p. 228.

40,000 men under arms; in 24 hours, he would not have been able to gather all that later arrived in three days, and a retirement could have had a moral effect on his army and on ours in the opposite direction.[*]

Langeron's statements provided an accurate assessment of Napoleon's intentions—but Langeron's sentiments did not reflect the prevailing views at the allied headquarters. Czartoryski reflected on the preoccupation at allied headquarters to seize the moment, "of not allowing so good an opportunity to escape of destroying the French army and dealing Napoleon a decisive and fatal blow."[†] While the fighting generals saw an opportunity to force the French to retreat, the neophytes surrounding Alexander had already won a decisive victory in their imaginations.

Langeron went on to fume at the problems the army encountered on the flank march.

> We continued our march on the 29th and 30th and 1 December over very bad roads smashed by the rains of autumn. Several of our columns were even obliged to chase off their [French] outposts to take the bivouacs that were assigned to them. One can understand what an army already suffering from fatigue and hunger had to endure in winter marches, in very short days, with insufficient supplies and no way to distribute them.[‡]

As if the time lost on the poor side roads were not enough, Langeron chafed under the complicated orders penned by the Austrian chief of staff.

> Incredible confusion reigned, with daily changes that had no place and no reason, not even a pretext. We marched in five columns, not including the advance guard. The five generals who commanded these columns ought to have been able, it seems to me, to keep under their orders the same troops they had received at Olschan . . . In these five marches, no general commanded on one day the regiments that he had commanded the day before. What could be the cause of these perpetual changes if not to delay the marches, to sow confusion, to destroy any advantage to the troops and their commanders?[§]

Langeron's frustration is clear, but his complaint is exaggerated. Far from daily shuffling of troops, the columns arriving on what would be the battlefield

---

[*] Langeron, p. 31.

[†] Czartoryski, II, p. 105.

[‡] Langeron, p. 32.

[§] Ibid. The orders for this flank march are logical enough, though plainly the method behind them was lost on Langeron and most likely the other Russian generals as well.

of Austerlitz on 1 December were nearly identical in composition to the columns that had left Olschan. The daily dispositions issued by Kutuzov, still titular commander of the army even if removed from any decision-making capacity, reveal that the only shuffling occurred on 29 December, the day the flank march began and the day when Langeron saw his army's opportunities slipping away.

By late afternoon on 1 December, the allied army was drawing into position on the Pratzen Heights. Kienmayer's Advance Guard, which had been in position on the southern end of the heights since the day before, stood in the south near Augezd. Behind it, encamped in two lines near Klein-Hostieradek, stood the 1st Column commanded by GL Dokhturov. To his right, on the southern end of the heights stood the 2nd Column of GL Langeron, also in two lines stretching toward Pratze. To the right of the 2nd Column and behind Pratze stood the 3rd Column of GL Prshibyshevsky. The 4th Column, formed into a line of Russians under GL Miloradovich and a line of Austrians under Kollowrath, bivouacked outside of Krenowitz.

The remainder of the allied forces stopped short of their intended positions. The 5th Column of Liechtenstein remained in the valley of the Littawa and did not reach its assigned position on the heights near Blaziowitz. Constantine's 1st Guard Column stood east of the Rausnitz Brook near Austerlitz, roughly in position, but the 2nd Guard Column had fallen behind and was still east of Buschowitz, well to the rear. Finally, Bagration's Advance Guard remained in its position astride the Brünn–Olmütz Road just southwest of Rausnitz with patrols pushed out as far as Holubitz and Posorsitz.

For the French, daybreak on 1 December brought preparations for what seemed an inevitable attack by the allies. As the day progressed and only the allied advance guard appeared on the Pratzen heights, Napoleon became impatient and decided to go himself to reconnoiter the allied positions. Accompanied by his escort, twenty chasseurs à cheval of the Imperial Guard commanded by Daumesnil, Napoleon rode over the ground from Augezd to Pratze and on to Girzikowitz to observe the positions and movements of the allies personally and to inspect his own troops. At one point the party drew too close to the Russian cavalry, provoking a charge by some Cossacks that sent Napoleon's party scampering. After spending most of the day in the saddle, around 3:00 Napoleon established his headquarters on the Zuran Hill south of the main road near Schlapanitz from which point he would have a clear field of observation of much of the battlefield.

The extended delay in the allied attack ensured the arrival of an additional 12,000 men of Bernadotte's I Corps and allowed the weary men of Friant's division to reach Raigern, placing an additional 4,000 troops within a few hours' march of the French positions. More importantly, though, the slow advance of the allies in the three days following their attack at Wischau removed any lingering doubts Napoleon may have had regarding his ability to concentrate his forces in time for the impending battle, while their visible shift to the south clearly revealed their intentions to maneuver on his right. For the first time since the allied offensive began, Napoleon committed to a single plan of action. Throughout 1 December, the French forces took the positions that Napoleon had conceived over a week earlier as a reaction to what had then been a hypothetical allied attack on his right.

Based on reports and his personal observations, Napoleon drafted a revised plan in which Soult would seize the Pratzen Heights after the allies had descended into the valley of the Goldbach to turn the French right. Then Lannes and Murat would advance on the far left, with Bernadotte close behind, and lead a sweep around the allied right, driving their entire army into the ponds and swamps to the south.

After taking a leisurely dinner with Murat and his staff, Napoleon proceeded on foot to the bivouacs of the Imperial Guard and other nearby regiments. At one point, someone lit a torch to light the emperor's way and soon others had followed suit, producing a dramatic torchlight procession as they escorted Napoleon back to his headquarters.* From the allied camp, the blaze fired the imaginations of a number of allied officers, who imagined that the French were torching their supplies in preparation for a hasty retreat.

During the night, the sound of firing to the south prompted Napoleon to send Savary to investigate. Savary returned with news of an Austrian attack on the small detachment at Tellnitz, composed only of one battalion of the 3rd Line and a detachment of about 100 men from the Tirailleurs du Po. With the apparent focus of the allied attack shifting further south, Napoleon made two additional adjustments to his dispositions, ordering the far right at Tellnitz to be reinforced and shifting Bernadotte's two divisions toward Girzikowitz, closer to the center. From the positions assumed by the allied forces the evening before and the aggressiveness of the Austrian attacks at Tellnitz, Napoleon concluded that the main allied effort would strike the French line well to the south of Kobelnitz, which he had assumed the allies were targeting. Around 4:00 A.M., with the apparent focus of the allied attack shifted to Sokolnitz and Tellnitz, Napoleon sent orders to the 3rd Corps at Raigern directing Davout to march on Sokolnitz instead of Kobelnitz. At 6:00 A.M., as the men of the 3rd Line were getting what little rest they could, GdB Heudelet

---

* It is certain that this torchlight procession occurred, but there are many variations of the story and many individuals claimed to know who lit the first torch.

de Bierre set off from Raigern with the 108th Line and the voltigeurs of the 15th Light, accompanied by the 1st Dragoons. A half hour later the remainder of the 3rd Corps set off for Sokolnitz. Having issued these final orders, Napoleon took the opportunity to grab a few hours sleep.

While Napoleon was enjoying his torchlit procession on what he declared to be "the finest evening of my life," the allied commanders were making their way to a council of war at their headquarters at Krenowitz. Weyrother had prepared very thorough and complex plans, and proceeded to brief the allied commanders who had assembled—all except Bagration, who appears to have demonstrated his disgust with the way operations were being handled by claiming that the distance was too far and that the proximity of the enemy required that he remain with his troops. The council convened at 1:00 A.M. on 2 December. Langeron, admittedly a hostile witness, described Weyrother's briefing, stating that "He read his dispositions to us in a loud voice, and with a boastful manner that announced his personal conviction of his own merit and our incapacity."* At any event, the instructions were detailed and therefore complex. The battlefield, which had been the site of Austrian army maneuvers the previous year and was therefore quite familiar to Weyrother, was entirely unknown to the Russian commanders who were moreover struggling to understand a foreign tongue. Langeron reported that Kutuzov dozed off, while Buxhöwden, Miloradovich and Prshibyshevsky listened without saying a word. Dokhturov examined the map attentively, and Langeron, if we can believe his own claims, asked probing questions about what would happen in the event the French attacked the heights after the allies had left them. This last bit would seem unlikely, as Langeron was taken entirely by surprise and initially denied that it was even possible when this in fact occurred during the battle.

Weyrother's plan called for the majority of the allied army to sweep around the French right flank, cross the Goldbach Brook at three points and then sweep north into the French rear, severing their line of retreat toward Vienna. To accomplish this, Kienmayer's Advance Guard and Dokhturov's 1st Column would advance through Tellnitz, crossing the Goldbach by the two bridges at that village. Langeron's 2nd Column and Prshibyshevsky's 3rd Column would march by two separate routes on Sokolnitz, with the 2nd Column crossing the Goldbach via the bridge at Sokolnitz village and the 3rd Column by the bridge slightly to the north by Sokolnitz Castle. This entire left wing of the army would be under the command of Buxhöwden. Weyrother emphasized that none of the columns was to advance beyond the Goldbach until the others were in line and ready to advance, an emphasis that would

---

* Langeron, p. 33.

have unfortunate results for the allies. The 4th Column, under the direct command of Kutuzov and composed of Miloradovich's Russians and Kollowrath's Austrians, would descend from the heights upon Kobelnitz. This left only Liechtenstein's considerable body of cavalry and Bagration's Advance Guard to hold the heights and the main road, with Constantine's 1st and 2nd Guard Columns in reserve.

Weyrother's plan might have had some chance of success had the allies been in a position to put it into action three days earlier. With the reinforcements Napoleon had received, however, the allies no longer had any significant numerical advantage. Moreover, the defiles along the Goldbach were ideal for a small force seeking to delay the passage of a much larger one and the French dispositions placed the majority of the French forces opposite the thinly held allied right. Based on faulty information of the French strength and position, the plan was handicapped by a complete absence of any contingency planning save a vague instruction that in the event of defeat the army would retire by the road to Hungary rather than toward Olmütz. The plan made no allowance for any reaction by the French. To the contrary, it assumed that the French would either remain stationary or flee, utterly unrealistic assumptions for an army commanded by a general already known for taking dynamic and aggressive action to surprise his opponents. The allies would pay a bitter price the next day for the miscalculations of Weyrother, Alexander's closest aides, and most importantly Alexander himself.

Chapter 4

The Battle Begins:
2 December, 7:00 – 10:00 A.M.

On the morning of 2 December Napoleon arose after only a few hours of sleep, greeting his staff with the words, "Now gentlemen . . . Let us go and begin a grand day!"* The air was cold and a fog lay across the landscape, particularly in the valleys and hollows. "There was a thick fog," related Savary, "which enveloped all our bivouacs, so that it was impossible to distinguish objects at the distance of ten paces."† After dressing, Napoleon summoned his marshals to a meeting at the location he had chosen for his headquarters, the Zuran Hill. The troops had already been roused before dawn and stood under arms, blanketed by the fog, with orders to maintain strict silence.

Soon the various corps commanders (all but Davout whose corps was still en route) emerged from the fog with their aides-de-camp and assembled on the Zuran Hill. Napoleon calmly gave instructions to each of them, revising his orders of the night before to counter the allied movement on the extreme right at Tellnitz. On their part, the marshals, many of them comrades in arms from past campaigns, "teased him to begin" the battle.‡ Soon the sound of firing signaled that the allies had engaged the French outposts on the lower Goldbach. "When the Emperor judged, by the briskness of the fire, that the attack was serious, he dismissed all the marshals, and ordered them to begin."§ Only Soult, whose corps was positioned immediately in front of the Zuran Hill, remained in the company of the emperor and his staff.

The calm professionalism of the French headquarters on the morning of 2 December contrasted sharply with the confusion prevailing in the allied camps. While Napoleon had produced a general plan of battle well in advance and had issued written orders the evening before, in the allied headquarters the plan of battle had not been completed until the evening of 1 December and the column commanders had only learned of the details after midnight. Written dispositions required translation into Russian, delaying the distribution of the final orders. As a result, at dawn on the day of battle

---

* Segur, p. 245. Other witnesses reported words to the same effect, although the exact phrasing varies slightly.

† Savary, I, pp. 132–3.

‡ Ibid., p. 133.

§ Ibid.

Napoleon was calmly making adjustments to the orders that his corps commanders had already fully digested, while the allied commanders only received their written orders about an hour before they were to march against the French. Under such circumstances, confusion was inevitable. Nonetheless, the allied columns set off more or less on schedule, though with their commanders unclear of their exact missions and almost universally distrustful of the plan and the man who had framed it. Only the commander of the allied army, the Emperor Alexander, and his equally inexperienced entourage seem to have been free of misgivings.

Opening Action at Tellnitz

As day broke on 2 December, the weary men of the 3rd Line and the Tirailleurs du Po at Tellnitz prepared for a renewal of the attack they had deflected during the night.* Around midnight they had driven off an attack by Austrian hussars. A few hours later the small force had beaten off a renewed attack by Austrian infantry. While the Austrians had not pressed this attack, they had been able to determine that a substantial body of French infantry occupied Tellnitz. After receiving Savary's report, Napoleon had ordered Tellnitz reinforced and GdD Legrand accordingly sent the two remaining battalions of the 3rd Line to reinforce the post. These battalions made the short march from Sokolnitz to Tellnitz in the darkness and arrived around 4:00 A.M. The mission given to Colonel Schobert of the 3rd Line was to hold Tellnitz for as long as possible in order to buy time for the development of the main attack to the north. The longer Schobert held out at Tellnitz and the more allied troops he could tie down, the better the French chances of achieving decisive results.

Once at Tellnitz with the two additional battalions of 3rd Line, Schobert pushed his three companies of voltigeurs forward into the vineyards and up to the crest of the hill in advance of Tellnitz. The remainder of the French battalions occupied the strong natural defensive position at Tellnitz while the 11th and 26th Chasseurs à Cheval, commanded by General Margaron, remained in position to the south to detect any broader flanking maneuver the allies attempted. In all, the French numbered about 1,800–2,000 men, supported by about 650 cavalry.†

---

* A detachment of the Tirailleurs du Po was at Tellnitz during the allied attack on the morning of 2 December. While the greater part of this battalion was engaged at Sokolnitz, it appears that the detachment originally occupying Tellnitz (apparently a single company of about 100 men) remained and operated with the 3rd Line. [Charles Theodore Beauvais de Preau] *Victoires, Conquêtes, Désastres, Revers et Guerres Civiles des Français, de 1792 à 1815* (Paris: C. L. F. Panckoucke, 1819), XV, p. 244.

† Margaron's third regiment, the 8th Hussars, was detached well to the south of Tellnitz and was in contact with Merveldt's small corps on 1 December. Napoleon ordered the 8th Hussars

Only a few kilometers to the east the allied camp was stirring and beginning to set in motion the plan outlined by Weyrother. For many of the allied commanders, their written instructions arrived only shortly before the hour set for them to march. In contrast to the confusion among the allied columns, however, General Kienmayer had a clear idea of what his command was expected to do that day. The advance guard of the allied left was to head the sweeping maneuver that would turn the French right and cut their communications with Vienna. Tellnitz stood in front of him and beyond Tellnitz lay the plain of Turas, in which the large columns of the allied left would sweep around on the flank and rear of the French. The job before him was obvious—drive the French from Tellnitz and open the way for the allied 1st Column. Kienmayer's forces, bivouacked in front of Augezd, were only a short distance from Tellnitz and pickets from the Székler Hussars had remained in contact with the French outposts through the night, provoking sporadic firing. By 6:30 Kienmayer's forces were assembled, the cavalry brigade of General Stutterheim in the lead with General Carneville's infantry brigade following. Apparently expecting to meet at most a single French battalion at Tellnitz, Kienmayer intended to throw the French out of Tellnitz at first light.

The village of Tellnitz was the southernmost of a chain of defensive positions that were extraordinarily well-suited to Napoleon's plans. The road from Augezd to Tellnitz ascended a small hill before descending into the town, which stood on the left or eastern bank of the Goldbach brook. Although sloping gently from the direction of Augezd and standing only ten meters above the level of the Goldbach, the hill was high enough to mask Tellnitz when approached from the east. Even quite close to the village only the roofs of the houses were visible. Vineyards and orchards stood on the western slope of the hill facing Tellnitz, creating good defensive positions for the French skirmishers and limiting the effectiveness of Kienmayer's considerable body of cavalry. To the south the hill sloped gradually for about 600 meters down to the Satchan Pond. The northern bank of the pond, running east–west, formed an angle with the Goldbach running northeast–southwest. The distance between the Goldbach and the Satchan Pond across the crest of the hill in front of Tellnitz was about 1,500 meters. The village of Tellnitz stood at the point of this triangle.

The village itself consisted of two rows of sturdy houses lining a single street that ran parallel to the Goldbach. Walled gardens behind the houses

---

northward and Colonel Francheschi arrived north of Sokolnitz after 3:00 P.M. Strength estimates for 3rd Line range from 1,640 (Bowden) to 1,888 (*Relations et Rapports Officiels*). To this must be added the detachment of about 100 men from the Tirailleurs du Po. *Relations et Rapports*, p. 118; Scott Bowden, *Napoleon and Austerlitz* (Chicago: The Emperor's Press, 1997), p. 494.

formed a ready-made fortification for the French defenders, while the houses themselves constituted a second line of defense. At the bottom of the hill at the edge of the vineyard stood a ditch, apparently dug for drainage from the cultivated hillside. This ditch formed a very useful entrenchment for forces defending the village from an attack from the east. Tellnitz commanded two bridges over the Goldbach Brook, one just north of the village and the other immediately south of it. The road from Augezd intersected the road running through the village at the northern end of the village before passing over the northern bridge. The Tellnitz church stood at this intersection with an open plaza in front of it. Beyond the Goldbach this road forked, one branch running north to Sokolnitz by the west bank of the Goldbach and the other ascending a hill to the northwest. South of Tellnitz, the road running through the village also forked, one branch passing over the Goldbach and running roughly due west past the inn of Ottmarau and on toward Raigern. The other branch continued on the west bank of the Goldbach about 2.5 kilometers to the southwest before crossing by another bridge near the village of Mönitz.*

Tellnitz was extraordinarily blessed with multiple lines of defense against an attack from the east—the vineyard on a reverse slope, a ditch, the garden walls and the houses themselves all gave great help to a small force intending to delay a larger one. Moreover, the narrow space between the Goldbach and the Satchan Pond offered a limited frontage to an attacker. The Satchan Pond, together with the Mönitz Pond beyond it, provided a barrier extending for over four kilometers to the south, except for a narrow isthmus between the two ponds. Although the ponds were frozen, the ice was not thick enough to guarantee safe passage for the allied columns. The stream and ponds served to form a narrow defile through Tellnitz. With only a few hours to prepare, the French had only to occupy the ready-made works to defend the approaches to Tellnitz and the bridges over the Goldbach. Margaron's small body of cavalry was sufficient to cover the narrow passage between the ponds and to watch for any wide, time-consuming, flanking maneuver south of Mönitz.

As the sun rose around 7:00, Kienmayer dispatched parties of his Székler Hussars to probe the mist-shrouded French positions alongside the Goldbach. As the hussars crested the hill in front of Tellnitz, the French voltigeurs opened fire, scattering the horsemen who nevertheless quite accurately assessed the French forces in front of Tellnitz to be several companies strong. To the left, the Austrian hussars observed the French cavalry on the far shore of the pond on the Mönitz road south of Tellnitz. With the information brought back by the hussars, Kienmayer appears to have underestimated the French strength, concluding that only the small French force that his men had

---

* Alombert and Colin, V, pp. 157-8.

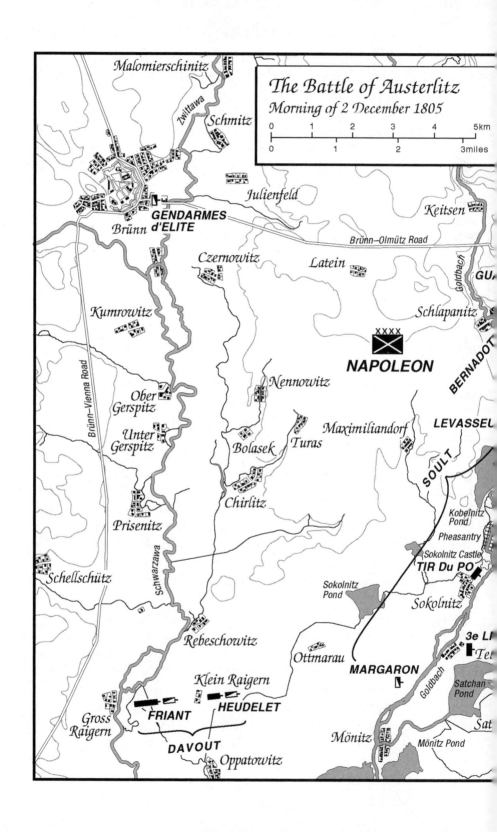

The Battle of Austerlitz
Morning of 2 December 1805

0   1   2   3   4   5km

0   1   2   3miles

Malomierschinitz

Zwittawa

Schmitz

Julienfeld

Keitsen

GENDARMES
d'ELITE

Brünn

Brünn–Olmütz Road

Goldbach

Czernowitz

Latein

GU

Schlapanitz

Kumrowitz

xxxx

NAPOLEON

BERNADOT

Ober
Gerspitz

Nennowitz

Maximiliandorf

LEVASSEU

Unter
Gerspitz

Bolasek

Turas

SOULT

Chirlitz

Kobelnitz
Pond

Prisenitz

Pheasantry

Sokolnitz Castle

TIR Du PO

Schellschütz

Sokolnitz
Pond

Sokolnitz

Rebeschowitz

3e LI

Ottmarau

Tet

MARGARON

Klein Raigern

Satchan
Pond

Gross
Raigern

FRIANT

HEUDELET

Goldbach

Mönitz
Pond

Sat

DAVOUT

Mönitz

Oppatowitz

Mönitz Pond

Brünn–Vienna Road

Schwarzawa

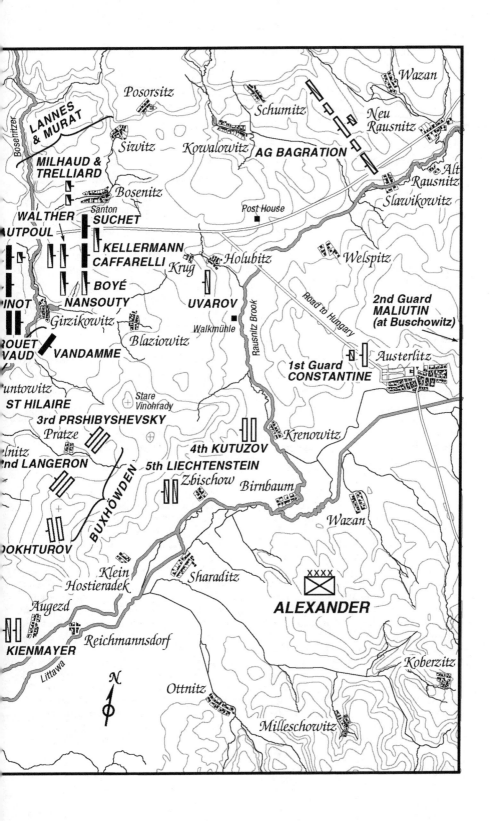

encountered during the night defended Tellnitz. Kienmayer immediately sent forward the 2nd Battalion, 2nd Székler Grenz Regiment, (about 500 men) to sweep the French skirmishers from the vines.* Kienmayer supported the infantry with a detachment from the Székler Hussars on their left to protect against any movement by the French cavalry to the south. The Széklers, coming from the wilds of Transylvania, were well suited to perform the mission at hand, but they were to suffer from Kienmayer's miscalculation of his enemy's strength. Around 7:30 or shortly before, the lone battalion, commanded by Major Diveky, advanced boldly over the crest of the hill with band playing, to be met with a withering fire from the French voltigeurs who immediately fell back to the cover of the vines. Diveky's men pressed forward and engaged in an intense firefight with the French defenders. With the appearance of the Székler, Schobert promptly reinforced his voltigeurs with additional troops from Tellnitz. As the additional French troops flooded into the vines and orchards in front of Tellnitz, the fire "became pretty warm," in Stutterheim's understated words. The Széklers suffered mounting casualties and were finally forced to withdraw.†

In the brief lull following this first assault, Schobert fed more fresh troops into the vineyards while wounded French made their way back to the village. Some of the French cavalry had shifted north toward Tellnitz in reaction to the firing and General Margaron sent an officer off to alert Marshal Davout at Raigern that the post at Tellnitz was coming under attack by a considerable enemy force. Schobert, however, was determined to hold his position for as long as he possibly could.

---

* The regimental history of the Székler Hussar Regiment explicitly identifies the battalion initiating the attack as the 2nd Battalion, 2nd Székler. This is supported by Schönhals who identifies Major Diveky (commander of the 2nd Battalion, 2nd Székler) as leading the attack. However, there is some disagreement as to which Székler regiment led this attack among recent secondary sources. Duffy and Bowden both identify 2nd Székler as the leading regiment, but inexplicably cite Stutterheim as the source for this information. Stutterheim does not specify the regiment involved but only mentions the "first" and then the "other" to indicate the order of engagement. Ian Castle draws the opposite conclusion, indicating 1st Székler as the leading regiment, apparently relying on Vanicek's account. However, Vanicek describes only the attack on the village itself and not the initial engagement that cleared the hill in front of the village. From the entire body of available sources, it is certain that the action in the vineyards involved 2nd Székler as specified by Schönhals and Treuenfest. Because the first attack on the village immediately followed the seizure of the approaches, the troops engaged in confused, open-order fighting in the fog-enshrouded vineyards regrouped while Carneville with the 1st Székler and Broder Regiments attacked the village as Vanicek described. Stutterheim, p. 82; Schönhals, p. 159; Alphons Wrede, *Geschichte der K. und K. Wehrmacht* (Vienna: L. W. Seidel & Sohn, 1898–1901), I, p. 153; Fr. Vanicek, *Specialgeschichte der Militärgrenze, aus Originalquellen und Quellenwerken geschöpft* (Vienna: Kaiserlich-Königlichen Hof- und Staatsdruck, 1875), IV, p. 112; Gustav Amon von Treuenfest, *Geschichte des k.k. 11. Huszaren-Regimentes Herzog Alexander v. Württemberg 1762 bis 1850 Székler Grenz-Huszaren* (Vienna: 1878), p. 233.

† Stutterheim, p. 82.

In the face of stiffer French resistance in the vineyards than he had expected, Kienmayer ordered the 1st Battalion, 2nd Székler, to support the 2nd Battalion in a fresh effort, placing General Stutterheim in charge of the attack. The presence of the French cavalry on the opposite side of the Goldbach prompted Kienmayer to support the attack with additional cavalry.[*] He ordered GM Nostitz with the regiment of Hessen-Homburg Hussars to the right of the hill and GM Prince Moritz Liechtenstein with the remainder of the Székler Hussars to the left, leaving the O'Reilly Chevauxleger and Carneville's three remaining Grenz battalions in reserve. With approximately 500 fresh troops, the Széklers pressed forward again in the face of the French fire from the vines.

This time the determined Széklers penetrated nearly to the foot of the hill, arriving at the open space between the vineyards and the village before being driven back by the French lining the ditch in front of Tellnitz. "The French defended themselves with obstinacy," wrote Stutterheim, "and the Austrians, who had been supported by another battalion, attacked with spirit."[†] On the flanks, the Austrian hussars, unable to come to grips with the French infantry in the vines, were also being picked off by the French skirmishers. "The Hussars, excellent ones of Hessen-Homburg, had many men and horses killed by the enemy skirmishers, but the enemy did not succeed in making them yield."[‡]

Determined to overcome the French resistance, Stutterheim urged his men forward for a third assault. With mounting losses of their own, the remaining French finally withdrew from the vineyards to the position of the ditch, having made the Austrians pay dearly for the ground they had gained. "Twice the Austrians were thrown back and twice moved anew up to the foot of the embankment which they had to take in order to come to the village. Finally General Stutterheim with two battalions became master of it."[§] Thus the victorious Székler swept through the vines and took the ditch, only to come up short as they again met French fire from the houses and walled gardens in the rear of Tellnitz.

Finally in possession of the approaches to Tellnitz, Kienmayer paused to assemble his forces for the seizure of the village itself and its bridges over the Goldbach. The two battalions of the 2nd Székler had already suffered

---

[*] Ibid., p. 83. This cavalry noted by Kienmayer may have been elements of Margaron's two regiments of chasseurs that had been drawn north from their positions toward Mönitz or may in fact have been the 1st Dragoons who had been sent ahead by Heudelet, although the timing seems to make this latter option unlikely.

[†] Stutterheim, pp. 82–3.

[‡] Amon von Treuenfest, *Geschichte des k. k. 11. Huszaren-Regimentes*, p. 233.

[§] Ibid.

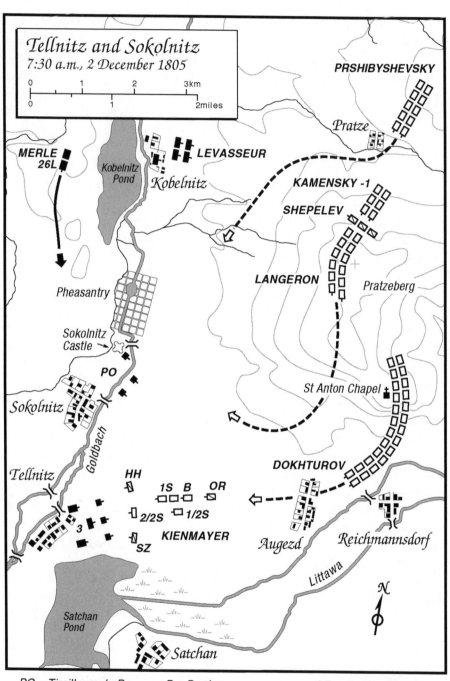

Tellnitz and Sokolnitz
7:30 a.m., 2 December 1805

0   1   2   3km

0   1   2miles

PRSHIBYSHEVSKY

Pratze

MERLE
26L

Kobelnitz Pond

Kobelnitz

LEVASSEUR

KAMENSKY -1

SHEPELEV

LANGERON

Pratzeberg

Pheasantry

Sokolnitz Castle →

PO

Sokolnitz

Goldbach

St Anton Chapel

Tellnitz

HH

1S B   OR

2/2S   1/2S

3

KIENMAYER

SZ

DOKHTUROV

Augezd

Reichmannsdorf

Littawa

Satchan Pond

Satchan

N

PO = Tirailleurs du Po

B = Broder
HH = Hessen-Homburg
OR = O'Reilly

SZ = Székler Hussars
1S = 1 Székler
2S = 2 Székler

considerable losses, the 2nd Battalion alone having lost nearly half its men (roughly 250) in its initial unsupported attacks on the vineyard. While the 2nd Székler rested and regrouped, Kienmayer called up General Carneville with the two battalions of the 1st Székler and a single depleted battalion of the Broder Grenz Regiment for the seizure of Tellnitz. Having expended a little more than half an hour just in taking the hill in front of Tellnitz, Kienmayer seems to have been painfully aware of the need to clear Tellnitz to allow the advance of the 1st Column to proceed according to plan. Between the ponds and French cavalry to the south and the bridgeless stretch of Goldbach to the north, he was left with one course of action. Carneville deployed one battalion of 1st Székler and the single battalion of Broder for a direct assault on Tellnitz, retaining the second battalion of 1st Székler and the two reforming battalions of 2nd Székler in reserve. Around 8:00, Kienmayer hurled the Grenzers against the French positions, intending to batter a passage through the village.*

> Now a very murderous musketry fire began and the smoke was so close because of the fog that one could not see a single step. The battalions were completely wrapped in smoke, which made the operation much more difficult.[†]

As Carneville's Grenzers advanced, they engaged the fresh troops of the 3rd Line occupying Tellnitz and another firefight ensued. Carneville's men pressed over the open ground beyond the ditch, through the smoke and fog, and reached the edge of the village before being driven back. The French, pressing their advantage, chased the Austrians back into the vines where they rallied. Kienmayer fed in the remaining three battalions of Grenzers and managed to push the French back again, once more seizing the ditch. As the exhausted French behind the garden walls and in the houses of Tellnitz faced their equally exhausted enemies in the ditch and the vineyards beyond it, the head of the allied 1st Column began arriving. Although Kienmayer had failed to clear the route through Tellnitz, the arrival of the fresh troops of the 1st Column provided overwhelming numerical superiority and there was little chance the French could hold out much longer.[‡]

Kienmayer reported the situation to General Buxhöwden, who immediately detached the battalion of 7th Jäger that headed the 1st Column to support Carneville's battered infantry. In addition, Buxhöwden moved the brigade of GM Leviz up to form a reserve.[§] Bolstered by the fresh Russian troops, and

* Vanicek, IV, p. 112; Stutterheim, pp. 84–5.

† Treuenfest, *Geschichte des k. k. 11. Huszaren-Regimentes*, p. 233.

‡ Ibid.

§ This brigade consisted of the New Ingermanland and Yaroslav Musketeers. Mikhailovski-Danilevski, p. 240.

with his men rested somewhat during the brief pause while the Russians advanced, Carneville attacked again with two battalions of Székler and the 7th Jäger. After an additional 20 minutes or so of fierce fighting, the allied forces finally managed to drive the last of the French from Tellnitz. Outnumbered and exhausted, the French streamed out of the village and across the brook, evacuating the defile of the Goldbach entirely and ascending the hill to the north toward Sokolnitz. With a cheer, the Russian 7th Jäger poured into Tellnitz while the Székler seized the bridge over the Goldbach north of the town.[*]

Though it had taken them over an hour and a half, the allied forces at Tellnitz had finally overcome all resistance and stood ready to advance against the French right and rear according to plan. All that remained was for General Langeron's 2nd Column to come into line with the 1st Column according to Weyrother's directives. The four battalions of Székler and the battalion of Broder began reforming at the northern end of Tellnitz in preparation to cross the Goldbach, while the battalion of 7th Jäger mopped up stragglers of the 3rd Line in the village to their left. To the rear, near the crest of the hill just beyond the vineyards stood the two regiments of Leviz's brigade, most likely formed in column with the two regiments abreast of each other. The remainder of the 1st Column stretched out behind Leviz. The Austrian cavalry remained on either flank, the Hessen-Homburg Hussars on the right (north) and Székler Hussars on the left against the Satchan pond. Although the fog was clearing across the battlefield, it still lay in the moist low areas that stretched the length of the Goldbach. Added to this was powder smoke, still lingering from the intense firing of the past 90 minutes. As the allies prepared to cross the Goldbach and advance to the northwest, a surprise attack struck them from an unexpected quarter.

Marshal Davout had received word of the action at Tellnitz from Margaron's messenger at around 8:00, about an hour and a half after he had left Raigern for Sokolnitz with Friant's main body. Davout reacted immediately and ordered Heudelet's Advance Guard, a half hour ahead of the main body, to redirect its march toward Tellnitz. Heudelet urged his troops forward, marching via the most direct route past Ottmarau and approaching Tellnitz from the west.[†] As they neared the village, the musket fire from the final storming of Tellnitz was gradually dying off, signaling the end of French resistance. Heudelet's brigade descended the gentle slope to the Goldbach into the still thick fog and smoke lining the brook, aware that the village of Tellnitz was now certainly in the hands of the enemy. Deciding to make the most of

[*] Ibid.

[†] Alombert and Colin, V, 165; "Davout à l'Empereur et Roi, 5 Nivose an 14," in *Relations et Rapports*, pp. 8–9.

the element of surprise, Heudelet ordered his men to fix bayonets for the storming of Tellnitz.

Heudelet's route had brought his men to the bridge over the Goldbach southwest of Tellnitz. Without even pausing, the French swept over the bridge and turned north, entering the village from the south. They first met the startled Russians of the 7th Jäger, who were most likely still searching houses for remaining French—or remaining food and loot that the French might have overlooked. Having driven the French out of the village to the northwest, the sudden irruption from the opposite direction came as a complete surprise to them. Scattered and utterly unprepared for the attack, the 7th Jäger simply fled before the onslaught. The momentum of Heudelet's attack carried the men of the 15th Light and 108th Line down the main street through the entire length of the village. At the north end, the fleeing Russian Jäger flooded through the reforming Grenz battalions and in moments the French charged into the Austrian forces. The Grenzers were as surprised as the Russians had been and were equally ill-prepared to receive an attack. The impetus of the French charge threw the Grenzers back as well and they fled in the wake of the Jäger.

As the French troops emerged from the northern end of Tellnitz, the momentum of the charge slowed and Heudelet began deploying his forces. The impetus of the allied rout, however, continued with the fleeing Jäger and Grenzers sweeping away much of the New Ingermanland (Novoingermanland) Musketeers who were positioned in the path of their flight. As the allied officers struggled to restore order and rally the fleeing troops, Heudelet prepared for the inevitable allied counterattack. The voltigeurs of the 15th Light took up position as skirmishers in the vineyard and the 1st Battalion, 108th Line, deployed in line in front of the village. The 2nd Battalion remained in column at the northern end of the town where the road emerged to the northeast. Detachments still clashed with pockets of Russian Jäger who had taken refuge in the houses of Tellnitz as the French swept through the village. Heudelet's men did not have long to wait for allied retaliation.[*]

As the allied infantry were sent fleeing eastward, the cavalry positioned to the right and left of the road to Augezd remained in position. General Nostitz, taking advantage of the same fog and smoke that had allowed the French to take Tellnitz completely by surprise, now wheeled into action with two squadrons of Hessen-Homburg Hussars under Colonel Mohr. The hussars, having been reduced to the role of spectators and targets for French marksmanship all morning, finally had their opportunity. The 1st Battalion of the 108th stood in line in the narrow strip of open ground between Tellnitz and the vineyards. Nostitz directed Mohr's men into the exposed flank of the

[*] Alombert and Colin, V, p. 165.

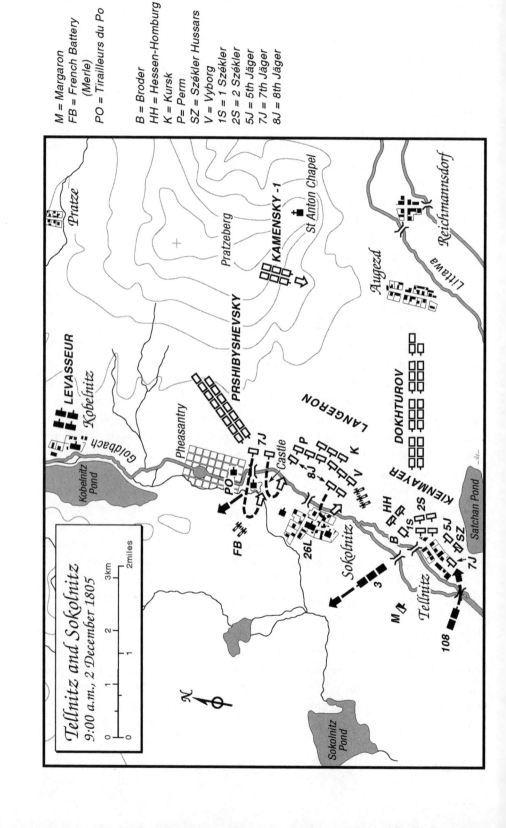

Tellnitz and Sokolnitz
9:00 a.m., 2 December 1805

0 1 2 3km
0 1 2miles

N

M = Margaron
FB = French Battery
(Merle)
PO = Tirailleurs du Po

B = Broder
HH = Hessen-Homburg
K = Kursk
P = Perm
SZ = Székler Hussars
V = Vyborg
1S = 1 Székler
2S = 2 Székler
5J = 5th Jäger
7J = 7th Jäger
8J = 8th Jäger

Pratze

Goldbach

Kobelnitz

LEVASSEUR

Kobelnitz Pond

Pheasantry

PRSHIBYSHEVSKY

Pratzeberg

KAMENSKY -1

St Anton Chapel

FB

PO

7J

Castle

8J

P

LANGERON

K

V

26L

Sokolnitz

3

HH

B

1S

2S

DOKHTUROV

Augezd

Littawa

Reichmannsdorf

KIENMAYER

5J

SZ

7J

Satchan Pond

M

Tellnitz

108

Sokolnitz Pond

French infantry and they swept through the French ranks, causing them to flee for the security of the village. Once through the 1st Battalion, Mohr wheeled his hussars around and charged the 2nd Battalion, hitting it in the flank as well. Heudelet credited the grenadiers of the 2nd Battalion with blunting the Austrian charge sufficiently to allow most of the French troops of 15th light and 108th Line in front of Tellnitz to escape into the village, but nonetheless many were cut off and captured.*

With the French cleared from the ground in front of Tellnitz, the allied infantry quickly advanced to occupy it. Unlike the previous assaults, by this time the allied artillery had arrived. A battery was soon in position and began bombarding the French positions while the Russian infantry advanced in two lines from the north and east, quickly engaging the 1st Battalion, 108th, in Tellnitz.† Hopelessly outnumbered and in an untenable position, Heudelet gave the order to retire to the north. The grenadier company of the 2nd Battalion, nearly surrounded by the attacking Jäger and musketeers, was forced to cut its way out between two battalions as the French force fell back to the north along the Goldbach between the cemetery and the brook. Behind them:

> . . . the artillery opened a violent fire from the hill on the retiring Frenchmen and after they had completely withdrawn from these points [on the east bank of the Goldbach] the cavalry brigade of Prince Moritz Liechtenstein along with that of General Stutterheim, passed without opposition through the defile and formed themselves beyond in battle order; Tellnitz and the defile were occupied with some battalions and artillery.‡

Still harassed by the allied artillery fire and the advancing cavalry to their rear, the French marched through the swirling fog and smoke until suddenly they were hit by a volley of musket fire from a column looming up through the fog ahead of them. Caught between two fires, Heudelet's men recoiled from the unseen enemy in front of them and staggered back toward Tellnitz where their rearguard still stood. Recognizing the column to the northwest as French, a party of men from 108th Line frantically called out to them and waved their regimental eagle, eventually managing to identify themselves as friends.§ With the mistake sorted out, Heudelet's men resumed their march

---

* Stutterheim stated that several hundred were taken prisoner as a result of this charge. Stutterheim, p. 87; Schönhals, p. 160.

† Details of the composition of this Russian force are not available but it seems likely to have included the 7th Jäger and possibly a battalion of the 5th Jäger that might have been with the 1st Column.

‡ Treuenfest, *Geschichte des k. k. 11. Huszaren-Regimentes*, p. 234.

§ Duffy, *Austerlitz*, p. 110.

toward Turas, this time in the company of their attackers from the 26th Light as the allied forces drove the rearguard from its toehold in Tellnitz and across the Goldbach. The whole action from Heudelet's arrival at Tellnitz until he recrossed the Goldbach had lasted little more than half an hour. Within that brief span, Heudelet's command had suffered severe losses.

The villagers of Mönitz had observed the two-hour struggle for Tellnitz from the vantage point of their church tower. After hearing an early-morning prayer for the success of their army against the backdrop of the noise of battle that was just opening, the 72-year-old priest and many of his congregation crowded into the church tower to see what they could of the course of the battle.

> The church tower was overcrowded with Mönitzers. Astonished and at a loss for speech, as far as the powder smoke would allow, they watched the the corps advancing with loud shouting and booming cannon and firing. The Russians [*sic*] in Tellnitz, where the Frenchmen had entrenched themselves, five times broke and were even hunted back to Augezd.*

By this time the fog was finally lifting, but despite this fact and despite having driven Heudelet's men from Tellnitz the allies proceeded with caution. The Austrian cavalry under Liechtenstein and Stutterheim proceeded across the Goldbach and pursued the retreating French a short distance before they met three regiments of dragoons from Bourcier's division.† Bourcier immediately charged the Austrian cavalry, driving them back toward the Goldbach to allow the infantry time to escape. As the French dragoons neared the stream, however, they were struck by a volley from fresh Russian infantry advancing from Tellnitz:

> In this moment [wrote Bourcier] the enemy infantry and artillery began a lively fire on my squadrons. The ball and canister carried away many men

---

* The account describes five consecutive attacks of the "Russians" but this must refer to the entire series of Kienmayer's attacks and the final attacks of the combined Austro-Russian force. There is no indication that the earlier attacks of Stutterheim and Kienmayer were ever driven back toward Augezd nor is it likely that they could have been driven off five times in the course of the thirty minutes between the arrival of the 1st Column and the final seizure of Tellnitz. The description of the allied forces being driven back to Augezd would appear to be a reference to the initial assault on Tellnitz by 108th Line that had put the allied forces in Tellnitz to flight. In all, the various accounts from French and Austrian sources indicate a total of at least five failed or semi-successful assaults prior to the initial seizure of Tellnitz and a sixth final assault that drove the 108th Line out of the village and placed it finally in allied hands. "Report of the Parish and school archives of Mönitz," in Clemens Janetschek, *Die Schlacht bei Austerlitz: 2. December 1805* (Brünn: Päpstliche Benedictiner-Buchdruckerei, 1898), p. 103.

† Bourcier had the 15th, 17th and 27th Dragoons with him. The 25th Dragoons had been left to cover the communications in Raigern while the 18th and 19th Dragoons under GdB Sahuc remained in reserve.

and several horses; they would have done more harm had they been directed better, being within half-range.[*]

Faced with enemy infantry and artillery, Bourcier withdrew his force to the northwest. The allied force that had fired on him, composed of the battalions of 7th and 5th Jäger, the Moscow Musketeers, Vyatka Musketeers and Bryansk Musketeers (eleven battalions in all) and supported by the Austrian cavalry, advanced cautiously, fearing other nasty surprises lurking in the fog and smoke, to occupy the high ground northwest of Tellnitz.[†]

The infantry of Kienmayer's Advance Guard, the bloodied Grenzers, rested in Tellnitz. Buxhöwden positioned the remainder of the 1st Column—twelve battalions—in the open ground between Augezd and Tellnitz.[‡] With his forces straddling the Goldbach, Buxhöwden turned his eye to the north, adhering to Weyrother's instructions to advance only in parallel with the other columns. As a result, instead of marching north to overwhelm the hard-pressed French forces engaging the Russian 2nd Column, Buxhöwden stuck to the letter of the plan and settled in to wait for the 2nd Column to clear its own way.

The fighting at Tellnitz had involved a small number of troops on either side, the nature of the terrain preventing the allies from taking full advantage of what had become considerable numerical superiority. In the initial phase the French had not more than 2,000 infantry occupying a remarkably strong natural defensive position. Opposing them were approximately 2,300 infantry and 2,200 cavalry, the latter being useless in attacking the French positions in the vineyards and village. By committing his forces piecemeal, Kienmayer squandered his modest numerical advantage in the initial assaults, allowing the French to prolong the fighting. With the arrival of the Russian 1st Column, an additional 400 Jäger, with about 3,000 additional infantry under Leviz providing nothing more than intimidation, were sufficient to sweep the French from Tellnitz.

For the second phase of the fighting at Tellnitz, the allies in and adjacent to Tellnitz numbered approximately 1,800 to 2,000 men while Heudelet's brigade mustered less than 900.[§] Once the initial surprise was spent,

[*] Alombert and Colin, V, p. 166.

[†] Ibid.

[‡] Ibid. These regiments were the Kiev Grenadiers, Yaroslav Musketeers, Vladimir Musketeers, and New Ingermanland Musketeers.

[§] Colin states a total of 3,800 men for Friant's division at Austerlitz (including the attached 1st Dragoons). Bowden includes Bourcier's dragoon division in the 3,800 figure and reduces Friant's infantry strength to 3,200 without explanation for his reasons for doing so. Based on the returns from Friant's division prior to the forced march to Austerlitz, the 108th Line and the detachment from 15th Light comprised roughly 30 percent of the division. Assuming an even distribution of the depletion in strength during the forced march among the regiments it is reasonable to conclude that Heudelet's force numbered no more than 1,140 based on 30 percent of a total

Buxhöwden massed at least 3,000 men, supported by cavalry and artillery, against them. Given the much greater disparity of force, the rapid expulsion of Heudelet from Tellnitz can be readily understood. But the half-hour of time bought by Heudelet's bold attack served the French well by allowing time for Bourcier's dragoons to arrive. This, in turn, prevented the Austrian cavalry from probing to the northeast where they would have encountered the rear of the French defenders of Sokolnitz and dramatically altered the dynamics of the events occurring to the north.

The Struggle for Sokolnitz

About two kilometers north of Tellnitz, Colonel Hulot commanded a small detachment manning another outpost in the French defensive cordon on the lower Goldbach. The Tirailleurs du Po, a battalion of Piedmontese troops who had found themselves in French service following the annexation of their country by Napoleon, defended the vicinity of Sokolnitz at a point where two bridges spanned the Goldbach. Hulot's small command had originally formed the extreme right of the French line and had stretched from the pheasantry (a game park on the banks of the Goldbach between Sokolnitz and Kobelnitz) to Tellnitz. With the allied activity at Tellnitz the night before, Legrand had sent the 3rd Line to reinforce Tellnitz while Hulot remained at Sokolnitz with his small command. About one hour's march to the north stood the remainder of Legrand's division at Kobelnitz—seven battalions of the 26th Light, 18th Line, 75th Line and the Tirailleurs Corse.[*]

Soon after first light, the sounds of musketry from Tellnitz alerted both Hulot at Sokolnitz and Legrand at Kobelnitz to the allied movement to the south. By 7:30 the firing had intensified, indicating a serious attack on Tellnitz. Concerned for the extreme right of the long French line, Legrand ordered GdB Merle with the two battalions of the 26th Light to reinforce Schobert at Tellnitz.[†]

Hulot's battalion numbered between 440 and some 580 men according to various accounts. Deducting the detachment of about 100 stationed at Tellnitz, perhaps as few as 340 men remained to defend Sokolnitz. Colonel Hulot positioned a large portion of his men in an orchard just east of the Goldbach. This orchard commanded the roads from both the villages of Augezd and Pratze immediately before each passed over the Goldbach. To the

---

strength of 3,800 or 960 based on 30 percent of a total divisional strength of 3,200. Other low-end estimates place 108th Line at 818, based on a 50 percent reduction from its previous reported strength of 1,637. It is not clear why Bowden claims that this brigade had been reduced to at most 800. Alombert and Colin, V, p. 134; *Relations et Rapports*, p. 116; Bowden, p. 494.

[*] "Rapport de la Bataille d'Austerlitz par Soult," in *Relations et Rapports*, p. 19.

[†] Ibid., p. 18; Alombert and Colin, V, p. 160.

west of the stream, detachments occupied Sokolnitz village and, to the north, the large stone buildings of the estate called Sokolnitz Castle.*

As Kienmayer's forces began their reconnaissance of Tellnitz and Buxhöwden was getting under way with the 1st Column, the 2nd and 3rd Columns were preparing to march. The 2nd Column of GL Langeron, encamped in two lines between the villages of Pratze and Klein-Hostieradek, and the 3rd Column of Prshibyshevsky positioned behind the village of Pratze, had been ordered to advance in parallel with the 1st Column. The 2nd Column was to cross the Goldbach between Tellnitz and Sokolnitz and the 3rd Column just north of Sokolnitz. Although both commanders had been briefed on their orders for the day during the previous night's meeting, their written orders only arrived around 6:00 A.M. and the two generals began preparing their columns to march at 7:00 as ordered but were unexpectedly disrupted by the cavalry of the 5th Column.[†]

The cavalry of the 5th Column had received its written orders at 6:00 A.M. as well. The 5th Column had been camped east of the 2nd and 3rd Columns, but on reading their orders it became clear to the commanders that their specified position for 2 December was immediately to the south of the village of Blaziowitz. Hurriedly breaking camp, the Austrian and Russian cavalry of the column proceeded to what they thought was the prescribed position, and were no doubt surprised to find it occupied by a large body of Russian infantry—the 2nd Column!

Langeron indignantly rode to confront the officers of the cavalry riding through the midst of his column as it was preparing to march. General Shepelev, *shef* of the St Petersburg Dragoon Regiment and commander of one of the two Russian cavalry brigades of the 5th Column, was equally indignant, indicating that Liechtenstein had specified the position and accusing Langeron of having his infantry in the wrong place. Shepelev appears to have then stubbornly led his brigade through the midst of Langeron's column, planting his men south of Pratze. Behind Shepelev, Hohenlohe apparently realized the mistake and hesitated, remaining east of Langeron's column. Langeron described the encounter:

---

* The official strength reported by 4th Corps for the Tirailleurs du Po was 587 officers and men. Bowden calculates the actual strength to be only 340 men by noting 308 men in a return of 22 November and indicating that some detachments rejoined the unit before the battle. It is not clear if the detachments in question include the portion of the battalion at Tellnitz. The 587 figure appears to date from 7 November. According to Bowden's data, a return dated 7 December shows 361 men present with the unit. Casualties sustained by this battalion at Tellnitz and Sokolnitz are described as heavy, suggesting that Bowden's figure for its strength on 2 December excludes the detachment of approximately 100 men at Tellnitz. This would indicate a loss of about 80 men or nearly 20 percent casualties which is reasonable in context. *Relations et Rapports*, p. 118; Bowden, pp. 467, 494, 508.

[†] Langeron, p. 69.

At six o'clock in the morning, I saw pass by the village of Pratzen [*sic*] all the Russian cavalry which came to occupy the heights where I was camped. As I knew by the dispositions that the cavalry was to be placed to my right two or three versts from the village, I told the cavalry generals this, but GL Shepelev said to me that Prince Johann Liechtenstein had sent an order to them to move to the place where he then was. I assured him that it was by error, but he persisted in remaining where he was. He said to me that if he were not where he was meant to be, he would take his place at daybreak, but that he could not go in the dark.[*]

Shepelev's cavalry, in position south of Pratze, now stood in the midst of the 2nd Column and squarely in the path of the 3rd Column, preventing both columns of infantry from proceeding with their march. While Langeron fumed at Shepelev, the Austrian staff officer with the 3rd Column plotted a course around the obstruction, allowing the 3rd Column to begin its march at 7:00 as scheduled. By around 7:30 as the sun began to burn off the fog on the heights, the error was realized. Langeron was able to set off with the head of his column while Shepelev and his wayward cavalry reversed their course and set off for their intended position. The tail of the 2nd Column, two regiments commanded by GM Kamensky-1, were apparently forced to wait for the passage of the cavalry before following Langeron with the main body.[†]

After incurring about a thirty-minute delay while the error of the 5th Column was unraveled, Langeron's column finally began its descent through the fog to the Goldbach. Because the ground immediately in front of his position was steep, Langeron directed his column down the road to the left toward Klein Hostieradek where the descent into the valley of the Goldbach was easier. From Klein Hostieradek the column passed through Augezd and then directly down the road to Sokolnitz. By around 8:30, Langeron had the head of his column aligned with the head of the 1st Column, which had paused between Augezd and Tellnitz while the 7th Jäger joined Kienmayer's forces in the storming of Tellnitz. Although thirty minutes behind schedule, Langeron had finally aligned with the 1st Column, but to the north there was no sign of the 3rd Column nor any sound of firing through the fog in that direction. Frustrated, Langeron sent the Austrian staff officer assigned to his column, Baron Wallenstädt, to make contact with Prshibyshevsky.[‡]

Soon after dispatching Wallenstädt on his mission, Langeron arrived opposite the southern end of the village of Sokolnitz. Unwilling to commit his forces to an assault on Sokolnitz until he could coordinate his attack with

[*] Ibid., p. 43; a verst was approximately equal to a kilometer.
[†] Ibid.
[‡] Ibid., p. 70.

Prshibyshevsky, Langeron deployed his advance guard and leading regiments in two lines opposite Sokolnitz. On the approach of the Russian column, French skirmishers positioned in an orchard east of the Goldbach and north of the road from Augezd opened fire on Langeron's advance guard. Scouting parties soon also identified French forces across the stream in Sokolnitz. Langeron immediately moved a battery into position to bombard the village. To counter the French skirmishers, Langeron detached the 3rd Battalion, 8th Jäger, supported by the Grenadier Battalion, Vyborg Musketeers. Fanning out in skirmish order, the more numerous Russian Jäger engaged the French just as the head of Prshibyshevsky's 3rd Column began arriving through the mist. Between the effective skirmishing of the Russian Jäger and the arrival of Prshibyshevsky's column, the French skirmishers melted away into the mist toward the Goldbach and Sokolnitz.[*]

Prshibyshevsky's 3rd Column had begun its march shortly before Langeron's, guided by the Austrian staff officer attached to it. The route indicated by the officer, however, cut across plowed fields interspersed with ditches. The ground slowed the march and the ditches formed obstacles that the company of pioneers attached to the column had to overcome to allow the passage of the artillery. Prshibyshevsky noted that the pioneers had to repair the "road" three times, suggesting a series of three ditches cutting across the route of march. In between the guns were dragged across the frozen furrows, plowed in neat parallel lines along the slope like so many speed bumps to impede the progress of the Russian column. With the passage of troops, the frozen ground turned to mud that clung to the wheels of the artillery and train. As they descended the slope, the sound of firing ahead signaled the arrival of Langeron's column opposite Sokolnitz. By 9:00 the 3rd Column had finally completed its descent from the heights, a hour-and-a-half-long trek that had brought them only four kilometers from their starting point.[†]

Although the two Russian columns had overwhelming numerical superiority at this point, the ground was well suited for defense by a small force. Like Tellnitz, the village of Sokolnitz consisted of stone houses with walled gardens. The bank of the Goldbach was somewhat marshy and broken

---

[*] Colin states that this battery was composed of thirty guns, but this would be the entirety of Langeron's artillery. Langeron had no position batteries, only regimental guns, which were typically distributed among the musketeer and grenadier battalions with one division (two guns) per battalion. It is probable that twelve guns remained with Kamensky-1's six battalions, leaving eighteen guns in Langeron's battery. Langeron, p. 70; Alombert and Colin, V, p. 163.

[†] The condition of the ground varies according to different accounts, sometimes being described as frozen (which is consistent with the reports of the frozen surfaces of the ponds). In other reports "clinging mud" is mentioned. It seems likely that the ground was frozen initially but was turned to mud by the passage of troops, aided by rising temperatures as the sun rose. "Raport I. Ya. Przhibyshevskogo Aleksandru I o Deistviyakh 3-i Kolonny v Srazhenii pri Austerlitse, 1806 g. Iulya 11," in *Kutuzov Sbornik Dokumentov*, pp. 269–70.

with scrub. From the stream the ground rose 20–30 meters to the village, the west bank commanding the lower east bank.

Although Langeron claimed later to have known that Sokolnitz was only lightly defended, it seems unlikely that the Russians had any idea what lay in front of them. Neither column had any cavalry for reconnaissance, while probes by parties of Jäger were deflected by the French skirmishers. As a result, the two allied columns groped their way through the fog without any clear idea what to expect, knowing only that there were French troops on the opposite bank of the Goldbach. Langeron's hindsight, however, was quite accurate. Only about 480 men at most held Sokolnitz and Sokolnitz Castle against the converging allied columns. Skillful use of the terrain and the fog that masked their weakness allowed the small force to hold the more numerous Russian Jäger back for about fifteen minutes. More importantly, though, their firing had attracted the attention of GdB Merle who was rushing his two battalions of the 26th Light toward Tellnitz.*

The 26th Light had just been approaching Sokolnitz from the north when Langeron's Jäger had engaged the French skirmishers east of the Goldbach. Although Merle had orders to reinforce the beleaguered 3rd Line at Tellnitz, the timing of his arrival near Sokolnitz could not have been better as the firing east of the village revealed a more pressing need close at hand. Merle immediately led the 26th Light to Sokolnitz, the 1st Battalion marching at the double down the main north–south street of the town and deploying in the houses, the 2nd Battalion dividing into two columns and advancing into position in the open ground between Sokolnitz village and Sokolnitz castle. The 1st Battalion arrived in the village just as Langeron's bombardment of Sokolnitz had begun and the 2nd Battalion was in position only minutes before the Russian infantry attacked. With the arrival of the 26th Light, most of the Tirailleurs du Po moved to take position in and around Sokolnitz Castle, with some skirmishers occupying the pheasantry immediately to the north, although some may have remained in Sokolnitz.

> The 26th Light [wrote Colonel Pouget] was put in line of battle behind this village; it was to be supported by a regiment of dragoons and two pieces of artillery. From where these troops were placed, they could see the enemy arriving only when they appeared at the top of the slope, within good gun range. Already the artillery of the line of battle could be heard, and the enemy were engaged. Fifteen minutes had hardly passed, when the 26th and the artillery, its neighbor, saw a Russian column go down to the village. Our artillery opened fire, while the first battalion, led by M. Brillat, its chief, under the direction of Brigadier-General Merle,

* Langeron, pp. 70–1.

penetrated Tellnitz [*sic*], going to meet the enemy; but seeing that they dealt with a deep column, supported by several artillery pieces, the second battalion was divided into two portions to go by two columns on the wings of the first, which was heavily committed.[*]

Pouget himself, having apparently remained with the 2nd Battalion, was offered command of the center by Brillat, and the colonel arrived in Sokolnitz as the Russian bombardment was reaching its peak:

> I suffered much during the combat of Tellnitz [*sic*] from the restlessness of the horse I rode which, startled by the whistling of the balls that flew around its ears and between its legs, did not allow me to go where I believed my presence necessary. Chef de Bataillon Brillat offered the center to me, which I accepted with eagerness. At the moment I dismounted, I was covered with dirt and stones launched at me with such force that I was bloodied and almost blinded. It was the impact of a ball that had fallen within three paces of me. I did not mount less peacefully the mount of my chef de bataillon, and rode with him to the center of my regiment, which I encouraged with voice and example to defend this post honorably, with that calmness that this force was known for.[†]

With Prshibyshevsky now in position and the head of his column aligned with Langeron's as stipulated by Weyrother's instructions, Langeron ordered his two battalions of 8th Jäger under the command of Colonel Laptev to cross the Goldbach opposite the south end of the village of Sokolnitz. The main body of the column, nine battalions under the command of GM Olsufiev, remained at the ready on the east bank of the Goldbach. To the north, Prshibyshevsky made similar dispositions, first directing his forces against what he considered to be the most important French position, Sokolnitz Castle. GM Miller-3 with two battalions of the 7th Jäger was to advance to the north of Sokolnitz and seize the castle. The main body of the 3rd Column under the command of GM Strik would follow in close support while the column reserve under GM Wimpfen remained some distance to the northeast as a precaution against the French forces known to be at Kobelnitz.[‡] The 3rd Battalion, 8th Jäger, appears to have remained in the orchard, serving to link the two columns although it may also have participated in this initial attack.

[*] Alombert and Colin, V, pp. 163–4.

[†] François-René Cailloux, dit Pouget, *Souvenire de Guerre (1790-1831)* (Paris: La Vouivre, 1997), p. 95; [bound with Florent Guibert, *Souvenirs d'un Sous-Lieutenant d'Infanterie Légère (1805–1815)*]

[‡] Langeron, pp. 44, 70; "Raport I. Ya. Przhibyshevskogo," in *Kutuzov Sbornik Dokumentov*, pp. 269–70.

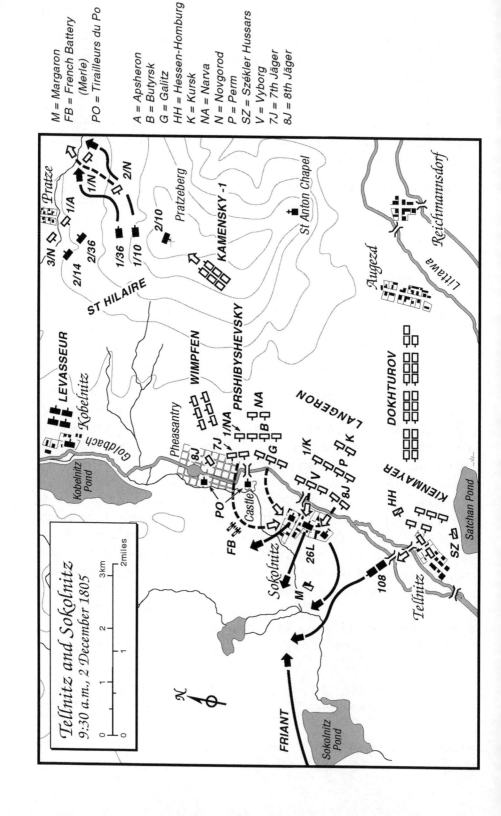

Tellnitz and Sokolnitz
9:30 a.m., 2 December 1805

M = Margaron
FB = French Battery
     (Merle)
PO = Tirailleurs du Po

A = Apsheron
B = Butyrsk
G = Galitz
HH = Hessen-Homburg
K = Kursk
NA = Narva
N = Novgorod
P = Perm
SZ = Székler Hussars
V = Vyborg
7J = 7th Jäger
8J = 8th Jäger

Pratze
3/N
2/14
2/36
1/A
1/N
2/N
1/36
1/10
2/10
Pratzeberg
ST HILAIRE
KAMENSKY - 1
St Anton Chapel
LEVASSEUR
Kobelnitz
Goldbach
Kobelnitz Pond
WIMPFEN
PRSHIBYSHEVSKY
Pheasantry
8J
7J
1/NA
NA
B
G
PO
Castle
FB
Sokolnitz
M
26L
108
LANGERON
1/K
V
P
K
8J
DOKHTUROV
HH
KIENMAYER
SZ
Tellnitz
Satchan Pond
Augezd
Reichmannsdorf
Littawa
FRIANT
Sokolnitz Pond

N

0   1   2   3km
0   1   2miles

Shortly after 9:00, GM Miller-3 advanced with two battalions of 7th Jäger to take Sokolnitz Castle from several hundred Tirailleurs du Po defending it. Miller ordered two companies to attack Sokolnitz Castle with the remaining six companies advancing in support. Outnumbered and in danger of being surrounded, the French quickly relinquished the strong point, which was occupied by the Russian Jäger. As Miller's men emerged beyond the castle and advanced across open ground through the fog, however, they found themselves under fire from the 2nd/26th Light and two guns positioned on the heights to the west. Surprised by a largely unseen enemy, the Russian Jäger retreated in confusion and Miller fell wounded. Taking advantage of their initial success, the 2nd/26th advanced, capturing Miller and other wounded Russians and retaking Sokolnitz Castle.[*]

About 800 meters to the south, Laptev's two battalions of 8th Jäger crossed the Goldbach and ascended toward the village. As the Russian Jäger came into view through the fog, Merle's men opened fire on them from their positions in the village. Laptev's men held on to their position for a short while, returning fire as best they could, but were quickly driven back with heavy losses and Merle's men were allowed a brief respite while the Russians regrouped. While the 26th Light braced itself for the next Russian assault, the Tirailleurs du Po took position as skirmishers in the pheasantry.

Although the initial Russian attacks on Sokolnitz had been beaten off, the French had now revealed their strength and positions. Langeron and Prshibyshevsky accordingly assembled their forces for a renewed effort, taking advantage of their vastly superior numbers to overwhelm the French. Prshibyshevsky placed GM Strik in command of five battalions for the main assault on Sokolnitz. Two battalions of Jäger would drive the French from Sokolnitz Castle and then wheel to their left to strike the village. The three battalions of Galitz Musketeers would advance between Sokolnitz Castle and the village, attacking the French in the village directly. As insurance, Prshibyshevsky moved the Butyrsk Musketeers and one battalion of Narva Musketeers to the west bank of the stream in close support, while the two remaining battalions of Narva Musketeers stayed in reserve on the east bank. Wimpfen, with two regiments, observed the French forces to the north at Kobelnitz, while Prshibyshevsky detached a battalion of Jäger (probably the battalion of 8th Jäger that had cleared the French skirmishers from the orchard opposite Sokolnitz) to move into the pheasantry and cover his right.[†]

In a mirror image of Prshibyshevsky's deployment, Langeron shifted his

---

[*] Zhmodikov, p. 44; *Sbornik Dokumentov*, pp. 269–70.

[†] One battalion of 8th Jäger, probably the 3rd Battalion, which had driven the French skirmishers from their position east of the Goldbach, operated with the 3rd Column after its arrival at Sokolnitz. It seems that this battalion was the one sent into the pheasantry.

two Jäger battalions to the south to attack the southern end of Sokolnitz village and placed the three battalions of Vyborg Musketeers to their right with GM Olsufiev-3 in overall command of the attacking forces. The Perm Musketeers and one battalion of Kursk Musketeers advanced behind the first line to support the attack while the remaining two battalions of the Kursk Regiment stood in reserve. The two Russian columns together composed a force of ten battalions, supported by an additional eight battalions, to assault the two battalions of 26th Light and Tirailleurs du Po holding Sokolnitz village and castle.*

Around 9:30 the Russian forces advanced. On the far right, the Jäger battalion detached to the pheasantry promptly drove the outnumbered French skirmishers northward toward Kobelnitz. Strik's Jäger made contact with the French forces in Sokolnitz Castle, and with their considerable numerical superiority they threatened to surround the estate. Once again the French defenders were forced to withdraw after firing a few volleys. To the left of the Jäger, the Galitz Musketeers advanced into the open ground between Sokolnitz Castle and the village. Strik's men met no serious resistance initially, but once they had emerged into the open ground between Sokolnitz Castle and the village they came under fire from the French lodged in the north end of Sokolnitz. To the left, however, Olsufiev's men ascended the bank of the stream in the face of a withering fire from the 26th Light in the village. The French, taking advantage of their strong defensive position and superior musketry, produced carnage between Sokolnitz and the Goldbach.[†]

Although inflicting severe casualties on their Russian attackers, the 26th Light was soon in a desperate situation. Five battalions were attacking the village from the east while the three battalions of Galitz Musketeers had swung around to strike the village from the north. Strik's Jäger battalions, advancing beyond Sokolnitz Castle with their right secured by the battalion detached into the pheasantry, first swept up the hill and captured the French battery that had surprised Miller-3. Then wheeling toward the south, they charged Sokolnitz from the northwest. The Russian and Austrian artillery attached to the battalions advanced with the infantry and poured canister into the defenders. Pouget estimated the enemy strength at "12,000 Russian Grenadiers" supported with "thirty pieces of ordnance" which is a reasonably accurate assessment of the ten battalions attacking with eight additional battalions supporting them in a second line. "The enemy canister inconvenienced us greatly," he wrote. "They came on both sides of us with the bayonet."[‡] The

* Alombert and Colin, V, p. 164.
† Ibid.
‡ Pouget, p. 94.

situation now hopeless, the men of the 26th Light began a mad flight from their doomed position. With fog and powder smoke still hanging thick over Sokolnitz and the lowlands lining the Goldbach, the jubilant Russians swept into the village, Strik's battalions from the north and northwest and Olsufiev's battalions from the southeast and south.

As the Russian battalions enveloped Sokolnitz, most of the 2nd/26th and scattered parties of defenders slipped out to the west and ascended the heights in the direction of Turas where they reformed behind the Sokolnitz Brook. GdB Margaron with his two regiments of chasseurs, freshly arrived from the vicinity of Tellnitz, quickly moved into position to cover their retreat and discourage any Russian pursuit, the timing of this arrival having been as fortuitous as that of Merle less than an hour earlier. Most of the 1st/26th, though, was cut off from the west by the Russian envelopment. About 100 men were trapped in the village by the Russian advance, while the remaining portion of the 1st/26th (roughly half) slipped out of Sokolnitz to the south before Laptev's Jäger sealed the southern exit to the town. Marching fast to put as much distance as possible between them and Sokolnitz, they were soon dismayed by the sudden appearance of a column in front of them marching north from the direction of Tellnitz. The men of the 26th Light immediately deployed and fired into the head of the approaching column, halting it and forcing it to fall back. After several rounds of fire, the outline of an Imperial eagle was seen through the mist, being waved on the end of its pole by Captain Livadot of the 108th Line. Immediately the order was given to cease fire and the two columns joined and made their escape to the northwest toward Turas.[*]

As the French fled, the still-thick fog aiding their escape as much as Margaron's cavalry, the Russians struggled to regroup. The same fog that had prevented the men of the 26th Light from recognizing their countrymen at short range now worked against their opponents. The converging attack on Sokolnitz, in the end coming from three sides, had resulted in the right of Strik's line penetrating the village south of the point where the right of Olsufiev's Vyborg Musketeers entered the village from the opposite direction. As a result the two commands became intermingled. The noise and confusion of the advance and the low visibility made separating and reassembling the battalions a challenge for their officers, resulting in a lull in the battle while the Russian officers sorted out their tangled units.[†]

By around 9:45 the fighting around Sokolnitz had died down to the sporadic firing of skirmishers in the pheasantry and west of the village. The French had

---

[*] Duffy, p. 110; Alombert and Colin, V, p. 165.

[†] Alombert and Colin, V, p. 164.

been scattered in several directions with the portion retiring to the west reforming northwest of the Sokolnitz brook while the portion of the 26th that had been ejected to the south retired toward Turas with the 108th Line. The fighting at Sokolnitz had lasted just over an hour and a half from the first arrival of Langeron's Advance Guard, but much of this time was spent by the Russians in waiting for the arrival of the 3rd Column. The actual assault on the French positions took perhaps forty-five minutes at most from the initial tentative attacks by the Russian Jäger to the final routing of the 26th Light.

The Russians had incurred significant losses, particularly east of the village toward the Goldbach. Despite this, the result was never in question and the ten Russian battalions easily evicted the two battalions of the 26th Light, taking 100 prisoners in the village. For their part, the French had performed well in an impossible position and had twice benefited from unplanned good fortune. First, the remarkably opportune timing of Merle's march had placed the 26th Light, destined for Tellnitz, in position to occupy Sokolnitz minutes before the Russian attack. Second, the timely arrival of Margaron from Tellnitz after covering the retreat of the 3rd Line effectively prevented any attempt at pursuit that the tangled Russian columns might have made.

While a bolder general might have stormed Sokolnitz and Sokolnitz Castle with overwhelming force in the initial assault, Prshibyshevsky and Langeron cannot be blamed too harshly for their caution in the face of an unseen enemy. Once the French positions were revealed in the initial attack by the Jäger of the two columns, the Russian generals had deployed sufficient forces to get the job done. Their subsequent actions, however, would expose both commanders to harsher criticism as the events on the Pratzen heights behind them made the successful seizure of Sokolnitz more of a liability than an asset.

The French Advance on the Pratzen Heights

As day broke on the morning of 2 December, the French forces poised for the seizure of the Pratzen Heights stood at the ready in the valley of the Goldbach.

> It was not yet eight o'clock [wrote Segur] and silence and darkness were still reigning over the rest of the line, when, beginning with the heights, the sun suddenly breaking through this thick fog disclosed to our sight the plateau of the Pratzen growing empty of troops from the flank march of the enemy columns. As for us who had remained in the ravine which defines the foot of this plateau, the smoke of the bivouacs and the vapours which, heavier on this point than elsewhere, still hung around, concealed from the eyes of the Russians our centre deployed in columns and ready for the attack.*

* Segur, pp. 248–9.

Napoleon had concentrated eight infantry divisions plus most of the army's cavalry in the five kilometers between Puntowitz and the Santon while a single division covered about six kilometers of the lower Goldbach. The instructions Napoleon had issued to his mist-enshrouded columns laid out a concerted plan of action. The four divisions of the 4th and 5th Corps under the command of Marshals Soult and Lannes would advance *en echelon* once the signal was given. St Hilaire's division, assembled near Puntowitz, was to begin the advance, moving forward in three lines. The two battalions of light infantry formed the first line and were followed by the remaining four regiments in columns of battalions, the 1st battalion of each regiment in the first line and the 2nd battalions in the third line. St Hilaire's right would be covered by the brigade of GdB Levasseur of Legrand's division, which would remain in position at Kobelnitz with five battalions (the 18th and 75th Line and the Tirailleurs du Corse). To St Hilaire's left, Vandamme's division would advance in parallel from Girzikowitz in an identical formation of three lines, two battalions of light infantry in front followed by the four remaining regiments in columns of battalions. Though beginning its march at the same time as St Hilaire's division, Vandamme's division would angle slightly more to the south, the first line drawing even with St Hilaire's second line at about the line of the Stare-Vinohrady and Pratze village.*

Once the French advance had begun and the two divisions of the 4th Corps had cleared the left bank of the Goldbach, the two divisions of Marshal Bernadotte's 1st Corps would cross the Goldbach at Girzikowitz and take

---

* The exact arrangement of regiments for the advance is subject to some disagreement. Some writers have concluded that Schiner with 4th Line and 24th Light advanced in parallel with Ferey (46th and 57th Line) with Candras and 28th Line in reserve. This accurately describes the deployment of the regiments after engaging the second allied line on the Pratzen plateau but contradicts several first-hand accounts. Soult's report clearly stated that he had recommended "two lines of battle and one of light infantry" to both divisions and that the advance of Vandamme's division was in three lines. In his comments on Colonel Frèche's memoirs, Beaucour indicated that the 24th Light stood alone in the first line and Major Bigarré of the 4th Line indicated that his regiment was on the extreme left with one battalion detached toward Blaziowitz. This is consistent with the arrangement described by Soult. In St Hilaire's division, GdB Morand with the two battalions of the 10th Light formed the first line, with GdB Thiébault's brigade (14th and 36th Line) behind on the right and GdB Varé's brigade (43rd and 55th) on the left. In Vandamme's division, GdB Schiner with the two battalions of the 24th Light formed the first line, with GdB Ferey's brigade (46th and 57th Line) behind on the right and the brigade of GdB Candras (4th and 28th Line) on the left. In both divisions about 300 meters separated each line, with the second line composed of the 1st battalions of the four line regiments and the third line composed of the 2nd battalions. Colin provides a detailed analysis of the orders issued by Napoleon and Soult for the formation the divisions of St Hilaire and Vandamme should use for their advance and I have adopted Colin's conclusions. Louis Frèche, *Mémoire de mes Campagnes (1803–1809)*, (Paris: Centre d'études Napoléoniennes, 1994), p. 50; Auguste Julien Bigarré, *Mémoires du Général Bigarré, 1775–1813*. Paris: Grenadier, 2002), p. 170; "Rapport sur la bataille d'Austerlitz, addressé par M. le maréchal Soult . . . au maréchal Berthier," in *Relations et Rapports*, p. 19; Alombert and Colin, V, pp. 174–6.

position east of that village ready to advance on receiving Napoleon's order.

To the left of Vandamme's division Marshal Lannes's 5th Corps stood ready with the divisions of GdD Caffarelli on the right and GdD Suchet on the left, straddling the main Brünn–Olmütz road. Two light cavalry divisions and two dragoon divisions from Marshal Murat's cavalry reserve supported Lannes's divisions. Lannes's two divisions, supported by the cavalry, would advance once Morand's light infantry, leading St Hilaire's division, had reached the Pratzeberg. Remaining behind the Goldbach were the Imperial Guard and Oudinot's grenadier division, along with the two cuirassier divisions, to form the reserve of the army.*

Shortly before dawn, as the French forces in the fog-shrouded valley of the Goldbach and the first three allied columns were rousing themselves, the titular commander-in-chief of the allied army, in the company of his staff, rode the short distance from Krenowitz to join the 4th Column which had bivouacked just west of that village. Kutuzov had shown his disdain for Weyrother's plan by napping during its presentation at the council of war the previous night. Now, a commander who was not allowed to command, he had been given the honor of leading the 4th Column in person. Opposed to the allied offensive in general, and to attacking on 2 December in particular, Kutuzov demonstrated an understandable pessimism and reluctance.

Of the four columns designated for the attack on the French right, the 4th Column was the weakest. Although composed of twenty-seven battalions, more than any of the other columns, in terms of total numbers it was comparable to the 2nd and 3rd Columns which had only seventeen and eighteen battalions respectively. Moreover, the quality of troops in the 4th Column was questionable. The Russian battalions in the column, forming the first division, commanded by GL Miloradovich, were composed of weary veterans who had endured the march to Braunau and back. These four regiments, severely depleted from combat losses at Dürrenstein, numbered only 5,000 in total according to Miloradovich's report.[†]

The second division of the 4th Column, commanded by FZM Kollowrath, consisted of fifteen Austrian battalions. A portion of these were frontline troops, specifically the five field battalions of the Salzburg IR and three field battalions that had been gathered in Vienna early in November from various

---

[*] "Relation de la bataille d'Austerlitz," in *Relations et Rapports*, 90–1; Alombert and Colin, V, pp. 185–6.

[†] Allied strengths are somewhat problematic as discussed in Appendix A, but the total can reasonably be estimated at 5,000–5,500 infantry. Stutterheim confirms Miloradovich's estimate, noting that the Russian battalions "were scarcely composed of 400 men each" (Stutterheim, p. 96). To this must be added several hundred men for the artillery battery, the dragoons and possibly also the hussars attached to Alexander's HQ. "1805 g. Dekabrya 3, Raport M. A. Miloradovicha M. I. Kutuzovu o Srazhenii pri Austerlitse," in *Kutuzov Sbornik Dokumentov*, p. 230.

garrisons where they had been stationed.* The remaining seven battalions were reserve (6th) battalions, composed of recruits and hastily mobilized in the crisis following the capitulation of Ulm. The reserve battalions present at Austerlitz represented the best of the 6th battalions available at Olmütz, which is to say the best of the worst. Ten other 6th battalions were so severely under strength and of sufficiently poor quality that they were left with the Olmütz garrison. Estimates of the total strength of the Austrian battalions vary as well, but they could not have reached much more than 7,000 men in all.[†] By contrast, the troops they were about to engage were among the finest the French had to offer. The divisions of St Hilaire and Vandamme had been under the command of Soult at the camp of Boulogne and had received exemplary training. The officers were seasoned veterans of many campaigns and the unbroken string of successes the army had enjoyed since crossing the Rhine ten weeks earlier had buoyed the morale of the men.

The 4th Column marched in two divisions, each formed in two lines. Unlike the 2nd and 3rd Columns, the 4th Column had some cavalry support, but this amounted to only two squadrons of Erzherzog Johann Dragoons under the command of GM Wodniansky.[‡] This cavalry formed a part of the Advance Guard of the 4th Column along with two battalions of the Novgorod Musketeers and the Grenadier Battalion of the Apsheron Musketeers, drawn from Miloradovich's division and commanded by the Russian Lt-Col Monakhtin.[§] The remainder of the column followed, each division formed in

---

* These battalions were replaced in their garrisons by the reserve battalions of their regiments.

[†] Schönhals, using the strengths recorded in the official returns in the Kriegsarchiv, itemizes battalion strengths to produce a total strength of 9,150. This figure is the most widely repeated. However, in the example of the 6th Battalion, Kerpen IR 49, the battalion strength at Austerlitz given by Schönhals is 700. Major Mahler, who commanded the battalion, confirmed a strength of about 700 at Vienna but reported considerable desertion and an epidemic at Olmütz that had left him with 312 men by the time his battalion reached Austerlitz. With 9,150 men in these battalions at Vienna, we can deduct nearly 1,000 prisoners the French reported taking from these regiments between Vienna and Wischau and estimate at least 1,000 additional deserters and victims of the epidemic at Olmütz if we consider the situation of IR 49 as typical. Schönhals, p. 177; Major Mahler, "Tagebücher ans dem Jahre 1805," *Mittheilungen des K. und K. Kriegs-Archivs. 6 (1881)*, pp. 516–23; Alombert and Colin, III, pp. 860–1.

[‡] These squadrons were the 2nd Squadron of the Lieutenant-Colonel's Division and the 2nd Squadron of the 2nd Major's Division. Gustav Amon von Treuenfest, *Geschichte des K. und K. Bukowina'schen Dragoner-Regimentes General der Cavallerie Freiherr Piret de Bihain Nr. 9 von seiner Errichtung 1682 bis 1892*. Vienna: 1893), p. 232.

[§] Sources vary on the composition of Monakhtin's force. A detachment of three squadrons (two of Hessen-Homburg Hussars and one of Székler Hussars) seems to have joined the 4th Column after the fighting had begun, but there are no details available on where (or if) it was engaged. Forty Elisabetgrad Hussars also appear in accounts describing the action of the 4th Column, but these seem to have been attached to either Alexander's or Kutuzov's headquarters. "1805 g. Dekabrya 3, Raport M. A. Miloradovicha M. I. Kutuzovu o Srazhenii pri Austerlitse," in *Kutuzov Sbornik Dokumentov*, p. 230; Mikhailovski-Danilevski, p. 245.

standard marching order, with the battalions in two parallel lines of march, the artillery and baggage marching between the lines.

Kollowrath had received his written orders at 5:00 that morning, obviously getting a copy of the original German dispositions, but Miloradovich most likely did not receive his orders until around 6:00 A.M., like the other Russian commanders. The 4th Column's orders were to break camp at 7:00 and to be prepared to begin its march on the French right after the first three columns had defeated the French posts on the lower Goldbach—roughly an hour later according to the plan. This would bring the 4th Column to Kobelnitz at the same time as the first three columns would be driving northward against the French rear to the west of the Goldbach. As the Austrian battalions formed into column, Major Mahler of the Kerpen IR 49 noted that:

> . . . the fog was so dense that one could hardly see fifty paces; a lively fire could be heard, but one could not differentiate which part of our allied army was attacking or had been attacked by the enemy.[*]

The end of Prshibyshevsky's 3rd Column was filing through Pratze when Emperor Alexander and his entourage arrived at the camp of the 4th Column near Krenowitz, around 8:00.[†] The conversation which followed has been described by one historian as "one of the most famous exchanges in military history."[‡] Prince Volkonsky, who was at Kutuzov's side and witnessed the exchange, later related it as follows. According to Volkonsky, Alexander approached Kutuzov and exclaimed "General, why don't you advance?" "I wait," answered Kutuzov, "for all the troops of the column to assemble." The emperor retorted, "We are not on a parade ground, where one awaits the arrival of all the troops to begin the parade." "Lord," answered the old warrior, "it is precisely because we are not on a parade ground that I do not begin . . . but if that is your order!"[§]

While Alexander was confronting Kutuzov, Prince Czartoryski was busy observing the scene around him:

> When we had arrived at this point, I looked round in every direction and saw a vast plain. A column of Austrian infantry, which seemed to me

---

[*] Mahler, p. 519.

[†] Mikhailovsky-Danilevsky states that Alexander and his entourage arrived at Kutuzov's headquarters at 9:00 A.M., but this would be at about the same time that St Hilaire's men were reaching the vicinity of Pratze, at which point the head of the 4th Column was already at least a half-hour's march from their bivouacs. Czartoryski states that the emperor left shortly after 7:00 to join Kutuzov. Mikhailovski-Danilevski, p. 244; Czartoryski, II, p. 106.

[‡] Duffy, *Austerlitz*, p. 103.

[§] Mikhailovski-Danilevski, p. 244–5; Duffy, *Austerlitz*, p. 103. I have used Duffy's translation of the exchange, which is true to the original Russian version. The French translation of Mikhailovsky-Danilevsky by Narishkine differs slightly.

rather loose in formation came to arrange itself in order of battle. Anxiety was impressed on the faces of the Austrian General, the officers, and even the soldiers. The artillery officers alone did not give way to the general depression, and expressed absolute confidence in the effect of their guns.[*]

Kutuzov issued the necessary orders and, by around 8:30 A.M., Miloradovich and Kollowrath had begun their march toward Pratze.[†] Miloradovich's Russians led the column, following the road from Krenowitz and passing just east of the heights of the Stare Vinohrady. Wodniansky led the column with his two squadrons of dragoons, followed by Lt-Col Monakhtin and his three battalions and two pieces of artillery detached from the brigade of GM Repninsky.[‡] Behind them in line was the remainder of the brigade of GM Repninsky, consisting of the remaining three battalions of the Novgorod and Apsheron Musketeers, followed by the brigade of GM Berg, composed of the six battalions of the Little Russia (Malorossiisky) Grenadiers and Smolensk Musketeers.

While Czartoryski had perceived gloom among the Austrian troops, the Russian troops were in good spirits according to one account, and their commander called out to them as they marched to bolster their fighting spirit:

> [Miloradovich] harangued the soldiers with his accustomed cheerfulness, and when those of the regiment of Apsheron passed in front of the Emperor Alexander, he reminded them of [the 1799 campaign in] Italy. He said to the soldiers "It is not necessary to teach you how to take villages."[§]

Miloradovich's confidence was based on the assumption that the French were on the defensive and that the Russians would be striking them at Kobelnitz. Because of this certainty, the column proceeded along the road with no effort being made to try to penetrate the fog hanging in the valley of the Goldbach that masked the French positions. Moreover, there appears to have been no attempt even to place pickets at the crest of the ridge, the Russian column advancing in perfect confidence and in complete ignorance of what might be developing over the slight rise to its right.

---

[*] Czartoryski, II, p. 107.

[†] Miloradovich notes the time as 8:00 in his report, but this seems too early given the timing of the march of the 3rd Column, which had cleared Pratze before the 4th Column set out, and the 4th Column's subsequent convergence with the French. Kollowrath gives the time as 7:30 in his report, which seems more likely to be the time at which his troops were ready to march, not the time they set out. *Kutuzov Sbornik Dokumentov*, p. 230; Alombert and Colin, V, pp. 176–7.

[‡] Two pieces of artillery are mentioned, but it seems that there should have been six battalion guns accompanying Monakhtin's three battalions. Schönhals, p. 161; Mikhailovski-Danilevski, p. 245.

[§] Mikhailovski-Danilevski, p. 245.

While Alexander was persuading Kutuzov to set the 4th Column in motion, the French forces in the valley of the Goldbach were waiting impatiently in the fog for their signal to advance. The entire French line from Kobelnitz in the south to the Santon in the north, placed in a state of readiness at 7:00, was under strict orders to maintain complete silence. Napoleon, his headquarters on the Zuran hill, would personally give the orders to advance once the expected allied movement to the right had developed sufficiently. After waiting for nearly an hour, the movement of the first three allied columns into the valley of the Goldbach had proceeded as Napoleon had hoped. By about 7:45 the tail of Prshibyshevsky's 3rd Column could be seen passing Pratze and beginning its descent of the slope toward Sokolnitz.

Once Prshibyshevsky's men were well clear of Pratze, Napoleon continued to wait. As the Russian column marched further down the slope toward Sokolnitz, the last ravine disrupting its march having been overcome by the Russian pioneers, Napoleon maintained a close watch on the heights. Seeing no further sign of Russian movement, Napoleon finally gave the order to advance. According to Segur, Soult was anxious to set his troops in motion:

> ... but Napoleon, calmer than he [Soult], still held him back that the enemy might rush upon his own ruin; and pointing to the Pratzen asked "How much time do you require to crown that summit?" "Ten minutes," answered the marshal. "Then go," resumed the Emperor, "but you can wait another quarter of an hour, and it will be time enough then."[*]

With the Russian columns in the valley of the Goldbach to the south, the divisions of St Hilaire and Vandamme would drive a wedge between the allied right and left and then descend on their rear. "The moment having arrived," wrote Segur, "the divisions of Vandamme and Saint Hilaire springing out of the mist which enveloped them, suddenly appeared on the scene. It was then eight o'clock."[†] Kutuzov's reluctance to begin the advance of the 4th Column, however, ensured that events would not go exactly as Napoleon had planned.

Monakhtin's Advance Guard had passed east of Pratze, through the camp that the 3rd Column had occupied the night before, by around 8:30. Wodniansky and the Austrian staff officer assigned to the 4th Column, Captain Ringesheim, rode at the head of the column with the two squadrons of the Johann Dragoons and a small party of Cossacks. As they emerged from behind the village, they were astonished to see a large French column ascending the heights from the west, marching rapidly toward the Pratzeberg.

---

[*] Segur, p. 249. In fact, it seems to have taken a little more than thirty minutes to reach the summit of the heights.

[†] Ibid.

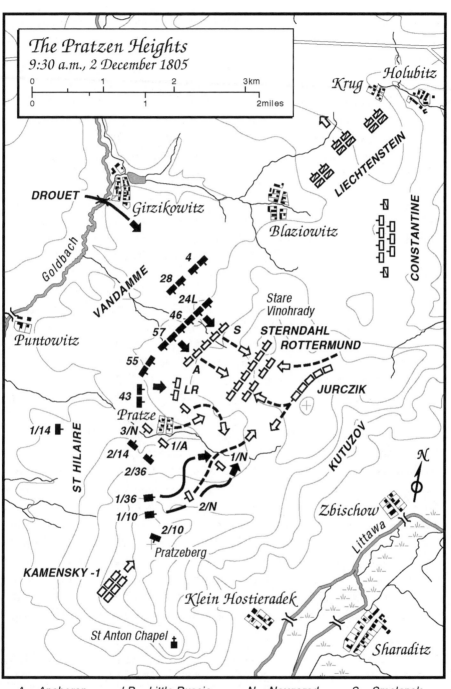

The Pratzen Heights
9:30 a.m., 2 December 1805

0   1   2   3km

0   1   2miles

Krug   Holubitz

LIECHTENSTEIN

CONSTANTINE

DROUET   Girzikowitz

Blaziowitz

Goldbach

VANDAMME

Puntowitz

4

28

24L   Stare Vinohrady

46   S   STERNDAHL ROTTERMUND

57

55   A

43   LR   JURCZIK

Pratze

3/N   1/A   KUTUZOV

1/14   1/N

ST HILAIRE   2/14

2/36

1/36   2/N

1/10   Zbischow

2/10   Littawa

Pratzeberg   N

KAMENSKY -1

Klein Hostieradek

St Anton Chapel   Sharaditz

A = Apsheron   LR = Little Russia   N = Novgorod   S = Smolensk

The two officers immediately rode back to alert Monakhtin and Miloradovich. As the French columns were sighted emerging from the fog, initially the Russians mistook them for friendly troops:

> Because the fog was heavy, the Russians believed that their Jäger or other troops wanted to retire on them, and dared not fire at all, but remained standing in best order . . . Only when the enemy, formed in masses, approached to approximately twenty paces did they notice the fact that they were mistaken and threw themselves against them in a desperate manner and with exceptional bravery.[*]

At this point, the head of the French column (10th Light) and Monakhtin's Advance Guard were about equidistant from the Pratzeberg. Recognizing the importance of the heights, Monakhtin immediately ordered his two battalions of Novgorod Musketeers to advance on the heights at the double in an attempt to reach the crest before the French. The two Russian battalions crossed a small brook that runs past Pratze and the leading battalion raced the 10th Light to the heights. The other Novgorod battalion deployed in the ravine the brook had carved in the side of the hill, the men concealing themselves behind the bank. Wodniansky's Austrian dragoons already stood beyond the stream in support, occupying a low rise near the village church, but the Apsheron Grenadiers appear to have remained in or behind Pratze.[†]

As the Russian battalion emerged from behind the village and headed for the Pratzeberg, the 10th Light continued at their steady pace and won the race. The leading battalion of the 10th Light occupied the Pratzeberg, while the other battalion faced to the north to meet the advancing battalion of Novgorod Musketeers. A short distance behind Morand's light infantry, St Hilaire's second line, accompanied by St Hilaire, was approaching Pratze village. Thinking Pratze abandoned (the general assumption by the French being that the allies had already abandoned the heights), St Hilaire directed GdB Varé with the four battalions forming the right of the second and third lines to march to the left of the village and GdB Thiébault to occupy the village itself. St Hilaire then rode up the hill to join Morand and the 10th Light.

Thiébault detached one of his four battalions, the 1st/14th Line under the command of Colonel Mazas, to occupy Pratze. As Mazas neared the village,

---

[*] Mahler, p. 519.

[†] Some accounts attribute this action to Miloradovich himself, but he was not with the Advance Guard and there was insufficient time between the sighting of the French and the rush to the Pratzeberg to have allowed even a fast rider to reach Miloradovich and return with orders. The actions of the Advance Guard were plainly performed on Monakhtin's own initiative. Miloradovich's first orders, according to his own report, were to send reinforcements to Monakhtin who was already engaged. *Kutuzov Sbornik Dokumentov*, pp. 230–1; Treuenfest, *Geschichte des K. und K. Bukowina'schen Dragoner-Regimentes*, p. 232.

however, his battalion was surprised by the sudden appearance of a full battalion of Novgorod Musketeers rising from the ravine in front of the village and opening fire on them. Taken completely off guard, the 1st/14th Line broke and fled in the direction of Puntowitz with Mazas riding after them, leaving a disgusted Thiébault to react to the unexpected appearance of the Russians in Pratze. "How an officer with his [Mazas's] experience of war could have fallen into such an ambush for want of sending forward some scouts to reconnoiter the ravine and find out the Russians, I do not know," Thiébault later marveled.[*]

Now faced with two Russian battalions and with the 1st/14th in flight, Thiébault immediately called in the remaining three battalions of his brigade, deployed them in front of Pratze, and placed himself at their head:

> But there was no time to waste on reprimands [Thiébault continued] so I rode forward calling to Mazas to rally his battalion. Then, having dismounted and ordered the 36th [Line] to march on the village and force their way in, I set off, crying "Long live the Emperor!" and charging at the head of the 2nd Battalion of the 14th, which deployed as it ran, I flung myself into the ravine where my horse could not have got down, attacked the Russians with the bayonet, and routed them, avenging on them the losses of the 1st Battalion.[†]

Thiébault's account, though reasonably accurate, oversimplifies the action with Monakhtin's advance guard and assigns Thiébault the majority of the credit for a broader effort. With Thiébault at the head of the 2nd/36th and 2nd/14th opposing the 3rd Battalion of Novgorod Musketeers in front of Pratze, St Hilaire addressed the other Novgorod battalion advancing on Morand's battalions. St Hilaire drew the nearest of Thiébault's battalions, the 1st/36th, closer to the 1st/10th Light, positioning it between the Pratzeberg and Pratze village to oppose the Russian battalion advancing on the heights. He then directed Varé's brigade, still several hundred meters from Pratze, to swing to the north of the village and operate in cooperation with Vandamme, thereby threatening the Russians in the village with envelopment.

While St Hilaire was deploying his forces to face the enemy to the north, the Russians were also reacting to the unexpected appearance of the French. The 1st (Grenadier) Battalion of Apsheron Musketeers quickly moved into position from behind Pratze to support the battalion of Novgorod Musketeers in front of the village. On hearing of the French force in front of him, Miloradovich had immediately relayed the news to Kutuzov. He then ordered GM Repninsky to advance with the remainder of his brigade. Repninsky

---

[*] Thiébault, II, p. 160.
[†] Ibid.

accompanied the 1st (Grenadier) Battalion of the Novgorod Musketeers, directing it toward the Pratzeberg where Monakhtin's other battalion was engaging Morand's two battalions.

The remaining two musketeer battalions of Apsheron Musketeers seem to have started toward Pratze but were almost immediately recalled. Within minutes of Repninsky being ordered forward with his brigade, French troops were also sighted emerging from the fog and ascending the heights from west. Now attacked from two sides, Kutuzov urged Kollowrath, still some distance to the rear, to hurry his division forward.

When the 24th Light at the head of Vandamme's division was first sighted it was less than a kilometer away from Miloradovich's column and closing fast. As the alert was sounded, orders were passed down the Russian line to face right, and it appears that the Russian column advanced to a position just over the crest of the heights to meet the French attack. The 2nd and 3rd Battalions of Apsheron Musketeers, which had just been ordered to the Pratzeberg, were recalled and moved into line with the three battalions of Smolensk Musketeers in the first line to meet the French attack while the three battalions of the Little Russia Grenadiers formed the second line. No sooner had this been executed than GdB Schiner reached the crest of the heights with his two battalions of the 24th Light and deployed to engage the Russians. Behind him, Vandamme directed GdB Ferey with his four battalions to move into position on Shiner's right to engage the entire length of the Russian line. Four battalions of Candras's brigade (the 28th Line and 4th Line) remained in reserve. On Vandamme's right, Varé's brigade had advanced around Pratze and was also drawing into line to engage the flank of Miloradovich's line.

With the additional French battalions emerging from the mist to the west, Kutuzov redirected the ten battalions at the head of the Austrian column to the Stare Vinohrady while the remainder proceeded on to the Pratzeberg.* Prince Adam Czartoryski, accompanying the Emperor Alexander's entourage, watched the events unfolding before him from Alexander's headquarters, which had been established on the summit of the Stare Vinohrady:

> Suddenly we perceived some French columns advancing rapidly and pushing back the corps opposed to them. When I saw the promptitude of

---

* Most secondary accounts overlook the formation of three Austrian lines of battle, which is described by Major Mahler of IR 49. Salzburg IR 23, at the head of the first line of march, formed the first line of battle and moved into position behind Miloradovich. The two battalions at the head of the second line of march joined the remaining two battalions of the first line of march to form the second line of battle. Finally, the remaining five battalions formed the third line of battle sent to reinforce Repninsky and Wodniansky by Pratze. Mahler, p. 520; *Kutuzov Sbornik Dokumentov*, p. 230; Thiébault, II, p. 160.

the French troops, it seemed to me to augur ill for the result of the day; the Emperor was also struck by the rapidity of this movement, which caused a real panic in the Austrian ranks.*

Given the high proportion of raw recruits in the Austrian battalions, the reaction of these troops assembled close to the Emperor's headquarters on the Stare Vinohrady can be readily understood.

Within about fifteen minutes of the first sighting of the French forces ascending the Pratzen plateau, twelve battalions of St Hilaire and Vandamme had engaged Miloradovich's twelve battalions. Varé, with four additional battalions, was advancing against the left flank of the main Russian line and the rear of Pratze. Behind the thin Russian line, stretched from the Pratzeberg to a point just west of the Stare Vinohrady, the Austrian battalions moved into position. Kollowrath shook out his two lines of march into three lines of battle, ten battalions marching toward the Stare Vinohrady to form behind Miloradovich while the remaining five battalions veered to the left toward the Pratzeberg. Excluding the battalion of the 10th Light occupying the Pratzeberg, the routed battalion of the 14th Line and Candras with four battalions of the 4th and 28th Line in reserve, the French had over 12,000 men opposed to 5,000 Russian infantry and Austrian cavalry with about 7,000 Austrian infantry rushing forward to help even the numbers.

Before the Austrian brigades could get into position, however, the French forces had deployed and initiated a firefight in which their superior training gave them an enormous advantage. Nowhere was this more telling than between the Pratzeberg and Pratze village. The 3rd Battalion, Novgorod Musketeers, in front of Pratze village was soon engaged in an unequal battle against two French battalions at once. Thiébault had deployed the 2nd/14th and the 2nd/36th. Monakhtin quickly committed the Grenadier Battalion of Apsheron Musketeers to reinforce it, and Captain Morozov led this battalion in a charge that drove the French back, capturing two guns in the process. To their left, however, the other Novgorod musketeer battalion, caught alone and in the open, was quickly overwhelmed before Repninsky could arrive to reinforce it with the grenadiers of the Novgorod Regiment

> Now the hand-to-hand fighting became general, which, with the determination of the Russians, forced back the first enemy troops . . . Finally the French infantry advanced in checkerboard formation and attacked impetuously, having noticed the retreat of their first line . . . The Russians, still without direction from their superiors, nevertheless remained perfectly formed and made an offensive thrust. The French

* Czartoryski, II, p. 107.

masses hardly noticed but opened their ranks so that cannon hidden in their midst, which had been pulled into position by their crews, could fire a salvo of canister. This collapsed the Russian column completely.[*]

As Repninsky drew past Pratze village with his battalion of grenadiers, the murderous fire of St Hilaire's men took its toll. The battalion of Novgorod Musketeers nearest the Pratzeberg broke and fled while Thiébault led his men forward in a charge that retook the captured guns and routed the Russian battalions near Pratze. The three routed Russian battalions streamed past Repninsky, who tried in vain to rally them. In a matter of moments the pursuing French had enveloped his battalion of grenadiers as well.

Wodniansky's dragoons, who might possibly have been able to stem the tide of Thiébault's advance, had seen the movement of Varé's brigade around the opposite side of Pratze village and had instead maneuvered to counter this threat. Colonel Ledru des Essarts of the 55th Line described what followed:

> I was going to enter Pratzen [*sic*] and destroy this column [Monakhtin's] completely when the cuirassiers of the Russian Imperial Guard [*sic*] arrived at a gallop to save it by charging me. I formed nimbly in a mass and since my tirailleurs were ready to kill many of them at 50 paces, they did not dare to attack me.[†]

Wodniansky thus held back from attacking Ledru's regiment but the presence of his cavalry did delay Ledru's encirclement of the Russian forces in and around Pratze.

The collapse of Monakhtin's Advance Guard on the left flank of the Russian line and the arrival of Varé's four battalions on Ferey's right made Miloradovich's position critical. GM Berg led the three battalions of Little Russia Grenadiers in an attempt to avert disaster. For about ten minutes Repninsky's battalion, surrounded by the French, also continued to resist, suffering appalling casualties. Repninsky himself fell wounded, struck by three musket balls. Berg led his grenadiers in a wild charge, hoping to break through the French to retrieve Repninsky's isolated battalion, but in vain. Berg fell wounded and the charge of the Little Russia was broken by the effective musketry of St Hilaire's men.[†]

---

[*] Mahler, p. 519.

[†] Ledru des Essarts (ed. Jean-Louis Bonnery), *François-Roch, Ledru des Essarts, un Grand Patriote Sarthois Méconnu, la Vie de ce Soldat Courageaux qui n'aimait que la paix.* (Le Mans: J. L. Bonnery, 1988); p. 42. Ledru mistook Wodniansky's Austrian dragoons for Russian Life Guard cuirassiers. In 1805, Russian cuirassiers wore no breastplates and the Cavalier Guard wore white uniforms and helmets, just like the Austrian dragoons.

[†] Miloradovich's report is brief and difficult to follow, but the main features of the action including the charges of Morozov and Berg, Repninsky's stand, and the final destruction of 1st/Novgorod can be traced. *Kutuzov Sbornik Dokumentov*, pp. 230–2.

The details of Berg's actions are impossible to unravel from the reports, but it appears that his forces formed a single line and moved into position to stem the French advance. The battalion on the far left had attempted to rescue Repninsky, only to be beaten back with heavy losses. The other two battalions faced Thiébault's forces emerging from Pratze. As Varé's brigade drew into line the situation became hopeless for the Russians. The three battalions of Little Russia Grenadiers, having taken heavy losses to French fire from St Hilaire's four battalions and now attacked in the flank by Varé's brigade, were forced to retreat. With their left crumbling, the remainder of the Russian line had no choice but to fall back as well. The French pushed forward in their wake, capturing the wounded generals Berg and Repninsky, along with most of the Grenadier Battalion of the Novgorod Musketeers. They then paused to consolidate their position, the right securely in possession of the summit of the Pratzeberg, the center occupying Pratze and the left now facing the Austrians who had formed a line anchored on the Stare Vinohrady.[*]

The initial action on the Pratzen Heights had been short and sharp. Just over an hour had elapsed since the two advancing columns had first sighted each other with only 30–45 minutes of actual fighting. In this short time the outnumbered and outmaneuvered Russian force had simply been overwhelmed. Initially, St Hilaire's four battalions routed the three battalions of the Russian advance guard (approximately 3,300 men versus 1,500) while the six battalions of Schiner and Ferey engaged the five battalions in the Russian first line (about 4,600 versus 2,500). St Hilaire, joined by Varé with four fresh battalions, then drove in the flank of the Russian position, forcing the deployment of the Russian second line, the 1,500 Little Russia Grenadiers, to counter them. When the Little Russia Grenadiers were overwhelmed, the entire Russian line was sent staggering to the rear just as Kollowrath's Austrians assumed position behind them.

In less than an hour, the allied army had been shocked from its complacency and was in danger of being driven from the heights and split in two by the aggressive French maneuver. Kutuzov, having been hit by a spent musket ball during the action, was urged by Alexander to move to the rear to have his wound tended. "There," Kutuzov declared in frustration, gesturing toward the Austrian battalions advancing toward the waiting French, "there is where we are hurting."[†] As the two Austrian brigades moved into position to contest the French position on the heights, Kutuzov sent urgent requests for reinforcements from Liechtenstein and Constantine to the north.

Although Kutuzov was not yet aware of it, reinforcements were already

---

[*] Alombert and Colin, V, p. 183.

[†] Mikhailovski-Danilevski, p. 247.

arriving. To the south, GM Kamensky-1 had heard the fighting starting up near Pratze. Having been delayed in his march by the passage of elements of the 5th Column through the midst of the 2nd Column, his brigade was still descending the heights and had not yet reached Augezd. Kamensky immediately notified Langeron of the fighting on the heights and countermarched toward the Pratzeberg with his two regiments. To the north, however, no reinforcements would be forthcoming. Liechtenstein's cavalry was already moving northward to engage about 17,000 French infantry and cavalry of Lannes and Murat advancing up the main Brünn–Olmütz road. Constantine, watching the gap between the 4th and 5th Columns widening, was painfully aware that his 10,600 men now stood as the last reserves of the allied army.

Napoleon receives the capitulation of Ulm. From the painting by Charles Thevenin. *RMN*

Marshals Murat and Lannes seize the Tabor Bridge, 14 November 1805.
From the painting by Guillaume Guillon Lethière. *RMN*

Napoleon visits the bivouacs of the army and the soldiers form a torchlight procession on the eve of Austerlitz, 1 December 1805. From the painting by Louis Albert Guillaumin Bacler d'Albe. *RMN*

GdD Savary. One of Napoleon's aides in
1805, Savary was entrusted with a variety
of missions, including the diplomatic
mission to Tsar Alexander in the days
prior to Austerlitz. Savary was also sent
to determine first-hand the situation at
Tellnitz on the night of 1 December.
His reports were very influential in
Napoleon's planning. *T&JB*

GM Dolgoruky. One of the more
controversial figures at Austerlitz,
Dolgoruky was an intimate of the Tsar who
became famous for his reported arrogance in
his interview with Napoleon. Bagration
praised his performance in his reports, but
Langeron viewed him as largely without
military talent, earning praise only because
of his political connections.
Alexander Mikaberidze

Napoleon gives the order to advance. From the painting by Antoine Charles Horace Vernet. *RMf*

GdD Friant. Friant's division conducted an epic forced march from Vienna, arriving in time to stem the allied advance from Sokolnitz. Although outnumbered, Friant launched his men in skillful attacks to keep the Russians on the defensive. *James Arnold*

GdB Morand. Morand's brigade participate in the rout of the Novgorod Musketeers an held the Pratzeberg against repeated attack by Kamensky-1. His performance at Austerlitz would earn him promotion to général de division. *James Arnold*

The Pratzeberg viewed from the south. Pratze village lies beyond the horizon in the center of the photo. Langeron's 2nd Column advanced across the open ground in the foreground *en route* to Sokolnitz. St Hilaire's division ascended the heights from the west (left of the picture). *Robert Ouvrard*

The stone wall surrounding the pheasantry and the woods formed a strong defensive position, first for the French Tirailleurs du Po and later for Russian Jäger and scattered elements of the Allied 3rd Column. *Robert Ouvrard*

The Pratze church. Both sides used the tower to observe enemy movements at different points during the battle. The original tower collapsed due to damage from artillery fire and was rebuilt in 1810. *Robert Ouvrard*

A panoramic view of the battle with the Santon and Bosenitz clearly visible in the foreground smoke rising from buildings at Blaziowitz and the action on the heights and near Sokolnitz marked by clouds of powder smoke. From the painting by Siméon Jean Antoine Fort. *RMN*

Right, top: GdD St Hilaire. His skillful deployment of forces on the southern end of the Pratzen Heights enabled him to beat off several attacks by Kamensky-1's Russians and Jurczik's Austrians until the French success to the north forced them to withdraw. *T&JB*

Right, middle: GdB Thiébault. Although he had a reputation for being difficult and spiteful, Thiébault performed well at Austerlitz. His brigade took Pratze from Monakhtin's Advance Guard and opposed the Austrians of General Jurczik for the better part of the morning. In the afternoon Thiébault led his brigade against the rear of the Russians at Sokolnitz where he was seriously wounded. *T&JB*

Right, bottom: GdD Vandamme. He led the assault on the Stare Vinohrady, engaging the larger part of the allied 4th Column and finally driving it from the heights. In the afternoon, Vandamme led the attack that took Augezd and cut off the main allied route of retreat. *T&JB*

GdB Merle. Merle was sent to reinforce Tellnitz against the allied attacks there on the morning of Austerlitz, but arrived at Sokolnitz just as the attack on that village was beginning. Merle deployed his forces at Sokolnitz on his own initiative and beat back the initial allied Jäger attacks before being driven from the position by the more numerous allied forces. His brigade fought alongside Friant's division through the afternoon. Merle was promoted to général de division for his performance at Austerlitz. *T&JB*

FML Kienmayer. Kienmayer enjoyed a reputation as a tough fighter, and his aggressive though unimaginative assaults on Tellnitz during the morning of 2 December support this reputation. A capable subordinate, Kienmayer demonstrated little initiative at Austerlitz. *Robert Ouvrard*

GM Olsufiev-1. Olsufiev's lack of experience was demonstrated many times over at Austerlitz. He led the attack on Sokolnitz, but then allowed the French to catch his forces off guard, enabling Friant's outnumbered command to get the better of them. *Alexander Mikaberidze*

The low rise of the Stare Vinohrady seen from the center of the heights (i.e. from the "allied" side). Some of the fiercest fighting on the heights occurred around this key position, held by the Austrians of Salzburg IR 23 for about an hour. *Robert Ouvrard*

GM Repninsky. Repninsky was sent to the aid of Monakhtin's outnumbered Advance Guard with the Grenadiers of the Novgorod Musketeer Regiment, only to find himself surrounded by the advancing French. His personal courage, despite the odds against him, resulted in five wounds to the leg, torso and head.
Alexander Mikaberidze

GM Kamensky-1. Demonstrating excellent initiative, Kamensky-1 returned to the heights with his brigade as soon as the news of the French attack reached him. His six battalions challenged the French possession of the Pratzeberg for two hours. His forces were among the last parts of the allied army to withdraw from the heights.
Alexander Mikaberidze

The view from the top of the Santon, looking east. In the days before the battle all the trees on the Santon were cleared and the entire eastern face excavated for gun emplacements. In 1805 the plain was much as it is today—ideal ground for cavalry. *Robert Ouvrard*

PK Gogel. Gogel had the unenviable task of leading the diversionary attack on Bosenitz and the Santon. While the attack and subsequent retreat were managed well, his Jäger were subsequently routed by French cavalry, compromising Bagration's defensive position. *Alexander Mikaberidze*

GM Uvarov. Vain, boastful and lacking in experience, Uvarov took over command of the Russian cavalry of the 5th Column after the mortal wounding of Essen-2. His series of charges was instrumental in stalling the French advance on the Brünn–Olmütz road for several hours. *Alexander Mikaberidze*

The death of General Valhubert in action against Bagration's forces on the Brünn–Olmütz road. From the painting by Jean-François Pierre Peyron. *RMN*

GdD Kellermann. Kellermann's hussars made several fierce charges and counter-charges against the Constantine Uhlans and Uvarov's cavalry, effectively neutralizing them. Kellermann was seriously wounded and his division did not play a major role in the afternoon's fighting. *T&JB*

GdD d'Hautpoul. In the afternoon of the battle, d'Hautpoul, the model of the French cuirassier, was instrumental in driving back the Russian cavalry near Siwitz and in outflanking Bagration's position in support of the attack of Suchet's division. *T&JB*

GdD Nansouty. Nansouty's skillful handling of his heavy cavalry division beat off several charges by Uvarov's cavalry and then drove them back across the Rausnitz brook. His cuirassiers also provided support for Caffarelli's attacks on Holubitz village. *T&JB*

GdD Caffarelli. One of Napoleon's aides at the beginning of the campaign, Caffarelli took command of Bisson's division of 3rd Corps at Austerlitz because Bisson was wounded. He led the attack on Holubitz that took the village and forced Bagration to retreat. *T&JB*

FML Prince Johann Liechtenstein. Liechtenstein commanded the 5th Column containing the majority of the allied cavalry His quick thinking prevented the allied forces from being divided in the north before Bagration's forces could close the gap His subsequent handling of the Austrian component of his column succeeded in slowing Bernadotte's advance and preventing the allied forces on the heights from being immediately outflanked. *Alexander Mikaberidze*

Napoleon observing several Russian columns escaping across the ice of the Satchan Pond from his position at the Chapel of St Anton. A broken causeway is visible to the left of the chapel and Augezd at the foot of the heights. From the painting by Siméon Jean Antoine Fort. *RMN*

dD Suchet. Famous as a future marshal, uchet commanded a division in Lannes's th Corps at Austerlitz. His division ngaged the Russians of Bagration's dvance Guard and launched a series of loody attacks that eventually drove back agration's forces. Suchet's success nearly urned into a rout of Bagration's forces but as stopped short by the arrival of ierenberger's battery. *T&JB*

General Rapp presenting his prisoners to the Emperor Napoleon. From the painting by François Pascal Simon Gérard. *RMN*

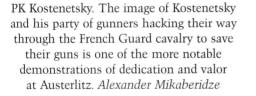

PK Kostenetsky. The image of Kostenetsky and his party of gunners hacking their way through the French Guard cavalry to save their guns is one of the more notable demonstrations of dedication and valor at Austerlitz. *Alexander Mikaberidze*

PK St Priest. A French émigré in the Russian service, St Priest commanded the Life Guard Jäger battalion. His skillful defense of Blaziowitz forced the deployment of no fewer than four French battalions to dislodge him. *Alexander Mikaberidze*

The Austerlitz Peace Monument, dedicated to the fallen soldiers of all nations, is located on the Pratzeberg. *Robert Ouvrard*

The crypt in the chapel within the Peace Monument holds the remains of French, Russian and Austrian dead. *Robert Ouvrard*

The interview between the Emperors Napoleon and Francis at Sarutitz on the morning of 4 December. From the painting by Pierre Paul Prud'hon. *RMN*

TIDDY-DOLL the great French Gingerbread-Baker, drawing out a new Batch of Kings. — his Man Hopping Talley, mixing up the Dough

January 1806 British caricature. Napoleon is portrayed in this caricature by James Gillray as "Tiddy-Doll, the Great French Gingerbread-Baker, Drawing out a new Batch of Kings" (identified as Bavaria, Württemberg and Baden) while his man "Hopping Talley" (Talleyrand) mixes up a new batch of dough (labeled Turkey and Poland). Naples and Holland would in fact be the next "batches of gingerbread." *RMN*

Chapter 5

The Outcome is Decided:
2 December, 10:00 A.M. – 12:30 P.M.

Napoleon had observed the initial action on the Pratzen Heights from his command post on the Zuran Hill. Although the mists still lingered in the low, damp areas, from his hilltop position the French emperor had a clear view of Vandamme's defeat of Miloradovich's Russians in front of the Stare Vinohrady and St Hilaire's successful seizure of the crest of the plateau in the south. Reports from the lower Goldbach indicated that the allied forces were heavily engaged along the Goldbach from Tellnitz to Sokolnitz. On his left, along the Brünn–Olmütz road, the remainder of Napoleon's first line had begun to advance around 9:15 A.M. and soon afterwards had been halted by allied cavalry and artillery.

Although the number of allied troops remaining on the Pratzen Heights was something of a surprise to him, Napoleon had good reason to be pleased with the success of his men so far. By 10:00, however, stiff resistance the forces of Marshal Lannes met on the northern end of the battlefield forced Napoleon to begin re-evaluating his original plan of turning the allied right and driving their entire army southward. The events of the next several hours would reveal new opportunities that Napoleon would exploit with devastating effect.

The First Cavalry Actions in the North and the Struggle for Blaziowitz

After the unfortunate tangling of Shepelev's cavalry regiments with Langeron's 2nd Column early that morning, Liechtenstein had reversed the course of his column and then headed it toward its proper position in the vicinity of Blaziowitz where it would form a link between the 4th Column and Bagration's forces on the Brünn–Olmütz road. The order of the column was now reversed, with FML Hohenlohe's Austrian cuirassiers leading the column, followed by GL Essen-2 with Shepelev's brigade of Russian cavalry. Uvarov's brigade had already been ordered to support Bagration's left and had moved into position the night before.* By 8:30 A.M., about the time that Monakhtin's advance guard sighted St Hilaire's division ascending the heights, Hohenlohe had taken position near the village of Blaziowitz. Shepelev

---

* Mikhailovski-Danilevski, p. 233.

moved into position between Hohenlohe and Uvarov around 9:00 just as Vandamme's division was engaging Miloradovich on the heights.

To Liechtenstein's right rear stood Bagration's command, now assigned the mission of securing the right flank of the allied army. Bagration occupied a position running perpendicular to the Brünn–Olmütz road on a line running roughly from Kowalowitz to Slawikowitz and facing southwest. At least three kilometers separated Liechtenstein's right from Bagration's left. Bagration's orders were to remain in position until the 4th Column had passed Kobelnitz, then to advance to engage the French left. Bagration, known to be an aggressive fighter, undoubtedly resented the role he had been assigned. His experience and aggressiveness, however, would make his presence on the Brünn–Olmütz road quite fortunate for the allied army.

Constantine's Guard columns formed the third body of allied troops in the northern sector of the battlefield. The 1st Column of the Russian Life Guard under the direct command of Grand Duke Constantine, had marched at dawn from its position in front of Austerlitz. The 2nd Guard Column under GM Maliutin (which included the Life Grenadiers and half of the Guard cavalry) had marched at about the same time from its position just east of Buschowitz, roughly nine kilometers to the east, but was two or three hours behind the 1st Guard Column. As the 1st Guard Column reached the Rausnitz Brook, its progress was slowed as the entire column filed over the narrow weir near the Walkmühle (fulling mill). As a result, Constantine's column arrived on the high ground just east of Blaziowitz around 9:00 (roughly at the same time the last of Essen-2's cavalry was arriving near Krug). About 850 meters west of Constantine's force stood the village of Blaziowitz. The village stood at one end of a valley that ran eastward from Girzikowitz, where Vandamme's division had been. From his position Constantine overlooked Blaziowitz and could see beyond the valley to the Brünn–Olmütz road to the north and the slope from the Stare Vinohrady to Girzikowitz to the south where Vandamme's division could be seen emerging from the mists and rapidly approaching the Pratzen heights.

Unlike the forces on the extreme left of the allied line advancing into the valley of the Goldbach, no overall commander had been named for the three formations—the 5th Column, Advance Guard and Imperial Guard—composing the right wing. This omission appears to have reflected the expectation that the allied headquarters, which would take position on the Stare Vinohrady, would be well placed to coordinate the activities of the entire allied right directly. In actuality, the columns received no direction from the allied headquarters (or what remained of it after the French exploded onto the Pratzen heights) beyond urgent pleas from Kutuzov for reinforcements.

Nevertheless, the three allied column commanders, operating independently of each other, managed to support each other more effectively than the three columns on the lower Goldbach which had the supposed benefit of a wing commander.

Facing these forces were no fewer than four French infantry divisions, four heavy cavalry divisions and eight regiments of supporting light cavalry. Napoleon had concentrated these forces east of the Bosenitzer Stream between Girzikowitz and the Santon, ready either to absorb the brunt of a direct frontal assault by the allies or to launch what Napoleon intended to be the decisive counterstroke. Lannes's infantry divisions straddled the main road with GdD Caffarelli on the right and GdD Suchet on the left. The four light cavalry regiments of Picard's and Marizy's brigades of Kellermann's division were positioned in front of the infantry. To the left of Suchet stood the light cavalry of GdBs Milhaud and Trelliard; to the right of Caffarelli the dragoon division of GdB Boyé. Behind the infantry, the dragoon division of GdD Walther and the two cuirassier divisions of Nansouty and d'Hautpoul formed the reserve.[*]

Standing to the right of the forces of Lannes and Murat had been Vandamme's division at Girzikowitz. With the departure of this to the southeast, the two divisions of Bernadotte's 1st Corps began advancing to take its place. The 1st Corps had left its bivouacs around 7:00 A.M. to move into position just west of the Goldbach opposite the village. As the last of Vandamme's division left Girzikowitz, the division of Drouet began filing across the bridges. By 9:30 Drouet's division was across. Rivaud's division followed Drouet's and had completed the crossing by 10:30.

Lannes's instructions were to begin advancing directly up the Brünn–Olmütz road once St Hilaire's troops were visible on the Pratzeberg. Around 9:15, when Morand's men could clearly be seen on the heights and in fact were beginning to engage Monakhtin's advance guard, Lannes gave the order to advance. With Kellermann's light cavalry in the lead, the entire body moved forward into the plain between Bosenitz and Blaziowitz.

The French movement was visible to the allies almost immediately and caused considerable alarm. With a three-kilometer gap between Liechtenstein and Bagration, Lannes's force was moving to separate Bagration from the remainder of the army. To the left, Vandamme had already engaged the Russians of the 4th Column near the Stare Vinohrady, threatening to separate Liechtenstein's 5th Column from the remainder of the army as well. Without waiting for orders, Liechtenstein, Bagration and Constantine each reacted individually to the crisis.

[*] "Relation de la bataille d'Austerlitz," in *Relations et Rapports*, pp. 90–1; Alombert and Colin, pp. 185–6.

Liechtenstein, his cavalry comprising the allied force closest to the advancing French, was the first to react. Kellermann's four regiments of cavalry leading the French columns formed a promising target for a cavalry charge, and Liechtenstein appears to have issued orders to Essen-2 to charge the head of the French column as it was drawing even with Blaziowitz. Uvarov ordered the Elisabetgrad Hussars to the inn of Holubitz on the main road, presumably to launch a charge in concert with the light cavalry of Shepelev's brigade, the Constantine Uhlans, which were deployed in line near Krug. According to one account, Constantine rode to meet Essen-2 and whip up the morale of the Uhlan regiment that bore his name. According to this account, Essen-2 launched the charge immediately with Constantine's approval.[*] However, reports of events occurring at about the same time place Constantine with the Guard, suggesting that this story might be apocryphal. What is known for certain is that, while Uvarov's hussars were maneuvering into position, the Constantine Uhlans, among the last of the cavalry to have arrived and itching for action, charged on their own with Essen-2 at their head.[†]

It was around 9:30 when Kellermann's troopers saw the ten squadrons of Russian Uhlans sweeping down on them from the southeast. The Uhlans had arrived from Russia with Buxhöwden's corps and as a result were fresher and closer to full strength than the forces that had endured the march to Braunau and then the rearguard actions of the previous two months. With ten squadrons organised into two battalions, the large Russian light cavalry regiments were comparable in size to a French cavalry division. Kellermann's four regiments consisted of twelve squadrons that had been largely untested during the victorious French advance. The larger size of the Russian squadrons, however, gave them a very slight numerical advantage over the French chasseurs and hussars (1,380 Russians versus 1,270 French).

The suddenness and fury of the Russian charge gave Kellermann little time to react. The 1st Battalion of Constantine Uhlans struck the 2nd Hussars directly while the 2nd Battalion passed across the front of the 2nd Hussars and struck the 5th Hussars, driving them into the 4th Hussars to their left.

---

[*] A. Vasil'ev, "Russkaya Gvardiya v srazhenii Pri Austerlitse, 20 Noyabrya (2 Dekabrya) 1805 g." Voin Nos. 3–4 <www.genstab.ru/voin/auster_01.htm>.

[†] Essen-2 is usually credited with jumping the gun and ordering this immediate charge, but it is also possible that Constantine ordered the immediate charge, that Essen-2's orders were misunderstood or that the lancers surged forward prematurely on their own account without express orders to do so, carrying Essen-2 with them. Uvarov, under Essen-2's command, appears to have had orders for the Elisabetgrad Hussars to charge as well and it seems odd that Essen-2, having issued such orders, would not have waited for them to be carried out. Essen-2 fell mortally wounded as a result of the charge, so his version of events was never recorded. Vasil'ev, "Gvardiya" <www.genstab.ru/voin/auster_01.htm>.

Kellermann did not attempt to resist the onslaught, instead wheeling the majority of his regiments around the left of the infantry columns and clearing their line of fire. Many of the 2nd Hussars escaped in the intervals between the battalions of the 17th and 30th Line which stood behind them. The Russian Uhlans pursued the French cavalry, sweeping across the front of the French infantry and between gaps in their ranks. The crews of three French guns abandoned their pieces to the Russians.* Much of the 1st Battalion of Constantine Uhlans, with the regiment's commander, GM Müller-Zakomelsky, found itself between the 17th Line and 61st Line, squarely in the center of Caffarelli's division while the remainder harassed the front of the French infantry. The front ranks of the infantry opened fire, causing appalling casualties among the Russians, while their third rank made a half turn to their right to allow them to fire at the Uhlans behind them. The impetus of the charge spent, the Uhlans milled around among the infantry, thrusting at whatever they could reach with their lances but making little impact in the face of a steady row of French bayonets.

While the Uhlans were doing what damage they could, Kellermann had reformed his four regiments on the left (north) of the French columns. Demonstrating the knack for timing that had proven decisive at the battle of Marengo, he launched his hussars at the disordered mass of Russian Uhlans. During the mêlée, Müller-Zakomelsky was struck in the chest by a musket ball, but the projectile was deflected by the Order of St Vladimir pinned to his coat. Nevertheless, he had the wind knocked out of him and was dazed. Directly in the path of Kellermann's charge, Müller-Zakomelsky was soon personally attacked by hussars from the 5th Regiment, and took several saber blows before his officers came to his rescue. However, groups of Uhlans, including Müller-Zakomelsky's party, were then surrounded by the French and captured. The remaining Uhlans escaped through the intervals between the infantry, whose fire dropped a considerable number of Russians as they fled leaving 28 of their 59 officers and 194 lower ranks killed, captured or severely wounded—16 percent of their total number. Among the severely wounded was Essen-2 who managed to escape only to die of his wounds several weeks later. The entire mêlée had lasted perhaps quarter of an hour.

While Essen-2 was leading his charge, Bagration was also springing into action, ordering his troops to advance to close the gap between his forces and the 5th Column. In order to buy time, he ordered Wittgenstein with the Mariupol Hussars and Yashvil's horse artillery battery to advance directly up the main road ahead of his main body. By shortly before 10:00, Yashvil had

---

* The pieces belonged to the 1st Company, 7th Artillery Regiment. Naturally the Russians claimed the guns as captured and then lost, but in these matters it is doubtful that the cavalry could have taken possession of the guns in any meaningful way.

unlimbered his guns in position across the main road adjacent to Holubitz. At this point they were partially protected by a shallow ravine in front of them. As the remnants of the Constantine Uhlans fell back, pursued by Kellermann's four regiments, Yashvil opened fire on the pursuing French cavalry.

Pausing briefly to assemble his regiments, Kellermann quickly launched them in pursuit of the Uhlans fleeing down the main road. Observing the action, Uvarov immediately ordered the Elisabetgrad Hussars forward against Kellermann's right. Approximately 800 Russian hussars quickly enveloped the 4th Hussars on the French right, capturing their commander, Colonel Burthe. Abruptly forced to abandon his pursuit of the Russian Uhlans, who took cover behind Yashvil's battery, Kellermann wheeled his remaining three regiments to face the new threat to the south and again charged, taking the Russian hussars in flank. In a brief mêlée, the French hussars managed to recover Colonel Burthe and rescue the 4th Hussars, driving the Elisabetgrad Hussars off to the south. Pausing to recover after the confused series of charges, Kellermann's hussars soon came under fire from the Russian artillery to the south and on the main road. Uvarov, however, was unable to take advantage of the situation to launch a fresh charge against Kellermann with his dragoons owing to a crisis developing on his left around the village of Blaziowitz.

About thirty minutes earlier, while Lannes and Bagration were advancing toward each other on the Brünn–Olmütz road and Essen-2 was launching his ill-fated charge, there seems to have been a sudden recognition on both sides of the fact that Blaziowitz remained unoccupied. After successfully beating back the first French assault on his line on the heights (see p. 197), Kollowrath launched a counterattack on the French left near the Stare Vinohrady, driving back the 24th Light. The Grenadier Battalion of the Salzburg IR 23, supported by the 6th Battalion of the regiment which stood on the extreme right of Kollowrath's line, pressed the French back a considerable distance, drawing away from the main part of the Austrian line in the process. Vandamme countered this move by detaching the left-most battalion of his third line, the 2nd Battalion, 4th Line, toward Blaziowitz to prevent the Austrians from turning the flank of the 24th Light and also turned his guns to bombard the advancing Austrians. Some of the French artillery fire reached the Russian Guards standing east of Blaziowitz, mowing down a file of the Preobrazhensky Regiment. This rude awakening alerted Constantine to the danger of the French seizing Blaziowitz and driving a wedge between the allied right and center. Immediately Constantine ordered GM St Priest with the Life Guard Jäger Battalion and two guns to occupy Blaziowitz.

While the Austrians pursued the 24th Light to the northwest and St Priest advanced on Blaziowitz with his battalion, Lannes's forces were drawing even with Blaziowitz on the Brünn–Olmütz Road. Lannes ordered GdB Eppler with the 13th Light, positioned on the extreme right of his line, to occupy Blaziowitz to secure his right flank with Boyé's dragoon division shifting to the south to fill the gap between Lannes's right and Vandamme's left until Bernadotte's corps could complete its crossing of the Girzikowitz Brook. Colonel Castex deployed four companies of the 1st/13th Light as skirmishers and sent them forward to occupy the village. Boyé's dragoon division passed west of Blaziowitz to take position south of the village. Thus, at the same time as the Constantine Uhlans were launching their charge with the results already described, the Russians and French were converging on Blaziowitz from both directions.

As the French skirmishers were approaching Blaziowitz, however, St Priest arrived with the Guard Jäger Battalion and immediately occupied the village. The first company, deployed as skirmishers, quickly took position at the northern end of the village while two more companies moved into the southern end. The Russian Jäger quickly infiltrated the village, establishing themselves in the houses and gardens. As the French arrived, they were surprised by the Russian Jäger and were immediately thrown back. Colonel Castex ordered forward the remainder of his regiment and personally led the 2nd Battalion in charging the Russians, only to fall dead with a bullet through his forehead at the edge of the village.

The regimental history of the Life Guard Jäger battalion describes the action in some detail:

> Meanwhile, the French Column (from the division of Rivaud [*sic*]), in order to cover itself from our batteries, inclined toward the right [south], skirmishers began to infiltrate the garden and go around our left [southern] flank, where Lieutenant Ofrosimov-2 commanded. After requesting permission from Captain Ridinger, he immediately took measures to stop the enemy and, after hiding his Jäger under the bushes and behind the fence which surrounded the garden, he waited for the approach of the Frenchmen, despite their heavy fire; when they approached, Lieutenant Ofrosimov gave the order to fire and, after doing serious damage, forced them to double the number of their skirmishers. Our two companies then rushed them with bayonets and, after driving away the enemy, again returned to the garden.*

---

* Both Russian and Austrian accounts confuse the names of the French generals. Caffarelli's division is identified as Rivaud's in both this source, Stutterheim's account and Schönhals's. Caffarelli is mistakenly identified as the commander of Suchet's division. Officers of the Regiment, *Istoriia Leib-Gvardii Egerskago Polka, 1796–1896 GG* (St Petersburg: 1896), p. 33.

The French light infantry fought the Life Guard Jäger from house to house, but met with fierce resistance. Seriously outnumbered, St Priest sent an urgent plea to Constantine for support. Constantine received St Priest's request for reinforcements at about the same time that he and Liechtenstein both received Kutuzov's urgent request for assistance. Faced with the large-scale French advance to his right and with Bagration's infantry still advancing and not yet even with Holubitz, Constantine determined to retain four of his battalions and his cavalry in reserve. He detached the 3rd Battalion of the Semenovsky Regiment from the extreme right of his first line along with two guns to reinforce St Priest and the 1st Battalion of the Ismailovsky Regiment from the extreme left of his second line to reinforce Kutuzov on the heights. At about the same time, GM Maliutin with the 2nd Guard Column was approaching Austerlitz from the east, and Constantine appears to have directed Maliutin toward Krenowitz to reinforce Kutuzov on the Pratzen Heights instead of following the 1st Guard Column and marching by way of the Walkmühle.[*]

As the 3rd Battalion of the Semenovsky approached Blaziowitz, Boyé observed an isolated Austrian battalion, the Grenadiers of IR 23, approaching from the southeast. Seeing the Austrian infantry in the open, Boyé sent several squadrons of dragoons to attack them. The dragoons quickly surrounded the grenadiers, who were taken by surprise. The 6th Battalion of IR 23, though in position to advance to relieve the grenadiers, threw down their guns and fled according to Russian accounts. Austrian accounts make no mention of the flight of the recruits of the regiment, but French reports indicate a large number of Austrian prisoners taken near Blaziowitz, an outcome consistent with the Russian version of events.[†]

Either concurrently with the attack on the Austrians of IR 23 or immediately after, French dragoons also attacked the 3rd Battalion of the Semenovsky as it advanced toward Blaziowitz. Seeing the French cavalry charging around the south end of the village, Constantine sent the first line of

---

[*] While there is no direct indication when, or even if, such orders were issued, the subsequent arrival of Maliutin's command opposite Krenowitz indicates that his route of march was redirected sometime during the battle. The logical assumption is that this occurred as a result of Kutuzov's plea for reinforcements.

[†] Many writers have overlooked the presence of Austrian infantry near Blaziowitz entirely. Colin notes French reports of hundreds of Austrian prisoners being taken at Blaziowitz (and later being mistakenly sabered by Uvarov's cavalry), but indicates that no Austrians were present at Blaziowitz, the reports resulting from a confusion in uniforms. Duffy concluded that the Austrians must have been horse artillery accompanying Liechtenstein. However, St Priest reported Austrian infantry being broken by the French attack on Blaziowitz just as his troops were engaging, confirming the French reports of Austrian infantry at Blaziowitz. Alombert and Colin, V, p. 192; Duffy, *Austerlitz*, p. 127; *Istoriia Leib-Gvardii Egerskago Polka*, p. 34; Anonymous, *Geschichte der k. und k. Infanterieregiments Markgraf von Baden No. 23* (Budapest: 1911), pp. 717–20.

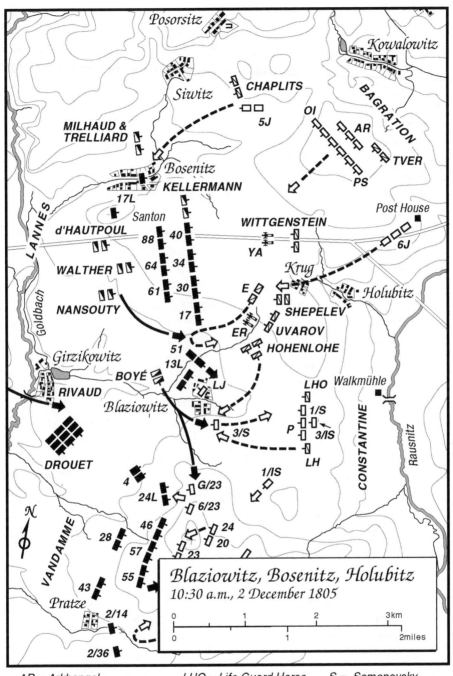

Posorsitz

Kowalowitz

Siwitz

CHAPLITS

BAGRATION

5J

OI

AR

TVER

MILHAUD & TRELLIARD

PS

Bosenitz

KELLERMANN

17L

Santon

Post House

d'HAUTPOUL

WITTGENSTEIN

6J

88

40

YA

WALTHER

64

34

Krug

Holubitz

61

30

E

NANSOUTY

17

SHEPELEV

ER

UVAROV

51

HOHENLOHE

13L

LHO

Walkmühle

Girzikowitz

BOYÉ

LJ

1/S

RIVAUD

Blaziowitz

P

3/IS

3/S

LH

DROUET

1/IS

4

G/23

24L

6/23

46

24

N

28

20

57

23

VANDAMME

55

43

CONSTANTINE

Rausnitz

Pratze

2/14

Blaziowitz, Bosenitz, Holubitz
10:30 a.m., 2 December 1805

0   1   2   3km

0   1   2miles

2/36

LANNES

Goldbach

AR = Arkhangel
E = Elisabetgrad Hussars
ER = Ermolov Battery
IS = Ismailovsky
LH = Life Guard Hussars

LHO = Life Guard Horse
LJ = Life Guard Jäger
OI = Old Ingermanland
P = Preobrazhensky
PS = Pskov

S = Semenovsky
YA = Yashvil Battery
5J = 5th Jäger
6J = 6th Jäger

the Life Guard Hussars (three squadrons) to drive them off. The Russian hussars struck the leading French dragoons and drove them back into the remainder, the entire body retreating behind the infantry around Blaziowitz. The pursuing Russians soon came under artillery fire and retired to their original position. However, as a result of the attack of the French dragoons, only two of the four companies of 3rd/Semenovsky appear to have joined St Priest's battalion at Blaziowitz but the action of the Life Guard Hussars had saved the remainder of St Priest's reserve from coming under attack and had stopped the French pursuit of the routed Austrian battalion and companies of the Semenovsky Regiment.*

The French movement on the Russian right at Blaziowitz signaled the arrival of the 51st Line, sent up by Lannes to reinforce Eppler's two battalions. The 51st quickly covered the short distance between the right of Lannes's position and Blaziowitz, joining the 13th Light around 10:30. The two battalions of the 13th Light renewed the attack on the Russians from the west while the 2nd/51st Line circled the village to the north to descend on their rear. St Priest, observing this flanking movement, shifted his reserve company, to which were joined two companies of 3rd/Semenovsky, to counter it. In the words of the regimental historian of the Life Guard Jäger:

> French skirmishers again attempted to turn our left [southern] flank, but they were repulsed for a second time by the bayonet and switched their attack to the right [northern] flank. Count St Priest, seeing this movement, sent his adjutant Lieutenant Prince Shcherbatov to call in the reserve. Prince Shcherbatov reported that Colonel Kridner had retired with his battalion [3rd Semenovsky]; then the company of Prince Bagration [the reserve company of the Life Guard Jäger Battalion] was ordered to support the right flank and the company of Graf St Priest [from the left] became the reserve.†

With no further reinforcement at hand, St Priest ordered his forces to withdraw and by 11:00 had rejoined Constantine.

The French report summed up the action succinctly:

> These [four] companies [of 13th Light] being put in skirmish order, the attack made little progress; the remainder of the regiment [then] received the order to advance. The 2nd Battalion arrived at the *pas de charge*; the

---

* This action is described as occurring during the charge of the Constantine Uhlans. Although it is not completely certain that the cavalry charge was directed at the same cavalry attacking south of Blaziowitz, the timing and circumstances of the attack make this the most likely explanation. Vasil'ev, "Gvardiya" <www.genstab.ru/voin/auster_01.htm>.

† *Istoriia Leib-Gvardii Egerskago Polka*, p. 33.

enemy fled and trailed their [artillery] pieces toward the plateau; 300 men were taken prisoner in the village. The 2nd Battalion of the 51st, which had come to support the attack, cut off the retreat of 250 fugitives. Colonel Castex, who had always demonstrated bravery, was killed at the head of his regiment [13th Light]. Five pieces of artillery which protected the defense of Blaziowitz were taken; they had been supported by a body of cavalry that was overthrown.*

While the struggle for Blaziowitz was raging, Liechtenstein had responded to Kutuzov's pleas by shifting his Austrian cavalry from its position northeast of Blaziowitz to the south of Blaziowitz to support the Austrian forces around the Stare Vinohrady. As a result, Uvarov was now required to cover the entire gap between Blaziowitz and Krug while Shepelev, with only the Empress Cuirassiers and the remains of the Constantine Uhlans, linked with Bagration's cavalry on the main road. Liechtenstein's cuirassiers arrived south of Blaziowitz around 10:30 to find the Austrians pressed hard by the French attack on their position at the Stare Vinohrady and the Austrian cavalry took position to cover the space between Blaziowitz and the heights.

The advance of Bernadotte's infantry from Girzikowitz presented a promising target for the Austrian cavalry, and Liechtenstein sent General Caramelli with the Lothringen Kürassier Regiment (KR) 7 to harass them.

> The Austrian General, Caramelli, made a charge with the Cuirassiers of Lorraine [Lothringen] upon the enemy's infantry, which coming out of Girschikowitz took advantage of the vineyards between that village and Pratzen [Pratze], to take the Russians in flank.†

Caramelli had his horse shot from under him and Major Count Auersperg, leading the charge, was killed. Following the modest success of Caramelli's charge, Liechtenstein sent in the Nassau KR 5 which had little effect against the large mass of French infantry and soon retired under the fire of the French infantry in the vineyard. However, the charge had delayed the French advance by at least thirty minutes. Events on the heights, however, made this delaying action futile as the Austrian line defending the western edge of the heights finally broke.

With the withdrawal of the Austrian line on the heights, Liechtenstein shifted Caramelli with the Lothringen and Nassau cuirassiers to the south to support the allied forces remaining on the heights. Bernadotte took this opportunity to resume his advance, Rivaud's division marching to the south of Blaziowitz. It appears that Liechtenstein had left the Kaiser 1 to slow the

---

* "Note on the Division Caffarelli," quoted in Alombert and Colin, V, p. 192.

† Stutterheim, p. 108.

advance of the French infantry, but the French pressed on and by 11:30 had drawn even with Blaziowitz. Constantine, eyeing the broadening gap between his column and the thin allied line that had formed on the eastern edge of the heights, ordered the Russian Guard to advance toward Blaziowitz in order to support the flank of the 4th Column on the heights and to prevent the army from being split in two. As Rivaud's division drew even with Blaziowitz, Constantine's Guard was advancing to meet them.

As the Russian Guard approached, Constantine ordered the four battalions of Preobrazhensky and Semenovsky to fix bayonets and charge the French. At 300 paces, the Russian guardsmen surged forward with their customary "urrah!" This charge, launched at too great a distance, met with Rivaud's seasoned troops who deployed and stood to receive the attack. The skirmishers that Rivaud had deployed in front of his first line were swept away by the charge, but the Russian troops were winded by the time they reached the main French line and the French fire inflicted heavy losses. Despite this, the three battalions of Rivaud's first line were driven back on the second line of battalions where the impetus of the Russian attack was halted. Colonel Rall, commanding the Russian Guard position battery, advanced his guns in support of the infantry. Before he could get them into position, however, Constantine received word of Kutuzov's orders for a general withdrawal from the heights.

Constantine appears to have conferred with Liechtenstein and resolved to retire on Krenowitz to support the 4th Column and maintain contact with the main body of the army. Liechtenstein ordered the Kaiser KR 1, still in the vicinity of Blaziowitz, to support Constantine while the remaining two Austrian cuirassier regiments attempted to cover the retreat of the 4th Column and to keep the route to Krenowitz open for Constantine. With French infantry threatening their line of retreat, GM Kaspersky, overall commander of the Guard artillery, expressed concern for the heavy guns and requested that Constantine send the artillery ahead to Krenowitz.* Constantine agreed and, over Rall's protests, ordered the Life Guard Jäger battalion to accompany Rall's battery and retire immediately while the main column followed. By around 12:30, the Russian Guard infantry, covered by their cavalry and the Kaiser KR 1 had disengaged, reformed, and set off for Krenowitz.

---

* Russian accounts indicate that Rall was ordered to the rear, which has been interpreted as countermarching back the way the column had come. However, Russian accounts place Rall's battery on the left bank of the Rausnitz stream opposite Krenowitz less than two hours later. This does not allow sufficient time for the battery to retire via the more northern Walkmühle, cross, and march down the left bank to Krenowitz. Clearly the march of Rall's battery "to the rear" indicates that they followed the same rearward direction that was taken by the entire 1st Guard Column.

Stand-off on the Brünn–Olmütz Road and the Attack on Bosenitz

While Liechtenstein and Constantine were occupied to the south of Blaziowitz, the withdrawal of the Austrian cuirassiers around 10:30 had left a gap to the northeast of the village. Uvarov accordingly shifted his attention toward that area. The Elisabetgrad Hussars had fallen back after the last furious charge of Kellermann's hussars and, with his left flank exposed by Liechtenstein's departure, Uvarov did not order a countercharge, choosing to cover St Priest's retreat instead. As Uvarov shifted his hussars toward Blaziowitz, Yashvil advanced his horse artillery into range and opened fire on Caffarelli's motionless troops formed up across the road. At almost the same time, Ermolov opened fire on the French flank from the south or southwest. "Eight pieces sitting on the plateau bombarded our line directly," noted Caffarelli's report. "Those brought in front of Blaziowitz took it in flank; in a few moments 400 men were rendered *hors de combat*. Our soldiers, motionless, endured this fire with the greatest intrepidity."[*]

Uvarov's shift toward Blaziowitz gave Kellermann time to reform his four regiments and charge the Russians between Blaziowitz and Krug. The French hussars drove Uvarov's dragoons back and were able to capture two guns from Ermolov's horse artillery battery (from Uvarov's brigade). Bagration, however, riding ahead of his infantry which had finally drawn even with the Posorsitz Post house, had brought up his cavalry and the three battalions of 6th Jäger, supported by Cossacks, toward Holubitz. Seeing Kellermann's charge, Bagration ordered the 6th Jäger to occupy Holubitz and Krug and ordered the Pavlograd Hussars, Tver Dragoons and three squadrons of St Petersburg Dragoons, (eighteen squadrons in all) to drive off the French hussars. The Russian cavalry hit Kellermann's hussars in flank and drove them off in disorder, recapturing the guns that had been captured and linking with the Elisabetgrad Hussars.[†]

Bagration's timely intervention allowed Uvarov to make an effort to provide some relief for the hard-pressed Russian infantry in Blaziowitz. Uvarov had observed the 51st Line advancing toward Blaziowitz, and sent his Elisabetgrad

---

[*] Colin identifies the guns firing from the south as coming from Blaziowitz, which would make these the guns sent with St Priest and the Life Guard Jäger battalion. However, the Life Guard Jäger were hard-pressed in Blaziowitz and it is unlikely the guns were targeting distant formations when they were urgently needed to repel French attacks on the village. It seems more likely that these additional guns were Ermolov's battery or possibly Austrian horse artillery. Ignatiev's battery seems to have remained near Holubitz and Krug. Alombert and Colin, V, ch. 18.

[†] "Raport F. P. Uvarova M. I. Kutuzovu o Srazhenii pod Austerlitsem, 1805 g. Noyabrya 25" (7 December 1805) in *Dokumenty Shtaba Kutuzova*, pp. 221–4.

Hussars in to disrupt any further reinforcements. Uvarov's cavalry surged forward, drove between the 51st Line and the remainder of Caffarelli's division and forced the 61st Line to form square.* Drawing up short in the face of the French square bristling with bayonets, Uvarov's cavalry took fire from the third rank of 17th Line that had turned and was pouring volley after volley into them as they sought to regroup. Uvarov finally managed to convey the order to retreat amidst the din and smoke and the Russian hussars headed back the way they had come.

Murat, from his position behind Lannes's infantry, had been reduced to a supporting role to this point, a role for which he was poorly suited. Itching for action, Murat observed Uvarov's incursion into the rear of Lannes's infantry and called on GdD Nansouty to drive them off with his six regiments of cuirassiers and carabiniers. Nansouty led his regiments forward and eighteen squadrons of elite French cavalry swept down on the ten squadrons of Russian hussars. Uvarov's retreat soon became a rout as the Russians fled before the fury of the charge. The 3rd Cuirassiers pursued Uvarov's hussars onto the bridge over the Holubitz Brook, but Nansouty's cavalry soon came under fire from Russian artillery—Yashvil's battery on the main road and Ignatiev's battery near Krug, most likely. A few rounds from the Russian guns soon forced Nansouty's heavies to fall back.

Nansouty's charge had driven Uvarov's cavalry back behind the Holubitz brook, leaving the entire area between Holubitz and Blaziowitz open. With French infantry (Rivaud) advancing south of Blaziowitz, around 11:30 Constantine advanced his column (six battalions and ten squadrons) approximately 750 meters to the west to counter the advancing infantry.† To support the right of the Guard, Uvarov left his exhausted hussars to regroup, formed his dragoons in two lines and launched them in pursuit of the retreating French cavalry.

With a large body of fresh Russian cavalry nipping at their heels,

---

* It seems that 51st Line may also have formed square, being directly in the path of the Russian charge. However, this regiment was marching toward Blaziowitz where the ground was broken by a small stream and ravine, which may have discouraged the Russian cavalry from attacking it directly.

† The advance of the Guard toward Blaziowitz is typically interpreted as an advance on the Pratzen Heights. However, this interpretation, which has the Guard infantry charging the 4th Line, is not supported by any evidence in French accounts or documents indicating that the 4th Line came under attack by the Russian Guard infantry. Russian accounts indicating a westward advance in support of the forces on the heights, followed by a withdrawal southeast toward Blaziowitz are consistent with the account of Bigarré and Estrabaut's *Livre d'Or du 8e Régiment*. Bigarré's account rules out an attack by the Life Guard infantry on the 4th Line while the *Livre d'Or* indicates that the 8th Line was the target of this attack. This advance involved the five Guard battalions of the Preobrazhensky, Semenovsky and Ismailovsky Regiments (1st/Ismailovsky had been detached) along with the Life Guard Jäger and Guard cavalry.

Nansouty's cuirassiers and carabiniers slipped between the gaps in the infantry columns, taking refuge behind Caffarelli's infantry. With the Russian dragoons nearly on them, the 30th and 17th Line opened fire, the first point-blank volley taking a murderous toll on the Russian cavalry, causing their charge to falter. With their momentum broken, the Russian cavalry milled about in front of the French infantry, suffering more casualties from the heavy fire the French were pouring into their ranks. Minutes later they were in full retreat while Nansouty, having reformed his division in two lines behind the cover of the infantry, led them forward again through the intervals in the lines of infantry. With the two carabinier regiments and the 2nd Cuirassiers in the first line and the remainder following in the second line, Nansouty quickly caught up with the Russians, who turned to meet them. In the ensuing mêlée, the French soon forced the Russian horse back. Nansouty, quickly reforming his division, launched a final charge that scattered the Russian cavalry, this time to the southeast and across the Rausnitz Brook. Uvarov, denying credit to the French cuirassiers, wrote that:

> . . . at this time the enemy infantry and artillery, after pressing on my flanks, produced such fire that despite the bravery of the regiments that I commanded, they were forced to retreat and to retire through the creek [Rausnitz Brook] that was located to our rear.[*]

The series of clashes between Uvarov and Nansouty marked the last of the major cavalry actions between Blaziowitz and Holubitz. On the allied side, the Russians of the 5th Column, particularly Uvarov's brigade and the Constantine Uhlans, had taken serious casualties and Uvarov's brigade in particular was spent and needed time to recover. Bagration's cavalry remained in better condition than that of the 5th Column, but Bagration had shifted much of it to the north to support a diversionary move on Bosenitz that he hoped would draw Lannes's attention northward. The series of charges and countercharges had kept Lannes's infantry immobilized, however, and provided ample time for Bagration's infantry to arrive.

As previously noted, Bagration had sent his horse artillery and the Mariupol Hussars ahead of his infantry to occupy a position on the main road. With this detachment and Liechtenstein's cavalry holding the French at bay, Bagration rushed his infantry forward, directing the 6th Jäger under GM Ulanius with supporting Cossacks to occupy Holubitz and Krug on the left where they

---

[*] "Raport F. P. Uvarova M. I. Kutuzovu o Srazhenii pod Austerlitsem, 1805 g. Noyabrya 25," in *Dokumenty Shtaba Kutuzova*, pp. 221–4. There is some disagreement as to which brook Uvarov was referring to in his report. However, his mention of "the narrowest of weirs" and subsequent position on the heights east of the Rausnitz Brook near the Walkmühle point to the Walkmühle crossing as the most likely location.

joined the Empress Cuirassiers and the remnants of the Constantine Uhlans. To his right, Bagration deployed Colonel Gogel with the 5th Jäger and GM Chaplits with the Pavlograd Hussars and supporting Cossacks toward Siwitz. Bagration's main line stretched between these two points, with the six battalions of the Old Ingermanland and Pskov Musketeers in the first line and the Arkhangel Musketeers in second line behind them. The remainder of Bagration's cavalry—the five squadrons of Tver Dragoons and three squadrons of St Petersburg Dragoons—stood behind the Arkhangel Musketeers.

With the French getting the best of the action around Blaziowitz, Bagration resolved on a diversionary attack on the extreme northern end of the French position, and around 11:00 ordered Gogel and Chaplits to advance on Bosenitz. The unexpected movement of the two battalions of Russian Jäger from the northeast surprised the French detachment in Bosenitz. Driving the detachment from Bosenitz, Gogel's men pursued them toward the Santon. Perched atop the hillock, GdB Claparède's 17th Light were soon under attack in the entrenchment they had dug on the face and crest of the hill. With the protection given by this position, the Russian assault was beaten off, the French artillery fire inflicting heavy casualties on the Russians, who fell back to Bosenitz.[*]

With his left flank exposed by the Russian occupation of Bosenitz, Lannes directed Claparède to retake Bosenitz before resuming the advance of his main body. Supported by the light cavalry of Milhaud and Trelliard (four regiments with a total of twelve squadrons), the 2nd/17th Light descended from their entrenchments on the Santon and stormed into the Russian Jäger in Bosenitz. After minimal resistance, Gogel withdrew his Jäger toward Siwitz under the cover of Chaplits and the Pavlograd Hussars.[†] Bagration's attack on Bosenitz had achieved little, but undoubtedly prevented the French from resuming their advance for at least thirty minutes which was perhaps his intended purpose in ordering the attack.

The entire series of poorly coordinated actions by the allied forces on the northern part of the battlefield received criticism from Ermolov, among others. Ermolov stated that "Our cavalry, like the rest of our army, acted largely without coordination, mostly on its own account, without any attempt at mutual support."[‡] This observation only serves to emphasize the fact that the allies had never anticipated being attacked in this sector, that there was no overall commander of the several columns composing the allied right, and that the entire series of actions from Blaziowitz to Bosenitz represented

---

[*] Alombert and Colin, V, p. 194.

[†] Ibid.

[‡] Ermolov, Notes, p. 56.

nothing more than isolated attempts by the allies to disrupt the French advance while they drew their own scattered forces closer together. Viewed in this light, the allied operations on the northern part of the battlefield can be considered moderately successful, the fact that the allied forces were not separated by the advancing French and driven from the field being in itself an achievement. If the allies incurred substantial losses as a result they certainly inflicted heavy casualties upon the French in the process.

On the French side, the unexpectedly fierce resistance of the allies had indeed disrupted Napoleon's plans. The turning of the allied right flank was no longer possible despite the seizure of Blaziowitz and the heavy losses of the greater part of the allied cavalry. As effective as the French cavalry had been in neutralizing the allied cavalry, the French infantry had been held paralyzed in position on the Brünn–Olmütz road and under fire from the Russian artillery. Despite this setback, events on the Pratzen Heights more than compensated for the very limited success on the French left.

As the 5th Jäger was being driven from Bosenitz to Siwitz, Constantine was receiving news of the desperate situation on the Pratzen heights. The Austrian line anchored on the Stare Vinohrady had finally been defeated around 11:00, though Kollowrath and Miloradovich had scraped together assorted Austrian and Russian battalions to form a third line on the heights east of the Stare Vinohrady. Constantine's advance toward Blaziowitz had drawn the Guard roughly even with this third allied line on the Pratzen heights, with Liechtenstein's Austrian cuirassiers filling the gap between the lines. Shortly after noon, however, this last line on the heights crumbled

The Battle's Climax: The Pratzen Heights

The rapid defeat of the astonished Russians of the 4th Column between 9:30 and 10:00 had left the divisions of St Hilaire and Vandamme in control of the western edge of the Pratzen Heights. This victory, however, was only the end of the beginning of the struggle to control this key position. To the south, the defeat of the Russian advance guard, along with the grenadiers sent to support them, had left the majority of St Hilaire's division facing northeast. In the north, Vandamme's action against Miloradovich's forces had occurred south and west of the Stare Vinohrady, leaving that prominence unoccupied. To consolidate their position on the heights, the crest of the heights had to be secured. This meant not only retaining the Pratzeberg, but also seizing the Stare Vinohrady.

The allies also were well aware of the strategic significance of the two high points on the plateau. To counter the two French divisions moving onto the plateau, the Austrians of the 4th Column had been divided in two parts, one sent to support the action on the Pratzeberg and the other to defend the Stare Vinohrady. The leading Austrian battalions, under the direct command of Kollowrath, had taken position behind Miloradovich's line, their right anchored in the vineyards of the Stare Vinohrady and the left stretching out to the south. The remainder of the Austrian forces marched directly toward Thiébault's brigade between Pratze village and the Pratzeberg. With Miloradovich's advance guard routed and the remainder of his command overwhelmed and soon to be sent reeling to the rear, Kollowrath's Austrians were all that prevented the French from immediately splitting the allied army in two.

The Austrians of the 4th Column consisted of eight regular battalions and seven reserve battalions of questionable combat value, and were the last forces Kutuzov had to oppose the twenty French battalions of St Hilaire and Vandamme until Miloradovich's shattered Russian units could reform. The Austrians advanced onto the heights in two lines of march and Kollowrath ordered them to deploy into three lines of battle as they drew up behind Miloradovich's position. The Salzburg IR 23, heading Rottermund's first line of march, faced right and moved into position behind Miloradovich's Russians, replacing the Little Russia Grenadiers who had moved southward against St Hilaire to shore up the collapsing left flank. The Salzburg Regiment's commander, Colonel Sterndahl, took command of this line under the direct supervision of Kollowrath. The two leading battalions of the second line of march also faced right and took position behind Sterndahl's men, while the remaining battalions of the first line of march drew into the second line to the right of these two battalions, with Rottermund assuming command of the second line. The remaining five battalions of the second line of march constituted the third line of battle, commanded by Jurczik, and pressed forward toward the Pratzeberg to support the hard-pressed Russians there. Kutuzov and much of the Russian staff rode forward with Jurczik's brigade, which was sighted by the French shortly after the collapse of Miloradovich's line and its retreat behind Kollowrath's Austrians. The Austrians had arrived in the nick of time and it seemed that Kollowrath's fifteen battalions, composed largely of recruits, held the fate of the allied army in their hands.*

---

* The more common interpretation is that Rottermund's first column of march (eight battalions) was directed toward the Stare Vinohrady and Jurczik's second column of march on the Pratzeberg. However, Major Mahler of IR 49 explicitly describes three lines of battle, his own battalion being in the third line commanded by Jurczik and the first line commanded by "acting brigadier" Sterndahl. This is consistent with French accounts describing a line of Austrian troops behind the Salzburg IR 23 at the Stare Vinohrady. From this evidence, in the initial deployment only five battalions marched on the Pratzeberg while ten battalions defended the Stare Vinohrady position against Vandamme's division. Mahler, p. 520; "Rapport de la bataille d'Austerlitz par Soult," in *Relations et Rapports*, p. 20.

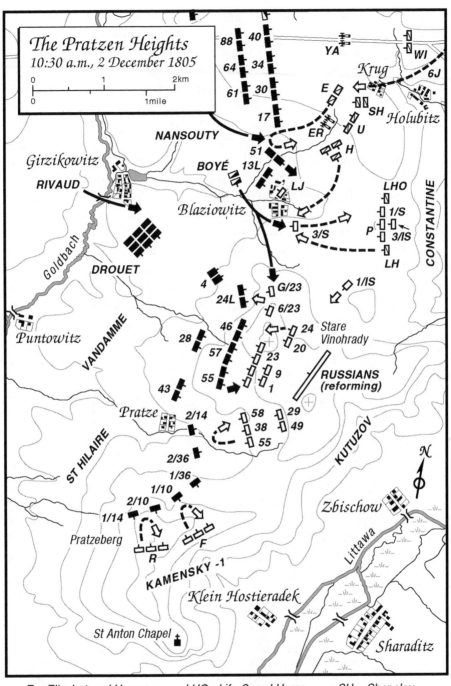

The Pratzen Heights
10:30 a.m., 2 December 1805

0   1   2km
0   1mile

YA   WI
Krug   6J
88 40
64 34   E
61 30   SH
17   ER   U   Holubitz
NANSOUTY   H
51   LHO
BOYÉ 13L   LJ   1/S
Girzikowitz   P   3/IS
RIVAUD   Blaziowitz   CONSTANTINE
3/S   LH
DROUET   1/IS
4   G/23   Stare
24L   6/23   Vinohrady
Goldbach   46   24
Puntowitz   28   23   20
VANDAMME   57   RUSSIANS
55   9   (reforming)
43   1
Pratze   58   29
2/14   38   49
55
2/36
1/36   Zbischow
1/10   N
2/10   Littawa
1/14   F
Pratzeberg   R
KAMENSKY -1
Klein Hostieradek
St Anton Chapel   Sharaditz

E = Elisabetgrad Hussars   LHO= Life Guard Horse   SH = Shepelev
ER = Ermolov Battery   LJ = Life Guard Jäger   U = Uvarov
F = Fanagoria   P = Preobrazhensky   WI= Wittgenstein
H = Hohenlohe   R = Ryazhsk   YA = Yashvil Battery
IS = Ismailovsky   S = Semenovsky   6J = 6th Jäger
LH = Life Guard Hussars

The French, however, knew before Kutuzov and Kollowrath that other allied reinforcements were at hand. To the south, GM Kamensky-1 had heard the fighting starting up near Pratze. Demonstrating excellent initiative, Kamensky immediately notified Langeron of the fighting on the heights and countermarched toward the Pratzeberg with his two regiments. The leading elements of his brigade approached Morand's single battalion of the 10th Light on the Pratzeberg around 10:00. Morand immediately reported the approach of the enemy column to St Hilaire, who faced the 1st/10th Light and the 1st/36th Line from northeast to southeast, and placed three of his divisional guns under Morand's command.

No sooner had this adjustment begun than some men of the 2nd/36th Line positioned in the Pratze village church reported the approach of a column from the north. According to Thiébault, there was some doubt whether the column was Austrian or Bavarian, causing both Thiébault and St Hilaire to pause and observe the approaching column.[*] With three of his five available battalions already deploying to oppose Kamensky-1's six battalions, only two battalions remained with Thiébault to oppose this new force. Thiébault deployed his three 8-pounders to the right of the 2nd/36th Line while the 2nd/14th Line took position to the left of the 2nd/36th at the end of the thin line.

> I ordered the 36th to deploy with all speed [Thiébault wrote] resting on Morand's regiment so as to form a pivot about which I might maneuver, and placed the 2nd Battalion of the 14th in column on the left of my line, so as to have a mass which I could oppose, if necessary, to those which were advancing toward us and a force with which I could, without disturbing my line, meet any cavalry or other corps that might try to surround us.[†]

As the Austrians drew closer and began to deploy, Chef de Bataillon Fontenoy arrived with six 12-pounders from the 4th Corps artillery reserve, yet another example of the fortunate timing that the French were to enjoy all day. St Hilaire deployed Fontenoy's artillery in two batteries of three guns each on either end of the 36th Line. "With my line thus bristling at three points," Thiébault stated, "I masked my guns with squads of infantry and galloped off at full speed to reconnoiter the newcomers."[‡]

---

[*] Thiébault did not explain why either he or St Hilaire might have thought that Bavarians would have been approaching from the northeast, but he went on to describe St Hilaire hesitating while the wise Thiébault offered the correct interpretation—that the approaching troops were Austrian. This is one of many similar events related by Thiébault in which he demonstrates his superiority to his commanding officer and must be taken as self-promotion of questionable veracity. St Hilaire was a capable and experienced officer who likely needed little advice from a braggart like Thiébault.

[†] Thiébault, II, p. 161.

[‡] Ibid.

As Kamensky-1's leading battalions were deploying to engage the 2nd/10th Light on the Pratzeberg, Thiébault and Morand, who had ridden in the same direction to observe the Austrian column, observed an officer from the approaching column ride to converse with an officer detached from Kamensky's column. This removed any lingering doubts the French generals might have had as to the column's identity:

> Returning to my line, I amended my arrangements [Thiébault continued]. I bade Major Fontenoy . . . load all the guns with roundshot and grape, and to his remark that this would ruin them I added, "It will be all right if they last ten minutes." I had them laid for a distance of thirty or forty meters, and had ten cases of grape and ten roundshot laid by each.*

The result of St Hilaire's dispositions left the two battalions of the 10th Light on the Pratzeberg facing roughly southeast with three 6-pounders positioned between the battalions. To their left stood three of Fontenoy's 12-pounders and the 1st/36th Line which occupied the corner of the L-shaped French position. Facing northeast were Thiébault's three 6-pounders to the left of the 1st/36th Line, followed by the 2nd/36th, the remaining three 12-pounders of Fontenoy and the 2nd/14th standing north of Pratze village. To the left of the 2nd/14th, Varé's brigade stood some distance away operating in conjunction with Vandamme's division. In all, St Hilaire had approximately 4,000 men deployed in the open in a single line with no reserve save the 1st/14th Line which was rallying in the rear. Engaging him were Kamensky's six battalions, roughly 3,000 men, and five Austrian battalions totaling another 2,500 men. Aside from occupying the high ground, there was little else to aid in the French defense of their position.

To the north, Vandamme had immediately launched an attack on the Austrian line as Miloradovich's Russians withdrew behind it. Although Soult's report stated that Schiner's brigade quickly cut the Austrians to pieces and forced their line back without firing a shot, the reality seems to have been a good deal more intense with the Austrians putting up fierce resistance. In the face of the initial French assault on their position, the Austrian line held firm. On the northern end of the line, near the Stare Vinohrady, Schiner's first assault faltered and the Austrian Lt-Col Hubler led the Grenadier Battalion of the Salzburg IR 23 in a counterattack with bayonets, driving a part of the French infantry off to the northwest. The grenadiers, and their regiment's 6th Battalion which was nearby, were then charged and forced back in disorder by some of Boyé's dragoons (as already described on p. 184).

---

* Thiébault, II, p. 162.

On the heights, Kollowrath reacted quickly, ordering the 6th Battalion, Auersperg IR 24, to plug the gap separating Hubler's battalion from the main line and to rescue Hubler. With the advance of the recruits of IR 24, Hubler was able to disengage from the French dragoons and draw back into line with the remainder of his battalion, leaving a large number of men dead and over 100, mostly wounded, as prisoners of the French.*

Hubler's counterattack, though costly, had blunted Schiner's advance and provided time for Miloradovich's Russian battalions to rally. The Novgorod Musketeers had largely ceased to exist, with the two musketeer battalions, which had been the first to be routed that morning, having fled to Krenowitz and the grenadier battalion having been surrounded and captured almost to a man. The remaining nine Russian battalions reformed behind Kollowrath's Austrians. With 6th/IR 24 advancing into what was now the first line, Miloradovich placed his steadiest battalions in the second line alongside the remaining Austrian battalions, holding the remainder in reserve.†

As the situation stabilized on his left, Vandamme detached the 2nd/4th Line toward Blaziowitz and then addressed the Austrian line in front of him. The key to the Austrian position was the Stare Vinohrady anchoring their line just to the north of center.‡ As the Austrian incursion toward Blaziowitz had been crushed by Boyé's dragoons, Vandamme shifted his forces northward to bring them to bear in a converging attack on the Austrian right. On the far left, Vandamme reinforced GdB Schiner with the 1st/4th Line and ordered him to attack the Austrian position from the northwest. GdB Ferey would simultaneously attack with his own brigade (57th and 46th Line) and the 55th Line drawn from Varé's brigade. Candras remained in reserve behind Ferey with the 28th Line. Varé, with only the two battalions of the 43rd Line, would stretch to link Vandamme's left to St Hilaire's right, which was anchored in Pratze. By drawing half of Varé's brigade into the action at the Stare Vinohrady, Vandamme had unwittingly removed any chance for St Hilaire to recall any portion of Varé's brigade to meet the unexpected threat posed by Kamensky.

As Vandamme's forces moved into position, the two opposing forces assembling on the heights were both deployed in a mirror image of each other,

---

* French reports claimed several hundred prisoners. IR 23 reported a total of 27 dead, 160 wounded, 245 prisoners and 797 missing. Some of the missing may have been among the prisoners taken by the French near Blaziowitz. Anonymous, *Geschichte der k. und k. Infanterieregiments Markgraf von Baden No. 23*, p. 720.

† There does not appear to be any Russian account of which battalions were rallied or where they were placed. Miloradovich's report only provides a vague idea of the deployment and regimental histories provide no additional details.

‡ From most accounts it seems that the Austrian force only occupied the Stare Vinohrady. However, given the fact that the first line was composed of six battalions and the Stare Vinohrady was but a small promontory, it is probable that the Austrian line stretched to the south and maintained contact with the other Austrian battalions engaging Thiébault's forces near Pratze.

with stronger forces massed to their left against the weaker part of their enemies' line. In the south, the allies opposed St Hilaire's 4,000 defending the Pratzeberg with approximately 5,500, while on the northern end of the plateau Vandamme was massing 7,000 men against approximately 5,000 Austrians around the Stare Vinohrady. The results of these two actions would decide the control of the Pratzen plateau and with it the fate of the allied army.

The opening clash of the next phase of fighting on the Pratzen Heights occurred near the Pratzeberg as the first of Kamensky's battalions arrived. Unaware of the disaster that had befallen Miloradovich's advance guard, Kamensky immediately deployed his leading battalions and they advanced to engage the French occupying the Pratzeberg. Although the 2nd/10th Light was outnumbered initially, Morand's men took advantage of their superior marksmanship, a legacy of their intensive training at the camp of Boulogne, to stop the Russians in their tracks. The Russians returned fire as best they could, but their lack of adequate musketry training coupled with the shock of a strong French column appearing on their rear reduced their effectiveness, while the French fire began inflicting serious casualties.

As the 1st/10th Light and the 1st/36th drew into line adjacent to the 2nd/10th Light, additional Russian battalions were also deploying to counter them. Kamensky, seeing an opportunity on the other side, deployed the leading battalion of the Ryazhsk Musketeers to turn Morand's right flank. The Russian maneuver caused the 2nd/10th Light to pull back slightly and might have produced a serious reverse and won the Pratzeberg for the Russians if not for the arrival of the 1st/14th Line, which had finally rallied after being routed at Pratze. St Hilaire directed this battalion on the extreme right of the French line to counter the Russian threat and the 1st/14th surged forward, the men eager to redeem themselves for their earlier embarrassment. The arrival of the 1st/14th stabilized Morand's line and arrested the forward progress of the Ryazhsk Musketeers. By 10:30 Kamensky's battalions had engaged the full length of Morand's line and were getting the worst of the resulting firefight as the French infantry and artillery took a heavy toll.

> Soon, the French lines initiated a very sharp and very murderous fire of musket and canister upon the brigade of Kamensky which in a moment had many men rendered *hors de combat*. [Kamensky's brigade] answered with a less sharp and badly directed fire; the majority of our soldiers fired in the air . . . in justice I ought to say that despite the critical situation they found themselves in, despite the superior number of the enemy, despite their little experience of war and the effect on them of an unforeseen attack on their rear, despite the noise of gunfire, which many

of them were hearing for the first time, they maintained themselves admirably for nearly two hours and in these two hours more than half of the two regiments were left lying dead.[*]

To the north of the Russians, Kutuzov had joined General Jurczik and shortly after 10:00 the Austrian battalions at the head of Jurczik's brigade were deploying to attack Thiébault's small force. Jurczik's three leading battalions—the 6th Battalion of Reuss-Greitz IR 55, and the 3rd Battalions of Württemberg IR 38 and Beaulieu IR 58—advanced against Thiébault's position while Jurczik's two remaining battalions. the 6th Battalions of Kerpen IR 49 and Lindenau IR 29, remained in reserve on a low rise to the rear. Thiébault watched the Austrians advance, instructing his men to hold their fire until the Austrians had closed to thirty or forty meters. Once the Austrians were in close range, the French batteries were unmasked and their fire ripped into the Austrian ranks with devastating effect. The Austrian advance slowed and then halted as Thiébault's men poured round after round into their ranks. As with Kamensky's Russians, the Austrians were incapable of matching the disciplined fire of the French and their ranks were thinned at an alarming rate while they inflicted far fewer casualties on their enemy. As the Austrian attack stalled, Thiébault ordered his infantry to attack.

Major Mahler, commanding the 6th Battalion of IR 49, described the action from the Austrian perspective:

> For defense against attack [by the French on the heights] I led my battalion, formed in mass, upon the aforementioned hill, and advanced to the front to cover where we were threatened in front and flank. Our comrades of the Beaulieu Regiment [IR 58] also advanced, and I was to follow and cover their flank. When the enemy skirmishers noticed this advance, and the placing of two cannon which could cover the whole enemy line, for a while their fire died down. As I made these dispositions to advance, General Jurczik called to me loudly: "Bravo, Major Mahler!" The advance had hardly been carried out when I noticed that the enemy were about to launch a frontal attack themselves. When they began on their brief advance, I let loose an orderly discharge and brought them to a halt. In the meantime the battalion of the Beaulieu Regiment was being attacked and thrown back by the French infantry. Now I counterattacked in conjunction with a battalion of the Reuss-Greitz Regiment; as we advanced we encountered heavy fire, Captain Nigl and many other men were heavily wounded and many were killed.[†]

---

[*] Langeron, p. 75.
[†] Mahler, p. 521.

From Thiébault's account the French quickly overcame the Austrians, but the duration of the action and Mahler's description tell a different story. In vivid words, Mahler described the actions of hastily trained recruits:

> In consequence of the losses we suffered, as well as from having my left flank exposed and now threatened by the enemy, my battalion began to falter, but I urged them to remain firm and not yield. My brave adjutant, Ensign Jlljascek, saw Captain Steinberg and Lieutenant Bayer fall wounded, sprang from his horse and placed himself at the head of the formation; he drew his sword and enforced good order among the troops. *

While the allied attack on Pratze and the Pratzeberg bogged down, Vandamme was launching his attack on the key allied position at the Stare Vinohrady. Around 10:30 GdB Ferey advanced against the Austrian position with his six battalions, engaging the Austrian line frontally from the northwest. Ferey's reinforced brigade was roughly equal in number to the whole of the Austrian first line at the Stare Vinohrady. While Ferey occupied the Austrians' attention, Schiner maneuvered his three battalions into position to strike the Austrians from the north. Soon after Ferey launched his attack on the Austrian left, Schiner launched the attack on the Austrian right with two battalions of the 24th Light and one battalion of the 4th Line. Ordering his men to fix bayonets, Schiner led them forward against the Austrians of Salzburg IR 23.

For at least half an hour, intense fighting raged across the entire length of the Pratzen heights from the Stare Vinohrady to the Pratzeberg. At the Pratzeberg, Langeron arrived to investigate the alarming reports he had received from an officer sent by Lt-Col Balk of the St Petersburg Dragoons.[†] Balk had sent the officer to Langeron for orders after Kutuzov had ordered Balk's detachment to join the 2nd Column. When the officer returned to the heights, St Hilaire's forces were already on the heights to their rear. Balk immediately sent the officer back to Langeron to report that a French column was attacking the Pratzen Heights in force and then joined his small force to Kamensky-1's brigade, though his few hundred cavalry failed to make any significant contribution to the action. As the breathless officer returned to Langeron at Sokolnitz, Langeron dismissed the officer's report of a French

---

* Ibid.

† Kutuzov had ordered Balk's cavalry detachment, two squadrons of St Petersburg Dragoons and two squadrons of Isayev Cossacks, to join Langeron's 2nd Column at Sokolnitz. Balk's command had been detached from the portion of 5th Column that had become entangled with the 2nd Column in the confusion early that morning. Langeron identifies GM Shepelev, *shef* of the St Petersburg Dragoons, as the Russian general who obstinately insisted that his regiment was in the correct position.

column attacking Pratze as an exaggeration of a French raid, sending him back with instructions to Balk to investigate the report. Almost immediately after he left, another officer arrived with a report from Kamensky giving details of the French attack. In the face of this disturbing news from Kamensky, Langeron had ridden off to investigate.

The situation Langeron found was utterly unexpected. When Langeron arrived (around 10:30), Kamensky's forces were faltering after an unequal firefight of at least 15–20 minutes and the Austrians to their right were falling back after the failure of their first advance.

> When I joined Count Kamensky he had deployed his brigade with its back turned to our columns [the 2nd and 3rd], and within 200 paces of him, the enemy had also deployed two to three lines of infantry which overflowed ours and were placed precisely in the camp we had just left. At the bottom, close to Sbetzau [Zbischow] and Hostieradek, I saw some battalions that had withdrawn in disorder, pursued by the enemy columns. They were the Austrians; I could not understand how they were then so far from the point of attack that had been indicated to them.*

Recognizing the futility of engaging in a duel of musketry with the better-trained French infantry, Langeron immediately ordered Kamensky's first line to fix bayonets. Placing himself at their head (according to his own account), Langeron led them in a furious charge against the French line. Helped by the impetus of the Russian charge, the attackers got the best of the ensuing mêlée, pushing the French back and one of the battalions nearly gaining the Pratzeberg.

> The 1st [Grenadier] Battalion of Fanagoria advanced vigorously against the enemy line, having at its head Major Brandt, who was wounded. It took two guns, but the French were too much more numerous, and the battalion was obliged to retreat leaving behind the captured guns.†

Morand, with St Hilaire himself also present, led the counter-charge that regained the original French position and then closed to within some 200 paces of the Russian defensive line. In the wake of the failed assault, Langeron sent an officer to Buxhöwden describing the situation and urgently requesting reinforcements.

Kutuzov, meanwhile, had sent his capable staff officer, GM Volkonsky, with instructions to coordinate a combined assault by the Russians on the left and the Austrians on the right. But while Jurczik and Kamensky reformed their

---

* Langeron, p. 74. In his official report Langeron said the distance between the lines was 300 paces.
† Ibid., p. 46.

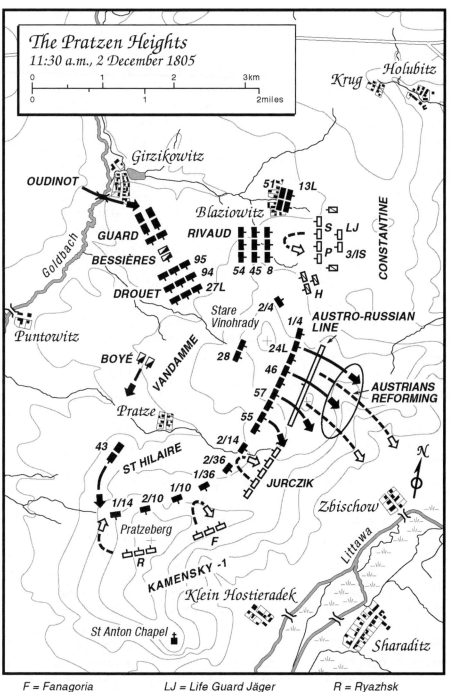

The Pratzen Heights
11:30 a.m., 2 December 1805

0   1   2   3km
0   1   2miles

Krug

Holubitz

Girzikowitz

OUDINOT

Blaziowitz

51   13L

GUARD

RIVAUD

CONSTANTINE

BESSIÈRES

95

S   LJ

94   54 45 8

P   3/IS

DROUET

27L

Goldbach

H

Puntowitz

Stare
Vinohrady

2/4

1/4

AUSTRO-RUSSIAN
LINE

BOYÉ

28

24L

VANDAMME

46

AUSTRIANS
REFORMING

57

Pratze

55

N

2/14

43

2/36

ST HILAIRE

1/36

JURCZIK

1/14   2/10   1/10

Zbischow

Pratzeberg

F

Littawa

R

KAMENSKY -1

Klein Hostieradek

Sharaditz

St Anton Chapel

F = Fanagoria   LJ = Life Guard Jäger   R = Ryazhsk
IS = Ismailovsky   P = Preobrazhensky   S = Semenovsky
H = Hohenlohe

troops for a renewed attack, Langeron observed a confused movement beyond them in the distance—Kollowrath's Austrians had finally broken and were retreating in disorder behind Miloradovich's Austro-Russian line.

The Austrian withdrawal had occurred after nearly an hour of intense fighting in and around the Stare Vinohrady. Ferey's men had slowly forced back the Austrian battalions in the south while Schiner's battalions had gradually bent back the Austrian right wing. Vandamme's divisional artillery took position and ripped into the Austrian ranks with canister at close range. Part or all of Boyé's dragoons had also joined Vandamme's division after cutting up the Grenadier Battalion of IR 23 and waited for opportunities on the Austrian right flank.

Making good use of his numerical superiority, Vandamme extended his frontage to bring greater pressure on Kollowrath's flanks. Finally, after about an hour of fighting, Austrian resistance crumbled. The fire on their flanks intensified and French cavalry attacked the regiment, throwing it into disorder. A large number of Austrian prisoners fell into the hands of the French and many simply fled. The artillery supporting the regiment (battalion gun's and Kudriatsev's Russian position battery) was also overrun by the French cavalry and many of the guns could not be withdrawn, their exhausted horse teams being unable to pull them through the deep mud that clung to their wheels. The French breakthrough appears to have begun on the Austrian right and, as the right of the line crumbled, the other Austrian battalions fell back in succession until Kollowrath ordered the entire line to withdraw around 11:00.*

In its stubborn defense, the Salzburg IR 23 suffered losses amounting to 1,229 killed, captured, missing or wounded, nearly 45 percent of its numbers. The victorious French surged onto the crest of the heights with a cheer, occupying the key ground that gave the French forces a secure position controlling the crest of the plateau from the Stare Vinohrady to the Pratzeberg.

Despite the Austrian withdrawal occurring to the right, Kutuzov ordered the attack on the Pratzeberg to proceed, hoping to recover the crest of the heights in the south and with it a position from which he could prevent disaster from falling on his army. With Jurczik and Volkonsky at their heads, the Austrian and Russian columns surged forward with the bayonet to be met with a withering fire from the French, dropping many Austrian and Russian soldiers and mortally wounding General Jurczik. The attack faltered and the allied infantry fell back yet again. With Vandamme's forces now advancing against Miloradovich's line, Kutuzov ordered a final charge against their

---

* Anonymous, *Geschichte der k. und k. Infanterieregiments Markgraf von Baden No. 23* (Budapest: 1911), pp. 717–20.

weakening enemy. Again Volkonsky led the allied forces forward, hoping finally to break through, but though the French had sustained heavy losses their fire remained steady and their line held firm. With the ground in front of the French line littered with Russian and Austrian dead and allied morale flagging, Langeron ordered Kamensky to hold his position and refuse his right in order to cover Augezd. Langeron then rode off on a desperate mission to Tellnitz to demand reinforcements from the 1st Column.

The defeat of Kollowrath's line and the simultaneous failure of the allies to retake the Pratzeberg marked the complete success of the first phase of Napoleon's plan of battle. Despite encountering a strong allied column where none was expected, the heights had been secured by two hours of intense fighting. Casualties on both sides had been severe, and while Kutuzov ordered the last desperate attempt to drive the French off the Pratzeberg to recover some advantage on the heights, Vandamme paused to regroup his weary and disordered battalions.

Observing from his command post on the Zuran Hill, Napoleon had suddenly lost sight of Vandamme's men as they surged over the crest of the heights. With his initial objectives achieved, the French emperor issued orders for the next phase of his plan, ordering the bulk of his reserve—the two divisions of Bernadotte's I Corps and the Imperial Guard—to advance. On the left, GdD Rivaud's division marched on Blaziowitz. On Rivaud's right, GdD Drouet advanced to reinforce St Hilaire, directing his march between the Stare Vinohrady and Pratze. Finally, behind Drouet, the twenty battalions of the Imperial Guard and Oudinot's grenadiers stirred from their position near the Zuran Hill and began crossing the Goldbach. As the powerful French reserves advanced, Napoleon with his staff and escort rode ahead of them to establish a new command post on the Stare Vinohrady from which point the entire Pratzen Heights would be visible.

While Napoleon and the French reserves ascended the heights, St Hilaire and Vandamme consolidated their positions. The Austrian withdrawal had shortened the allied line, which now ran roughly in a straight line from east of the Stare Vinohrady to Kamensky-1's position east of the Pratzeberg. Vandamme ordered Varé with the 43rd Line to march to St Hilaire's aid while he formed the remainder of his command to attack Miloradovich's line of shaken and battered Russians and Austrian recruits. With Rivaud's division now advancing toward Blaziowitz, Vandamme recalled the 2nd/4th Line to rejoin the division.

The final allied defense of the Pratzen Heights constituted nothing more than a last desperate attempt to block the French advance with exhausted and demoralized men. The composition and deployment of the allied line is not clear, but it appears to have included most of Miloradovich's Russian battalions.[*] These were supported by the reserve battalions of Kollowrath's force on the right and the Austrians of Jurczik on the left, who were still engaged against Thiébault's men. Flagging morale and heavy losses among the battalions made the last allied line on the heights shaky at best.

Vandamme's columns again engaged the Russians and Austrians in their final defensive stand on the Pratzen Heights between about 11:15 and 11:30. Vandamme ordered his men forward and the victorious French made short work of the shaken enemy in front of them. Miloradovich attempted to rally his Russians behind the remnants of the Salzburg IR 23 that Kollowrath was attempting to form in line, but Kollowrath's men had not had enough time to recover and attempts to maintain an orderly retreat failed. Within 20–30 minutes the third allied line had been swept away and the Austrians and Russians alike were fleeing from the heights toward Krenowitz and Zbischow in a confused mass.

To the south, Kutuzov watched the defeat of Miloradovich and Kollowrath and observed the leading elements of the 7,000 fresh French troops of Drouet's division arriving on the western edge of the heights between Pratze village and the Stare Vinohrady. The final charge on St Hilaire's position had failed and the hopelessness of retaining any hold on the heights was now all too clear. Further, Thiébault had resumed the offensive as Vandamme's forces advanced against the final allied position.

Major Mahler provided a vivid description of the final action of the Austrians of Jurczik's brigade:

> Now the battalion of the Reuss-Greitz Regiment standing beside me also began to retreat, while the commandant of the battalion, Lieutenant-Colonel Scovaud, was severely wounded by a gunshot to the belly and backbone. I was now almost completely alone and left with only a few remaining men formed in a mass. I already had one officer and 72 men dead, two officers and over 100 men wounded and finally 50 men captured . . . the battalion, which had been 312 strong before the battle, amounted now to hardly 80 men.[†]

---

[*] The three battalions of Monakhtin's advance guard had routed in the initial engagement and attempts to rally them by Miloradovich and even Alexander had failed as they streamed past the senior officers with the 4th Column. Secondary accounts have interpreted this to mean that these forces refused to rally for the rest of the day. This is not supported by any after-action reports and in fact the only unit that appears to have been absent in this last phase of the action on the Pratzen is the Grenadier Battalion of the Novgorod Musketeers which was surrounded and almost entirely captured after the rout of Monakhtin's advance guard. However, it should be added that all these battalions, weak before the battle had begun, had lost heavily and were thoroughly demoralized.

[†] Mahler, p. 522.

Around noon, as the confused mass of Miloradovich's line merged with the Austrians behind them and dissolved into a rout, Kutuzov calmly ordered Miloradovich and Kollowrath to withdraw toward Krenowitz and Zbischow, hoping to hold the route open for the withdrawal of the allied army toward Hungary. Kutuzov issued similar orders to the forces under his direct command, the Austrians of Jurczik's brigade and the Russians of Kamensky-1, to retreat toward Zbischow and Klein Hostieradek. Kutuzov also sent an officer to Grand Duke Constantine instructing him to retire on Krenowitz to safeguard the right of the fleeing 4th Column. The sounds of firing on the northern end of the Pratzen heights slowly died down as Vandamme's exhausted troops caught their breath. Jurczik's Austrians managed to disengage from Thiébault's brigade in reasonably good order and presented at least some small protection for the remainder of the 4th Column along with Wodniansky's two squadrons of Johann Dragoons and Rakovsky's three squadrons of light cavalry.*

Kamensky, however, was faced with a fresh crisis. Varé and the 43rd Line, had marched from a position northeast of Pratze to the extreme right of St Hilaire's line just south of the Pratzeberg. In addition, Boyé's dragoons, sent by Napoleon to reinforce St Hilaire after the French seizure of Blaziowitz, had now arrived on the heights. With reinforcements at hand, Morand's men made a fresh effort, engaging Kamensky's men as they tried to withdraw. The 43rd, arriving on the left of the Ryazhsk Musketeers, turned the Russian left flank while Boyé's dragoons threatened to encircle them. By 12:30, Kamensky's brigade, which had bought the 4th Column a fighting chance for survival, was in danger of envelopment. With 1,200 men and 30 officers dead and wounded from three hours of desperate fighting, the remnants of the Ryazhsk Musketeers and Fanagoria Grenadiers finally broke and fled toward Klein Hostieradek, with Balk's small cavalry force covering the retreat as best it could.

The fighting on the Pratzen Heights between 9:00 and noon had marked the climax of the Battle of Austerlitz. More so than any other part of the battle, the fighting on the Pratzen Heights demonstrated the mismatch between the armies, pitting some of the weakest battalions of the allied armies against some of the best of the French Army. Despite this, the allies held the French back for a surprisingly long time, demonstrating a toughness and resilience for which they rarely receive credit. Miloradovich and Kollowrath, abruptly thrust into an impromptu defense of the heights, scrambled to put up three

---

* Rakovsky's three squadrons had started the day near Holubitz and were ordered to rejoin Kienmayer near Tellnitz. This force was crossing the Pratzen Heights just as the French attack on the heights began, and Kutuzov had joined them to the 4th Column. Treuenfest, *Geschichte des k.k. 11. Huszaren-Regimentes*, p. 232.

reasonably solid lines of defense. To the south, Kamensky-1 demonstrated excellent initiative, which was rare among allied commanders during the day of battle, his troops fighting well despite being severely outclassed by the French musketry. Finally, the Austrians of Jurczik and Rottermund performed better than could be expected of a force that was half composed of raw conscripts. Ultimately, however, the superb performance of the French facing them made their brave attempts futile.

For the French there is little to criticize. The appearance of a strong allied column on the heights was as much a surprise to the French as the abrupt appearance of the French columns out of the mist was to the allies. Better discipline and training, however, allowed St Hilaire to hold superior numbers of the enemy at bay while Vandamme massed for a crushing blow on the allied right. In the end, the confidence of the French troops remained unshaken and even battalions severely depleted by casualties could resume the offensive when called upon to do so.

The importance of possession of the Pratzen Heights to the allied army appears to have been recognized by the allied commanders witnessing the action there, but down in the Goldbach valley, Buxhöwden and Prshibysshevsky in particular remained focused on pursuing the original objectives issued to them. Kutuzov's failure to issue direct orders for reinforcements appears to have been due to his replacement as *de facto* commander of the army by Alexander and his entourage which left him in a position where he had to request support from his fellow column commanders. Alexander's failure to issue any orders of any kind appears to have resulted from his complete lack of experience. As a result, the lack of any higher-level command left the allied army to drift into disaster. Nowhere was this more evident than in the actions of the first three allied columns in the valley of the lower Goldbach.

The Struggle for Sokolnitz

To the south of the Pratzen Heights, the 2nd and 3rd Columns had continued their attempt to drive west from Sokolnitz, apparently in complete ignorance of the broader conflict evolving around them. By 9:30, the success of the allied attack on Sokolnitz had left the 2nd and 3rd Columns with the majority of their forces on the right bank of the Goldbach and in a position to begin their advance toward Turas in concert with the 1st Column to the south. First, however, Langeron and Prshibysshevsky had to sort out their battalions which had become intermingled during the final attack on Sokolnitz. The French forces defending Sokolnitz had been driven off in two directions, one portion to the south and the other northwest toward Turas. Their small number made it unlikely that they would be able to launch an immediate counterattack. Langeron kept the three battalions of his second line (two of Perm and one of Kursk) between the Goldbach and the village while the battalions that had been involved in the attack on Sokolnitz regrouped south and west of the village. Prshibyshevsky reformed the five battalions of the 3rd Column that had been involved in the attack on Sokolnitz north of the village.

While the Russian forces were regrouping for their advance into the French rear toward Turas, Langeron had received the first report from Balk concerning events on the heights. Balk's officer had arrived at Sokolnitz requesting orders from Langeron shortly after 9:00. Roughly one hour later the same officer returned to Langeron with news that the French had attacked the heights in force. Dismissing this as exaggeration, Langeron sent the officer back to Balk:

> This news did not seem believable to me [wrote Langeron], seeing on my right the column of Prshibyshevsky, which had passed by Pratzen [sic], knowing that [the column] of Kollowrath and Miloradovich was to the right of Prshibyshevsky and also had to cross Pratzen to get to Kobelnitz, it did not appear probable to me that the French were already in the camp which we had just left.*

Balk's aide having been dismissed, another breathless staff officer rode up to Langeron moments later, this one sent by Kamensky-1, with the same news. Leaving Olsufiev in command of the column, Langeron rode off with Kamensky-1's staff officer to observe first-hand what was occurring on the heights. "This second opinion confirming the first seemed most important and I did not hesitate a moment to go to join Count Kamensky."† Almost immediately after Langeron left, all hell broke loose at Sokolnitz.

Lacking cavalry to reconnoiter the western approaches to Sokolnitz and apparently also lacking the foresight at least to push out infantry patrols—failings that must be assigned equally to Langeron and Olsufiev—Olsufiev proceeded with the task of reforming his units. Langeron and Olsufiev appear to have both suffered from considerable overconfidence and assumed that the defeat of the French in Sokolnitz meant that they were in full retreat. Lulled into a false sense of security, for nearly thirty minutes they proceeded to reform their battalions in the open ground west of the village in what appears to have been a leisurely fashion while the second line, which had not been involved in the attack on the village, remained between Sokolnitz and the Goldbach.

While neither Langeron nor Olsufiev made any attempt to secure the high

* Langeron, p. 71.
† Ibid., p. 72.

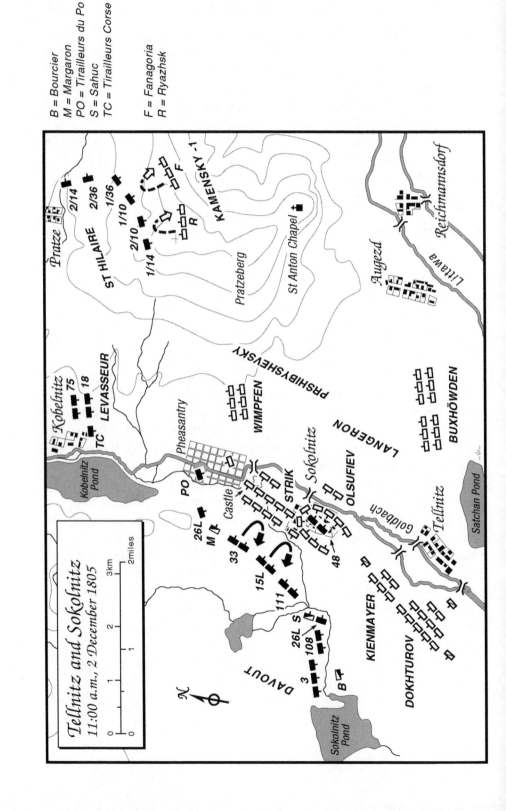

B = Bourcier
M = Margaron
PO = Tirailleurs du Po
S = Sahuc
TC = Tirailleurs Corse

F = Fanagoria
R = Ryazhsk

Tellnitz and Sokolnitz
11:00 a.m., 2 December 1805

Pratze

ST HILAIRE
2/14
2/36
1/36
1/10
2/10
1/14

KAMENSKY - 1
F
R

Pratzeberg

St Anton Chapel

Augezd

Reichmannsdorf

Littawa

PRSHIBYSHEVSKY

WIMPFEN

LANGERON

BUXHÖWDEN

Kobelnitz
75
18
TC
LEVASSEUR

Kobelnitz
Pond

Pheasantry

PO

Castle

STRIK

Sokolnitz

OLSUFIEV

Goldbach

Tellnitz

Satchan
Pond

26L
M

33

15L

111

26L
108
3
S
B

DAVOUT

48

KIENMAYER

DOKHTUROV

Sokolnitz
Pond

N

0   1   2   3km
0   1   2miles

ground overlooking Sokolnitz, nor advance fresh troops nor withdraw their men to a more secure position, to their right Prshibyshevsky demonstrated more foresight. Apparently detecting the approach of Friant's division and coming under fire from French artillery, Prshibyshevsky realized the vulnerability of his forces north and west of Sokolnitz. He therefore withdrew those battalions involved in the attack on Sokolnitz to a more secure position between the village and Sokolnitz Castle and advanced his second line to take their place:

> As my column was found in an exposed position [wrote Prshibyshevsky in his report], so that the fire of the enemy battery should not do so much harm I ordered my troops to move toward the castle toward the point of passage [over the Goldbach] while I myself, with the regiments of Narva and Butyrsk, immediately passed forward through the castle against the reinforced enemy; and at the same time ordered General-Lieutenant Wimpfen with the regiments of Azov and Podolsk, forming the reserve, to remain behind until receiving further orders.*

Neither the fog nor the powder smoke that must have still lingered in the valley can excuse Olsufiev's complete surprise in the face of an attack he had half an hour to prepare for.

While the 26th Light had indeed been soundly defeated and was not in any condition to oppose the allied forces arrayed around Sokolnitz, GdD Friant with GdB Lochet's brigade was nearing Sokolnitz. As they approached the village from the west, it seems likely that they met some elements of the 26th Light and were well informed as to the strength and situation of the allied forces. Although considerably outnumbered by the allied forces at Sokolnitz, Friant did not hesitate to attack in order to forestall any allied advance west of the Goldbach. Lochet's brigade consisted of four battalions of the 48th and 111th Line, totaling about 1,350 men. Olsufiev had nine battalions west of the Goldbach and Prshibyshevsky had as many more to the north of Sokolnitz totaling nearly 8,000 men. Like Heudelet at Tellnitz, however, Friant had the element of surprise on his side. Friant directed his leading regiment, the 48th Line, to circle slightly to the right and strike the Russians from the south. The 111th would proceed due east toward the village and join the battle to the left of the 48th. Sending word to Davout, who was accompanying Kister's brigade a short distance to the rear, Friant rode forward with his men.

Whether lingering mists and powder smoke in the valley of the Goldbach or inexcusable inattention by the Russian forces at Sokolnitz were more to blame, the Russians south of Sokolnitz were caught utterly unprepared when

---

* "Raport I. Ya. Przhibyshevskogo Aleksandru I o Deistviyakh 3-i Kolonny v Srazhenii pri Austerlitse, 1806 g. Iulya 11," in *Kutuzov Sbornik Dokumentov*, pp. 269–70.

the well-disciplined 48th, led by GdB Lochet, swept down upon them from the southwest. To their credit, the Russian troops south of the village, part of the Perm Musketeers, did not immediately break and run back across the Goldbach in the face of the onslaught. Instead, the Russian officers managed to organize a confused fighting retreat into the south end of Sokolnitz village. Friant reported that "The 48th marched on them, attacking with the bayonet, defeated them, and managed to seize the first houses on the extreme right of the village. It made astonishing progress considering its strength, because it had to attack each house individually, and it seized some in turn."[*]

Capturing two Russian standards and several guns in its assault, the 48th Line soon met determined resistance as it pushed its way into the village, with the Russians making the French fight for each house. To the northwest, the Vyborg Musketeers and 8th Jäger were alerted to the sound of firing south of Sokolnitz. Apparently unaware of the approach of the 111th Line from the east, Olsufiev immediately reacted by facing at least a portion of his battalions to the southeast to counterattack the 48th. At the same time, the battalions held in reserve between the Goldbach and the village responded by advancing from the east. Within fifteen minutes of the victorious sweep of the 48th into the south end of Sokolnitz, Russian forces had surrounded the regiment.

Once again, however, the absence of any effective allied reconnaissance or pickets left them unprepared for the arrival of Lochet's second regiment. By around 10:30 the 111th had arrived on the heights west of Sokolnitz and Friant immediately sent it into action. Charging down from the heights and into the plain west of the village, the 111th met the still-disorganized Russian forces, most likely elements of the Vyborg Musketeers and 8th Jäger, driving them into the village and to the south and taking two guns in the process. With the ground west of Sokolnitz cleared, the 111th made contact with the 48th which had been isolated for about quarter of an hour and was desperately fighting off Russians on all sides.

> The 111th Regiment [reported Friant], which had remained in line of battle at some distance behind [the 48th], went ahead at once; it charged with vigor a great mass of men advancing without order, without commanders, and making a horrible clamour; it repulsed them, then it attacked a numerous corps that marched to cut the communications of Lochet's brigade with that of General Kister, who arrived and deployed on the left.[†]

---

[*] "Le Général de Division Friant à M. le Maréchal Davout (8 décembre 1805)," in *Correspondance du Maréchal Davout, Prince d'Eckmühl, ses Commandements, son Ministère, 1801–1815* (Paris: Plon, Nourrit et cie, 1885), p. 215.

[†] Ibid.

Despite the fact that the 48th still retained its hold on the south end of Sokolnitz, stubbornly defending from the cover of the sturdy houses, the Russians in the northern part of Sokolnitz were proving themselves to be equally obstinate. The 111th, unable to dislodge the Russians from the houses on the western side of Sokolnitz began suffering increasing losses from being in the open, despite the indifferent quality of the Russian musketry.

Having recovered from the surprise and fury of the French attack, GM Olsufiev assembled his forces to strike back. Gathering fresh troops from the east of Sokolnitz, Olsufiev brought them through the village and launched them against the 111th. The composition of this force is unclear due to the confused nature of the fighting, but it appears to have included one battalion of Kursk Musketeers and one or two battalions of Perm Musketeers. The Russian attack quickly drove the 111th back to the heights west of Sokolnitz and allowed the Russian forces again to surround the 48th Line.

Friant described the fierce back-and-forth fighting around Sokolnitz:

> However, the enemy continually received many reinforcements for their line; they managed to reform their scattered and beaten troops and brought them back to the fighting for the village, in the plain and on the heights; twice in succession they were pushed back there [into the village], twice the enemy returned to the charge and managed to force us in the same way to retreat.*

By around 11:00, Olsufiev's forces were securely lodged in the northwestern part of Sokolnitz and had surrounded the 48th Line still holding the southern tip of the village.† During the fierce hour-long struggle between the forces of Olsufiev and Friant, Prshibyshevsky had remained stationary with the majority of his forces in the open ground between the village and Sokolnitz Castle. During this time, the disordered Jäger battalions and Galitz Musketeers had reformed and established a first line with its right (Galitz) anchored on Sokolnitz castle and the left (7th Jäger) extending toward Sokolnitz village. The three battalions of Butyrsk Musketeers and one battalion of Narva Musketeers stood behind them in a second line, with the remaining two Narva battalions forming the reserve. To the right of this force, a battalion of Jäger was scattered through the pheasantry in open order from

---

* Ibid., pp. 215–6.

† Colin has suggested that the 48th was surrounded for fifteen minutes. Friant's report noted that the 48th was surrounded for forty-five minutes. The 48th appears to have been isolated during the period between the initial Russian reaction and the attack of the 111th (roughly between 10:15 and 10:30). After the 111th was driven off, the 48th was isolated for an additional thirty minutes before the arrival of Kister's brigade around 11:00 which resulted in the relief of the 48th. While the 48th was not surround for the entire forty-five minutes between about 10:15 and 11:00, it was surrounded for the majority of this time. Alombert and Colin, V, p. 167.

where they exchanged fire with French skirmishers. On the left bank of the Goldbach, GL Wimpfen with the remaining six battalions covered the right rear of the column, facing the French forces at Kobelnitz.

Prshibyshevsky does not appear to have been at all aware of the events unfolding behind him on the Pratzen Heights, nor does it seem he had received any orders from Buxhöwden. Langeron, who had immediately sent word to Buxhöwden of the crisis on the heights that he had observed first-hand, expected Buxhöwden to react appropriately and issue orders to the columns assigned to him. Instead Buxhöwden had remained fixed in position, neither reacting with the forces under his immediate command nor informing the other columns making up his wing of the army. Ignorant of the larger picture and without any orders to disengage or to adopt a defensive posture at Sokolnitz, Prshibyshevsky proceeded with the execution of his orders which were to align his column with the 1st and 2nd Columns and drive the French back onto the plain of Turas. Friant's unexpected arrival had forestalled any advance and had kept Olsufiev's battalions occupied, but does not appear to have been severe enough to have required Prshibyshevsky's forces to assist in driving them back.

Around 11:00, however, Davout arrived with Kister's brigade (the rest of Friant's division). The remainder of the 15th Light (the voltigeurs of this regiment had accompanied the 108th Line to Tellnitz) headed the column followed by the two battalions of the 33rd Line—approximately 900 men. The 15th Light arrived on the heights overlooking Sokolnitz just as Olsufiev was driving back the 111th. Davout immediately sent them forward against the Russians and they swept down the hill against the right flank of the Russian forces, making contact with them near the culvert over the Sokolnitz Brook near the northwestern end of the village. The Russian troops broke off their pursuit of the 111th and fell back into the village, the 15th Light following them and penetrating the village, where the French and Russians engaged in house-to-house fighting.

> No sooner had the 15th and 33rd arrived and deployed than they marched on the enemy; nothing could resist their vigorous attack; the 15th was directed at the bridge and chased a corps ten times more numerous than they, penetrated Sokolnitz, intermingled with the Russians, slaughtering with the bayonet all that dared oppose them.[*]

Behind the 15th Light, the 33rd Line also rushed into action at the double. Davout directed it to the left of the 15th Light where it attacked the Russian

---

[*] "Le Général de Division Friant à le Maréchal Davout," *Correspondance du Maréchal Davout,* I, p. 215.

forces arrayed in the open between the village and Sokolnitz Castle. GM Strik immediately launched a counterattack with the three battalions of Galitz Musketeers in the first line to drive the French off but, under the withering French musketry, they fell back in disorder. Prshibyshevsky reinforced the Galitz Musketeers and sent Strik forward against the French once again. At the same time, Prshibyshevsky ordered several battalions of the Narva and Butyrsk Regiments to advance through the castle on the right to flank the French. While the flanking maneuver developed, Strik's forces were again beaten back, and regrouped for a third try.

While Prshibyshevsky struggled to bring his superior numbers to bear against the small but surprisingly stubborn French forces in front of him, Olsufiev was making slow but steady progress against the French in the village. Finally, after nearly thirty minutes of reducing the stubborn French defense of each house, Olsufiev managed to drive the 15th Light out of Sokolnitz and behind Sokolnitz Brook where Major Geither took refuge on the heights adjacent to the 111th Line. With the defeat of the 15th Light, the 33rd Line stood in a precarious position with its right now uncovered and Russian troops emerging from Sokolnitz Castle on its left. General Kister pulled the 33rd Line back to prevent it from being enveloped.

Strik's battalions attacked once more, driving the 15th Light and 33rd Line back to the heights, as Colin described: "The 15th had been obliged to withdraw to the heights . . . the 33rd, which was exposed and turned on this flank, was also forced to retreat."[*] To the south the 48th appears to have withdrawn from the southern end of Sokolnitz at about the same time that the 15th Light withdrew to the heights, although the exact timing of this withdrawal is not certain.[†]

By noon the French forces had fallen back to the heights overlooking Sokolnitz and for the next half hour both sides regrouped for a renewal of the battle. The 48th Line stood on the heights to the southwest, while the remainder of Friant's division stood on the heights beyond the Sokolnitz Brook. The 111th Line occupied a position almost due west of the village. To its left and extending northwards stood the 15th and 33rd. Friant assembled the other scattered battalions that had joined them behind the Sokolnitz

---

[*] Alombert and Colin, V, p. 216.

[†] Colin never mentions the withdrawal of the 48th Line from Sokolnitz, but Russian reports do not indicate any fighting in the south following the repulse of Kister's attack. If the 48th had remained in the southern end of Sokolnitz, it is puzzling that there is no mention of further fighting or any concerted effort to drive it out, as was the case with the 15th Light in the northwestern part of the village. Further, it is difficult to see how the Russian forces south of the town could have been withdrawn over the bridge east of Sokolnitz without interference considering that they would have had to pass within range of any French infantry lodged in the southern end of the village.

Brook and formed them north of the 33rd Line in preparation for a concerted attack on the allied positions at Sokolnitz. It appears that a portion of the 26th Light and the Tirailleurs du Po occupied the pheasantry to the left of the 33rd Line and continued skirmishing with the Russian Jäger there. On the opposite side of Friant's division, Heudelet with the 108th and 3rd Line stood on the heights straddling the road to Turas and observed the stationary allied forces northwest of Tellnitz.

On their side, the Russians were also in need of regrouping after the confused series of attacks and counterattacks of the preceding hour. If Prshibyshevsky accurately recorded the chronology of events in his report, it was only at this point (around noon) that he received word of the fierce fighting occurring behind him on the Pratzen Heights. Apparently not realizing the seriousness of it, he only sent word to Wimpfen to keep an eye on the heights to the rear in addition to watching the French force at Kobelnitz, reinforcing Wimpfen with only a single battalion of Narva Musketeers sent from his reserve. Prshibyshevsky arrayed the main part of his column to continue operations against Davout's forces to his front. The Galitz and Butyrsk Regiments and the two remaining Narva battalions had pursued the 33rd Line for some distance in its retreat behind Sokolnitz Brook and had drawn up between the brook and the French position on the heights just to the northwest of Sokolnitz Castle. To their left stood the two battalions of 7th Jäger, just north of the northwestern corner of Sokolnitz.

To the south, Olsufiev was also busy once again sorting out his tangled battalions. In the village and the open ground to the west stood the three Perm battalions and one Kursk battalion, the Kursk battalion occupying the northwestern projection of Sokolnitz. South of the village, the three Vyborg and two 8th Jäger battalions regrouped. The remaining two Kursk battalions stayed between the village and the Goldbach.

The engagement between the French of Davout's 3rd Corps and the Allied 2nd and 3rd Columns had seen two hours of severe fighting and had resulted in little change in position. While the allies now stood west of Sokolnitz Castle and village, the French were still securely in possession of the heights overlooking the Goldbach. More importantly, however, Davout had fixed the attention of the Russians to their front. The aggressive French attacks had kept the more numerous allied forces off guard, forcing them to react to each successive attack and preventing them from regaining the initiative. The French had accomplished much with little, but by noon they had sustained significant losses and had been pushed back onto the heights where they regrouped for one final effort.

The performance of the allies at Sokolnitz must be regarded as poor.

Repeatedly surprised due to overconfidence, negligence or incompetence, they were continually pushed back by inferior forces and were unable to organize themselves for a concerted effort against the French until after 11:30. The rank and file had fought well, stubbornly defending and attacking as ordered. In particular, the seesaw action in Sokolnitz saw both Russian columns demonstrating excellent discipline although, as at other points on the battlefield, their efforts were less effective than those of the French, resulting in heavier losses.

At a higher level, the allies rate even more poorly. While Buxhöwden had twelve fresh battalions from the 1st Column east of the Goldbach that were immediately available to intervene in the fighting on the Pratzeberg and an even larger force west of the Goldbach that could have assisted in driving the French off from Sokolnitz and allowed the 2nd and 3rd Columns to disengage, he did neither. Instead he chose to wait until the 2nd and 3rd Columns had cleared their own front and held his forces east of the Goldbach in reserve, never considering the circumstances on the heights sufficiently serious to warrant committing them. While Prshibyshevsky's shortsightedness can perhaps be understood considering the close proximity of an aggressive enemy, Buxhöwden's unwillingness to issue orders to the 2nd and 3rd Columns in his capacity as commander of the left wing of the army is more difficult to understand. What is certain is that while Kutuzov was issuing orders for the withdrawal of the allied forces on the Pratzen Heights toward Austerlitz and Krenowitz, Prshibyshevsky and Buxhöwden remained blind to the magnitude of the disaster about to descend on the allied left wing as events to the north reached their climax.

Chapter 6

The French Victory is Decisive:
2 December, 12:30 – 3:00 P.M.

The morning's action had resulted in the defeat of the allied army and Napoleon's army had the remainder of the day before it to complete the destruction. Although Napoleon had defeated the allied army, shattered its leaders' offensive plans and forced them to order a full withdrawal, the victory was far from complete. The decisive victory Napoleon had envisaged, turning the allied right and driving the entire allied army into the ponds and swamps to the south, was no longer possible due to the stiff allied resistance in the north. The seizure of the heights in the center of the allied position, which effectively divided the allied army into two separate pieces, and the presence of substantial uncommitted French reserves provided other opportunities to make the results decisive, however. Napoleon now planned to wheel the divisions of Vandamme and St Hilaire to the south and descend on the allied forces locked in combat in the Goldbach valley in accordance with the original plan. With strong allied forces to the north remaining undefeated, however, Bernadotte's two divisions were required to hold the heights and to cover the right of Lannes's infantry advancing up the Brünn–Olmütz Road.

For the Allies, the three hours of fighting on the Pratzen heights had driven in their center, split their army in two and forced Alexander to authorize a general retreat. The circumstances that the allied army found itself in, however, made retreat all but impossible. A total of thirty-seven battalions and some Austrian cavalry stood near Tellnitz and Sokolnitz. Sixteen of these battalions stood idle near Tellnitz; the remaining twenty-one were regrouping around Sokolnitz after several hours of fierce fighting, and thirteen of them were on the west bank of the Goldbach. With a substantial and aggressively led French force in front of them, the withdrawal of the thirteen battalions and attached artillery on the right bank of the Goldbach over the two bridges near Sokolnitz would be difficult. To the north, Bagration's Advance Guard held a position stretching from the Rausnitz Brook to the hills near Siwitz. To his left, Constantine's 1st Guard Column and the cavalry of the 5th Column had covered Bagration's flank from Blaziowitz to Holubitz during the morning's action. The crisis on the heights, however, had prompted Constantine to move south in the company of the Austrian contingent of the 5th Column, leaving only the Russian brigades of the 5th Column to cover Bagration's left.

Around noon, Segur had returned to Napoleon's command post, now atop the Stare Vinohrady and the French emperor immediately sent him off to urge Bernadotte to hurry his two divisions forward. Sometime before 12:30, Vandamme's division had driven the last of the Austro-Russian forces of the 4th Column off the heights toward Krenowitz and Zbischow. With Kamensky's Russians continuing to resist near the Pratzeberg, Napoleon ordered the majority of Vandamme's forces to support St Hilaire. The 55th Line, Ferey's brigade (46th and 47th Line) and Candras with the 28th Line marched southward to support St Hilaire in driving the last Russians from the heights. Once the heights were cleared, the sixteen battalions on the southern end of the heights would descend on the rear of the allied forces in the valley of the Goldbach. Drouet's division, composed of nine fresh battalions, was just completing its ascent of the heights and was directed to support St Hilaire as well. The remaining four battalions of Vandamme's division (4th Line and 24th Light) were to remain on the heights and join with Rivaud's division (advancing from Blaziowitz) to harass the retreating allies at Krenowitz and Zbischow. As Vandamme's regiments moved into position but before Drouet and Rivaud could arrive, the unexpected arrival of the Russian Guard on the Pratzen Heights once again threw Napoleon's plans into confusion, and produced some of the most dramatic fighting of the day.

Drama on the Heights: The Clash of the Guards

After their brief attack on Rivaud's division near Blaziowitz, between about 12:15 and 12:30, Constantine had reformed his column and set off to the southeast. Any thoughts of taking offensive action against the French on the heights had been rudely interrupted when Constantine received Kutuzov's orders for a general withdrawal. Despite the high spirits of his troops, who were eager to continue their engagement with Rivaud's division, Constantine called them back to continue the withdrawal to Krenowitz. The Life Guard Hussars headed the column, followed by the infantry in two columns. The four battalions of Preobrazhensky and Semenovsky formed the right-hand column and the remaining battalion of Ismailovsky formed the column on the left with the Guard artillery between the two columns.* The Life Guard Horse brought up the rear. Constantine planned to join Maliutin's 2nd Guard Column, which was approaching the heights west of Austerlitz, and link up with the remnants of the 4th Column that had been driven back on Zbischow and Krenowitz. As the 1st Guard Column retired to the southeast,

---

* 1st/Ismailovsky disappears from all accounts after being sent to the heights except for the brief observation that it got caught up in the withdrawal of the 4th Column. Most likely the battalion formed part of the final Austro-Russian line referred to in Soult's report.

Constantine sent orders to Maliutin to hurry forward to secure the bridges at Krenowitz and help cover the allied retreat. As the Russian Guards proceeded with their march, however, they discovered French infantry standing on the heights to the immediate right of their route.

The better part of Vandamme's forces had set off to the south to support St Hilaire at about the same time that Constantine had set off from Blaziowitz. Major Bigarré with the 4th Line stood east of the Stare Vinohrady facing Krenowitz while the 24th Light stood a short distance to the south facing Zbischow. The French forces on the heights did not immediately detect the movement of the Russian Guard on the plateau, and it appears that they were first sighted by Napoleon's staff from the high ground of the Stare Vinohrady. "It was now one o'clock," Segur wrote. "Napoleon from the summit of this commanding plateau, could see before him Alexander's guard advancing in a mass to drive him away and retake it."* Segur's memoirs, however, do not reflect the uncertainty in the minds of the French at the time. The column, marching southeast from Blaziowitz, was at first not definitively identified as a hostile column.

Vandamme was getting his wounds dressed a short distance from Napoleon's command post at the summit of the Stare Vinohrady when he received a report of the approach of an unidentified column. On orders from Vandamme, Major Bigarré advanced his battalion a short distance to the northeast to investigate the column and determine its identity. As Bigarré was advancing at the head of his 1st Battalion, an officer he had sent out to scout out the column returned to report the approach of the enemy. Bigarré immediately sent word to Vandamme and requested support from the nearest French troops, the 24th Light of Colonel Pourailly and the 2nd Battalion of his own regiment, located a short distance to the south. Before help could arrive, however, Russian cavalry was upon them.

Bigarré provided a vivid account of the cavalry attack, though the sequence of events differs slightly from the Russian accounts:

> I was about a quarter of a league from my division, when Captain Vincent, who preceded my scouts, discovered on the reverse slope a considerable mass of cavalry. He came to me at a gallop, signaling me to direct my column to the left. I hurried to do so, but kept the battalion marching in column with the correct intervals in order to be able, if circumstances required, to form square. Once I had given orders to *Chef*

---

* Segur, p. 251. Most secondary accounts place the arrival of the Russian Guard on the heights at 12:00. Segur states very clearly that this occurred around 1:00 following his return to Napoleon's headquarters. He had been sent to prod Bernadotte to move faster shortly after noon by his own account. This timing of events is the most consistent with both French and Russian reports of the morning's actions.

[*de bataillon*] Guye, I went in person with Captain Vincent to see what this enemy column was. Hardly were we on the plateau that dominated the two reverse slopes, than we saw them advancing at a fast trot to meet us. I returned to the battalion and ordered it form square.*

The advance of the 1st Battalion, 4th Line, had placed it to the west of the Russian column. Upon sighting the lone French battalion, Constantine ordered GM Yankovich with the five squadrons of Life Guard Horse from the rear of the column, to attack. Yankovich, assuming personal command of the first line of three squadrons of the regiment, immediately launched them against Bigarré's nearby battalion. As the Russian heavy cavalry thundered toward them, Bigarré quickly ordered his battalion to form square. Yankovich's squadrons closed on the dense mass of bristling bayonets and circled the square, but suffered heavy casualties from the French musketry and were unable to break it.

Behind Yankovich, however, Lieutenant-Colonel Kozen, commanding four guns of the Guard horse artillery, had advanced with the second line of two squadrons of Life Guard Horse commanded by Colonel Olenin-1. Kozen unlimbered his guns 200 meters from the French square while Yankovich's men were swarming around it. As Yankovich withdrew, Kozen fired five successive rounds of canister into Bigarré's tightly packed battalion, inflicting heavy casualties. Immediately following the fifth round, Olenin led the two fresh squadrons charging forward. The Horse Guards broke through the square, which had been thrown into disorder by Kozen's artillery, captured the eagle and hacked wildly at Bigarré's dazed men. This rare example of effective combined arms operations by the allied forces at Austerlitz was a resounding success. The battalion was scattered, the men fleeing from the Russian cavalry. Only 18 were killed, but over 200 were injured and Bigarré himself reportedly suffered 25 saber wounds. Bigarré noted that the enemy:

> . . . unmasked six pieces of light artillery and fired canister on this battalion, causing disorder in the ranks. [Immediately after,] the Grand Duke Constantine, wanting to benefit from the isolation of my battalion, made a charge with two regiments of his column. The first charge did not penetrate the square, and was on the receiving end of a volley of musketry, but a second [charge] that a third Russian regiment made, after our weapons had been fired, rode over the square both while advancing and retiring and sabered more than 200 men.†

---

* Bigarré, pp. 170–1.

† Ibid., p. 171. Although Bigarré noted three cavalry regiments participating in the attack, Russian accounts indicate that there were only five squadrons of one regiment in position at this point.

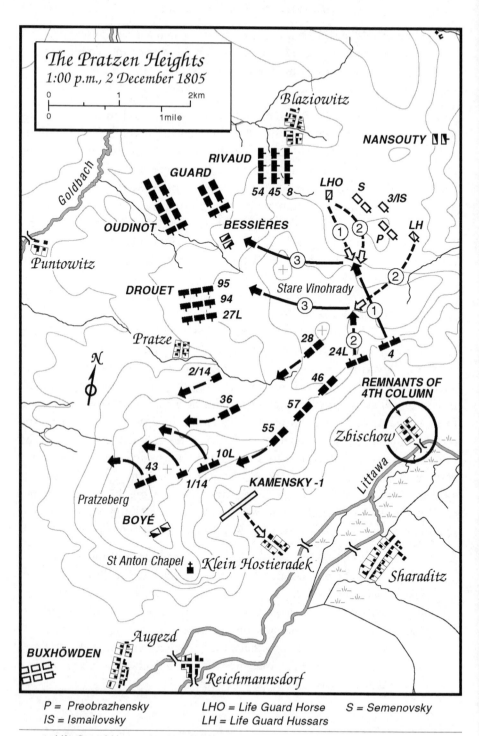

The Pratzen Heights
1:00 p.m., 2 December 1805

Blaziowitz

NANSOUTY

RIVAUD

GUARD

54 45 8

LHO   S

3/IS

LH

OUDINOT

BESSIÈRES

Puntowitz

Goldbach

DROUET   95
          94
          27L

Stare Vinohrady

Pratze

28

24L

4

2/14

46

REMNANTS OF
4TH COLUMN

36

57

Zbischow

55

10L

KAMENSKY -1

Littawa

43

1/14

Pratzeberg

BOYÉ

St Anton Chapel   Klein Hostieradek

Sharaditz

Augezd

BUXHÖWDEN

Reichmannsdorf

P = Preobrazhensky   LHO = Life Guard Horse   S = Semenovsky
IS = Ismailovsky   LH = Life Guard Hussars

1. Life Guard Horse charge 1/4 Line
2. Life Guard Horse & Artillery break 1/4 Line; Life Guard Hussars rout 24 Light
3. Rout of 4 Line & 24 Light

While the Guards regrouped after overwhelming the 4th Line, Constantine observed the two battalions of the 24th Light approaching from the south toward the head of his column and ordered his cavalry to drive them off as well to clear the route to Krenowitz. As they neared the Russian column, Colonel Pourailly inexplicably ordered his battalions to deploy in line instead of in square, despite the presence of the considerable body of Russian cavalry. Yankovich, having reformed his five squadrons of Life Guard Horse, ordered them forward and struck the 24th Light on their left. GL Kologrivov of the Life Guard Hussars observed Pourailly's men deploying and ordered his hussars, who were at the head of Constantine's column, to charge their right. Struck from both sides by the Life Guard Hussars and Life Guard Horse, the 24th Light broke and ran, abandoning an eagle that, unseen, was trampled under the hooves of the Russian cavalry.*

The action between the Russian Guard cavalry and the infantry of Vandamme's division had occurred in the folds of ground that characterized the landscape and was thus out of sight of Napoleon from his command post. The sounds of fierce fighting were obvious enough, however, and caused some concern on the Stare Vinohrady, as Segur related:

> On this side, the action in the hollow was hidden from [Napoleon]. The sound of its tumult was becoming so threatening, that, withdrawing his glance from the decisive attack that was going to take place in front, and seeing behind him a black mass of moving troops, he exclaimed: "What! Can those be the Russians?"†

Segur quickly verified that the column approaching the Stare Vinohrady from the west was in fact a brigade of Oudinot's grenadiers marching from the heights toward Kobelnitz. The story emphasizes the confusion and uncertainty caused at Napoleon's headquarters by the unexpected arrival of Constantine's men on the heights, even amidst a stunning French victory.

The routing of the 4th Line and 24th Light occurred a short distance to the east of the French headquarters, and the routed French battalions almost passed through the imperial headquarters in their flight. "The unfortunate fellows were quite distracted with fear and could listen to nothing; in reply to our reproaches for thus deserting the field of battle and their Emperor they shouted mechanically 'Vive l'Empereur!' while they fled faster than ever," recalled Segur. Napoleon dismissed them with a scornful gesture, saying

---

* It is not clear whether the 2nd Battalion of the 4th Line was operating under Pourailly's orders and also deployed in line and was routed with the 24th Light or if it was further to the rear. Some men of the 4th Line, marching over the same spot after the ensuing cavalry action, spotted the lost eagle of the 24th Light on the ground and retrieved it, thinking that it was the lost eagle of their own 1st Battalion.

† Segur, p. 251.

"Let them go," and then sent one of his aides-de-camp, General Rapp, to bring up the Imperial Guard Cavalry.*

Rapp galloped off to Marshal Bessières, who stood with the Guard cavalry a short distance from the Stare Vinohrady, to deliver Napoleon's orders to throw back the Russians. Bessières had already been alerted, however, as related by one of his aides-de-camp:

> The Marshal was standing with the other officers mentioned in front of the chasseurs and grenadiers of the Guard. The ground before him rose to a height that cut off our distant view. He was on his way to investigate, as was his custom, when he noticed some infantry running rapidly down the slope and constantly looking back. Then he said "Laville, we are going to have a cavalry engagement." . . . The evening after the battle I asked him how he had guessed so opportunely that a cavalry engagement was imminent. He replied: "Because the retreating soldiers kept looking back. When infantry retires before infantry they never turn their heads."†

Bessières deployed the Guard cavalry in three lines. In the first line, Bessières placed the first two squadrons of the Chasseurs à Cheval of the Guard under the command of Colonel-en-Second Morland and gave Rapp the honor of commanding the company of Mamelukes on their right. The 3rd and 4th Squadrons of the Chasseurs à Cheval along with the 5th Squadron (velités) of the Grenadiers à Cheval formed the second line under the command of GdB Dahlmann. Bessières himself with the first four squadrons of the Grenadiers à Cheval brought up the rear.

As the French Imperial Guard cavalry advanced, Drouet's division was also reacting to the sounds of battle on the northeastern corner of the heights. The division had already passed between Pratze and the Stare Vinohrady and was approaching the Pratzeberg when Drouet redirected his division to the northeast to meet this new threat.‡

> My division was ordered to join [Soult's Corps]. But during my march, the Emperor learned that the Russian reserve, composed of the Guard infantry and cavalry, had made an attack on our center, and had overthrown a brigade of infantry from Vandamme's division and strongly shaken the Chasseurs of the Imperial Guard, whose colonel was later killed. This circumstance changed the plans made by the Emperor. He directed my division to support the center. To arrive earlier at the threatened point, I

---

* Ibid., p. 252.

† Henry Lachouque and Anne S. K. Brown, *The Anatomy of Glory: Napoleon and His Guard* (London: Greenhill Books, 1997), p. 64.

‡ There is some dispute over who ordered this movement. Drouet claimed Napoleon ordered it while Bernadotte also claimed to have ordered it on his own initiative.

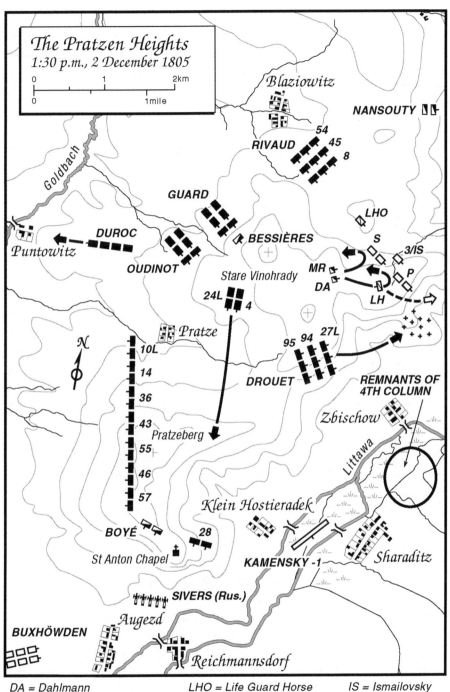

The Pratzen Heights
1:30 p.m., 2 December 1805

0 _____ 1 _____ 2km
0 _____ 1mile

Blaziowitz

NANSOUTY

54
RIVAUD   45
          8

GUARD

LHO

DUROC

Puntowitz

BESSIÈRES   S
                    3/IS
OUDINOT   MR
Stare Vinohrady   DA   P
                       LH
24L   4

Pratze
10L
14
N
36
43   95 94 27L
Pratzeberg
55   DROUET
46
57   REMNANTS OF
                      4TH COLUMN

Zbischow

BOYÉ   28
                Littawa
St Anton Chapel
            Klein Hostieradek
            KAMENSKY -1   Sharaditz
SIVERS (Rus.)
Augezd
BUXHÖWDEN
        Reichmannsdorf

DA = Dahlmann   LHO = Life Guard Horse   IS = Ismailovsky
MR = Morland/Rapp   LH = Life Guard Hussars   S = Semenovsky
✛ = French skirmisher (27L) P = Preobrazhensky

crossed a marsh [probably an area on the heights where the ground had been churned into mud by the earlier fighting] and I formed my division in column by half battalions [keeping advancing all the while].*

Drouet sent out a cloud of skirmishers from the 27th Light and a battery of eight guns in advance of his division. Behind them followed GdB Frère with the remainder of the three battalions of the 27th Light on the right and GdB Werle with the six battalions of the 94th and 95th Line on the left adjacent to the Imperial Guard cavalry. Drouet's infantry advanced on a course to intercept Constantine's column before it reached Krenowitz.

While Bessières and Drouet converged on the Russian column, the Russian Guard cavalry was still reassembling after becoming scattered in the pursuit of the fleeing French infantry. Yankovich, well off to the north, reformed his Horse Guard squadrons and rejoined the tail of the main column where some of the artillery had fallen behind. GL Kologrivov, commanding the Life Guard Hussars, began reforming his scattered hussar squadrons directly in the path of the advancing French cavalry. As the French cavalry advanced at a trot, Kologrivov remained rooted to the spot, his squadrons only half-formed, and neither charged nor fled. The French Guard horse artillery, under the command of General Dogereau, advanced ahead of Morland's line, deployed and was able to fire several rounds into the flank of the Russian cavalry. Moments later, Morland and the first line of the French smashed into the first line of Life Guard Hussars and drove it into what had formed of the second line, causing the entire regiment to rout. Colonel Kostenetsky, with six guns of the Russian Guard horse artillery, was unable to help Kologrivov. His horse artillery had been advancing with the Life Guard Hussars at the head of the Guard column which had just reached an area of vineyards on the heights northwest of Krenowitz. When the hussars had wheeled to the right and passed through the rows of vines to engage the 24th Light, however, Kostenetsky had been unable to follow the hussars when the wheels of the guns had become tangled in the narrow rows of the vineyard. Kostenetsky watched helplessly as the French Imperial Guard cavalry routed the Life Guard Hussars and swept down upon the Russian Guard infantry.

With the Russian hussars now in full flight and the horse artillery too far off to help, the French Guard Chasseurs à Cheval, along with the company of Mamelukes, swept down on the Russian Guard infantry marching for Krenowitz. The Preobrazhensky Regiment, at the head of the column, was near the same vineyard that had prevented Kostenetsky from deploying his guns and fled to the relative safety of the vineyard. The Semenovsky

---

* Jean-Baptiste Drouet d'Erlon, *Le Maréchal Drouet, Comte d'Erlon : Vie Militaire* (Paris: G. Barba, 1844), p. 27.

battalions, however, were further to the rear, vulnerable on open ground. They quickly formed square in the face of the onrushing French cavalry. Morland and Rapp swept down on the Russians and managed to penetrate the Russian columns, some of the French horsemen sweeping down the rows of the vineyard in an attempt to get at the Preobrazhensky. But, between the squares of the Semenovsky battalions and the vineyards, they could not inflict much damage. In the confusion, Kaspersky's gunners managed to unlimber the light guns accompanying the infantry and canister fire from eight guns ripped into the ranks of the French cavalry. Between the artillery and musket fire, the French cavalry were soon driven off, with Colonel Morland being mortally wounded by a ball in the chest.

With the French cavalry beaten off temporarily, Constantine hurried his column along on its retreat. The 3rd Battalion, Ismailovsky Regiment, marching to the left of the main column, was able to continue its retreat unmolested and reached Krenowitz by around 2:00. The remaining battalions, though, soon came under fire from Drouet's skirmishers as well as being harassed by the Mamelukes and Guard Chasseurs of Rapp and Dahlmann. Nevertheless, the Russian Guard infantry managed to extricate itself, although forced to abandon one of the artillery pieces attached to the Semenovsky battalions due to some damage to the carriage. Second Lieutenant Demidov remained with the piece, firing one last round of canister before being taken by the French cavalry. Demidov, the first officer taken prisoner from the Russian Guard, was immediately brought to Napoleon. Segur recounts his interview with Napoleon (though he recalls his name incorrectly):

> Just then a young officer of artillery, named Apraxin [actually Demidov], whom our chasseurs had taken, was brought before the Emperor struggling and weeping, wringing his hands in despair, and exclaiming: "That he had lost his battery! That he was dishonored!" Napoleon tried to console him, saying: "Calm yourself, young man! And remember this; there can be no shame in being conquered by Frenchmen!"*

The Life Guard Hussars, still rattled from their earlier rout at the hands of the French Guard cavalry, remained disordered after the Russian Guard infantry had beaten off the French cavalry attack. Assuming command of Morland's chasseur squadrons, Rapp now charged the Russian hussars. Three squadrons scattered immediately, but the last two squadrons held firm and managed to hold Rapp's eager men briefly before being driven off themselves.†

---

* Segur, p. 254.

† According to French accounts, Rapp led only the single company of Mamelukes in this charge. Russian accounts indicate several squadrons, however, which is more likely considering both the proximity of the other squadrons and the results of the action.

Having routed the Life Guard Hussars and driven them off toward Krenowitz, Rapp next turned to the horse artillery they had been accompanying. Kostenetsky had managed to disentangle his guns from the vineyards, but had not moved very far toward Krenowitz when Rapp's cavalry swept down upon them. As the French cavalry approached, Kostenetsky and his officers drew their swords and bravely defended their pieces.

On leaving the vineyards, the Mamelukes rushed at the guns with a shout and began to hack at the crews. Then the "Russian Hercules" as Kostenetsky was called in the army, rushed forward with another strong soldier, Fireworker Maslovym, in front of the horse company, clearing the way by sword.* Shifting their crews to two guns, they abandoned the other four and escaped toward Krenowitz. After seeing his two guns to safety, Kostenetsky returned with his remaining crews and seized two more of the abandoned guns, managing to elude the French cavalry once again.

On the other end of the Russian Guard column, the Life Guard Horse and Kozen's four horse guns had fallen behind the infantry because the guns had become mired in the mud churned up by the passage of the column ahead of them. They appear to have passed unnoticed by the French forces intent on attacking the head of the column and the cavalry managed to hold back some of Rivaud's infantry that had followed Constantine's column from Blaziowitz while the artillery struggled to catch up with the rest of the column.† When they finally approached the descent to Krenowitz around 2:00, they met a scene of mass confusion. About 400 paces from the bridge over the Rausnitz Stream at Krenowitz, the forces of the Russian Guard formed a tangled mass. The four battalions of Preobrazhensky and Semenovsky had deployed in line across the road descending to Krenowitz while the Life Guard Jäger Battalion had occupied the houses and gardens of Krenowitz in the valley below to secure the passage. In between, the Russian artillery along with some infantry and cavalry and a mass of stragglers and men who had broken ranks streamed toward the bridges over the Rausnitz Brook. Yankovich and Kozen slipped behind the Guard infantry and proceeded toward Krenowitz.

Drouet's infantry and the Guard cavalry had converged on this point, and Drouet had deployed skirmishers to harass the Preobrazhensky Regiment on the southern end of the Russian position. Dogereau advanced his battery of Guard horse artillery and brought it to bear against the Preobrazhensky as well, quickly inflicting serious casualties. To the north, Rapp and Dahlmann faced the two battalions of the Semenovsky. The Russian infantry stood alone,

---

* Vasil'ev, "Gvardiya" <www.genstab.ru/voin/auster_01.htm>. A fireworker (*Feuerwerker*) was an artillery NCO responsible for the preparation of ammunition.

† It is not clear from French accounts whether Rivaud's entire division pursued Constantine's column or only part.

nearly all of the artillery having already been sent to the rear or captured. The French squadrons, having regrouped after their action with the Life Guard Hussars and Kostenetsky's artillerists, charged the two Semenovsky battalions, which immediately formed square. Although Dahlmann is not specifically mentioned in French accounts, it seems his squadrons were unable to make any headway against the 3rd/Semenovsky. A lieutenant of the Mamelukes, however, managed to hack his way into the square of the 1st/Semenovsky, suffering multiple bayonet wounds and having his horse killed beneath him. His comrades immediately exploited the breach in the square, breaking it and sending the battalion fleeing toward Krenowitz, leaving ten men and their battalion standard in the hands of the Mamelukes.

The hole left in the Russian line by the rout of the 1st/Semenovsky necessitated a general retreat and the remaining battalions began filing down the slope, still harassed by Drouet's skirmishers on their left and now Rivaud's arriving on their right. The 3rd/Ismailovsky had already crossed the Rausnitz Brook along with three of Kostenetsky's guns, taking position on the heights on the opposite side. The light guns accompanying the infantry also seem to have crossed to the left bank by this point except for the one gun with the Semenovsky Regiment that had been taken by the French. The infantry, however, were suffering from the steady fire of the French skirmishers and horse artillery. In addition, the French Guard cavalry still roamed nearby, waiting for opportunities to charge when they could catch the Russian Guard infantry unprepared.

Segur recorded the view from Napoleon's command post:

> From afar could be seen the remains of the Russian reserves abandoning the central plateau to us, and the left of their army retiring in close ranks upon Austerlitz. They were retreating under the cannonading of our guard, with which the commandant Doguereau [sic] . . . was furrowing into their ranks.*

With the last Russian reserves decisively beaten, Napoleon at this point felt secure in sending news of his victory to Paris and then proceeded with his staff to the south to observe the destruction of the allied columns on the Goldbach firsthand.

On the opposite side of the Rausnitz Stream, Maliutin had led his cavalry in advance of his column and drawn it up on the heights overlooking Krenowitz while the three battalions of Life Grenadiers and his artillery still approached from Austerlitz. An adjutant sent by Constantine met Maliutin on the heights overlooking Krenowitz shortly after 2:00, urgently requiring his

---

* Segur, p. 254.

assistance. Maliutin immediately ordered his cavalry forward to help retrieve the forces remaining on the opposite bank. Maliutin's seven squadrons, five of the Cavalier Guard and two of Life Guard Cossacks, forded the stream just north of Krenowitz near where Colonel Rall had positioned his battery to cover the crossing.*

The ensuing clash between the Russian Cavalier Guard and French Imperial Guard cavalry has become legendary. It has been elevated in importance and even shifted to the Stare Vinohrady, the key point on the Pratzen Plateau, to make it the climax of the battle of Austerlitz. While this certainly produces a memorable piece of melodrama, there is no indication that the clash occurred anywhere near the imperial command post on the Stare Vinohrady but rather at a distance from it at the eastern edge of the plateau near Krenowitz. Moreover, the charge did not constitute a last desperate offensive action in a Russian attempt to regain the heights but rather was intended to engage the French cavalry and skirmishers long enough to allow the Russian Guard infantry and artillery to make the descent to Krenowitz and secure their escape across the Rausnitz stream. Even placed in its proper perspective, however, the charge of the Cavalier Guard remains a dramatic encounter. The Cavalier Guard was composed of the offspring of the Russian nobility and enjoyed an elite status that had nothing to do with actual battlefield ability. Facing it were the elites of the French army, the Imperial Guard cavalry composed of officers and men who had served for at least ten years and had proven their abilities in several campaigns. The action encapsulated the broader struggle, that of the French Imperial meritocracy versus the old privileged order.

Upon crossing the stream, Maliutin's cavalry formed into three bodies: GM Depreradovich-2 assumed command of 2½ squadrons of the Cavalier Guard on the left, Colonel Repnin-1 the remaining 2½ squadrons in the center and Colonel Chernozubov-5 the two squadrons of Life Guard Cossacks on the right. Depreradovich led his squadrons of the Cavalier Guard up the slope on the far side of the stream, the Russian cavalry threading their way through the retreating mass of the two Preobrazhensky battalions. Once through, they immediately attacked a chain of French skirmishers that had been working

---

* Many accounts, both Russian and French, place this action at 1:00. However, this contradicts the eyewitness account of Segur, who placed the initial approach of the Guard toward the heights at 1:00. The erroneous timing given for the attack stems from a misunderstanding of the earlier action on the Pratzen heights and the mistaken assumption that Segur's statement that the Stare Vinohrady had been seized at 11:00 meant that the 4th Column had been driven from the heights at that time. This overlooks the later action with the third allied line referred to in the reports of both Soult and Miloradovich as well as Bigarré's memoirs and official accounts of the battle on both sides. The charge of the Cavalier Guard occurred roughly one hour after the initial action of the Guard on the Pratzen heights, or roughly around 2:00.

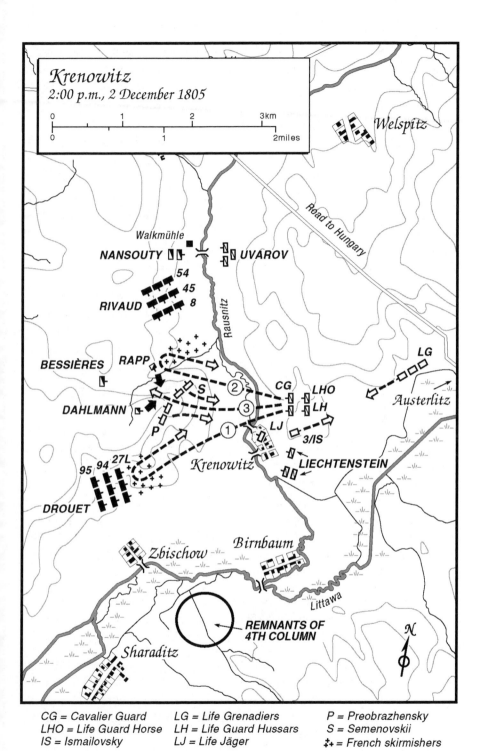

Krenowitz
2:00 p.m., 2 December 1805

0 — 1 — 2 — 3km
0 — 1 — 2miles

Welspitz

Road to Hungary

Walkmühle

NANSOUTY — UVAROV

54
45
RIVAUD — 8

Rausnitz

LG

BESSIÈRES — RAPP

② S

CG — LHO

Austerlitz

③

LH

DAHLMANN

P

LJ

3/IS

①

27L

95 94

Krenowitz

LIECHTENSTEIN

DROUET

Birnbaum

Zbischow

Littawa

REMNANTS OF
4TH COLUMN

N

Sharaditz

CG = Cavalier Guard	LG = Life Grenadiers	P = Preobrazhensky
LHO = Life Guard Horse	LH = Life Guard Hussars	S = Semenovskii
IS = Ismailovsky	LJ = Life Jäger	✛ = French skirmishers

1. 2.5 Sqs. Cavalier Guard – Depreradovich -2
2. Leib Cossacks – Chernozubov-5
3. 2.5 Sqs. Cavalier Guard – Repnin -1 + 2 Sqs. Life Guard Horse – Olenin -1

their way down the slope to harass the Russian retreat. Behind this cavalry screen, the Preobrazhensky battalions, their attached guns and the four horse guns of Kozen gained the bank of the Rausnitz at Krenowitz and began streaming across. Depreradovich held the French skirmishers at bay, securing the retreat of the infantry and artillery.

To the north, the Life Guard Cossacks ascended the slope and lunged into the fray with the French light cavalry that were busy harassing the Semenovsky battalions. Taken off guard, the French horsemen fell back to the west behind Drouet's infantry to regroup, Rapp's squadrons apparently following. Chernozubov-5 then wheeled his two squadrons to the right and drove off a party of French skirmishers, probably Rivaud's. At this point, it appears that Depreradovich-2 made a bold decision to attack the French Guard cavalry that had retired behind Drouet's infantry:

> Their cavalry took a high resolution and decided to pass through the intervals of my troops, again to charge the chasseurs of the Imperial Guard, which were rallying behind my division. In spite of this very bold operation, I did not stop the march of my division, which approached the Russian infantry frankly and impetuously with the bayonet, without firing a single gun, and defeated [the Russian infantry] by the village of Krenowitz.[*]

Both Depreradovich and Chernozubov had achieved their purpose, however, and the three remaining Preobrazhensky and Semenovsky battalions seized the opportunity to fall back, though the effects were only temporary. As a result of the persistent pressure from Drouet's troops, the retreat of the Russian Guard became increasingly disorderly until it became a mad panicked flight down the steep slope to the river. Behind Drouet's infantry, Rapp quickly reformed his squadrons and led a countercharge that drove Depreradovich's squadrons back between Drouet's columns and down the hill toward Krenowitz:

> When the Russian cavalry again passed by in the intervals, it received even more intense point-blank fire; in this retrograde movement, it received great losses, and was completely routed.[†]

While Depreradovich and Chernozubov were busy on the heights, the remainder of Maliutin's cavalry (2½ squadrons of the Cavalier Guard under the command of Repnin-1) had been joined by two squadrons of the Life Guard Horse under Colonel Olenin-1 and were slowly making their way up

---

[*] Drouet, p. 27.

[†] Ibid.

the slope between the two other bodies of Guard cavalry. These five squadrons advanced directly up the slope, intending to arrive at the top between Depreradovich's squadrons and the Life Guard Cossacks. Before they reached the top of the slope, however, the routed 1st Battalion, Semenovsky, swept around them, slowing their progress. As they pressed onward, more Guard infantry were falling back toward Krenowitz with the Russian Guard cavalry slowly forcing their way through the mass. When they finally reached the top of the slope the cavalry were met with a startling spectacle. Across the heights in front of them stood the masses of French infantry, the entire nine battalions of Drouet's division to the left already descending the slope toward Krenowitz, and part or all of Rivaud's division to their right. In between them, Rapp's squadrons had already driven off the Life Guard Cossacks and stood at the edge of the plateau. Repnin, demonstrating more valor than sense, immediately charged Rapp's admittedly weary squadrons without even waiting for Olenin's squadrons to join him.

The fresher Russian horsemen quickly gained the advantage over Rapp's tired Chasseurs and Mamelukes, driving them back. Seeing this, Dahlmann, with the second line of French Guard cavalry, launched his squadrons into the fray, the 3rd and 4th Squadrons of the Guard Chasseurs charging the left of Repnin's squadrons while the 5th Squadron of the Grenadiers à Cheval struck the right. Engaged on both sides and with Rapp's men holding their ground to the front, most of Repnin's small force was quickly surrounded.

While Dahlmann was charging at the head of his squadrons, Olenin had managed to struggle up the slope behind Repnin. Seeing Repnin surrounded, Olenin threw his two squadrons into the action along with the one squadron of Cavalier Guards that had escaped encirclement, attempting to hack a passage for the remaining Cavalier Guards to retreat. After about quarter of an hour of confused mêlée, Marshal Bessières, calmly advancing from behind the French infantry with his four squadrons of the elite Grenadiers à Cheval, came upon the struggle. Bessières ordered his four squadrons of imposing horse grenadiers forward at a trot and quickly drove the three Russian squadrons back toward Krenowitz. The Grenadiers à Cheval pursued them for some distance toward Krenowitz until they were halted by canister fired from a single gun that the intrepid Kostenetsky had retained on the right bank under his personal command. The remaining Russian Guard cavalry re-forded the stream under the cover of Kostenetsky's gun and regrouped on the left bank. Soon afterwards, the infantry completed its crossing followed by Kostenetsky and his gun, leaving only the Life Guard Jäger battalion occupying the village on the west bank of the stream. On the heights, Repnin's small party of Cavalier Guard continued their futile struggle for a short while longer before surrendering, the majority of their officers and men killed or wounded.

By 3:00 the remaining Russian Guard infantry was regrouping behind the Life Grenadier Regiment, which had taken position on the heights on the east bank of the Rausnitz stream about 1.6 kilometers east of Krenowitz. French skirmishers had already begun filtering across the stream to harass the Russians on the other side and Drouet had brought his artillery forward to the edge of the plateau to command the crossing at Krenowitz and was preparing to storm the village and drive out the Russian rearguard.

The losses of the Russian Guard had been substantial. The regimental histories of the Guard cavalry regiments detail 291 officers and men killed and missing (including those captured). The Guard infantry and artillery recorded 639 officers and men killed and missing. The number of wounded among the infantry and cavalry of the Guard is not documented, but an estimated 600–700 seems reasonable, with total casualties therefore exceeding 1,500.*
On the French side, casualties had been substantially lighter. The French Guard Cavalry had demonstrated its superiority over the Russian Guard Cavalry by consistently defeating forces of equal or larger size. Reported losses in the Guard cavalry regiments were 130–140 men, the majority suffered among the Guard Chasseurs and Mamelukes.† Drouet's division suffered negligible losses to the skirmishers that had harassed the Russian retreat. The main role of this division had been that of a deterrent, forcing the precipitate withdrawal of the Russian Guard infantry before the advance of Drouet's division cut them off from Krenowitz.

Despite the initial routing of the handful of French battalions left on the northern end of the heights, between about 1:30 and 3:00 Constantine's Russian Guard had been decisively defeated, crushed between the anvil of Drouet's infantry and the hammer of the Imperial Guard cavalry. With the defeat of the Russian Guard, the allied army was irretrievably split in two. The Rausnitz Brook and the presence of Maliutin's fresh infantry and considerable artillery on the opposite bank secured their retreat, however. But the events to the north, on the Brünn–Olmütz road, and to the south in the valley of the lower Goldbach, were to determine the true severity of the Allied defeat.

Lannes vs. Bagration on the Brünn–Olmütz Road

With Constantine abandoning his position opposite Blaziowitz and the Russians now retreating from Bosenitz in the north, by around 12:30 the French were again free to resume their advance. Napoleon had originally

---

* These figures are taken from regimental histories and Vasil'ev's article, which includes data from regimental histories not available to the author.

† These losses are detailed as 19 killed and 65 wounded in the Guard Chasseurs, 2 killed and 25 wounded in the Horse Grenadiers, and an estimated 20–30 Mamelukes killed or wounded.

envisioned a bold sweep up the Brünn–Olmütz road to turn the right flank of the allied army and drive it southward, but events had shifted the focus of the maneuver from the road to the Pratzen Heights. Nonetheless, Lannes had been champing at the bit all morning and was anxious to launch his troops forward to sweep the Russians away. Only Bagration's forces remained to oppose him.

Lannes's infantry had remained in position for over three hours while the cavalry on both sides charged and countercharged, but now he ordered them to attack Bagration's position astride the main road. Caffarelli with the six battalions of the 30th, 17th and 61st Line, received orders to advance on Krug and Holubitz where Bagration had positioned GM Ulanius with the three battalions of the 6th Jäger. To Caffarelli's right, Rivaud's division of 1st Corps was nearing Blaziowitz, allowing the four battalions at Blaziowitz to march on Krug and Holubitz as well. To Caffarelli's left, Suchet's eight battalions would engage Bagration's main body north of the Brünn–Olmütz road, while the 17th Light and the light cavalry of Trelliard and Milhaud continued to press on the Russian flank near Siwitz.

Bagration had deployed his forces carefully, the extensive cavalry actions having allowed plenty of time to prepare for the French attack. Bagration's main line ran roughly northwest–southeast with the left anchored behind the Holubitz ravine and the right on the heights near Siwitz. With the main road on his left and another road running through Kowalowitz to Rausnitz on his right, Bagration left himself two converging avenues of retreat that would allow his forces to retire easily to a second defensive position running between Kowalowitz and Welspitz or to the heights behind Rausnitz. Bagration's first line, commanded by GM Engelhardt, was composed of the six battalions of the Old Ingermanland and Pskov Musketeers. The Arkhangel Musketeers, commanded by GM Kamensky-2, formed the second line. Bagration positioned his Jäger on either flank, the seasoned GM Ulanius occupying Holubitz and Krug with the 6th Jäger while the less experienced GM Gogel occupied Siwitz on the right with two battalions of the 5th Jäger.*

Bagration positioned his horse artillery, cavalry and Cossacks to support both parties of Jäger with a cavalry reserve behind his center. Colonel Yashvil's

---

* The allocation of the three battalions of 5th Jäger remains unclear. Langeron asserts that one battalion of the 5th Jäger was with the 1st Column but he seems to be the only writer to make this claim. On the other hand, Schönhals specifically mentions the actions of only two battalions of 5th Jäger at Siwitz and Bosenitz, with no specific mention of a third battalion with either the 1st Column or the Advance Guard. The most probable placement remains a matter of opinion, but because of the intensity of fighting in the northern sector of the battlefield, it would seem highly likely that all three battalions would have been engaged if they had been present in that sector. The absence of any mention of a third battalion makes it seem more likely that it stood with the 1st Column, which remained idle for the majority of the day.

battery remained on the main road with GM Wittgenstein's Mariupol Hussars to anchor the left of the line. GM Chaplits and the Pavlograd Hussars supported Gogel's Jäger on the right while three squadrons of the St Petersburg Dragoons along with what remained of Shepelev's brigade (the Empress Cuirassiers and the remnants of the Constantine Uhlans) supported Ulanius on the left. While details on the deployment of Cossack regiments are always uncertain, it is reasonable to assume that two Cossack regiments were positioned on each flank. Ignatiev's horse artillery battery also appears to have been positioned to support Ulanius, aligned with Yashvil's battery on the road while the five squadrons of Tver Dragoons remained in the rear in reserve.[*]

Facing Bagration, Lannes's forces were deployed in much the same order as they had been all morning. Suchet's division stood in two lines of four battalions each straddling the main road itself. GdB Beker's four battalions of the 40th and 34th Line formed the first line with GdB Valhubert's 88th and 64th Line behind them. On their left rear a detachment of the 17th Light occupied Bosenitz with the remainder of the regiment anchoring the left of the entire French army in the key fortified position of the Santon. Aligned with Suchet's division south of the main road stood Caffarelli's division. GdB Demont with the 30th and 17th Line stood adjacent to Beker's brigade. In the second line commanded by GdB De Billy stood the two battalions of the 61st Line positioned behind the 30th Line. The 13th Light and the 51st Line occupied Blaziowitz to the right.

With the withdrawal of the Guard, the Russian cavalry was no longer roaming the open ground between Blaziowitz and Krug, and Nansouty's cuirassier division remained in this area observing Uvarov's brigade which had taken position on the opposite side of the Rausnitz Brook near the Walkmühle. Kellermann's light cavalry, along with Walther's dragoon division, remained in close support of the infantry. On the extreme left around Bosenitz stood the light cavalry brigades of Trelliard and Milhaud. Finally, to the rear of the infantry stood d'Hautpoul's cuirassier division.

With the severity of the morning's fighting, it is difficult to estimate the total strength of the opposing forces. Bagration had 14 or 15 battalions, 43 squadrons of regular cavalry, an additional 20–30 squadrons of Cossacks and 53 guns. Lannes and Murat had between them 20 battalions, of which two were positioned to the rear at the Santon and Bosenitz, 72 squadrons and

---

[*] Several sources place the Mariupol Hussars with the Pavlograd Hussars on the right of Bagration's line. Also, there is some confusion over the position of Uvarov's brigade. His report says that his forces were driven over a stream crossed only by a narrow weir. This matches the description of the Rausnitz Brook near the Walkmühle, although some writers have interpreted this to refer to the Holubitz brook and have considered Uvarov's cavalry to have supported the action at Holubitz. However, there is no indication of Uvarov's cavalry participating in this action.

about 32 guns, not including the heavy pieces in position at the Santon.* Of these forces, most were relatively fresh except for Uvarov's cavalry and the Constantine Uhlans on the Russian side and Kellermann's cavalry in particular on the French side which had suffered heavy losses in the morning's action.

Lannes's position didn't leave much opportunity for fancy maneuvering. With the foothills of the mountains rising north of Siwitz and the marshy banks of the Rausnitz Brook restricting maneuver on the right, Lannes planned to launch a straightforward frontal attack with emphasis on the Russian positions at Krug and Holubitz that anchored the left flank of the Russian line. Accordingly, Lannes ordered Caffarelli's division toward Holubitz, the main body of six battalions marching due east and the detachment of four battalions at Blaziowitz advancing northeast to converge on the village. Nansouty's cuirassiers would support this movement and keep Uvarov in check while the advance of Rivaud's division of the 1st Corps south of Blaziowitz secured their right. Suchet's division, less the 17th Light, would angle north of the main road to strike the center of Bagration's main line frontally with his eight battalions. Kellermann and Walther would fill the gap that would open between the two divisions on the main road with d'Hautpoul advancing to take position in a second line behind the leading cavalry and Suchet's infantry. The light cavalry of Milhaud and Trelliard would deploy to secure Suchet's left.

By 12:30, the entire mass of French troops was in motion and about fifteen minutes later Ulanius's outposts at Krug came under intense fire as Caffarelli's main body deployed and engaged the village. The detachment from Blaziowitz, commanded by Colonel Bonnet d'Honnières, approached Holubitz from the south, flanking the Russian outpost at Krug. Ulanius ordered the severely outnumbered detachment at Krug back to the main position behind the Holubitz stream while Caffarelli deployed his forces to attack. With d'Honnière's two regiments drawing into position on his right, Caffarelli shifted GdB Demont's infantry to the left behind the cavalry of Kellermann and Walther to secure his link with Suchet. GdB De Billy, with the 61st Line, stood in and behind Krug. With his forces positioned, Caffarelli ordered the six battalions opposite Holubitz to attack. However, Caffarelli's first attack on the position of Holubitz met with a storm of canister fire from the Russian artillery, particularly Ignatiev's battery positioned just northwest of Holubitz, and was quickly beaten off.

Suchet had meanwhile maneuvered his division into position on the plain

---

* The exact number varies and Bowden indicates that several pieces had been put out of action during the morning's fighting.

facing Bagration's main line. Halting his infantry just out of effective range of the Russian artillery, Suchet advanced his own artillery and opened a bombardment of the Russian lines. On his left, the 17th Light and the supporting light cavalry moved on the Russian position at Siwitz. The advance of Suchet's main body placed Chaplits and Gogel in a perilous position, in danger of being cut off and driven north into the mountains. Gogel therefore resolved to withdraw his infantry from Siwitz to a new position on the right of Bagration's main line, a small hill southeast of the village of Posorsitz. Chaplits moved his cavalry between the Jäger and the light cavalry of Milhaud and Trelliard to cover its withdrawal. To the south, however, GdD d'Hautpoul, in position behind Suchet's infantry, saw the column of Russian Jäger filing out of Siwitz. Seizing the opportunity, d'Hautpoul led the 1st Brigade of his cuirassier division northward, charging the unsuspecting Russian infantry.

As the six squadrons of armored horsemen swept down on them, Gogel ordered his two battalions to form square. French accounts report that the Jäger were initially broken but then managed to form square, suggesting that d'Hautpoul's cuirassiers had caught one battalion in the process of forming square and scattered it while the other formed square and fired on the cuirassiers. The 5th Jäger managed to withdraw to the north into Posorsitz while Chaplits rushed to cover them. In the face of the larger body of Russian cavalry, d'Hautpoul withdrew his six squadrons to the south. With the Russian cavalry from Siwitz now massing southeast of Posorsitz and preparing to charge d'Hautpoul, Murat shifted his remaining cavalry northward from its position on the main road to counter it. Some of Kellermann's light cavalry moved into position in the first line,* followed by Walther's dragoons in the second line with d'Hautpoul cuirassiers forming the third line. While the opposing cavalry maneuvered into position, Gogel began withdrawing toward Kowalowitz.

While Murat was massing his cavalry, Suchet was engaging Bagration's main position. After softening up the Russian position with his initial artillery barrage, Suchet ordered his infantry to attack at around 1:30. The exact sequence of events remains unclear, reports on either side being vague, but between 1:30 and 2:00 Suchet's infantry engaged Bagration's main line and were beaten off after a fierce struggle. Russian musketry and artillery inflicted heavy casualties on the French, wounding Suchet and GdB Beker. GdB Valhubert fell dead on the field, although it is not clear whether this occurred in the first assault or the subsequent one. His division's initial charge beaten

---

* It is not clear whether all four of Kellermann's regiments were shifted north at this point or not. The 4th Hussars is the only regiment of Kellermann's division that is mentioned in the attack. It seems likely that at least some of the hussars were left in position to oppose the Russian cavalry massed north of Holubitz while the remainder shifted north.

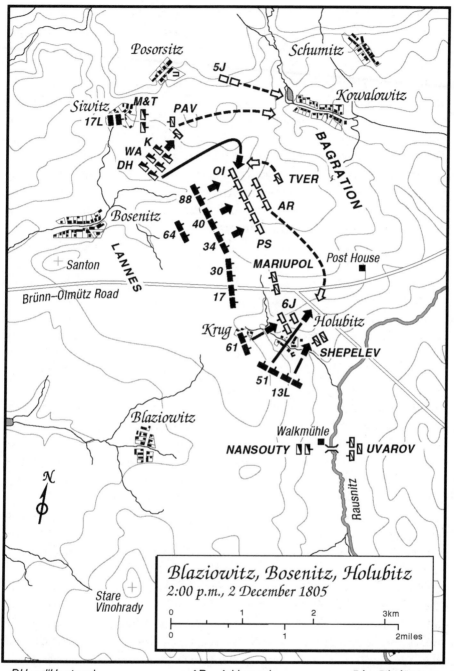

Posorsitz

Schumitz

5J

Kowalowitz

Siwitz
17L
M&T
PAV

K
WA
DH

BAGRATION

OI
TVER
88
AR
40
64
34
PS
30
MARIUPOL
Post House
17
6J
Krug
Holubitz
61
SHEPELEV
51
13L

Bosenitz

LANNES
Santon
Brünn–Olmütz Road

Blaziowitz

Walkmühle
NANSOUTY
UVAROV

N

Rausnitz

Blaziowitz, Bosenitz, Holubitz
2:00 p.m., 2 December 1805

Stare
Vinohrady

0   1   2   3km

0   1   2miles

DH = d'Hautpoul   AR = Arkhangel   5J = 5th Jäger
K = Kellermann   PAV = Pavlograd   6J = 6th Jäger
M&T = Milhaud & Trelliard OI = Old Ingermanland
WA = Walther

off, Suchet ordered a pause to regroup for another effort. At the same time, Murat's cavalry prepared to launch a coordinated charge against Chaplits's cavalry and the right of Bagration's line.

On the French right, Caffarelli had launched a fierce attack on Holubitz with the six battalions of the 61st and 51st Line and the 13th Light, and the Russians fought fiercely to retain the post. By 2:00, however, the French had managed to drive the Russian Jäger from Holubitz. As Ulanius pulled back with his 6th Jäger, Colonel Witt of the Empress Cuirassiers pulled back as well, failing to cover Ulanius's retreat much to Ulanius's disgust. Witt, one of the infamous Russian officers who had been enrolled in a Guard regiment as a child and who received a commission without ever receiving any relevant experience, certainly proved the foolishness of the Russian practice of patronage appointments. Bagration responded quickly, ordering his reserve, the three battalions of Arkhangel Musketeers under GM Kamensky-2, to come to the aid of the retreating Jäger. Kamensky drew his forces up on the hill behind Holubitz, roughly parallel to the highway running southeast toward Austerlitz, stemming the French pursuit while Ulanius rallied the remnants of his three battalions behind them.

With the French now in possession of Krug and Holubitz and his only reserves committed, Bagration's situation was perilous. The six battalions of 6th Jäger and Arkhangel Musketeers formed a line southwest of the Posorsitz Post House, its left anchored on the Rausnitz Brook and its right supported by the three squadrons of St Petersburg Dragoons and the Empress Cuirassiers. On the main road stood Yashvil's horse artillery battery, apparently still supported by Wittgenstein's Mariupol Hussars. GM Engelhardt and the six battalions of Old Ingermanland and Pskov Musketeers formed a thin line running to the northwest, backed up only by the five squadrons of Tver Dragoons. Finally, on the far right GM Gogel had emerged from Posorsitz village under cover of Chaplits's cavalry and was occupying the hills southwest of Kowalowitz. Opposing them, Lannes and Murat were determined to make one concerted push that would sweep the Russians from their position and drive them back on Rausnitz.

The concentration of artillery on the road and near Holubitz, coupled with the ravine formed by the Holubitz brook, made any effort in the south difficult. However, the shifting of the Arkhangel Musketeers to the south weakened the Russian center while the seizure of Siwitz by the 17th Light and the light cavalry placed the bulk of the French forces opposite Russian forces deployed on open ground. For the final push, Lannes ordered Caffarelli to hold his position while Suchet renewed the attack on the center. Murat would support this attack by launching his cavalry against Chaplits, driving this force back and then turning on the Russian infantry. The French attack probably began soon after 2:00.

Suchet again ordered his infantry forward and they soon met with intense fire from the Russian line. At the same time, Murat launched his cavalry forward, charging Chaplits before the Russian general was quite ready to charge himself. The 4th Hussars were the first to reach the enemy, followed by Sebastiani's brigade of dragoons. Roget's dragoon brigade and d'Hautpoul's cuirassiers followed in support. Chaplits's position was soon made more difficult by the activity of Milhaud and Trelliard, who finally managed to drive the Cossacks from around Siwitz and placed themselves on Chaplits's right flank. As the French light cavalry engaged Chaplits, d'Hautpoul's cuirassiers drew up from the rear and engaged Chaplits frontally, allowing the 10th Cuirassiers to overflow the left of the Russian hussars, turning their flank. Beset on three sides, the Pavlograd Hussars and the supporting Cossacks were all driven back in a mass toward Kowalowitz.

While Murat was driving in the Russian right, Suchet's infantry was charging the Russian center. Suchet deployed three regiments, the 34th, 40th and 88th Line for the attack, retaining the 64th Line in reserve. The six French battalions fixed bayonets and advanced steadily toward the Russian line. Engelhardt's battalions maintained a heavy fire, but the French were soon upon them. According to French accounts, Suchet's men inflicted 2,000 casualties, captured sixteen guns and took many prisoners. In fact, these figures exceed the total casualties reported by the Russians for the Pskov and Old Ingermanland Musketeer regiments for the entire day. But despite the exaggerated numbers in the French reports, the French had inflicted severe casualties on Engelhardt's men and broken the center of the Russian line.

By 2:30 the center and right of Bagration's line had been broken and the troops were fleeing eastward in disorder, some toward Kowalowitz and others back toward the main road. A portion of Engelhardt's command, covered by the Tver Dragoons, attempted to form a line along a ravine northeast of the Posorsitz Post House. The French cavalry now operating in this sector of the battlefield was far more numerous, however, with Chaplits having been driven back through Kowalowitz and Wittgenstein covering the retreat of the Russian left. General d'Hautpoul had advanced his cuirassiers to support the French infantry in their pursuit of the Russians, and now launched the 10th Cuirassiers to the left of the ravine. Circling behind the Russian infantry, they struck them in the rear, sabering many and scattering the rest. By 3:00 the entire plain between Bosenitz and the Posorsitz Post House had been cleared of the Russians after two hours of fierce fighting.

Slaughter on the Goldbach

To the south of the Pratzen Heights, the allied forces in the valley of the Goldbach stood paralyzed with uncertainty. Finally realizing the magnitude of the allied defeat on the heights between 12:00 and 12:30, Prshibyshevsky and Olsufiev were unwilling to engage the French further yet they still lacked any orders from Buxhöwden to withdraw. For the French, the absence of any Russian pursuit after the earlier French attacks had been beaten back hinted at the confusion and hesitation on the part of the Russian commanders. Now, after a thirty-minute respite, Davout's forces around Sokolnitz were again ready to attack while the Russians remained frozen in place. By around 12:30, Davout had reformed his battered battalions and prepared to launch them again on the Russians around Sokolnitz. Davout issued orders for all French forces remaining opposite Sokolnitz to converge on the Russians in an arc extending from the pheasantry past Sokolnitz Castle to their positions south of Sokolnitz village. Such was the position when Langeron arrived, breathless and panicked by the desperate situation he had just witnessed on the Pratzen to the rear.

Langeron later claimed that he had informed Buxhöwden of developments on the Pratzen Heights almost immediately after arriving there—at least by 11:00. Despite this, Buxhöwden had done nothing, the twelve battalions near Augezd remaining in position only 20–30 minutes away from the scene of the crucial fighting on the Pratzeberg. With no reinforcements arriving from his superior, Langeron had decided to take matters into his own hands and had returned to Sokolnitz to withdraw a portion of his own column from Sokolnitz in order to reinforce Kamensky's beleaguered battalions on the heights. Langeron apparently had left the heights shortly before Kamensky received Kutuzov's order for a general withdrawal and was unaware of this order. This unfortunate timing—a matter of perhaps fifteen minutes—would produce a series of catastrophes for the Allied 2nd and 3rd Columns, worsening what was already a desperate situation.

On arriving at Sokolnitz, Langeron immediately issued orders for the regiments of his column to withdraw to the east bank of the Goldbach in preparation for launching a counterattack on St Hilaire's right flank on the heights. He also claims to have informed Prshibyshevsky of events on the heights at this point, which appears to have been the first Prshibyshevsky had heard of it—demonstrating that Buxhöwden had not even notified the other column commanders of the developing situation. Two battalions of the Kursk Musketeers had remained as a reserve on the east bank of the Goldbach. To these Langeron planned to add the three battalions of Vyborg Musketeers and two battalions of the 8th Jäger, which stood south of the village. Langeron ordered these five battalions to recross the Goldbach to join the two Kursk battalions, intending to march the entire body—between 2,500 and 3,000 men—to the aid of Kamensky on the heights. The remaining four battalions of his column, three battalions of Perm Musketeers and one of Kursk Musketeers, were to remain in position in Sokolnitz to cover this withdrawal and were to follow once the other forces were across. Around 12:30 or shortly thereafter the five battalions of Vyborg Musketeers and the 8th Jäger began their withdrawal over the Goldbach, apparently passing between the village and the stream to cross via the bridge near the northern end of Sokolnitz.[*] While this movement was occurring, the French attack on Sokolnitz was also developing.

The intense fighting that would occur around Sokolnitz for the next several hours defies any attempt to sort out the details definitively. Friant's report, for example, details the morning's actions in five paragraphs setting out the activities of each of his regiments. By contrast, the afternoon's fighting, though of longer duration, is described in a single paragraph devoid of specifics. Memoirs provide glimpses into the character of the fighting, but none of the participants seem to have been able to capture the sequence of events in any coherent fashion. The picture that emerges from the reports and the memoirs is one of confused and desperate fighting that raged the entire length of the line from the pheasantry to the south end of Sokolnitz for about two and a half hours.

What is certain is that between 12:00 and 12:30 the 111th Line occupied a position almost due west of the village with the 15th Light and the 33rd Line to its left and the larger part of the Tirailleurs du Po on the extreme left in the pheasantry. The 48th Line appears to have stood on the heights to the southwest.[†] GdB Merle, with at least a portion of the 26th Light, did not participate in the morning attacks on Sokolnitz launched by Friant's division, but seems to have stood on the defensive, probably to the north opposite Sokolnitz Castle and anchored on the pheasantry. Some accounts place the 26th Light to the left of the 33rd Line while other accounts seem to place it to the right of the 48th Line. It seems entirely possible that the two portions of the 26th Light that had been driven from Sokolnitz in two directions may well have operated on either flank, the fragment that was driven to the south

---

[*] The Vyborg Musketeers appear to have had their battalion guns with them on the west bank of the Goldbach. The battalions therefore seem likely to have withdrawn over the bridge at the northern end of Sokolnitz to allow the withdrawal of their artillery, the column marching either through the village or between the village and the stream.

[†] Some writers, most notably Colin, have asserted that 48th Line remained lodged in the south end of Sokolnitz through this period. However, this seems unlikely given that the five Russian battalions south of the village passed beyond this point to the Sokolnitz bridge unmolested.

having remained on the heights to the southwest.* This splitting of the 26th Light seems the most likely explanation given the conflicting accounts placing the regiment on both the northern and southern extremities of Davout's line. Supporting the infantry, Margaron's two chasseur regiments appear to have remained in reserve behind the French center. In all, eleven battalions (less several companies previously detached) and six squadrons ringed the Russian forces in Sokolnitz and Sokolnitz Castle.

The presence of the allied forces of Dokhturov and Kienmayer northwest of Tellnitz remained a cause of concern for Davout, despite the fact that they had remained inactive since crossing the Goldbach around mid-morning. Davout left the troops that had been forced from Tellnitz under the command of GdB Heudelet, along with most of Bourcier's cavalry, in position facing Dokhturov and Kienmayer. These forces included the remnants of the five battalions of the 3rd and 108th Line (with their accompanying detachments of Tirailleurs du Po and the 15th Light) from Tellnitz.† The five regiments of Bourcier's dragoon division and the 1st Dragoons stood at the extreme right of the French line to contain the 20 squadrons of Austrian cavalry there. In all, Heudelet and Bourcier opposed about 5½ battalions and 18 squadrons to the 16 battalions and 20 squadrons of the allies northwest of Tellnitz.

Davout targeted Sokolnitz village as the focus of his next attack. Leaving only two battalions from the 4th Corps under GdB Merle on his left and the five battalions under Heudelet on his right, Davout planned to launch nine battalions against the Russians. Davout replaced the understrength 15th Light opposite the northwest projection of Sokolnitz with the stronger 33rd Line, shifting the 15th Light to the left where it would apply pressure on

---

* Most of the 1st Battalion of the 26th Light had been driven to the south, possibly with some elements of the 2nd Battalion. For simplicity, the two fragments can each be considered as a battalion in strength even though each fragment may have included men from both battalions.

† Colin places the 3rd and 108th Line along with the 26th Light with Merle between the 48th and 111th Line but does not specify why he believes this to be so. Duffy places Merle with the 3rd Line and the 26th Light on the extreme right based on the testimony of Col Pouget of the 26th who said that his regiment advanced adjacent to the Goldbach. Bowden places Merle with the 26th Light on the left of the 15th Light near the pheasantry, but this overlooks Pouget's statement that his men advanced adjacent to the Goldbach against an enemy already retiring (obviously 8th Jäger and Vyborg Musketeers, no other Russian forces were retreating at the time of the initial French advance). Neither Duffy nor Bowden mention the 108th Line. The placing of the 108th Line with Merle's brigade or between the 48th and 111th Line seems unlikely in context. Russian forces found few French troops in position to the northwest later in the afternoon, suggesting these battalions were not in position northwest of Sokolnitz as has been asserted. Further, the presence of Dokhturov and Kienmayer northwest of Tellnitz would require some body of troops to observe them and contain any offensive movement on the French rear when they maneuvered for their flank attack on the south end of Sokolnitz. The later positioning of the 108th at the head of Friant's division advancing south to Tellnitz also supports the idea that the 108th remained southwest of Sokolnitz. In the absence of firm evidence placing the 3rd Line with Merle, it seems most likely that this regiment operated with the 108th. Alombert and Colin, V, p. 206; Duffy, *Austerlitz*, p. 141; Bowden, p. 339.

Prshibyshevsky's forces drawn up just north of the village. With these regiments, Davout hoped to drive the Russian forces north of Sokolnitz and away from Dokhturov and their main line of retreat. From the west, the 111th Line would attack the center of Sokolnitz, while the remaining three battalions would converge on the southern end of the village, the 48th Line from the southwest and Pouget with his battalion of the 26th Light from the south. These nine battalions directly opposed nine Russian battalions in the village and to the south, along with the two battalions of 7th Jäger immediately north of the village.

Many of the battalions on both sides had incurred substantial casualties during the morning's fighting, making it impossible to derive an accurate assessment of comparative strengths. Given the larger initial size of the French battalions but reducing this strength for the reported attrition suffered during Friant's forced march, it would seem that the forces opposing each other at Sokolnitz village were roughly equal. The Russians had probably suffered at least equal casualties with the French in their struggle with Friant's division and had certainly sustained heavy losses in the initial storming of Sokolnitz, so this would make the opposing strengths on this sector of the battlefield perhaps 4,000–4,500 men on either side.

Because the Russian forces were jammed into the narrow space between the Goldbach and the French positions on the high ground opposite Sokolnitz, it was difficult for them to shift forces from their right to their left to meet this onslaught. Nevertheless, Merle was assigned the mission of holding the attention of the nine Russian battalions—about 4,500 men—in front of Sokolnitz Castle and in the pheasantry. Merle's force was composed of a portion of the 26th Light and the larger part of the Tirailleurs du Po and cannot have totaled more than about 1,000 men.

The French forces began their attack around 12:30. In the northern sector, the 15th Light and the 33rd Line came to grips with the Russians almost immediately, crossing the Sokolnitz Brook and advancing the short distance that had separated them from the Russian forces in minutes. The Russians deployed west of the village were soon driven into the cover of the houses, and the two battalions of the 33rd Line converged on either side of the northern projection of Sokolnitz where the Russian defenders, the grenadiers of the Kursk Musketeer Regiment, put up a stubborn defense. To their right, the men of the 7th Jäger held their ground against the assault of the 15th Light.

On the Russian left the situation soon became critical. The two battalions of the 111th Line advancing from the west engaged the Perm Musketeers as planned. As the two battalions of the 48th Line and Pouget's battalion of the 26th Light wheeled around to strike the Russian forces south of the village, however, they found that these had already been withdrawn. Instead of fighting five Russian battalions, Colonels Barbanegre and Pouget found themselves on the exposed flank of the Russian battalions defending the village.

Pouget describes the unopposed advance of his regiment, stating:

> The victory . . . was decided for the French in the center of the two armies. Those Russians who were opposed to the 26th had been advised of this first, and retired at once, leaving the field to this regiment as well as their wounded and prisoners.*

Advancing along the river, Pouget quickly found himself on the Russian rear between the village and the river. Colonel Barbanegre of the 48th Line led his regiment forward against the left flank of the Perm Musketeers. Attacked by two battalions of the 111th in front and the two battalions of the 48th in flank, the Russian forces were quickly driven into the village, hotly pursued by the French. The speed of the French attack had once again caught the Russians by surprise, the Russian 2nd and 3rd Columns again suffering from the absence of even a small Cossack contingent for reconnaissance and cavalry support. Langeron, recognizing the seriousness of the situation, halted the eastwards move of the 8th Jäger and Vyborg Musketeers and ordered the 2nd Battalion, Vyborg Musketeers, to counterattack the French who were busy surrounding the remainder of his column. Olsufiev led the battalion across the bridge once again, making some progress before being halted by French fire from the houses in the village.

Reinforcing the Vyborg battalion with a part of the 8th Jäger, Langeron made a second attempt to relieve the forces in the village, but again without success:

> . . . the French, cut off in the houses, maintained a dreadful fire, and we also fought with the bayonet. In a moment we lost many men, and, not having enough to retake the village, General Olsufiev and I were forced to retreat. I gathered the 8th Jäger Regiment and that of Vyborg. I placed them opposite the village and I deployed a battery composed of the guns of the Vyborg Regiment in front of the bridge. The French stopped then, and I met them a hundred paces from the village.†

With the four battalions of his column remaining on the west bank of the Goldbach pressed into the northern part of the village by a substantial body of French, and the allied forces on the heights to his rear in desperate straits, Langeron's position was unenviable. Acting quickly, shortly after 1:00 he

---

* Alombert and Colin, V, p. 206.
† Langeron, p. 76.

ordered Olsufiev to continue the attempt to relieve the forces in Sokolnitz with the Vyborg Musketeers and 8th Jäger. At the same time, Langeron ordered Colonel Seleverstov with the 2nd and 3rd Battalions, Kursk Musketeers, to proceed to the Pratzen heights to reinforce Kamensky-1. Langeron himself rode off to Tellnitz again to try to convince Buxhöwden of the desperateness of the situation and to bring back reinforcements.

Prshibyshevsky appears to have lacked Langeron's sense of urgency. Having received word of the action on the Pratzen Heights around 12:30 at about the same time as the French attack had begun, Prshibyshevsky had immediately sent off a report to the "Commander-in-Chief" stating that he was under attack and intended to bring the action to a quick and successful conclusion. Prshibyshevsky had easily beaten off the diversionary attacks of Merle and the 7th Jäger seems to have successfully fended off the attacks of the 15th Light. One participant wrote:

> Having marched through the village into a vast valley, we were deployed in front and advanced; the enemy cannonballs reaped our front, killing people [as they passed through the ranks] on the diagonal . . . We were moved back and stopped in a small ravine. The enemy line was soon deployed and fired at us with guns and muskets, while their cavalry charged us as well. A few of us volunteered to drive back the French skirmishers [strelki] who, under cover of cavalry, advanced very close to us. I volunteered as well. The French cavalry attacked us at that moment. We heard a shout from the front, "Beware, skirmishers!" We dispersed to the right and left, the French cavalry also dispersed to the sides; [a French] officer galloped past me and I fired at him—he fell down but his horse ran away. I ran to him, took his coat and threw mine away. I did not have time to check Frenchman's watches and was very glad I got the coat. It was very cold, wintertime and it snowed a bit. *

Prshibyshevsky would later write, "As I was in time in my enterprises, having completely defeated the enemy, at that moment a part of the 2nd Column and the Austrian horse artillery retired to the village of Sokolnitz, directing against my left flank even more enemies."† The collapse of the Russian left had enclosed Prshibyshevsky's forces in a quadrilateral surrounding Sokolnitz Castle, with a single bridge over the Goldbach to his rear. Prshibyshevsky's intention quickly to drive off the French attack prior to

---

* Popaditchev, pp. 11–12.

† "Raport I. Ya. Przhibyshevskogo Aleksandru I o Deistviyakh 3-i Kolonny v Srazhenii pri Austerlitse, 1806 g. Iulya 11," in *Kutuzov Sbornik Dokumentov*, pp. 269–70. During the advance into Austria, several batteries of Austrian guns were attached to the Russian columns, some of the light pieces serving as battalion guns. Prshibyshevsky is undoubtedly referring to some of these.

withdrawing, never particularly realistic, had become impossible. To the south, the four battalions in Sokolnitz, cut off from the rest of their column, continued to hold out in the village, conducting an intense defense of each house. Olsufiev continued to attempt to storm across the Sokolnitz bridge, supported by a battery of assembled battalion guns pouring fire into the French on the opposite bank of the Goldbach.

Davout's attack on Sokolnitz had succeeded beyond all expectations, the withdrawal of the Russian left giving the French forces substantial numerical superiority at the key point of the attack and producing quick and dramatic results. Despite this initial success, however, the French advance soon stalled. Merle's attack in the north had been intended only as a diversion and this small force stood little chance against the superior Russian forces in front of it. To the south, the collapse of the Russian flank had driven four Russian battalions into a narrow space of perhaps 500 meters between the Goldbach and Sokolnitz Brook, and the densely packed Russians obstinately defended the houses stretching almost the entire length of that space. Nevertheless, Davout maintained the pressure on the Russian forces, intense house-to-house fighting continuing in the village and several attacks and counterattacks occurring along the river near the bridge over the next thirty or forty-five minutes. This standoff came to an abrupt end, however, when the full impact of the French success on the Pratzen Heights came crashing down upon Sokolnitz.

The French attack on Sokolnitz started at about the same time that the 43rd Line and Boyé's dragoons were flanking GM Kamensky-1's brigade on the Pratzen Heights. With the Russian forces near the Pratzeberg finally defeated and retreating, Marshal Soult, operating on Napoleon's orders, prepared to spring the trap that would destroy the allied columns engaged in the valley of the Goldbach. Soult sent orders to GdB Levasseur to advance southward from Kobelnitz and ordered St Hilaire to wheel to his right and advance westward toward Sokolnitz.

St Hilaire paused briefly to reassemble his forces for the descent from the Pratzen Heights onto the rear of the allied forces in the Goldbach valley. St Hilaire's six battalions on the south end of the heights had already been reinforced by the return of the 43rd Line from the far side of Pratze village and the arrival of Boyé's dragoon division. The remainder of Varé's brigade, the 55th Line soon joined the 43rd. St Hilaire ordered his forces to deploy on the edge of the heights facing Sokolnitz in preparation for attacking the rear of the Allied columns on the Goldbach, and then went to get his wounds dressed while his orders were being carried out. Morand with the 10th Light simply changed front to his right while Thiébault's brigade moved into position to the left of Morand.* Varé's 43rd and 55th Line moved into position on Thiébault's left. Thiébault obviously had been unaware of Varé's orders to operate in cooperation with Vandamme's division, and reported being astonished by Varé's tardy arrival.[†]

On the northern end of the Pratzen Heights, Vandamme was at this point reforming his division after driving the Austro-Russian 4th Column from the heights. With the defeat of the 4th Column, Napoleon had ordered six of Vandamme's ten battalions to advance on Augezd and around 12:30 Vandamme ordered Ferey's four battalions and Candras with the 28th Line to take a position on St Hilaire's left facing Augezd. Boyé's dragoons skirted the edge of the heights to take position between St Hilaire and Vandamme.

Thiébault relates that the Russian positions in the valley of the Goldbach were clearly visible from his positions on the heights, though undoubtedly shrouded in powder smoke. "This château [Sokolnitz Castle] was still occupied by the Russians with the advance guard of one of the corps which had marched on Turas, and were covering the hill opposite to that which we had reached," he noted.[‡] Thiébault's description supports Prshibyshevsky's assertion that he had defeated the attacks on his column as the only Russian forces that could have been occupying the high ground beyond Sokolnitz Castle were Galitz and Butyrsk Musketeers. What Thiébault did not mention, however, was that while he was fascinated by the view of the action in the valley, to his left a Russian column was advancing toward the heights from Sokolnitz.

After a pause of about fifteen minutes while the field surgeons finished dressing St Hilaire's wounds, St Hilaire returned to the head of his division and gave orders to advance. Between about 1:15 and 1:30 the French battalions, somewhat refreshed by the brief pause in the action and their

---

* It remains unclear whether the two battalions of the 14th Line, separated on either flank of the French line on the Pratzen Heights through the morning's fighting, were reunited at this point or if they remained separated. In the absence of clear evidence one way or the other, I have assumed that the 2nd Battalion of the 14th joined the 1st Battalion in line adjacent to the 10th Light when the French advanced to the edge of the plateau.

† As with most of the afternoon operations, accounts are confused and imprecise. The deployment of St Hilaire's regiments has been interpreted in several different ways, apparently relying on Thiébault for details. Thiébault related that his brigade deployed in the center with Morand's brigade to his right and Levasseur's brigade (which should have been in Kobelnitz) on his left, and this has been taken as an error in direction on Thiébault's part, Levasseur plainly being on Thiébault's right. In mentioning Levasseur's brigade, however, Thiébault notes that his brigade stood between Levasseur's brigade, "which at last to our astonishment had joined us," and Morand's brigade on the opposite side. At the same time, Thiébault fails to mention Varé's brigade at all. Since it is unlikely that Levasseur's brigade would have ascended the heights, joined up to Thiébault's right, and then descended the heights again to attack Sokolnitz, especially given the fact that Levasseur engaged Wimpfen's forces frontally, it seems that Thiébault must have mistakenly referred to Levasseur when he meant Varé. Thiébault, II, p. 167.

‡ Thiébault, II, pp. 166–7.

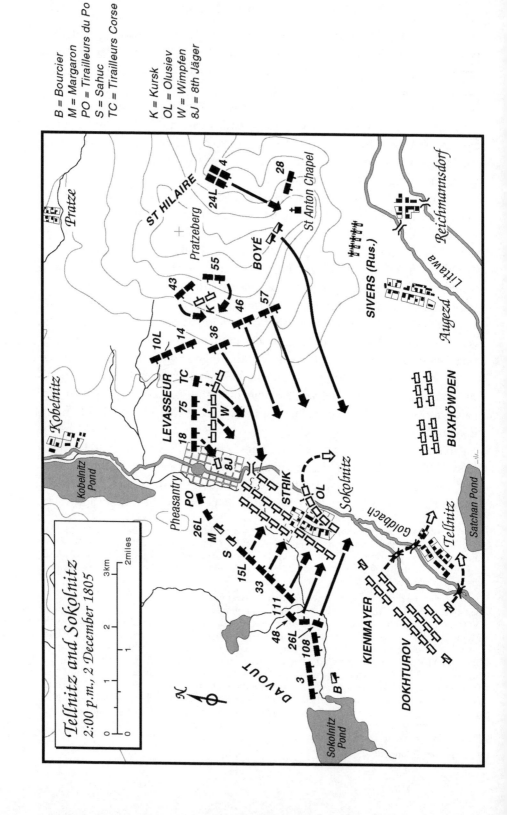

B = Bourcier
M = Margaron
PO = Tirailleurs du Po
S = Sahuc
TC = Tirailleurs Corse

K = Kursk
OL = Olusiev
W = Wimpfen
8J = 8th Jäger

Tellnitz and Sokolnitz
2:00 p.m., 2 December 1805

0   1   2   3km
0   1   2miles

Pratze

Kobelnitz
Kobelnitz Pond

Pheasantry

LEVASSEUR

ST HILAIRE

Pratzeberg

St Anton Chapel

BOYÉ

Sokolnitz

Goldbach

SIVERS (Rus.)

Augezd

BUXHÖWDEN

Reichmannsdorf

Littawa

DAVOUT

STRIK

OL

KIENMAYER

DOKHTUROV

Tellnitz

Satchan Pond

Sokolnitz Pond

morale buoyed by their victory on the heights, began their march down the slope toward Sokolnitz. At the same time, the two battalions of Kursk Musketeers, under the command of Colonel Seleverstov, were advancing up the slope, unaware that Kamensky-1 had retreated. The emergence of the French columns from the heights must have come as a nasty surprise to the Russians. Seleverstov halted his force in confusion as the French columns swept down upon him. It appears that the small Russian force stood directly in the path of Varé's brigade. Varé's four battalions immediately enveloped the flanks of the two Kursk battalions as Ferey and Thiébault continued their advance unimpeded to either side of Varé. Seleverstov managed a brief stand of not more than a quarter of an hour during which it became obvious that no relief was forthcoming. Some men seem to have managed to escape the encirclement and flee but the majority were forced to surrender.

While St Hilaire's division was advancing, Langeron was finding the day increasingly nightmarish. He had arrived at Buxhöwden's headquarters around 1:30 to find the general doing nothing to help retrieve the situation. Whether because he had been drinking heavily or was simply overcome by stress and an absence of direction from higher authority, Buxhöwden was behaving erratically. An Austrian staff officer, Captain Jurczik, was also at Buxhöwden's headquarters seeking his assistance, and both Langeron and Jurczik frantically tried to impress upon Buxhöwden the urgency of the situation. Buxhöwden, however, had finally received Kutuzov's general order to withdraw and refused to advance any portion of his command to aid the beleaguered forces on either side of his column. Realizing that the order to withdraw meant that Kamensky-1 had already withdrawn from the heights and that Buxhöwden would not be sending any assistance to Sokolnitz, Langeron rode back to Sokolnitz. En route he most likely witnessed the French advance from the heights and the envelopment of the two battalions he had sent to their doom. Rejoining Olsufiev, Langeron learned that the situation had not changed since he had left. With St Hilaire bearing down on his rear, Langeron determined to save what he could and leave the remainder of his command to their fate. Disengaging the Vyborg Musketeers and the 8th Jäger, Langeron drew them off to the south just as the French forces began arriving. With Varé preoccupied with securing the large number of prisoners—nearly all of Seleverstov's two battalions—Langeron was able to disengage the five battalions east of the Goldbach unmolested.

To the north, Levasseur's brigade, rested and ready after a morning of inactivity, appears to have advanced from Kobelnitz immediately upon receiving orders. Shortly after 1:00, Levasseur's five battalions engaged Wimpfen's forces (seven understrength battalions) east of the Goldbach adjacent to the pheasantry. The two forces were roughly equal in size and the Russian brigade appears to have been holding its own when St Hilaire's troops appeared on its right rear. Wimpfen immediately drew in his right to face the new threat, but Morand's depleted battalions of the 10th Light and possibly portions of the 14th Line quickly drove in his right flank. The combined forces of Levasseur and Morand soon pushed the majority of Wimpfen's forces back toward the Goldbach and across the stream into the pheasantry. A few, including Wimpfen himself, became separated and were able to slip off to the south in an attempt to join the 1st Column. Meanwhile, Thiébault's brigade (the 36th and 14th Line) had advanced between Varé and Morand. Passing through the gap between Seleverstov and Wimpfen largely unopposed, Thiébault's brigade soon found itself directly opposite Sokolnitz castle.

By around 2:15, all the Russian forces of the 2nd and 3rd Columns east of the Goldbach except for Langeron's five battalions had been killed, captured, or driven back across the Goldbach. For the Russian forces remaining west of the Goldbach, there was now no chance of rejoining the rest of the army. To the south of Sokolnitz, Davout had massed the seven battalions of the 33rd, 111th and 48th Line and the 26th Light. To the east, there were now fourteen battalions on the line of the Goldbach, St Hilaire's ten battalions and Levasseur's four. To the north and northwest, however, stood only the 15th Light and about a battalion of the 26th Light, three battalions that had been depleted by detachments and casualties, plus the Tirailleurs du Po slightly to the east of them covering the pheasantry.

Any thoughts Prshibyshevsky may have had of holding the line of the Goldbach against the French attacking his rear were abruptly shattered by the aggressive French advance. As the French forces arrived at the Goldbach, St Hilaire ordered Thiébault to pursue the fleeing remnants of Wimpfen's rearguard and seize Sokolnitz Castle while Morand (with Levasseur) and Varé supported him on the right and left. Thiébault launched his 36th Line in pursuit of the fleeing Russians, sweeping across the bridge before the Russians could reform to mount a defense. Many of the Russian soldiers took refuge in the buildings of the castle where they desperately tried to hold back the French onslaught. In the confusion of battle, the troops facing Merle had no idea that they had been attacked in the rear. One participant described the action vividly:

> I fired another four times with my musket, when I suddenly felt a burning in my right leg; I could not step or walk since I was wounded and two other soldiers quickly helped me leave the front. Meantime, the French advanced and one of their detachments flanked us on the right. Rapid musket fire came from both sides, our troops held ground and nobody

thought we were doing badly. I do not know how it happened but our commander, Strik, lost his sword. He was wandering about without it, saying again and again, "Lads, throw your guns away or they [the French] will slaughter us all." But despite this, our soldiers continued loading and firing. The firing gradually increased and the situation turned into a mess. We were muddled up with the French, and because we were not supported the enemy overwhelmed us. Two healthy lads who were with me asked me, "Why are we still here? They will kill you and us as well." They threw my musket away, grabbed me by the arms, and dragged me into a house, where we found many of our wounded.[*]

While Thiébault's men were penetrating the castle complex, Davout mounted a renewed assault from the west. Just as Thiébault could see the Russian troops arrayed on the low rise northwest of Sokolnitz from his vantage point on the heights, Davout could plainly see the French troops arrayed on the edge of the Pratzen and their advance toward Sokolnitz from his command post on the heights west of Sokolnitz. Judging the timing perfectly, Davout ordered a change of frontage for the 15th Light, shifting it to the north and launching it in an attack on Sokolnitz Castle from the west just as Thiébault's men were storming the position from the east. The result was to split the Russian forces west of the Goldbach in two: six battalions (two of the 7th Jäger, three of the Perm Musketeers and the remaining battalion of the Kursk Musketeers) were in the northern part of Sokolnitz village and the open ground just north of it, and the remaining ten battalions were to the north.

The fierce resistance of the Russian forces in the buildings of Sokolnitz Castle was soon reduced to confused fighting of isolated detachments as the French fought building to building. The forces cut off in the village, realizing the French were across the river to their rear, began to falter in their resistance as the 33rd and 111th hunted them from house to house. Toward 3:00 a portion of these forces—a mass of about 1,000 men—appears to have taken advantage of the shifting of the 15th Light toward Sokolnitz Castle to break out to the northwest, leaving large numbers of their comrades to be surrounded in the houses of Sokolnitz. The confused mass of refugees from Sokolnitz was apparently pursued by elements of Legrand's division (possibly the 3rd Line, which had been freed up with the withdrawal of Dokhturov to the south). Over the next few hours these fugitives from Sokolnitz were scattered, hunted down and mostly either killed or captured, although small parties eventually managed to escape and make their way back to Russia. Some of those escaping brought the regimental flags of the battalions that had

---

[*] Popaditchev, p. 12.

surrendered at Sokolnitz, having torn them from the standards and hidden them in their uniform coats.*

The 48th Line then pushed its way through Sokolnitz to join the 36th Line in mopping up the last resistance at Sokolnitz Castle while Davout ordered the 15th Light into the castle complex from the west. Beyond the castle complex, the larger portion of Wimpfen's command, now commanded by GM Selekhov, had found refuge in the pheasantry where it successfully held back the combined efforts of Levasseur and Morand for perhaps as long as half an hour. The Russian resistance became increasingly disorganized as the French forces penetrated the game park and isolated small parties of Russians.† Some refugees from the pheasantry escaped to join Prshibyshevsky's force while the remainder maintained sporadic fighting in the game park until they either ran out of ammunition or were hunted down by the French.

The largest body of Russian troops west of the Goldbach, under the direct command of Prshibyshevsky, was composed of eight comparatively fresh battalions positioned northwest of Sokolnitz Castle. This force does not appear to have been under any significant pressure from Merle's small force, but French artillery was pummelling the Russian ranks with shot. Operating on the advice of his Austrian staff officer, Prshibyshevsky resolved to retreat to the north where, the staff officer assured him, he would be able to recross the Goldbach and attempt to rejoin the army. However desperate the attempt, there was plainly no alternative.‡ Prshibyshevsky led his eight battalions (three battalions each from the Galitz and Butyrsk Musketeers and two battalions of the Narva Musketeers) plus assorted refugees from the pheasantry, not more than about 3,000 men in all, and headed north. Prshibyshevsky's column appears to have remained in good order, and he seems to have intended to pass to the west of the Kobelnitz Pond and then head east to cross the Goldbach north of Kobelnitz. Lochet, with the 36th and 48th Line, set off in pursuit of Prshibyshevsky while Margaron's two regiments of light cavalry harassed the rear of the retreating Russians.

* Serge Andolenko, *Aigles de Napoléon Contre Drapeaux du Tsar, 1799, 1805–1807, 1812–1814* (Paris: Eurimprim, 1969), pp. 84–8.

† It seems that the 18th Line from Levasseur's brigade penetrated the pheasantry from the east while the Tirailleurs du Po had remained in the northern part since that morning. As the Russian defenses became more fragmented, so did the French forces pursuing the various elements. It is likely that portions of several regiments ended up fighting in the pheasantry.

‡ This version of events is as related in Prshibyshevsky's report. While other accounts assert that Prshibyshevsky broke out to the north in an attempt to find the 4th Column that should have been around Kobelnitz, Prshibyshevsky's report reveals that he was not so deluded. His statement of his motives needs to be taken into consideration along with the motives others later ascribed to him. Although Prshibyshevsky's account was written after the fact and in part as a defense of his actions, there is no way that others would have a more accurate insight into Prshibyshevsky's motives. While the plan was utterly unrealistic, it is not at all implausible that Prshibyshevsky seized upon it as the only chance to avoid certain envelopment and surrender.

For the French forces remaining east of the Goldbach there remained little to do. Around 2:30, Soult ordered the 75th Line and Tirailleurs Corse from Levasseur's brigade to follow Langeron's battalions to the south to support Vandamme near Augezd and Tellnitz. At about the same time, St Hilaire collected the 10th Light, 14th Line and 43rd Line, which had seen little action in the fighting around Sokolnitz, and directed them to Kobelnitz to prevent the Russian forces west of the Goldbach from escaping to the northeast.* By around 3:00, the fighting around Sokolnitz was effectively over. As resistance diminished, Davout assembled the majority of his battalions and marched south toward Tellnitz where they joined Heudelet and Bourcier, leaving parties to continue hunting down the fugitive Russians. The allied 2nd and 3rd Columns had ceased to exist.

With Their Backs to the Ponds

While the 2nd and 3rd Columns were fighting for survival at Sokolnitz, Vandamme was moving against the 1st Column at Augezd and Tellnitz. Buxhöwden had remained with what Langeron termed his "guard of honor" between Tellnitz and Augezd all morning. This force, composed of the twelve battalions of the Kiev Grenadiers and Vladimir, Yaroslav and New Ingermanland Musketeers, could have exercised considerable influence on events on the Pratzen Heights. Instead, Buxhöwden had kept it in reserve, ignoring the pleas of Langeron and others to release the troops to reinforce the beleaguered allied forces on the heights. The remainder of the 1st Column, under the command of GL Dokhturov, stood on the opposite side of the Goldbach a short distance from Tellnitz. Dokhturov's eleven battalions, including one battalion each from the 7th and 5th Jäger along with the Bryansk, Vyatka and Moscow Musketeers, had also remained motionless after assuming their position west of the Goldbach following the defeat of the French at Tellnitz. Kienmayer's Austrians (five battalions of Grenzers and twenty squadrons of light cavalry) supported Dokhturov.

Kutuzov's orders for a general withdrawal reached Buxhöwden sometime after 12:30, but he had failed to take any action. Only after Langeron had left Buxhöwden's headquarters to return to Sokolnitz, around 1:30–1:45, did the commander of the allied left wing act at all, and even then he moved slowly. Buxhöwden, reportedly demonstrating no sense of the urgency of the situation, issued orders to Kienmayer and Dokhturov to recross the Goldbach and retire by way of the narrow causeway between the Satchan and Mönitz ponds. Kienmayer's command split to form the advance and rear guards for

---

* The 55th Line is not mentioned in the French reports and its disposition at this point in the battle is uncertain. It seems probable that it would have been employed toward Tellnitz.

Dokhturov's battalions. Kienmayer and Nostitz, with the six squadrons of Hessen-Homburg Hussars, three squadrons of Székler Hussars and the small parties of attached Uhlans (about ten squadrons in all) headed up this column. The remaining ten squadrons (eight of O'Reilly Chevauxleger and two of Székler Hussars) and the Grenz battalions crossed the Goldbach and occupied Tellnitz and the vineyards northeast of the town to form the rearguard. Buxhöwden's own twelve battalions were to retire by way of Augezd and would cross the Littawa at Reichmannsdorf. The two bodies would then link with the remnants of Kamensky-1's brigade and the 4th Column that were crossing the Littawa at Klein-Hostieradek and Zbischow.

Had Buxhöwden put his columns in motion immediately, there is little doubt that he could have withdrawn the entire force without loss. However, at this point Buxhöwden seems to have belatedly recognized his broader responsibilities as overall commander of the first three columns. While Kienmayer and Dokhturov began withdrawing their forces over the two bridges at Tellnitz, Buxhöwden distributed his immediate command in a line between Reichmannsdorf and Tellnitz, apparently intending to wait for the 2nd and 3rd Columns to withdraw—despite knowing the desperate circumstances of the 2nd and 3rd Columns related to him by Langeron (if Langeron's account of this conversation is accurate).

While Buxhöwden was methodically arranging his forces for withdrawal, the French forces on the Pratzen Heights were converging to oppose him. The brigade of Ferey had been sent from its position on the eastern edge of the Pratzen plateau overlooking Zbischow to join St Hilaire's left around 12:30. The advance of this column had forced Kamensky-1 to retire toward Klein-Hostieradek rather than joining the 4th Column at Zbischow. Behind Ferey's brigade marched GdB Candras with the 28th Line, which had remained in reserve for most of the morning's action. The infantry soon outpaced the artillery, which became mired in the soft clay on the heights. With Ferey operating on the left of St Hilaire's division, Vandamme had only Candras with the two battalions of the 28th Line immediately at hand. The French battalions arrived on the southern edge of the heights around 1:00, just as the sound of intense firing to the rear signaled the arrival of the Russian Guard on the heights to the north.

Vandamme, who had paused to have his wounds dressed, had remained to the rear during the initial actions with the Russian Guard but soon after rejoined the bulk of his division north of Augezd. Between about 1:15 and 1:30, the French forces on the heights began their descent. While St Hilaire's forces (with Ferey's brigade) descended toward Sokolnitz, the two battalions of the 28th Line moved toward Augezd, and Boyé's dragoons advanced toward

Tellnitz between the two bodies of infantry. As they cleared the crest of the ridge and began their descent, the position of the Russian troops along the road through Augezd came into view.

The massing French forces on the plateau appears to have been detected before they began their descent, perhaps by the cavalry of Lt-Col Balk, who had joined Buxhöwden at Augezd after covering Kamensky-1's retreat with his small party. As Vandamme's forces descended toward Augezd, they came under the massed fire of two heavy 12-pounder batteries (twenty-four guns) under the command of Colonel Count Sivers that Buxhöwden had positioned northeast of Augezd. Vandamme halted his two battalions of infantry at a small plateau midway down the slope near the chapel of St Anton to wait for his own artillery to arrive. To the right, Boyé drew up his dragoons adjacent to the infantry. For the next hour, Sivers's artillery held the French at bay while they waited for their own artillery to come up.

While the French infantry sat paralyzed, Marshal Soult sent orders to Boyé to advance toward the Goldbach to sever the allied forces at Sokolnitz from Tellnitz. Boyé led the 5th and 8th Dragoon Regiments down the slope at a trot, forcing the Russian forces along the river to withdraw into Tellnitz. Boyé pursued them to the edge of the village, but Colonel Geringer charged the rear of the French dragoons with two squadrons of Székler Hussars and a party of Cossacks, scattering them and driving them back to their original position.

Napoleon, having seen the Russian Guard driven back toward Krenowitz, then rode forward to join Vandamme near the St Anton Chapel, arriving shortly after 2:00. Almost immediately after his arrival, Napoleon witnessed Boyé's pursuit of Langeron's column and expressed his great displeasure with the results. He immediately ordered his aide-de-camp, Gardanne, to assume command of the remainder of the dragoon division and "do better." Gardanne took position at the head of the four regiments of dragoons that had not been previously committed and launched them against the Austrian cavalry that remained massed in front of Tellnitz, eight squadrons of O'Reilly Chevauxleger. As the dragoons got to within a hundred paces of the Austrians, the Austrians scattered to either side, uncovering a horse artillery battery that ripped the French lines with canister. For the second time, the dragoons fell back in disorder, this time pursued by the Austrian Chevauxleger. As the French and Austrian horsemen rode back up the slope, Gardanne's dragoons in turn suddenly split to either side to uncover a newly arrived battery of Imperial Guard horse artillery commanded by Colonel Digeon. Giving the Austrians a taste of their own medicine, Digeon's guns also fired a round of canister at point blank range, sending the Austrians streaming back toward Tellnitz.

While Gardanne was leading Boyé's dragoons in futile (though presumably more vigorous) charges against the Austrians, Boyé had been left to observe with the 5th and 8th Dragoon Regiments. Now, with Gardanne occupied toward Tellnitz, Boyé spotted a Russian column near the Goldbach, a party of refugees from Wimpfen's brigade, led by Wimpfen himself, that had eluded St Hilaire's advance toward Sokolnitz and was seeking to join Buxhöwden's forces. Undoubtedly eager to restore his reputation with his emperor, Boyé charged the Russian column with his two regiments, driving them back toward Tellnitz. Part of the 5th Dragoons forced their way between the Russian lines, hacking the Russian infantrymen right and left. The Austrian cavalry at Tellnitz charged almost immediately, driving off Boyé's dragoons and killing or wounding twenty of them, but not until after Boyé's men had managed to capture General Wimpfen.

With French artillery now in position on the heights commanding the Russian positions in the valley, the French prepared to resume the offensive. Four additional battalions (the 4th Line and the two battalions of the 24th Light), eager for revenge after having rallied following their defeat at the hands of the Russian Guard, joined Vandamme's forces around 2:30, giving him a total of six battalions near the chapel of St Anton. In addition, Soult ordered seven more battalions of French infantry that had not been needed at Sokolnitz to join the left of Vandamme's division. Ferey's four battalions of the 46th and 57th Line, the 75th Line and Tirailleurs du Corse drew into line shortly before 3:00. Hemmed in, the allied forces, numbering perhaps 6,000–8,000 men, had available for their retreat the bridge at Reichmannsdorf, two narrow causeways west of the Satchan pond and the fragile ice of the pond itself. What had been a defeat for the Allies had now turned to disaster.

Chapter 7

The Allied Remnants Escape:
2 December, 3:00 P.M. – Midnight

By 3:00 P.M. the situation of the two opposing armies was all Napoleon had hoped for. While the day's events had not occurred exactly as Napoleon had anticipated, he had achieved essentially the same results by exploiting the opportunity that had presented itself in the center. Eight of his ten infantry divisions and all of his cavalry had been or were now in contact with the allied army. The remaining two infantry divisions, composed of twenty battalions of elite infantry, stood in reserve. Oudinot's grenadier division had detached one brigade to the west of Puntowitz to help contain Prshibyshevsky. The remainder, with the Imperial Guard infantry, stood at the ready on the Pratzen Heights.

Napoleon's troops had been victorious in every direction and had driven the allies from their positions with heavy losses. The cost to the French had not been light. The divisions of Vandamme and St Hilaire in particular had sustained heavy casualties during the struggle for the heights, while Friant's division and the regiments of Legrand's division that had been strung out along the lower Goldbach had also suffered serious losses. Despite the fact that a number of battalions had been reduced to half-strength and one battalion reportedly had been reduced to only 150 men, all of the French forces remained in excellent fighting order. Segur had been shocked to see the state of several of Vandamme's battalions, and Vandamme had reportedly quipped in reply, "It is impossible to make a good omelette without breaking a great many eggs!"* This exceptional resilience and endurance can be credited to discipline and thorough training as well as high morale boosted still higher by what even the rank and file recognized as a day of victory.

On the allied side, the high hopes of the morning had been entirely replaced by demoralization. While some of the more experienced allied units remained in good fighting order despite the heavy losses that they had sustained, some of the units with a higher proportion of recruits had been reduced to panic-stricken mobs. Despite this, the allied army still had some capability to oppose the French. The three battalions of Life Grenadiers now defending the heights between Krenowitz and Austerlitz and the larger part of the 1st

---

* Segur, p. 256.

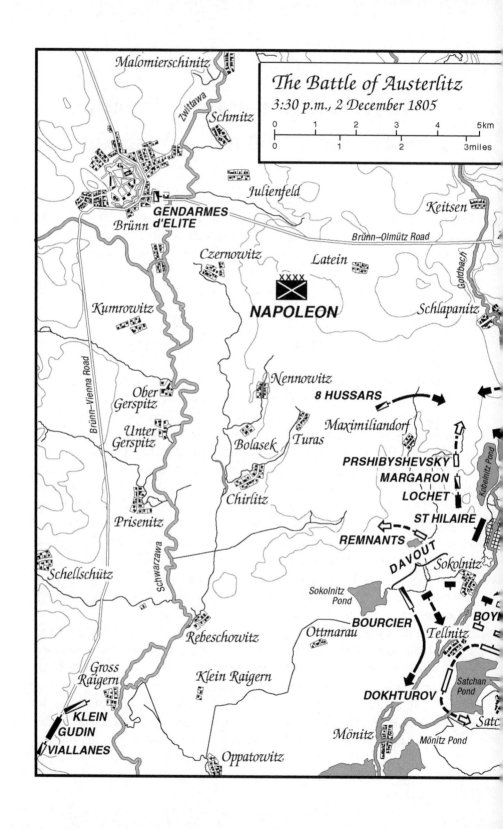

The Battle of Austerlitz
3:30 p.m., 2 December 1805

0   1   2   3   4   5km
0   1   2   3miles

Malomierschinitz

Schmitz

Zwittawa

Julienfeld

Keitsen

Brünn—Olmütz Road

GENDARMES
Brünn d'ELITE

Czernowitz

Latein

Schlapanitz

XXXX
NAPOLEON

Goldbach

Kumrowitz

Nennowitz

8 HUSSARS

Ober
Gerspitz

Maximiliandorf

Unter
Gerspitz

Bolasek

Turas

PRSHIBYSHEVSKY

Kobelnitz Pond

MARGARON

LOCHET

Chirlitz

ST HILAIRE

Prisenitz

REMNANTS

DAVOUT

Sokolnitz

Schwarzawa

Schellschütz

Sokolnitz
Pond

BOURCIER

BOY

Rebeschowitz

Ottmarau

Tellnitz

Gross
Raigern

Klein Raigern

Satchan
Pond

KLEIN
GUDIN

DOKHTUROV

Satc

VIALLANES

Mönitz

Mönitz Pond

Oppatowitz

Brünn—Vienna Road

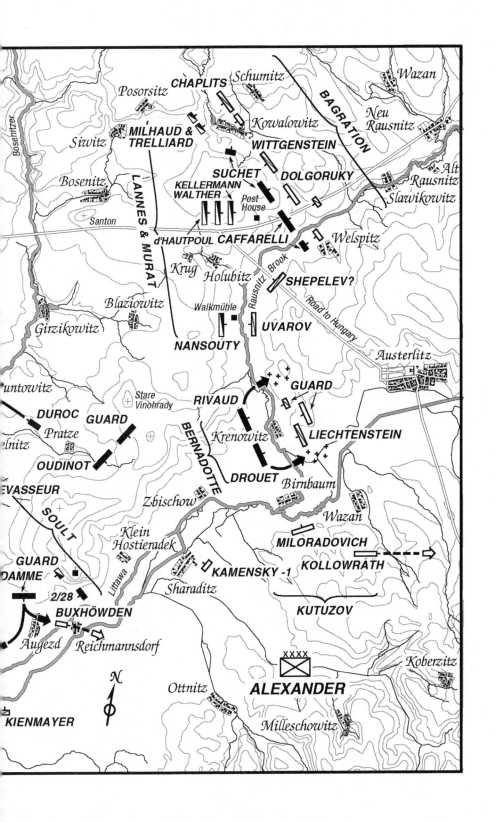

Column had not yet come under French fire, and the line of the Rausnitz Brook and Littawa River afforded a significant barrier to any French pursuit of the defeated allied center.

But the circumstances the allied army now found itself in prevented any effective coordination of effort. The army had been splintered into five separate bodies: the first in the north on the Brünn–Olmütz road, the second behind the Rausnitz Brook near Austerlitz, the third southwest of Austerlitz behind the Littawa River, the fourth around Tellnitz and Augezd, and the fifth west of the Goldbach near Sokolnitz. Communication between the scattered bodies had been severed by the French advance, forcing each of them to fend for itself in complete ignorance of the overall situation or the location of other friendly forces. But perhaps the most decisive blow had been the complete defeat of the allied headquarters. Tsar Alexander, never really capable of commanding the army, had withdrawn to Austerlitz after the 4th Column had been forced from the heights, while the officers he had gathered around him, including Weyrother, wandered about on their own seeking to do something to minimize the extent of the disaster. Lacking any sort of central direction, the individual commanders were left to their own devices.

The French conquest of the heights had completely severed the two fragments of the allied left and Bagration's forces on the allied right from the debris of the allied center. Kutuzov, with most of the remnants of the 4th Column, had retreated behind the Littawa by way of Zbischow, where he was joined by Kamensky-1. The French had made no effort to pursue these forces beyond the Littawa. The remainder of the allied center stood between the Littawa and the Rausnitz. Some elements of the 4th Column seem to have withdrawn through Krenowitz and had been joined by Constantine's battered Life Guard and Hohenlohe's Austrian cuirassiers behind the Rausnitz Brook. Most of the Russian cavalry of the 5th Column under Uvarov had retired behind the Rausnitz Brook by way of the Walkmühle and had established contact with Maliutin opposite Krenowitz. Facing them on the right bank were the divisions of Drouet, Rivaud and Nansouty's cuirassiers, though the swampy ground lining much of the Rausnitz Brook afforded the allies the opportunity to contest any immediate French pursuit with the limited forces that remained combat-worthy. The allied forces behind the Rausnitz were separated from Kutuzov's forces by the marsh-lined Littawa, and the two groups do not seem to have been in communication with each other.

In the north, Bagration's forces had finally broken after several hours of fierce defense and were retiring northeast toward Rausnitz. The advance of Caffarelli's infantry along the Rausnitz Brook had severed direct communications between Bagration's Advance Guard and Uvarov's cavalry.

Bagration still maintained tenuous contact with the center via a roundabout route through Slawikowitz and Rausnitz but was in imminent danger of being severed from the rest of the army entirely by the French advance. Unlike in the allied center, no river stood between Bagration's forces and the advancing French.

Finally, the allied columns to the south had basically disintegrated. Most of the 2nd and 3rd Columns had been surrounded or driven away from the rest of the allied army. The larger part of the divisions of Friant, Legrand and St Hilaire, along with the cavalry of Bourcier and Margaron, were busy hunting down the remnants. Twelve battalions of the 1st Column, none of which had seen any fighting, stood pinned against the Satchan Pond and Littawa River under fire from French artillery and harassed by Vandamme's division and Boyé's dragoons. To the west of them, Dokhturov's eleven battalions along with Kienmayer's Advance Guard were still filing across the two bridges at Tellnitz.

From his command post at the Stare Vinohrady three hours earlier, Napoleon had seen that he had already achieved a decisive victory, and had sent Lebrun to Paris with the news. Now, overlooking the shattered Allied 1st Column from his position near the chapel of St Anton, Napoleon knew that his army had achieved a victory of unparalleled magnitude. The mass of men jammed into a narrow space without an adequate means of retreat recalled a scene from the Egyptian campaign to the emperor's mind, and prompted him to exclaim "It is Aboukir!"* With about ninety minutes of daylight remaining, it seemed impossible that the allied army could avoid being utterly destroyed as the Turkish army had been at Aboukir in 1799. The battalions arrayed at Augezd under the watchful eye of their emperor and French forces across the entire length of the battlefield from Sokolnitz in the south to Posorsitz in the north advanced to deliver the *coup de grâce*.

The South

Near Sokolnitz, organized resistance by the allies had largely ceased by 3:00 and the refugees of the allied 3rd Column were desperately seeking to escape encirclement. Two bodies of troops had slipped through the French net at Sokolnitz. The first, about 1,000 men from the immediate vicinity of Sokolnitz village, had fled to the northwest—all that remained of about six battalions.† Pursued by GdB Merle with several battalions, the force quickly

---

* Segur, p. 255.
† Colin mentions 1,000 men being pursued into the pheasantry and 3,000 escaping to the north with Prshibyshevsky. Duffy asserts that the 1,000 refugees from Sokolnitz escaped to the northwest. Duffy's interpretation seems to match the confused accounts best, but the exact course taken by these men remains uncertain.

dissolved and the pursuing French captured a large portion of it, as already described.

Further north, Prshibyshevsky had led his more substantial body of refugees, still in formation, onto the heights west of the Kobelnitz Pond, intending to circle the pond and recross the Goldbach near Kobelnitz. Prshibyshevsky had approximately 3,000 men remaining, primarily the remains of eight battalions (Galitz Musketeers, Butyrsk Musketeers and two battalions of Narva Musketeers). To his rear, Friant had launched GdB Lochet in pursuit with the 36th and 48th Line supported by Margaron's two regiments of light cavalry. On the opposite side of the Goldbach, St Hilaire and Levasseur marched on a parallel course with six battalions of the 10th Light, 43rd Line and 14th Line. Closing the trap, one brigade of Oudinot's grenadier division commanded by Duroc had marched from the Pratzen Heights and recrossed the Goldbach (probably at Puntowitz) and was on a course to intercept the fleeing Russians.[*]

From his position on the heights west of the pond, Prshibyshevsky had a clear view of the forces closing in on him from three sides. Shortly after 3:30, the Russian commander was alerted to a column of French cavalry approaching from the west, Colonel Francheschi's 8th Hussar Regiment that had just arrived after a long day's march from the south where it had been observing Merveldt's corps near Auspitz. With no hope remaining, Prshibyshevsky surrendered the remainder of his command to Francheschi. Prshibyshevsky's last attempt at rejoining the army is most notable for robbing Lochet of the honor of receiving his surrender and providing Oudinot's elite grenadiers with their only action of the battle—escorting the prisoners back to Brünn.

To the southeast of Sokolnitz, the drama unfolding at Augezd would provide some of the most memorable scenes of the battle of Austerlitz. The Russian battalions stood in a long column between Augezd and Tellnitz, the frozen Satchan pond in the background. On the heights in front of them stood Vandamme's six battalions, with the Imperial Guard artillery raining death on the assembled allied troops below. To their right, Boyé's dragoons, which had been joined by two squadrons of the Chasseurs à Cheval of the Imperial Guard and the seven French battalions sent from Sokolnitz, stood between the slope of the heights and the Goldbach.[†] By around 3:00 Vandamme was ready to strike.

The situation in the valley had become increasingly gloomy for the fifteen Russian battalions now jammed in the narrow space between the heights and

---

[*] Alombert and Colin, V, pp. 207–8.

[†] Ibid., p. 209. These seven battalions included the four from Ferey's brigade (46th and 57th Line), 75th Line from Varé's brigade, and the Tirailleurs Corse from Levasseur's brigade.

the Littawa River and Satchan Pond. With the arrival of Langeron's five battalions from Sokolnitz, it seems Buxhöwden at last realized that the remainder of the 2nd and 3rd Columns had been irretrievably lost. As the Russian forces came under heavy fire from the French Imperial Guard artillery from its commanding position on the heights, Buxhöwden set the forces between Tellnitz and Reichmannsdorf in motion. Placing GM Leviz in command of the rear of the column, Buxhöwden placed himself at the head of the column and began the march toward Reichmannsdorf and its bridges over the two branches of the Littawa. As the Russian column was beginning its eastward march, however, the French infantry swept down from the heights upon them.

The confused series of actions occurring around Augezd are difficult to unravel, but it seems clear that Vandamme focused his attack on the head of the allied column in accordance with Napoleon's orders to separate the first three allied columns from the center. Vandamme ordered one battalion of the 28th to descend the slope to the left to cut the road running from Augezd to Klein-Hostieradek and prevent any possibility of escape to the north. Vandamme then ordered his other five battalions positioned near the chapel of St Anton to attack the village of Augezd. This attack would be supported on the right by the seven battalions just arriving from Sokolnitz, which would pressure the Russian forces between Augezd and Tellnitz.

Vandamme's men attacked ferociously, the 4th Line in particular winning praise for its conduct because of its desire to redeem itself after having been routed on the Pratzen Heights a short time earlier. In less than thirty minutes Augezd was in French hands and the Russian column was split in two, with two battalions east of Augezd and the remainder cut off between Augezd and Tellnitz. Stutterheim, commanding the Austrian cavalry covering the 1st Column, wrote that:

> As soon as the [Allied] column arrived in Aujest [sic], the French rushed like a torrent down upon the village, in which a sharp fire of musketry at first took place, but which was of short duration, before they gained possession of the village.*

Buxhöwden, with two battalions that had already made their way east of Augezd, led this small force across the Littawa at Reichmannsdorf, apparently without making any attempt to free the remainder of his column. Czartoryski met Buxhöwden later that night and found him dazed and despondent and entirely convinced that it was his small force, not the majority of the column, that had been cut off:

---

* Stutterheim, p. 121.

The poor General had lost his hat and his clothes were in disorder; when he perceived me at a distance he cried, "They have abandoned me! They have sacrificed me!" He continued his retreat and I hastened to join the Emperor.[*]

The Russian forces west of Augezd now faced a strong French force firmly in possession of the village, while French artillery continued firing on them from the heights. With their situation now desperate, the allies sought other avenues of retreat. Several narrow causeways spanned the Littawa and its bordering swamps north of the Satchan pond and the regiments nearest Augezd began filing across. Kienmayer split his cavalry into two bodies to support the withdrawal of the 1st Column. Fearing that the French might cross the Littawa and cut off the remaining avenues of retreat, he hurried nine squadrons of cavalry (six squadrons of Hessen-Homburg Hussars and three of Székler Hussars) through the narrow defile between the Satchan and Mönitz ponds. Once beyond the ponds, the Austrian cavalry took position between the towns of Satchan and Ottnitz in order to secure the line of retreat.[†]

The remaining cavalry, under the command of Stutterheim, covered the retreat. The eight squadrons of the O'Reilly Chevauxleger, along with two squadrons of Székler Hussars under the direct command of Colonel Geringer and a small party of Cossacks, advanced beyond Tellnitz to support attempts to retake Augezd. When these counterattacks failed, these ten squadrons positioned themselves in front of Tellnitz to safeguard the passage around the western end of the ponds. Dokhturov directed the Austrian and Russian infantry that had been west of the Goldbach to follow Kienmayer's cavalry through the narrow passage between the Satchan and Mönitz ponds. Both the causeways and the gap between the ponds were so narrow that the men had to march only two abreast. Probably about 12,000–14,000 men had to funnel through these narrow passages.

Leaving the detached battalion of the 28th Line to cover his left, Vandamme closed in for the kill. The five French battalions at Augezd assembled and advanced toward the masses of Russians along the banks of the Satchan pond while the seven battalions to their right closed in on Tellnitz. As Vandamme's forces advanced, one of the causeways over the Littawa broke under the weight of a cannon. The Russian troops who had been funneling onto the causeway plunged into the swamps on either side in panic while the remainder reversed their course to join the densely packed forces retiring around the other side of

---

[*] Czartoryski, II, 110.

[†] Treuenfest, *Geschichte des k. k. 11. Huszaren-Regimentes*, pp. 235–6; Schönhals, p. 168. Schönhals notes that Kienmayer took two squadrons of Hessen-Homburg Hussars and the Székler Hussars, but plainly this is not accurate as Colonel Geringer with two squadrons of Székler Hussars participated in the later actions in front of Tellnitz.

the pond. As the French increased the pressure on the Russians, order began to break down and isolated groups of Russians fled across the ice of the Satchan pond. The success of some encouraged others to use this avenue of escape, but the increased weight and the continual French artillery fire broke the ice, drowning a number of men and more horses:

> Many of the fugitives betook themselves to the lake, which was frozen over, but not sufficiently so to prevent many from perishing in it. The [French], who in the meantime had received their artillery, vigorously plied the fugitives with it . . .*

Near Tellnitz, GM Leviz had placed the three battalions of Moscow Musketeers in a strong position outside the town—lining the same ditch that Schobert and the 3rd Line had defended seven hours earlier. While a portion of the ten Russian battalions cut off at Augezd had managed to escape by the causeways and over the ice, the majority were being pushed back on Tellnitz by Vandamme's advance. This frightened mass soon converged with Dokhturov's column, which had been retreating in an orderly fashion between the Satchan and Mönitz ponds, generating more panic in the ranks. The entire body stood jammed onto a small hill that divided the pond from the Goldbach, under fire from French artillery that had been brought into position near the opposite bank of the pond.

Determined to maintain pressure on the retreating allies, Vandamme urged his weary troops forward from Augezd. After bringing up their artillery, the French fired several salvoes of canister at close range, dropping a large number of Austrian cavalry, among them Colonel Geringer of the Székler Hussars who fell from his horse unconscious with a head wound. While this was occurring, several French battalions skirted the edge of the Satchan pond and charged Tellnitz. The Moscow Musketeers fought desperately against this onslaught, finally beating the French back. The Austrian cavalry then advanced to harass the retreating French infantry, but their final charge was quickly beaten back by an alert Boyé with a party of dragoons and two squadrons of Imperial Guard Chasseurs.†

Developments on the opposite side of the Goldbach soon made the position north and east of Tellnitz untenable, however. While Vandamme was pressuring the allies from the front, Friant had assembled the larger part of his division on the heights between Sokolnitz and Tellnitz following the destruction and dispersal of the remaining allied forces at Sokolnitz. Six battalions (the 15th Light, and 33rd and 111th Line) joined Heudelet's two

---

* Stutterheim, p. 122.
† Treuenfest, *11. Geschichte des k. k. 11. Huszaren-Regimentes*, pp. 236–7.

battalions of the 108th Line, with Bourcier's five regiments of dragoons forming on their right. After a brief pause to rest his troops, Friant marched toward the intense firing at Tellnitz.

Cossack patrols on the right bank of the Goldbach sounded the alarm and galloped off to the south, pursued by Bourcier's dragoons. With Friant's substantial force closing in on them from the west, Leviz retired with his rearguard (the three battalions of Moscow Musketeers) toward Mönitz, covered by the Austrian cavalry. Skirmishers from Friant's division, taking cover in the scrub lining the banks, maintained a steady fire on the Russians as they retreated and Heudelet with the 108th Line advanced toward Mönitz on the west bank of the Goldbach.[*]

By around 4:00 the Austrian cavalry had pulled back from its position between Augezd and Tellnitz to the hill that separated the Goldbach from the Satchan Pond in order to cover the retreat of the infantry from this position. They held Vandamme's infantry at bay but at the same time took substantial casualties from French artillery fire from across the pond. "It was nearly 4:00, night had arrived, wet and cold snow had been falling for an hour, the ground was muddy and close to the canals one sunk to one's knees: nothing was lacking in the horror of our position."[†] Most of Dokhturov's half of the 1st Column (eleven battalions), and apparently also Kienmayer's Grenzers, had already passed through the narrow passage between the Satchan and Mönitz ponds, forming up on the other side in good order, roughly 8,000 men including the light cavalry that had led the way. The remainder, already disordered, were in the process of crossing when French artillery fire struck a caisson on the causeway, blowing it up and setting the Satchan Mill on fire. The dramatic explosion sparked a panic among the Russian troops remaining to cross. The Cossacks accompanying the Austrian cavalry covering the retreat bolted, riding through and over the infantry to reach the other side. Several gun crews abandoned their guns and fled.

With the causeway jammed with fleeing men and abandoned vehicles, many of those remaining behind attempted to cross the ice of the Satchan Pond, producing the scene immortalized by Napoleon's 30th Bulletin: ". . . one saw a horrible spectacle, such as one had seen at Aboukir: 20,000 men throwing themselves in the water and drowning in the lakes!"[‡] While the ice did break beneath them due to a combination of artillery fire and the weight of their numbers and a small number did drown, still others managed to cross to the safety of the other side or were pulled from the pond, which was

[*] "Rapport de la bataille d'Austerlitz par Soult," in *Relations et Rapports*, p. 24.

[†] Langeron, p. 51.

[‡] "30th Bulletin of the Grande Armée," in *Bulletins de la Grande Armée : Campagne d'Austerlitz, 1805*, p. 91.

only 1.5 meters or so deep. Segur claims personally to have helped to pull a Cossack from the icy water. Comeau, a French staff officer who witnessed the action, later scoffed at the exaggeration of the bulletin, and asserted that the pond actually preserved the 1st Column from destruction rather than claiming a large number of lives:

> The bulletin says that this pond absorbed thousands of them [Russian soldiers]. I was near enough to see what occurred there. The Russian army skirted the pond and put it between them and the cavalry that would have harassed them. While some parties might have got their feet wet, they did not drown. The few corpses of men and horses that I saw there had been killed by gunfire; they were on the bank, and even nearer. I would say in fact that it was not 2,000 men who perished, but fewer than 200 while without this obstacle [the pond] the column would have been crushed.*

When the ponds were drained after the battle, only three human corpses were found, along with thirty cannon and the corpses of about 130 horses, fully corroborating Comeau's eyewitness account.[†]

Seeing the ice breaking on the pond, most of the remaining allied troops west of the pond escaped to the south toward Mönitz, some continuing south from that village, others attempting to cross the ice of Mönitz Pond, which soon also broke up. Ironically, the troops which had maintained order and were left behind, including the Austrian cavalry forming the rearguard, still managed to cross between the ponds before the French closed in on their rear.

With the greater part of the allied forces now safely beyond the ponds and the Littawa, Vandamme's units paused to secure their numerous prisoners and regroup. Vandamme's exhausted men, including battalions from both his own and St Hilaire's divisions, remained in the vicinity of Tellnitz while other forces took up the pursuit. According to Langeron, only the fatigue of the French troops prevented the complete destruction of the fleeing allied forces: "If the French had pursued us . . . they would have sabered or taken 20,000 men."[‡] Only two squadrons of Imperial Guard Chasseurs under the command of Major d'Hallerman pursued the allies in this sector of the battlefield, chasing parties of infantry fleeing around the southern end of the Mönitz Pond and netting a large number of prisoners in the process.[§] On the opposite side

* Comeau, p. 231.
[†] Janetschek, p. 108.
[‡] Langeron, p. 52.
[§] French reports give the total number of prisoners taken by the Guard Chasseurs around the ponds as 1,200. This approaches the total number of prisoners taken from the forces retreating around the ponds. This figure may be somewhat exaggerated since it is close to the total number

of the Goldbach, Davout ordered Friant to cross the stream at Mönitz and advance toward Neudorf to cut off the allied retreat. Friant led his weary troops four or five kilometers down the road to Neudorf before darkness and the fatigue of his men forced him to halt for the night.

The North

While the forces in the south had been scattered or driven against the ponds and the swamps lining the Littawa, the Allied troops in the north at least had an open line of retreat. By 3:00, with Engelhardt's men now a tangled mass of refugees fleeing toward Rausnitz, Bagration was desperately trying to save his command from destruction. On his left, Ulanius and Kamensky-2 had begun retreating soon after the main line had been broken, with Caffarelli pursuing them from Holubitz. Marching at the double, they had paused at the ravine behind the Posorsitz Post House, only to continue their retreat when the French cavalry turned that position to the north.*

The ground east of the Posorsitz Post House presented a narrower field of operations, which was advantageous to Bagration against the more numerous French. Bagration used the series of ravines running perpendicular to the Russian line of retreat to prevent the regiments on his left flank from being cut off by holding each ravine in turn, forcing the French to deploy, and then retreating to the next position. Two successive positions were used to delay the French pursuit before Bagration determined to make a stand. He ordered the six battalions of 6th Jäger and Arkhangel Musketeers, covered by Wittgenstein's cavalry and Yashvil's horse artillery, to occupy a position at right angles to the Rausnitz Brook behind a ravine running northwest from Welspitz. A detachment of perhaps a few companies of infantry, probably Jäger, appears to have been sent to hold Welspitz (located south of the brook).†
Shepelev's cavalry disappears from all reports at this point, but must have either remained with Ulanius or joined Uvarov south of the Rausnitz Brook. Ulanius and Kamensky-2 were joined by what was left of Engelhardt's Old Ingermanland and Pskov Musketeers, although a portion had been routed and the fleeing mob had reached Rausnitz before they could be rallied. To the right of Bagration's main position, GM Gogel and the 5th Jäger, supported by Chaplits's cavalry, took position behind the Kowalowitz Brook just east of the

---

of prisoners taken from the 1st Column and Kienmayer's Advance Guard and does not account for the many prisoners that were taken by the French infantry in front of the ponds. It is also possible that small parties from the 2nd and 3rd Columns had made their way to Tellnitz, increasing the number of prisoners taken near the ponds.

* "Report of P. I. Bagration to M. I. Kutuzov," in *Dokumenty Shtaba Kutuzova*, pp. 220–1.

† This detachment is not mentioned in Bagration's laconic report, but French reports indicate a small Russian force. "Note on the Division Caffarelli (A. W.)," in Alombert and Colin, V, p. 221.

village of Kowalowitz with some companies pushed forward to occupy the village itself.

As Bagration's forces took position for a final stand against the pursuing French, the Austrian Major Frierenberger fortuitously appeared with two Austrian artillery batteries that had been brought up from the artillery park by the Olmütz Road. Bagration positioned these guns on a commanding rise north of Welspitz, approximately midway between the Rausnitz Brook and Gogel's forces in Kowalowitz.

As Bagration was assembling his line, Lannes was also regrouping his forces. Caffarelli detached several companies of the 13th Light and the whole of the 51st Line to cross the Rausnitz Brook, apparently via the main road running from the Posorsitz Post House toward Austerlitz. These forces were to operate on Caffarelli's right flank south of the Rausnitz Brook and attempt to cut off Bagration's line of retreat toward Austerlitz.* North of the brook, Caffarelli drew up the remainder of his division and advanced against the Russians. Caffarelli placed the rest of the 13th Light and the 61st Line along the Rausnitz brook while the 17th and 30th Line advanced straight up the main road. To Caffarelli's left, Suchet drew up his eight battalions facing Kowalowitz and the ravine in front of the Russian position. Suchet deployed the 64th, 40th and 34th Line on the Kowalowitz Heights facing Gogel's Jäger in and behind the town with the 88th Line to their left facing Kowalowitz. Suchet's main body was supported on its left by the 17th Light, which had just been ordered up from Siwitz and Bosenitz, and the light cavalry of Trelliard and Milhaud. The rest of Murat's cavalry stood along the road by the Posorsitz Post House.

It was after 3:30 before the French infantry drew up in front of Bagration's position, and they were welcomed by fire from Frierenberger's artillery. Yashvil opened fire from his position on the main road soon after. Suchet and Caffarelli called up their own artillery, and for the next 30–45 minutes the two opposing armies engaged in an artillery duel in the center of the position. With daylight fading, however, Suchet and Caffarelli were uncertain whether or not to launch an assault against the main Russian position, and Suchet sent to Lannes for orders. While waiting for his reply, both generals advanced against Bagration's flanks. At Kowalowitz the voltigeurs of the 88th Line launched a raid on the Russian position and succeeded in capturing a cannon, two caissons and a small number of men. On the far right, Caffarelli's detachment that had crossed the Rausnitz Brook prepared to seize Welspitz:

---

* The account of the operations of Caffarelli's division states that these forces advanced on Krenowitz, but this contradicts the stated intention of cutting off Bagration's line of retreat. To intercept Bagration they must have marched on Welspitz.

272 <i>The Allied Remnants Escape</i>

Already our tirailleurs had crossed the brook and spread themselves on the opposite heights. The enemy, by extending his lines considerably, sought to mislead us of his true force while his baggage pulled back. Three pieces [of artillery] kept up a constant fire; the 1st and 2nd Battalions of the 51st [Line], which had just joined, had arrived at the foot of the heights and were prepared to attack them. The 13th prepared to attack by the right. The order to pull back was given by Marshal Lannes, and the day was finished.[*]

Murat and Lannes, who had received no information on the course of the battle from Imperial Headquarters since Napoleon's departure from the Stare Vinohrady, decided that it would be wisest to remain in position around the Posorsitz Post House in order to be able to support the remainder of the French army if necessary. At around 4:30, Suchet and Caffarelli received Lannes's orders calling off any further action.[†]

To Lannes's right, Bernadotte had advanced his two divisions to the Rausnitz Brook. Rivaud's division, advancing from the vicinity of Blaziowitz, drew up on the heights occupied by the Russian Guard that morning, and Rivaud sent out parties of skirmishers to cross to the other side, moving his main body closer to the Walkmühle and its weir over the brook. The Rausnitz Brook between the Walkmühle and Krenowitz was characterized by low marshy ground that made fording difficult. The Walkmühle weir constituted a narrow defile, covered on the opposite bank by what remained of Ermolov's battery and possibly also Ignatiev's. Uvarov's cavalry roamed the opposite bank, at least twenty squadrons of regular cavalry, even if somewhat the worse for wear, and a substantial body of Cossacks who were now in their element seeking out isolated bodies of French who managed to work their way across.

At Krenowitz, Bernadotte and Drouet faced an equally difficult situation. Drouet's skirmishers had descended from the heights toward Krenowitz as the Russian Guard retreated, coming under fire from the Life Guard Jäger occupying the village and lining the far side of the stream. Drouet reinforced his skirmish line, quickly forced the Life Guard Jäger to the opposite bank and pursued them a short distance up the slope. The French were then soon driven back by skirmishers from the 3rd Battalion, Ismailovsky Guards, that Maliutin deployed to oppose them, a section of guns from Resleyna's company and the remaining three battalions of the Cavalier Guard led by Depreradovich-2. The French skirmishers reported a strong force composed of infantry, cavalry and artillery occupying the heights between Krenowitz and Austerlitz.[‡]

---

[*] "Notes sur la Division Caffarelli (A. W.)," in Alombert and Colin, V, p. 221–2.
[†] "Rapport du Général Belliard," in Alombert and Colin, V, p. 221.
[‡] <i>Istoriya Leib-gvardii Egerskago</i>, p. 34.

The forces opposing Drouet's division were stronger than he had anticipated and also stronger than most historians have reported. Here were assembled the three fresh battalions of the Life Grenadiers, the 3rd Battalion, Ismailovsky Guards, (which had not yet been engaged), and the Life Guard Jäger which had fallen back from Krenowitz. Behind them stood the four battalions of the Preobrazhensky and Semenovsky Guards, severely weakened during their retreat, bringing the total up to nine battalions, four of which were fresh. The infantry was supported by the remaining artillery of the Guard—at least ten position guns (12-pounders) of Rall's battery, Kostenetsky's remaining horse artillery, assorted light pieces from the 1st and 2nd Guard Columns, and most likely also Zocchi's Austrian battery. The artillery had been positioned on the heights commanding the crossing and, while ineffective against small parties of skirmishers, the guns posed a formidable threat to any attempt to cross in force. In addition, Liechtenstein's Austrian cavalry supported the infantry, along with the remaining fourteen squadrons of Guard cavalry.

The strength of the allied forces behind Krenowitz seems to have come as an unpleasant surprise, the precipitate retreat of the Guard having been taken as a rout. Drouet, with nine battalions and no cavalry, positioned his artillery on the slope of the opposing bank and continued to feed skirmishers across the brook. The difficulty of the position, the absence of supporting cavalry and the possibility that the fresh forces constituted the advance guard of Essen-1's column (known to be approaching from the east) prompted Bernadotte to exercise justifiable caution. Bernadotte determined that the considerable losses his forces must incur in crossing the river over the two available bridges under enemy fire and engaging infantry and cavalry up a steep slope during the short time remaining before nightfall would be pointless given the magnitude of the victory already achieved. Around 4:00 he called off the attack. Bernadotte's decision would earn him the wrath of his emperor, who remained convinced that the Russian Guard had been utterly routed and that Bernadotte had only to pursue a fleeing enemy.

The Retreat Begins

With the French forces in the north relaxing their pressure, the allied forces enjoyed a brief rest and began preparations for their retreat. Alexander had made his way to Austerlitz and by 4:00 stood just south of the town, "impatiently awaiting Kutuzov" in order to get his advice on dispositions for the retreat.* The shock of the defeat apparently had given the Russian emperor a new-found respect for the opinions of the old general to whom he

---

* Mikhailovski-Danilevski, p. 277.

would not listen before the battle. After his aides had failed to locate Kutuzov, Alexander determined to stick with the plan of the day before, which had called for retreat by way of Hodiegitz and Hungary should the battle be lost. Alexander ordered Miloradovich, who formed the rearguard of the 4th Column with his severely depleted battalions between Wazan and Austerlitz (south of the Littawa), to hold his position until Bagration arrived to replace him.* Alexander then sent Uvarov, who had ridden to Austerlitz for instructions, to Constantine and Maliutin with orders to hold their position between Krenowitz and Austerlitz until twilight and then retreat by way of Austerlitz. Bagration received similar instructions. Having issued his orders, Alexander proceeded to Hodiegitz to await the assembly of his army.

By around 5:00 the Russian Guard had begun its retreat, screened by the cavalry of Hohenlohe and Uvarov deployed between Krenowitz and Welspitz. The Guard passed through Austerlitz and proceeded on to Hodiegitz, arriving there very late at night. Wittgenstein and Chaplits covered the withdrawal of Bagration's infantry to Rausnitz and over the Rausnitz Brook. Bagration's infantry crossed the Littawa at Austerlitz in the small hours of the morning and all of the Russian cavalry north of the river followed, leaving only Hohenlohe's Austrians north of the Littawa to hold back any French pursuit until morning.

South of the Littawa, Kutuzov marched with Kollowrath's Austrians toward Hodiegitz while Miloradovich with several thousand Russian troops held the heights east of Wazan to hold the road from Austerlitz open should the French pursue. Once Bagration's forces had crossed to the left bank of the Littawa from Austerlitz, Miloradovich was to follow the remainder of the 4th Column. Kamensky-1's brigade seems to have retired through Wazan as well and may have formed a part of Miloradovich's rearguard.

While the allied forces north of the Littawa and the 4th Column retired without interference from the French under Lannes, Murat and Bernadotte, to the south the battle raged on even after night had fallen. For the pursuit of the main body of the allies, Napoleon ordered Boyé and Margaron to assemble their cavalry at Augezd and, after allowing them a short rest, Napoleon placed his aide-de-camp Junot at their head and ordered him to pursue the Russians. Junot scattered his regiments and they picked their way through the swamps and across the Littawa via several defiles, assembling on the far side and setting off to seek the enemy. The allies had retreated to the southeast toward Boschowitz with Kienmayer's cavalry covering the retreat on a line running from Mautnitz through Neudorf to Ottnitz.† Junot's cavalry squadrons came

* Kutuzov, with Kollowrath's Austrians, met up with Kamensky-1's brigade near Sharaditz and together they marched on toward Hodiegitz.
† Major Molitor commanded the detachment in Mautnitz, consisting of one squadron of O'Reilly Chevauxleger and one squadron of Székler Hussars. Treuenfest, *11. Huszaren-Regimentes*, p. 237.

upon the Austrian rearguard near Ottnitz around 8:00 pm, harassing them for about an hour or so before breaking off the action.*

Alexander's mood was understandably low. Czartoryski described that:

> Night came on and we proceeded at a foot pace on the road that leads to Holitsch [in Hungary]. The Emperor was extremely depressed; the violent emotion he had experienced affected his health, and I was the only one to bring him some relief.[†]

A staff officer, Major Toll, claimed to have come upon the Russian Emperor riding in the company only of his surgeon and groom. He went on to relate how he followed Alexander at some distance, "not wishing to intrude on his privacy," and then watched as he "dismounted and sat on the damp ground beneath a tree, where he covered his face with a cloth and burst into tears."[‡] Toll also claimed to have comforted the distraught Alexander.

The Russian emperor reached Hodiegitz with Czartoryski, and an officer managed to find Kutuzov. After a brief meeting with the restored commander-in-chief, Alexander went on to Urschitz. "As we went through the villages," noted Czartoryski, "we heard nothing but the confused exclamations of people who seek forgetfulness of their reverses in drink. The inhabitants suffered, and scenes of disorder were everywhere around us."[§] At the end of his miserable day, the Russian Emperor spent a miserable night, snatching three hours of sleep on a bed of straw in a peasant's hut in the village of Urschitz.

On the opposite side of the Littawa, Napoleon had left the chapel of St Anton after issuing the final orders for the pursuit of the allied 1st Column. From the vicinity of Augezd, Napoleon made his way north in the company of his staff, surveying the battlefield. Segur describes the scene:

> Night surprised him whilst he thus walked over the whole line of battle, strewn with the wounded, stopping to speak with every one of them. The morning mist was then falling back in frozen rain, which rendered the night even darker; but ordering complete silence, the better to hear the groans of his poor maimed soldiers, he would himself hasten to their help, making Yvan [his personal surgeon] and his mameluke give them brandy out of his own canteen.[¶]

Savary related much the same story, adding that "The squadron of his escort spent the whole night stripping the Russian corpses of their greatcoats,

---

* Alombert and Colin, V, p. 217.
[†] Czartoryski, p. 110.
[‡] Duffy, p. 150.
[§] Czartoryski, p. 110.
[¶] Segur, p. 257.

with which to cover the wounded."* The Emperor Napoleon finally reached the Brünn–Olmütz road around 10:00 P.M., stopping at the Posorsitz Post House where he dined on food scavenged by troops bivouacked nearby and started dictating a victory proclamation for his army before being overcome by the fatigue of the day.

The Butcher's Bill: Losses of the Two Armies

The day's fierce fighting had taken a toll on both armies. While estimates of losses vary, the data compiled from French and allied documents provide a reasonably accurate assessment of the total losses suffered by each. On the French side, the overall losses were remarkably light considering the magnitude of the victory they had wrought. However, the forces that had borne the brunt of the fighting had suffered severely. The 4th Corps alone, with all three divisions heavily engaged on the Pratzen Heights and the Goldbach valley, had lost between 4,000 and 4,800 men killed and wounded in the three infantry divisions, about 20 percent of initial strength. Friant's division was hit even harder. With only an estimated 3,800 men reaching Austerlitz on 2 December after its epic forced march from Vienna, no fewer than 1,990 were rendered *hors de combat*, a high price to pay for their remarkable effort. Lannes's 5th Corps, which only saw heavy action in the afternoon, recorded 1,538 killed and wounded for its two divisions—still significant, but in proportion just over half of the losses suffered by Soult's three divisions.

The cavalry suffered less than the infantry. Collectively, the French cavalry sustained in the vicinity of 1,000 killed and wounded, 750 of whom were from the cavalry originally massed on the Brünn–Olmütz road. Proportionally, Kellermann's four regiments of light cavalry sustained the heaviest losses, with 152 killed and wounded, mostly during the initial cavalry actions. The cuirassier divisions sustained only slightly fewer casualties, with 152 killed and wounded among Nansouty's six regiments and 129 from d'Hautpoul's four. Boyé's dragoon division, engaged around Blaziowitz for most of the morning, on the heights around midday and near Augezd and Tellnitz in the evening, lost 143 men killed and wounded from six regiments. The remaining cavalry suffered only minor losses: 104 from the Imperial Guard, 91 from the brigades of Trelliard and Milhaud on the northern extremity of the field and Margaron's three regiments on the southern extremity. The six regiments of Walther's dragoon division reported 83 killed and wounded, while Bourcier's five regiments, which could boast of taking part in at least one memorable charge, lost only 36 men.

---

* Savary, I, 136.

While the allied army had left their mark on the portion of the French army that was most heavily engaged, the remainder of the French army was nearly untouched. Drouet's division had lost only 280 killed and wounded during its protracted harassment of the retreating Russian Guard. Rivaud's division, which had only been engaged briefly near Blaziowitz, recorded a total of three killed and fourteen wounded. Bernadotte's decision to call off the storming of the Russian position on the heights behind Krenowitz, though much criticized, did leave two intact divisions for the next day. In the face of determined Russian resistance, moving Drouet's division across the two bridges at Krenowitz, deploying them under enemy artillery fire, and charging the Russian position at the top of the hill would surely have resulted in a steep butcher's bill with losses likely to rival those of Soult's divisions and with little likelihood of dramatic results. Beyond Bernadotte's two fresh divisions, Oudinot's grenadier division and the infantry of the Imperial Guard remained untouched.

In all, the French had lost between 8,000 and 10,000 men killed, wounded or captured. Duffy places the total French losses at 8,000. Colin summarizes French losses as 1,305 killed, 6,940 wounded and 573 prisoners for a total loss of 8,818 men. However, in itemizing losses by division, Colin uses a figure of 1,197 for Vandamme's division, 1,410 for St Hilaire's and 1,400 for Legrand. Together with his figures for other formations these produce a total of over 10,200. By contrast, Duffy reports 1,456 for Vandamme, 1,776 for St Hilaire and 1,494 for Legrand, suggesting that French losses could be considered slightly over 9,000, rather than the 8,000 total he suggests.* Any calculation of losses is difficult and, as Bowden points out, the figures were subject to change on a daily basis as those who had fallen out of the ranks lightly wounded rejoined the colors. Because of this, the French quickly recovered a significant number of wounded while the allies, forced into a rapid retreat, lost many of their lightly wounded as stragglers who were quickly snapped up as prisoners of the victorious French. In sum, 9,000–10,000 seems to be the most probable range for total French losses.

On the allied side, the losses had been more severe. In terms only of killed and wounded, the allies had lost around 6,000 men dead and dying, with another 9,600 wounded. The much higher proportion of dead among the total allied casualties, over 38 percent compared to just under 16 percent for the French is worth some additional analysis. Reported Russian losses amount to

---

* Colin details the losses of all divisions except Vandamme's. The figure used by Colin for Vandamme's division can be derived by subtracting the itemized losses from the total given. See Alombert and Colin, V, pp. 227–9 and Duffy, pp. 156–7 for summaries of losses. Russian losses are detailed in *Kutuzov Sbornik Dokumentov*, II, pp. 235–6. Life Guard losses are documented in Vasil'ev, "Gvardiya" <www.genstab.ru/voin/auster_01.htm>.

approximately 5,500 dead and mortally wounded with an additional 6,000 seriously wounded reported left behind—nearly 48 percent of total casualties dead. For the Austrians, the number killed amounts to an estimated 500–600 out of a stated 4,236 killed and wounded, roughly 12–14 percent which is comparable to the proportion of French dead to total casualties.

The extraordinarily high proportion of Russian deaths among the total casualties could be explained by a number of factors. First, several accounts relate the fanatical resistance of the Russian soldier and the extraordinary measures therefore taken against them. Thiébault mentioned standing orders he had received, presumably from Soult:

> Up till the last hour of the battle we took no prisoners, except those who contrived to constitute themselves such. It is true we had been warned that the Russians, even when too severely wounded to be able to march, would take up their arms again after their enemy had gone forward, reload them, and put their conquerors between two fires. Now, in a struggle of such obstinacy . . . it would not do to run any risk; one could stick at nothing, and thus not a single living enemy remained to our rear.[*]

In addition to Thiébault's statement, Ledru des Essarts recorded something very similar, noting that ". . . the soldiers had killed without mercy and had not wanted to capture anybody, in reprisal for the cruelty of the Russians."[†]

If this is indeed the explanation for the substantially higher proportion of Russians killed, then we can calculate the grisly statistic of up to 4,000 wounded Russians, possibly fighting to their last breath, being slaughtered at the hands of the French.[‡] Of course losses from other factors including poor or absent medical care, inability or unwillingness to seek medical attention, or weak general health and inadequate nutrition might reduce this figure somewhat and also we must consider that many of the prisoners on both sides were wounded prior to being captured. Even including all prisoners as wounded in calculating the proportion of Russian dead, however, the Russian death rate remains double that of both French and Austrians, apparently due to standing orders to take no Russian prisoners.

While a comparison of the total number of killed and wounded reveals 15,736 reported casualties for the allies, compared to 8,818 (perhaps slightly more) for the French, the disparity becomes enormous when prisoners are considered. Russian losses at the Battle of Austerlitz come to nearly 21,000, with 9,000 of these being prisoners. Total reported Austrian losses of 5,922

---

[*] Thiébault, II, p. 166.

[†] Ledru des Essarts, p. 42.

[‡] The figure of 4,000 is based on 12–16 percent of 11,500 total casualties being killed or mortally wounded, as was the case with both French and Austrian forces at Austerlitz.

(1,686 being prisoners) bring losses for the Allied army to just under 27,000 men or roughly 33 percent (based on a total strength of 81,000). When we consider that these figures were compiled on 6 January 1806 after some stragglers and parties of fugitives had managed to rejoin the Russian columns, the number absent from the ranks on the day after the battle is likely to have been even higher.

Computing Allied losses by column requires a good bit of guesswork, but unsurprisingly the first three columns were hit hardest. Of these, Prshibyshevsky's 3rd Column was almost entirely destroyed. Of some 8,500 men composing the 3rd Column, the French reported capturing about 4,000, nearly half. Reported combat losses for the regiments of this column on 2 December amount to an additional 2,000, leaving roughly 2,500 men (less than 30 percent) who eluded the French in small parties and rejoined the army between 3 December and 6 January. The 2nd Column also took heavy losses, with a reported 2,436 prisoners taken by the French and combat casualties (killed and wounded) of 2,454, leaving about 6,308 men (about 56 percent of initial strength) at the end of the day. Most of these men were in Kamensky-1's two regiments and the five battalions that had escaped with Langeron, although some refugees from other regiments also managed to rejoin the army. The 1st Column, which had seen virtually no action until after 2:00, still lost 1,200 prisoners and 759 combat casualties while pinned against the ponds, losses amounting to over 17 percent. Taken as a whole, losses for the first three allied columns amounted to nearly 42 percent of their initial strength.

Kienmayer's losses are not well documented. The Székler infantry had sustained severe losses in the initial attacks on Tellnitz, some battalions losing more than 50 percent of their initial strength. In addition, the cavalry units that were responsible for covering the retreat appear to have suffered heavy losses as well. Computing the total losses of the other columns and subtracting this from the totals given for allied losses, it appears that Kienmayer's small force lost nearly 2,000 men, over half of these from the infantry.

Allied losses on the Pratzen Heights were slightly less severe, but only because they had avoided being surrounded. Miloradovich's Russian contingent of the 4th Column, driven back quickly on two occasions, only lost a total of 252 prisoners according to French accounts, nearly all of these (250) being taken from the Novgorod Musketeers. Combat losses were also comparatively light, amounting to 787 men according to official Russian returns, total losses amounting to just under 20 percent. The Austrians of the 4th Column, however, suffered more severely as a result of their attempt to cover the retreat of the column. With the rapid defeat of the Russians in the third allied position on the heights, the French had quickly descended on the

Austrian battalions that were still attempting to form. As a result the French netted 1,400–1,500 Austrian prisoners from the 4th Column and inflicted a reported 1,886 casualties, making the total Austrian losses 45 percent and total losses for the 4th column roughly 33 percent.

On the far right of the allied army, Bagration's forces suffered comparable total casualties. Russian returns indicate total losses of 4,438, approximately 32 percent of their total numbers at the beginning of the battle. Of these, only about 1,000 were prisoners. Over 2,700 of the 4,438 men lost were from the Arkhangel and Old Ingermanland Musketeers, testifying to the devastating slaughter that resulted when the center of Bagration's position was turned by d'Hautpoul's cuirassiers.

Table 5:
Losses of the Two Armies

French	Killed	Wounded	Prisoners
1st Corps	297		
3rd Corps	1,990		
4th Corps	4,726		
5th Corps	1,538		
Cavalry Reserve	1,000		
Army Reserve	104		
Total Estimated	1,305	8,350 *	573
Total Reported	1,305	6,940	573
Allies			
Kienmayer	2,000		180
1st Column	759		1,200
2nd Column	2,454		2,436
3rd Column	2,000		4,000
4th Column	2,673		1,752
5th Column	772		10
Advance Guard	4,438		1,000
Life Guard	607		110
Total Estimated	6,100	9,603	11,834
Total Reported	No consolidated report exists		10,686

Finally, the 5th Column and Guards recorded the lightest casualties. The two Russian cavalry brigades reported total losses of 772, approximately 10

* Derived from the itemized killed/wounded figures presented by Colin and stated total prisoners. This figure does not match the total given by Colin, suggesting use of different returns for the itemized and total figures. See Alombert and Colin, V, ch XXVI.

percent of their total strength with only a handful of prisoners taken (mostly from the Constantine Uhlans). Not surprisingly, Uvarov's losses were distributed evenly among his three regiments while Shepelev's losses were primarily from the Constantine Uhlans. Adding in the losses from Hohenlohe's Austrian cuirassiers, total losses remain roughly 10 percent for the whole of the 5th Column. For the Guards, the losses were similarly light. French records indicate a total of 110 prisoners taken from the Guards while Russian returns indicate an additional 607 casualties; this represents roughly 7.5 percent of the forces most heavily engaged. The Life Grenadier Regiment, though not engaged to any significant degree, still reported 75 casualties, presumably lost to skirmishers and French artillery fire.

In addition to the considerable loss in manpower, the allied army suffered an enormous loss in artillery and equipage. French reports indicate a total of 143 Russian artillery pieces and 37 Austrian pieces captured, along with accompanying caissons and a vast amount of material from the army's baggage. Russian sources indicate a total of 160 pieces lost, suggesting that 17 guns had been destroyed or were irretrievably lost in the ponds or swamps lining the Littawa and Rausnitz. Some Austrian pieces may also have been destroyed or otherwise lost. While the total number of artillery pieces with the allied army at Austerlitz is not entirely certain, it appears that 231 Russian and 92 Austrian guns accompanied the army in its advance from Olmütz. This produces a total of 323 guns, excluding the artillery park (including Frierenberger's battery) and heavy companies left behind when the army advanced. The losses therefore amounted to more than 55 percent of the total allied artillery at Austerlitz.[*] Artillery losses by type are given below.

Table 6:
Allied Artillery Losses

	Heavy artillery			Light artillery			Horse artillery		
	Present	*Lost*	*%*	*Present*	*Lost*	*%*	*Present*	*Lost*	*%*
Russian	54	33	61	132	113	86	45	14	31
Austrian	8	8	100	72	29[†]	40	12	0	0
Total	62	41	66	204	142	70	57	14	25

[*] Russian records show 12 Austrian guns with Kienmayer, 36 with the 4th Column, and 8 with the 5th Column. Records detail several Austrian artillery companies being attached to Kutuzov's column during his advance from Radzivilov. As of 12 October, 32 Austrian guns had been attached to Kutuzov's columns. The total number of battalion guns indicated as attached to Russian regiments exceeds the total number of light pieces reported being with the army at Austerlitz by 36, indicating a total of 36 Austrian light guns used by Russian regiments as battalion guns. Duffy, pp. 182–5; Langeron, pp. 37–42; *Kutuzov Sbornik Dokumentov*, pp. 237–9.

[†] Excludes guns destroyed or abandoned and not captured by French.

Even the enormous magnitude of the artillery losses does not fully account for the situation of the army's artillery immediately after the battle. Colonel Kudriatsev, commanding the Russian position battery accompanying the 4th Column, had given up his entire battery for lost. However, ten days after the battle a small party of gunners turned up with two or three of the guns after having managed to elude the French and avoid capture.* The disruption of the allied columns had been so severe that it is not certain that the guns that had been saved could have counted on an adequate supply of ammunition in a subsequent action with the French. Therefore, the numbers above under-represent the artillery lost or rendered ineffective in the days immediately following the battle.

Overall, the allied army had been shattered. Bagration's mauled but disciplined force still had about 8,000 men who were retiring in good order. On the opposite flank, Dokhturov and Kienmayer had managed to preserve 8,000–12,000 men to cover the retreat of the left and center. Between these two bodies stood the Imperial Guard with Liechtenstein's cavalry, about 17,000 men. In all, between 35,000 and 40,000 men remained in any sort of condition to oppose the French, less than half of the proud army that had taken the field that morning.

The Causes of Victory/Defeat

The events of 2 December 1805 have been recorded in history as Napoleon's finest victory and the most glorious moment of La Grande Armée. The superlatives heaped upon the French army at Austerlitz are certainly justified. At all levels, the French army had performed as well as any army could be expected to perform. The key to French success has been much debated over the past two centuries. For some, the tactical proficiency demonstrated by the French at Austerlitz has led to the conclusion that French tactical doctrine was inherently superior to that of the allies. This conclusion is typically based on the assumption that the allied armies at Austerlitz were incapable of skirmishing and were locked into an archaic system of Frederican tactics. Research of the past twenty years or so has dispelled these myths, which nevertheless persist. In fact, the allied armies were using tactics that were essentially the same as those used by the French. In numerous examples throughout the battle, the allied forces demonstrated flexibility in tactical formations, skirmishing, advancing in column and deploying in line to engage the enemy. Allied forces stood toe to toe with French forces and held their own, sometimes pushing the French back and sometimes being pushed back

---

* Duffy relates this account, but does not cite his source. Russian accounts indicate that three of the twelve guns in Kudriatsev's battery were eventually recovered. Duffy, p. 160; *Kutuzov Sbornik Dokumentov*, pp. 237–9.

themselves. More often than not, superior numbers took their toll for one side or the other. Yet if the claim of inherent superiority of French tactical doctrine fails to hold up under close scrutiny as the root cause, what then accounts for the dramatic magnitude of the French victory at Austerlitz?

For the French, the victory was the culmination of a remarkable campaign conducted by an army that had been blessed with exceptional leadership, a level of training hitherto unparalleled, considerable depth of experience, and an uncanny ability to capitalize on the errors of their enemy for maximum gain. While credit for this can and should be granted at all levels, these qualities were exemplified in the person of Napoleon and much of the success is directly attributable to his abilities. His planning from the outset was designed to allow reaction to enemy operations based on a range of possible situations. These plans evolved with each report that arrived, and Napoleon modified them several times throughout the night before the battle. Unlike the allies, Napoleon had from the outset determined to concentrate all available forces as quickly as possible, refusing battle if necessary until such time as the outlying corps had arrived. Dynamic planning produced a readiness to shift dispositions to reflect the changing realities. A key factor in Napoleon's successful planning came from French leaders at all levels who supported Napoleon's planning by providing a steady stream of detailed and accurate information on the enemy's movements, a task made easy by the carelessness of the allies.

Two "textbook" principles are exemplified by Napoleon's operations at Austerlitz: economy of force and use of local numerical superiority. Throughout the battle, small French forces made use of narrow defiles, villages or broken terrain like the pheasantry to oppose numerically superior enemy forces. In these situations, allied forces were unable to make use of their numerical superiority to overwhelm the French and instead were forced to meet them at roughly equal odds under conditions that favored the defender. While allied numerical superiority eventually told at both Tellnitz and Sokolnitz, the fierce resistance of the French along the Goldbach delayed the allies' broad flanking maneuver. This prevented the allied columns from moving beyond the Goldbach for over an hour and a half at Tellnitz and for nearly three hours at Sokolnitz, tying down the first three allied columns until events on the heights to their rear decided the day. This use of economy of force enabled the majority of the French forces to be massed against the weakest point of the allied army on the Pratzen Heights. The defeat of the 4th Column then allowed the French forces on the heights to descend into the valley of the Goldbach, providing a comfortable numerical superiority first near Sokolnitz and then near Augezd and Tellnitz in addition to the morale advantage gained as the situation unraveled for the allies.

Savary summed up the root cause of the French success quite nicely in his conversation with Alexander in Holitsch several days after the battle. Alexander commented to Savary, ". . . the rapidity of [Napoleon's] manoeuvres never allowed time to succour any of the points which he successively attacked: you were every where twice as numerous as we." In reply, Savary assured Alexander that the army had in fact been numerically inferior to Alexander's and that "We manoeuvred, indeed, a great deal: the same division fought successively in different directions—this is what multiplied us during the whole day."[*]

While the superb grand tactical effort resulted primarily from the considerable abilities of Napoleon himself, the execution of Napoleon's orders fell to the entire army, and here also the French are deserving of high praise. In sharp contrast to the allied army, which suffered serious problems with command cohesion from the outset, Napoleon remained in contact with his subordinate commanders throughout the battle, maintaining firm central control and issuing clear, concise mission-oriented directives. On their part, the subordinate commanders, particularly those charged with the defense of the lower Goldbach, demonstrated excellent initiative and made effective command decisions. Heudelet's impulsive penetration of Tellnitz, Lochet's aggressive attack on Sokolnitz and Davout's coordinated attacks on Sokolnitz are all examples of experienced commanders effectively adapting to the situation before them to achieve mission objectives. Lannes and Bernadotte on their own initiative called off potentially costly attacks at the end of the day against an enemy already badly defeated. While these last examples are perhaps subject to second-guessing, they demonstrate the willingness of French commanders at the corps, division and brigade levels to adapt their orders according to the circumstances. This reflects not only the experience and ability of the generals involved, but also the climate engendered by an army that not only accepted but also rewarded independent action—at least when positive results were achieved. Stutterheim praised the performance of the French officer corps, stating that ". . . the French generals manoeuvred their troops with that ability which is the result of the military eye, and of experience, taking advantage of the inequalities of ground to cover their troops from fire, and to conceal their movements."[†]

Finally, even at the lowest levels the French enjoyed a significant advantage. The months of intensive training conducted at the Camp of Boulogne had allowed the Grande Armée a unique opportunity to train not only within their companies, battalions and regiments but also in large-scale exercises. This

[*] Savary, I, p. 142.
[†] Stutterheim, p. 104.

standing army, with talented and experienced officers and men with a level of training never before achieved by an army of its size, enjoyed substantial advantages over the allied army. This was demonstrated repeatedly by the effectiveness of their musketry, their cool maneuvering under fire, effective coordination of combined arms operations and larger-scale maneuvers, and a superb discipline produced by high morale and complete confidence in their commanders. Stutterheim praised the French infantry in particular, noting that "The French infantry manoeuvred with coolness and precision, fought with courage, and executed its bold movements with admirable concert."* In short, superior tactical execution rather than any systemic advantage in tactical doctrine appears to have provided the key advantage in ensuring the French victory.

Among the advantages noted above, the ability to exploit weaknesses and errors committed by the enemy requires some assessment of the allied army's role in engineering its own defeat, and with the allied army at Austerlitz the weaknesses and errors are not hard to find. The situation the allied army had found itself in by 27 November produced a large number of difficulties from the outset. The first phase of the war had been characterized by faulty strategic planning and a fixation on preconceived ideas of how the French army would react. The shockwaves of the capitulation of Ulm reverberated throughout the rest of the campaign. The surrender severely undermined morale, exacerbated the feelings of distrust of the Austrians among the Russians which had persisted since the end of their disappointing 1799 campaign, and left the remaining Austrian and Russian forces no alternative but to beat a hasty retreat in the face of the numerically superior French army.

Austro-Russian cooperation was further strained by Merveldt's abrupt departure from the line of the Enns and the Austrian failure to destroy the Tabor Bridges at Vienna. This last failure, occurring at a point in the campaign when Kutuzov had placed the formidable barrier of the Danube between his army and Napoleon's, forced a rapid retreat into Moravia and necessitated the severe losses incurred by the allied (mostly Russian) rearguard at Hollabrunn-Schöngrabern. By the time Kutuzov's army met up with Buxhöwden's forces, morale had deteriorated so severely that it affected the newly arrived troops as well. To many Russian officers, it seemed that their Austrian allies were more of a liability than an asset. In such a climate, the reliance Alexander placed on the Austrian Weyrother produced even more discontent.

The psychological differences between the two opposing armies could not have been more different. The French army was exultant after having achieved a dramatic string of relatively easy victories and driven its enemies deeper into

---

* Stutterheim, p. 132.

their own territory than in any of the prior wars. On the other hand stood an army that had been retreating constantly for a full month, its circumstances made more difficult by poor planning or plain incompetence. The general mood was one of anger, frustration and disappointment, and finger-pointing had already begun by the time the allied forces were assembled at Olmütz. This dismal situation formed the background for the allied offensive against the French in Moravia.

At the grand tactical level, the allied plan for the campaign in Moravia was in itself not a bad one. In its essence, the plan called for a bold stroke against the right of the French forces in front of Brünn that would sever them from their direct line of communications through Vienna and force them to use the more difficult line through the mountains to Budweis and Linz. This line of communications would be more vulnerable and could possibly be disrupted by allied forces in Bohemia. The allies made three fundamental errors in the execution of this plan, however. First, instead of waiting a few weeks for the arrival of the corps of Essen-1, the arrival of Bennigsen's corps in Bohemia, the expiry of the Prussian ultimatum or for Charles's army to be ready for offensive operations, the allied high command was determined to attack immediately. This resolve was motivated primarily by political concerns, and significantly reduced the size of the forces that could be brought against the French. While Napoleon could draw in additional forces from Iglau and Vienna, the allies advanced at a time when they could not expect any significant assistance from other forces nearby.

Secondly, once the offensive had begun, the operations were executed poorly. The initial advance from Olmütz had caught the French by surprise, and we have already seen how Napoleon had determined to retreat if the allies had advanced directly on Brünn on 29 November. From this point, however, the allies failed utterly in the execution of the plan. The broad flanking maneuver developed slowly and without any effort to seize the commanding heights between the two armies to mask their movement to ensure some measure of surprise. The failure to mask their own movements also meant leaving the heights in the hands of the French, allowing the French to mask their own dispositions, leaving the allies in the dark about the enemy they were maneuvering against.

In addition, the difficulties of coalition warfare also manifested themselves in the allied army and contributed to problems of execution. While both the Russian and Austrian armies had the same fundamental structure and tactics, there were numerous differences in detail in the ways the two armies operated. Basic activities like conducting a march produced friction. Austrian staff officers complained that the Russian commanders were incapable of following even the simplest instructions, while the Russian officers complained about the incomprehensible orders and pointless paperwork emanating from the Austrian staff. Under such circumstances, smooth execution of any plan became difficult.

Thirdly, allied plans for the battle were based on a set of fixed assumptions regarding the strength and expected reactions of the French forces and their commander. As the allied army methodically advanced at the pace of its slowest and least experienced units, Napoleon was busy rapidly bringing in additional forces to even the odds against him. When Weyrother formulated his plans for the battle itself on the night before, his dispositions to a large degree assumed that the French army had the same strength and approximate dispositions it had three days earlier in the immediate aftermath of the action at Wischau. Against a force of that size, his plan might have succeeded had Napoleon been foolish enough to remain in the same position. In fact, the French had been reinforced by three additional infantry divisions and some cavalry, over 25,000 more men.

Additional factors inherent in Weyrother's planning included the assumption that the French army would remain passive to be acted upon, and that its only alternative action would be a precipitate retreat. Any awareness of the events of the past decade should have warned Weyrother of the possibility of reinforcement by the notoriously fast-marching French, and the greater likelihood of a bold offensive movement over a passive withdrawal, common characteristics of every campaign in which Napoleon participated. Weyrother's underlying assumptions led to a bold plan to throw the majority of the army against the French right with a small screening force in front of them. Only a small reserve (12–15 percent of total strength) would be retained to react to the unexpected. Clearly Weyrother gave little thought to any possibilities that went beyond the script he had already written for the French to follow. At the grand tactical level, then, the allied army had been utterly outclassed by Napoleon. Alexander's inexperience, coupled with Weyrother's theoretically sound but hopelessly flawed planning, produced a mindset within the allied headquarters that promoted self-delusion.

During the battle itself, the performance of the allied army deserves somewhat higher marks. Hampered as it was by unrealistic planning and with direct orders to adhere to the letter of the plan, it is not at all surprising that things went awry. At the lowest levels, though, the allied troops fought well, earning the praise of their enemies for their toughness. "The Russians shewed themselves on that occasion [Austerlitz] such excellent troops as they have never appeared since; the Russian army of Austerlitz would not have lost the battle of the Moscowa [Borodino]," Napoleon would note while in exile on

St Helena.* For the most part discipline remained solid among both the Austrian and Russian units, the Novgorod Musketeers being the notable exception. In the fierce fighting in front of Tellnitz and at Sokolnitz the Austrian and Russian troops attacked repeatedly, despite sustaining heavy losses, until they had achieved their objectives. During the defense of the heights, the Austrians and Kamensky-1's brigade over-achieved in a very difficult situation. But overall, the troops had been poorly served by their commanders, which has to be regarded as the most serious failing of the allied army.

The quality of the officers commanding the allied army was certainly inconsistent, but evaluating their performance is difficult. Even before the fighting had ended on 2 December, the various generals had already begun their accusations and this would persist long after the war had ended. Langeron provided a scathing condemnation of Miloradovich's performance during the battle despite never having been in a position to witness his actions. Miloradovich, like many of the Russians, sniped at the "foreign" elements in the army, with Langeron, Prshibyshevsky and anyone Austrian high on the list of scapegoats. Stutterheim dismissed many of his Russian colleagues as being incapable of following simple instructions. With all of their personal vendettas and political motives and their desire to exonerate themselves and cast blame on others, the opinions of the participants must be handled carefully.

At the brigade level, a number of generals distinguished themselves and would later achieve greater fame. Kamensky-1 stands out for his rare example of initiative and effective intervention at a critical point in the battle. His brother, Kamensky-2, did a solid job anchoring Bagration's left, and Ulanius's stubborn defense of Holubitz is certainly worthy of praise. In the center, Rottermund and Jurczik, along with Colonel Sterndahl, did an excellent job with their brigades despite the extraordinarily high proportion of inexperienced recruits. Finally, among the cavalry commanders, Nostitz, Stutterheim and Chaplits each demonstrated a good eye for opportunities. Though there were some solid performances, there were as many failures. Olsufiev-3 was plainly out of his depth at Sokolnitz after Langeron's departure while Wimpfen and Strik were reportedly ready to surrender long before their troops were. Engelhardt, Berg, Repninsky, and most of the other brigade commanders failed to make any significant impact on the outcome.

At the column level the allied leadership was solid, if unspectacular for the most part. Bagration, Liechtenstein and Kollowrath all seem to have

---

* Count Las Cases, *Memoirs of the Life, Exile, and Conversations of the Emperor Napoleon* (New York: A. C. Armstrong & Son, 1883), I, p. 336.

performed as well as could be expected under the circumstances, and despite Langeron's spiteful commentary, Miloradovich seems to have done reasonably well in a difficult situation. Even Constantine reacted appropriately to the threats he saw, detaching forces to Blaziowitz on his own initiative, and appears to have been entirely competent. Dokhturov, under the direct command of Buxhöwden, played a limited role in commanding the 1st Column, but once Buxhöwden was removed from the picture he stands out as a cool, competent commander and deserves credit for salvaging much of the 1st Column.

Several of the column commanders performed well enough in the initial operations but lacked the sort of initiative that might have made a difference to the outcome. Langeron, upon realizing the danger to the rear of the allied columns in the Goldbach valley, reacted too slowly and when he did act he accomplished little. Nevertheless, in his defense it should be noted that he lacked the authority to do much more than he actually attempted, and he freely admitted his own failure to reinforce the heights with the whole of his column immediately upon confirming the situation there. In the case of Prshibyshevsky, evaluation is more difficult. Although it appears that he was informed only around noon of the circumstances evolving on the heights, the sounds of the battle there would seem to have been audible near Sokolnitz. However, when the news had reached Langeron earlier in the day after the fighting on the heights had begun, he too had been surprised, suggesting that wind direction, the lay of the land or some trick of acoustics muffled the sounds. In other words, it is conceivable that Prshibyshevsky remained unaware of the French seizure of the heights until explicitly informed by Langeron. Prshibyshevsky's complete lack of any sort of reaction to the events occurring to his rear may have resulted from ignorance, fixation on adhering to the letter of his orders, or a paralysis resulting from absence of higher orders (or, alternatively, a complete lack of initiative). None of these possible explanations speaks well for Prshibyshevsky's capabilities as a column commander despite his competent job in prosecuting the attack on Sokolnitz.

While allied command at the brigade level was uneven and at the column level was reasonably solid, at the highest levels allied leadership was utterly inadequate and ineffective. Emperor Alexander, commander of the allied armies, certainly demonstrated his inexperience. Despite some hostile characterizations portraying his actions as cowardly, there is evidence that Alexander was actively observing the battle on the heights throughout the morning and remained near Krenowitz through the afternoon. Czartoryski noted that "I constantly met the Emperor at the different points which he visited in succession." Members of Alexander's staff were also in the thick of the battle. Czartoryski noted that one of Alexander's aides-de-camp, Prince Michael Dolgoruky (the younger brother of the hot-headed Prince Peter who had met with Napoleon a few days before), had been wounded in the thigh. Weyrother "had wandered from point to point and by bravely exposing his life strove to remedy the evil of which he had been one of the chief causes."[*] While Mikhailovsky-Danielevsky and other Russian writers have described Alexander's actions on 2 December in more heroic, if tragic, terms, Czartoryski's portrayal rings true. Alexander and his staff appear to have remained near to the crucial point of the battle on the Pratzen Heights, fluttering about helplessly trying to figure out what could be done to save their army. Alexander's performance is characterized not by cowardice, it seems, but rather by plain ineptitude. Incapable of grasping the situation or of conceiving of any positive action to take, Alexander exhausted himself riding from point to point while his army drifted rudderless into disaster.

However much blame Alexander deserves, his inexperience as a military commander was certainly well known among his staff and senior generals. Of these, two in particular must share the blame for allowing the situation to become far worse that it had to. Kutuzov was later blamed by the *Bulletin of Europe* (a Russian literary journal) for his "excessive compliance to the will of his sovereign."[†] This criticism is well founded. Prior to the battle, Kutuzov had resigned himself to the role he had been given to play—the mouthpiece for the orders crafted by Weyrother (in consultation with Alexander's inner circle) and commander of the allied center (the 4th Column). In the midst of the command crisis, when Alexander was riding aimlessly from point to point, Kutuzov remained dutifully in position commanding his column. There is no evidence that he ever attempted to persuade Alexander to take any particular action until he issued the order to withdraw shortly after 12:00. While Langeron reported the presence of an Austrian staff officer, presumably sent by Kutuzov, also exhorting Buxhöwden to send reinforcements to the heights, there is no evidence that Kutuzov urged Alexander to issue direct orders to Buxhöwden. In his defense, it can be imagined that disagreement with the emperor of Russia might be detrimental to one's career, and it is entirely possible that Alexander might have been hard to locate. But it is difficult to imagine any of the more dynamic Russian commanders—a Suvorov or a Bagration—adopting Kutuzov's passive role on 2 December.

The third of the three key senior commanders, Buxhöwden, seems the most deserving of condemnation. Despite being informed of the situation on the

---

[*] Czartoryski, II, pp. 108–9.

[†] D. A. Zharynov, "Pervye Voiny s Napoleonom I Russkoe Obtshestvo" ("The First Wars with Napoleon and Russian Society"), in Sytina, I.D. *Otechestvennaya Voina I Russkoe Obtschestvo*, Vol. I (Moscow: 1911) <www.museum.ru/MUSEUM/1812/Library/Sitin/book1_14.html>.

heights, Buxhöwden failed to issue any orders to the three columns under his command to discontinue the offensive movement or to reinforce the heights. For three hours after the initial French attack on the heights, Buxhöwden held twelve fresh battalions inactive within thirty minutes' march from the Pratzeberg and another sixteen battalions (including Kienmayer's infantry) on the other side of Tellnitz. Throughout the desperate struggle on the heights, the entire 1st Column remained frozen, and neither Alexander nor Buxhöwden thought to call off the attack on Sokolnitz nor to send reinforcements to the heights. Beyond this, Buxhöwden made no attempt to position the unengaged 1st Column to cover the withdrawal of the remainder of the army, resulting in the debacle at Augezd and at the end of the day his own separation from all but two battalions of the sixty-three he had commanded.

Ultimately, the initial planning and deployment of the allied army, based on erroneous assumptions regarding the French strength and intentions, had placed the allied army in a situation where defeat was likely from the outset. The severity of that defeat, however, was amplified by the absence of effective army and wing-level command: from the inexperience of Alexander, who was quickly overwhelmed by the reality of commanding an army; to the resignation of Kutuzov, snubbed, superceded and stubbornly subordinating himself to the will of his sovereign without complaint; and to the utter incompetence of Buxhöwden, who has only the allegation of drunkenness to explain his deplorable performance. As a result, although there were some excellent isolated efforts by the allies that succeeded in stalling the French advance for several hours, the allied high command was unable to use the time gained to bring in additional forces or to organize any sort of coordinated defense, leaving the individual commanders to their own devices.

To sum up the allied performance, given the situation the allies had found themselves in by noon on 2 December, they had been fortunate to have survived as well as they had. The distraction caused by the Russian Guard on the northeastern corner of the Pratzen Heights and the determined resistance of Bagration's forces on the Brünn–Olmütz Road had allowed the allied right and center to withdraw after dark without any serious interference from the French. On the opposite end, the desperate efforts of Sivers's artillery, Kienmayer's cavalry and Leviz's infantry had prevented the 1st Column from sharing the fate of the 2nd and 3rd Columns. The allied army had suffered a monumental defeat, sustaining heavy losses in every column save Maliutin's 2nd Guard Column, but it seems clear that it could have been far worse in the end.

With the approach of the fresh troops of Essen-1's corps and the proximity of Merveldt's corps to the route of retreat toward Hungary, the allies still had the capability of defending themselves against the inevitable French pursuit. Napoleon was also well aware of the threat posed by the Archduke Charles, who was ready to resume the offensive toward Pressburg and Vienna which had been left vulnerable with the departure of Davout's two divisions. In Bohemia, Ferdinand's makeshift army was pressing back the Bavarian division left to contain it, but this still constituted a minor threat. But the ensuing days would reveal the broader effect that the Battle of Austerlitz had produced on the Third Coalition and its willingness to continue the struggle against Napoleon's France.

Chapter 8

The End of the Third Coalition and the Origins of Napoleon's Grand Empire

Around 4:00 A.M. on 3 December, Prince Johann Liechtenstein appeared at the outposts of the French 1st Corps west of Austerlitz, having been sent by the Emperor Francis to arrange an armistice with Napoleon. In the ensuing interview, Liechtenstein also proposed a meeting between Francis and Napoleon to discuss the terms of a general peace between France and Austria, revealing to Napoleon that he had done more than defeat an army. He had shattered the Third Coalition and forced Austria into negotiating a separate peace. Unwilling to give up his advantage, Napoleon refused to commit to an immediate armistice, but suggested meeting with Francis on the morning of the 4th on the road between Austerlitz and Göding at whatever point the French outposts had reached by that time. Napoleon's intention was to inflict as much damage on the retreating Russians as he could manage before an armistice ended the fighting.

Following his meeting with Liechtenstein, Napoleon completed the proclamation to his victorious army that he had begun the night before, eloquently fixing the battle's place in history:

> Soldiers! I am pleased with you. On the day of Austerlitz you have justified what I had expected of your intrepidity. You have decorated your eagles with an immortal glory. In less than four hours an army of 100,000 men, commanded by the emperors of Russia and Austria, has been cut down or dispersed. Those who escaped your iron have drowned in the lakes. Forty flags, the standards of the Russian Imperial Guard, 120 pieces of artillery, 20 generals and over 30,000 prisoners are the results of this day, to be celebrated forever. That infantry, so vaunted, and superior to you in numbers, could not resist your impact, and henceforth you have no rivals to fear. Thus, in two months the third coalition is conquered and dissolved. Peace can no longer be at a great distance; but, as I promised to my people before crossing the Rhine, I will only make a peace that gives you some guarantees and assures some recompenses to our allies.

Soldiers! When the French people placed the Imperial Crown on my head, I entrusted you to keep it always in a high state of glory, which alone could give it value in my eyes; but at that moment our enemies thought to destroy and demean it; and that Iron Crown, which was gained by the blood of so many Frenchmen, they would have compelled me to place on the head of our cruelest enemies; an extravagant and foolish proposal, which you have ruined and confounded the very day of the anniversary of your Emperor's coronation.

You have taught them that it is easier for them to defy us and to threaten us than to vanquish us.

Soldiers! When everything necessary to the happiness and prosperity of our country has been achieved, I will lead you back to France. There you will be the objects of my most tender solicitudes. My people will see you again with joy, and it will be enough for you to say: "I was at the battle of Austerlitz," for them to reply, "There is a brave man!"*

For the heroes of Austerlitz, French and allied alike, there remained one final effort as Napoleon ordered his army to pursue the allies and the allies sought to escape further destruction.

The Pursuit, Armistice and the Treaty of Pressburg

The destruction of the allied army, as Napoleon noted in his proclamation to his troops, had ended the allied offensive in Moravia and made the minor successes of the outlying allied corps meaningless. Schwarzenberg, advancing against Wrede's Bavarian division from Bohemia, had driven the Bavarians back after a minor engagement at Stöcken on the same day as Austerlitz, but the Bavarians still stood between Schwarzenberg and Napoleon's line of communications. To the south, French cavalry outposts had withdrawn before the advance of Merveldt's small corps, allowing Merveldt to advance past Auspitz, dangerously close to the Vienna–Brünn road. However, the approach of the remainder of the French 3rd Corps and Klein's dragoon division, along with the defeat of the main allied army on his right, forced Merveldt to beat a hasty retreat to avoid being cut off from Hungary.

With the allied army shattered and driven from the field of battle in considerable disorder, Napoleon envisioned a devastating pursuit that would result in the utter destruction of the remnants. Marshal Soult's three divisions had been severely battered in the previous day's victory and Friant's troops had endured an epic forced march followed by fierce fighting around Sokolnitz and Tellnitz and required rest. Marshal Lannes's two divisions were in somewhat better shape and Bernadotte's two divisions and the two divisions

* Markham, pp. 55–6.

of Napoleon's reserve (the Imperial Guard and Oudinot's grenadier division) remained fresh. To these forces could be added Gudin's division, which had arrived at Nikolsburg the night before, and Klein's dragoons which had reached Raigern.

But while the French forces were well positioned for the pursuit of the allies on the morning of 3 December, during the night they had largely lost contact with them. The large body of allied cavalry in the north had effectively screened the withdrawal of the Life Guard and Bagration's forces through Austerlitz and beyond the Littawa. Unaware that the allied commanders had orders to withdraw toward Hungary in the event of defeat, Napoleon had assumed that they would be falling back on their line of communications toward Olmütz. Napoleon's orders to his marshals for 3 December were simple: "pursue the enemy."* But, by morning, several of those marshals had only the vaguest idea of where the enemy might be.

On the morning of 3 December, the French set off in pursuit of the allied army. In the north, Murat initiated a vigorous advance through Rausnitz and Wischau, with Lannes's infantry following. It was not until 6:00 P.M. with the French forces strung out along the road to Olmütz from Wischau to Prossnitz that it was realized that no allies had retired along that route. While this has been taken by some as being indicative of extreme sloppiness on the part of Murat and symptomatic of poor reconnaissance by the French light cavalry, it may in fact indicate that Bagration's forces withdrew in excellent order, leaving little behind in their retreat to mark their route. By contrast, the main army had left a trail of wreckage behind it, allowing Bernadotte to pick up its traces and follow it southeast from Austerlitz.

During the night, the desperate retreat of the allies had put a considerable distance between them and the French and it was not until around 2:00 P.M. that the head of Bernadotte's corps encountered the allied rearguard under Bagration near Zaroschitz. Bernadotte reported contact to headquarters and his advance guard exchanged fire with the enemy while he brought up his remaining forces. Bagration had deployed parties of skirmishers in a broad patch of woods spanning the road in front of the town of Urschitz with cavalry deployed to either side of the woods. Once again hampered by a lack of cavalry support, Bernadotte's actions were limited to engaging the Russian skirmishers in the woods. The Russian forces held the French back for about two hours, falling back slowly to the position of Bagration's main body around Urschitz as darkness fell. Bernadotte's forces continued a sporadic firing until about 6:00 P.M. Under cover of darkness, Bagration withdrew to a new position in front of Czeitsch, where he was joined by Kienmayer's column. In Czeitsch,

---

* Alombert and Colin, V, p. 232.

Francis awaited dawn and his meeting with Napoleon while the remainder of the allied army reached Göding and began crossing the March. Merveldt also arrived at Göding and took position to defend the crossing.

French light cavalry sent out to the southeast to determine the location of the allied forces retreating in that direction brought back concrete information to Napoleon's headquarters only around 3:30 P.M., with the 3rd and 4th Corps therefore enjoying a well-deserved rest for most of the day. Gudin's division, Viallanes's light cavalry brigade and Klein's dragoons all drew nearer, but in this sector the allies were allowed to withdraw with only minor pressure from the light cavalry sent out to determine their whereabouts. It was not until after 9:00 P.M. that the forces on the French right were ordered to advance. Davout directed Friant and Gudin, preceded by the cavalry, toward Göding to intercept the retreat of the allied army.

As a result of the failed French pursuit on 3 December, what remained of the allied army eventually escaped, though only by executing forced marches and leaving behind much of their baggage, supplies, ammunition, and a large number of wounded and exhausted men. Napoleon, however, continued to maneuver to gain maximum advantage in the event negotiations with Francis the next day failed to result in an armistice. As the reports came in on the evening of the 3rd, Napoleon expressed his displeasure at Murat's error in judgement, firing off orders for Lannes to march due south from Wischau to be in position to turn the right flank of Bagration's rearguard by the evening of the 4th. With Davout's forces already moving on Göding to cut the allied line of retreat, he hoped to be able to trap any allied forces remaining northwest of the March.

Among the allies, the sense of desperation had reached its height by midday on the 3rd. Francis had met with Kutuzov and Alexander at Czeitsch to discuss their prospects. While details of the discussion can only be guessed, it can well be imagined that Kutuzov advised retreat beyond the River March and joining forces with the corps of Essen-I (which was achieved on the 6th). Francis reported that Alexander "strongly urged the total withdrawal of the Russians, if he did not actually demand it."[*] The climate at Alexander's headquarters confirmed Alexander's resolve to withdraw from Austria. Czartoryski discussed what happened in a letter he wrote to Alexander in April 1806:

> . . . if your Majesty had not been on the battlefield, you would have been able to issue your orders calmly and without precipitation. How could you do this in the midst of the confusion at Holitsch, where you were surrounded by people who loudly accused the Austrians of treachery and

[*] Duffy, p. 152, citing Angeli, *Mittheilungen*, p. 360.

declared that the Russian army was absolutely incapable of fighting any longer? In the midst of the agitation and clamour it was impossible to say anything in favour of Austria or of the interests of Europe. People declared that your Majesty had done enough for others and that you must now think of yourself . . . and you told the Emperor Francis that he could not reckon any longer upon your army.[*]

While the armistice had already been scheduled at the time of this meeting, Alexander's position dramatically changed the situation that Francis faced. Where he had instructed Liechtenstein to hint at the possibility that Austria might negotiate a separate peace with France, this course of action now appeared to be a necessity.

On the morning of 4 December, the two emperors, each with a cavalry escort, approached their outposts on the Austerlitz–Göding road. The meeting occurred in the open with warmth provided by a large bonfire. After a little more than an hour of discussion the two Emperors had agreed to the terms of an armistice. "The parties seemed to be in excellent humour," noted Savary, "They laughed, which seemed to us all to be a good omen; accordingly, in an hour or two the sovereigns parted with a mutual embrace."[†] Under the terms of the armistice, hostilities between the French and Austrian troops were to be suspended the following day. Hostilities between French and Russian troops would be suspended on the day following Alexander's formal acceptance of the terms. Napoleon ordered Savary to accompany Francis to meet Alexander and get his confirmation of the terms of the armistice. Francis paused to dine at Czeitsch, inviting Savary to join him, while messengers raced to Göding with news of the armistice.

While the French and Austrian emperors were meeting, Marshal Davout was urging his men forward toward Göding to strike a final blow against the retreating allied forces. Davout's cavalry (Klein's dragoons and Viallanes's light cavalry) made contact with Merveldt's Austrians around 3:00 P.M. on the 4th. Behind them, Davout's infantry began arriving over the next hour and deploying for an immediate attack. As soon as the French arrived, Merveldt hastily sent a messenger to Davout informing him of the armistice. In addition, he sent a letter written by Kutuzov and confirmed by Alexander stating that the armistice was in effect and that hostilities had effectively ceased. Technically this was not true. Savary, having paused for dinner with Francis, had not yet met with Alexander and at any rate the armistice was not supposed to go into effect until the following morning. Davout, demonstrating a justified suspicion, agreed only to suspend hostilities until 6:00 the next

[*] Czartoryski, II, p. 127.
[†] Savary, I, p. 139.

morning and to provide one hour's advance notice prior to resuming hostilities. He immediately penned a report to Napoleon describing the situation at Göding.[*]

Following his meal with Savary, Francis ordered Stutterheim to escort Savary to Alexander. At Göding, Savary observed Russian pioneers preparing to destroy the bridge over the March. Proceeding on to Holitsch, Savary met with Alexander around 4:00 A.M. on 5 December. Savary presented Napoleon's terms, indicating that upon Alexander's acceptance he would notify Davout to suspend hostilities. Alexander accepted, "with a look of great satisfaction," according to Savary. Savary then returned to Göding with Stutterheim, where he was forced to wait for Bagration's rearguard to file across the bridge. Once Savary and Stutterheim crossed to the other side, the bridge was destroyed behind them and Savary was conducted through Merveldt's lines to Davout's headquarters where he learned of the premature cessation of hostilities the night before.

While there is justification for viewing this as a last bit of trickery on the part of the Russians, claims that this robbed the French of an opportunity to destroy the remainder of the Russian army are exaggerated. Much of the Russian army had already crossed the March by the evening of the 4th and was secure from attack. Merveldt's forces, about 5,000 reasonably fresh troops, stood in position between Davout and Göding and would certainly have defended themselves against a French attack given the fact that the armistice between France and Austria would not go into effect until the following morning. With only an hour and a half until nightfall, Merveldt's corps already well-established in their defensive position, and Davout's forces still strung out behind his advance guard, it is doubtful that he could have brought off an attack much before 4:00 P.M., if then. This attack, launched in twilight, would have been a hurried frontal assault against a rested and prepared enemy with only a portion of Davout's troops. Given the situation and the likelihood of determined opposition, the seizure of Göding on the night of 4 December would have been highly unlikely, despite Savary's conviction that "Marshal Davout might in half an hour have been master of Göding and of the bridge over the March, when the Russian army [in fact Bagration's rearguard] was still two or three leagues off on the Austerlitz road, facing Bernadotte."[‡] According to Savary, the remaining Russian forces filed over the bridge at Göding between 2:00 and 4:00 A.M. As at Hollabrunn-Schöngrabern, it seems that both sides were attempting to mislead each other

---

[*] "Au Ministre de la Guerre, Major Général, Josephsdorf, 13 frimaire an XIV (4 décembre 1805)," in *Correspondance du Maréchal Davout*, p. 196.

[‡] Savary, I, p. 146.

to some degree. Davout's report reveals that he agreed only to a limited cessation of hostilities and was using the time to position his troops for attacking at first light. When Savary arrived at Davout's headquarters around 6:00 A.M. with the news that Alexander had accepted the armistice, Davout's forces were already in position for the attack, belying the claim that Davout had been misled and missed a final opportunity to destroy the retreating allies.

With the conclusion of the armistice, Napoleon returned to Vienna where he finally met with the Prussian ambassador, Haugwitz, on 7 December. Haugwitz, an opponent of war with France from the beginning, determined that the results of Austerlitz had changed circumstances sufficiently to warrant his withholding of the ultimatum he had been sent to deliver, presenting instead the congratulations that Frederick William had expected to be delivered to Alexander and Francis. Over the next several weeks, Napoleon worked with Talleyrand to finalize the details of the terms he would demand of both Prussia and Austria. Talleyrand, viewing Russia as a more dangerous rival to French ambitions than Austria, favored leniency with the Habsburgs. Napoleon, however, aware that he had fought Austria in three wars in less than a decade, was determined to deal harshly with his most persevering, if not most dangerous, foe.

While Napoleon was preparing the terms he intended to offer to Austria, the Archduke Charles wrote to his brother, urging him to do whatever it would take for peace.

> The monarchy is shaken, its constituent parts have been torn from their connections, confusion has taken the place of order, the foundation threatens to collapse, if the spirit of providence does not watch over you and lead your resolutions. Peace alone, so necessary, so indispensable to the state, will not heal the deadly wounds unless the unworthy men are displaced. The voice of the people still differentiates between the probable intentions of their monarch and his councillors of ill-repute, but soon they will be only more sensitive to their wrecked prosperity, to the bloody victims of the war and to its inevitable terrible consequences![*]

Even the fall of the house of Habsburg seemed possible to the pessimistic Charles if peace was not achieved immediately and the main architects of Austria's move to war dismissed. For the moment, at least, Francis embraced his younger brother's advice, fearing the dire consequences described in the letter. On 24 December Francis dismissed his most prominent pro-war ministers, Cobenzl and Colloredo, and two days later he signed the Treaty of Pressburg. Under the terms of the treaty, Austria ceded to France the Venetian

---

[*] Oskar Criste, *Erzherzog Carl von Österreich* (Vienna: W. Braumuller, 1912), pp. 372–3.

territory gained at Campo Formio in 1797 (Dalmatia and Istria). In Germany Austria would also cede all of its scattered Swabian possessions, the Vorarlberg and the Tyrol. Napoleon used these territories to augment Bavaria, Baden and Württemberg, with Bavaria given the lion's share including the whole of the Tyrol. Austria gained the small former archbishopric of Salzburg, displacing the former Grand Duke of Tuscany who had been granted Salzburg in 1803. In exchange, the former Grand Duke received Würzburg from Bavaria. This pragmatic shuffling of provinces produced for the first time a collection of states in southern Germany whose territories were entirely contiguous.

For Prussia, Napoleon determined that he would demand an exclusive treaty of alliance between Prussia and France. As a key prerequisite for the alliance, Hardenberg, Frederick William's chief minister who was known to be an adamant opponent of France, would be dismissed. In return, Prussia would finally receive Hanover, effectively alienating Prussia from Britain, but would cede the tiny outlying principalities of Ansbach (which Napoleon would give to Bavaria) and Neuchatel (which would later be given to Berthier). On 14 December, Napoleon met with Haugwitz and presented his terms. Haugwitz did not immediately take the bait, prompting Napoleon to suggest that perhaps Hanover would be given to the former Grand Duke of Tuscany who was being displaced from Salzburg. Haugwitz considered the offer overnight and found he had little alternative. Austria had been knocked out of the war and the Russian army had been badly beaten and was retreating eastward. This left France free to concentrate its forces against Prussia and the allied forces in Hanover. Since the conclusion of the armistice on 5 December, French forces had been on the move to oppose the small allied forces in Hanover and Naples. St Cyr marched with his corps back down the Italian peninsula from Venice while Augereau shifted his 7th Corps northward from the Vorarlberg to Mayence. While Hardenberg had calculated that no fewer than 299,000 men would be available to oppose the French, Haugwitz considered the risk too great in light of the astounding successes the French had just achieved.* On 15 December, Haugwitz agreed to all of Napoleon's terms and signed the convention, forwarding it to a dismayed government in Berlin for ratification. In Berlin, every attempt was made to modify the terms, but Napoleon refused to budge. Two months later, with the entire Grande Armée encamped in southern Germany and war with France threatening, Prussia accepted the Treaty of Schönbrunn.

---

* Czartoryski, p. 116. Czartoryski reports Hardenberg's calculations as follows: 193,000 from Prussia (not including reserve battalions), 15,000 from Saxony, 16,000 from Hesse-Kassel, 8,000 from Hesse-Darmstadt, 3,000 from Brunswick, 24,000 British and Hanoverian troops and 40,000 Russians in the corps of Tolstoi and Bennigsen. In mid-December, many Prussian troops remained in Poland and East Prussia and would not be immediately available to strike at the French. It is interesting to note that Hardenberg did not count on the Swedes in his calculations.

Austerlitz and the Fate of Europe

Despite Alexander's bitter disillusionment in the aftermath of the great battle, Russia was the first of the defeated allies to recover its spirits. News of Austerlitz reached Moscow on 12 December 1805, "Moscow is sad, as gloomy as an autumn night," wrote contemporary Russian writer, Zhikharev.[*] But within a few days the mood had already improved. As late as January 1806 the papers published articles doubting the veracity of the reports of the disaster, attributing them to French propaganda. An article in the *Bulletin of Europe* asked, "Why, because of all the successes of the French, should anyone despair?" Russians had become used to victories but, while the news of Austerlitz was a severe blow to Russian vanity, it caused no great alarm and provoked no outcry for change. Informed individuals considered the role of the Austrians in the campaign, the good fortune of the French and Kutuzov's "excessive compliance to his sovereign" to be the root causes of the catastrophe.[†] Only Czartoryski seems to have had the courage to blame Alexander for Russia's misfortune in an April 1806 letter filled with the wisdom of hindsight:

> If you had listened to the advice we were constantly giving you, at first not to go to the army, and afterwards not to remain with it, but to ask the King of Prussia for an interview in order to move him to decisive action, the battle of Austerlitz would not have been fought and lost, or, if lost, would not have had the results which followed upon it.[‡]

The finger-pointing extended to all levels as the Russian Army sought to explain its catastrophe. Buxhöwden, whose performance at Austerlitz was most open to censure among the allied generals, was quick to blame Langeron and Prshibyshevsky, claiming they had become so fixated on adhering to the letter of the original plan that they had failed to react to events. Kutuzov adopted Buxhöwden's version of events in his official report and also placed perhaps excessive emphasis on the rout of the two musketeer battalions of the Novgorod Musketeers for the defeat of the column under his direct command. On top of Buxhöwden's accusations and Kutuzov's acceptance of them, the ethnic Russians in the army began pointing fingers at the non-Russians, starting with the Austrians and then extending to the French émigré, Langeron, and the Pole, Prshibyshevsky.[§] Although Langeron fired back,

---

[*] D. A. Zharynov, "Pervye Voiny s Napoleonom i Russkoe Obshestvo" <www.museum.ru/ MUSEUM/1812/Library/Sitin/book1_14.html>.

[†] Ibid.

[‡] Czartoryski, II, p. 127.

[§] Buxhöwden was from an old Livonian family, in Russian service since the time of Peter the Great. Like Bagration, a Georgian, he seems to have been considered "Russian" by the nationalists.

sniping at Miloradovich for being an incompetent toady responsible for the defeat of the center, the voice of a general who had lost nearly his entire column had little effect. Langeron was discredited, though he would later serve in the Army of Moldavia against the Turks. Prshibyshevsky, conveniently absent for six months as a French captive, faced a court-martial on charges of cowardice after his return to Russia and, while he was able to clear himself, never again held a prominent command. Buxhöwden inexplicably escaped any negative repercussions from Austerlitz, apparently having managed to deflect blame onto others by getting his report in first. With the outbreak of war in the fall of 1806, Buxhöwden received one of the two main army commands and would once again hold back to allow others to bear the brunt of the fighting.

Others, predominantly the ethnic Russians in the army, managed to derive some glory from the defeat. With the formation of permanent divisions in the Russian Army in the spring of 1806, Miloradovich, Dokhturov, and Kamensky-1 would be among those named to command the thirteen original divisions. Kutuzov, while absorbing much of the blame, remained in command of the army while it returned to Russia and in mid-February 1806 he was appointed to the command of a new army formed on the frontier from the fresh units of the armies of Bennigsen and Rimsky-Korsakov in preparation for a renewal of hostilities with France. When war did resume in the fall, however, Kutuzov was left behind in an administrative post as military governor in Kiev.

From the magnitude of the Russian defeat it might have seemed likely that probing investigations into the causes of the calamity would be conducted and major reforms would follow in its aftermath, as would be the case with Prussia after its disastrous campaign with France in 1806–7. To the contrary, however, in St Petersburg and Moscow there was little official reaction to the defeat. Official reaction in Russia corresponded with public opinion, blaming the obvious failings of the Austrians, Prussia's vacillation, and the "duplicity" of Bavaria.[*] Alexander to some degree blamed Kutuzov, who fell from favor after Austerlitz, though it seems from the Tsar's actions in later campaigns— particularly 1812—that he understood his own responsibility for the disaster well enough. Beyond this, there was no immediate reaction. Unlike in Prussia eighteen months later, there was no officer purge, no re-examination of tactical doctrine, and no complete redesigning of the military infrastructure.

While Russia suffered a severe blow to its national pride from the outcome of the campaign of 1805, Austria had been thoroughly humiliated and substantial parts of its empire had been stripped away in the ensuing peace.

---

[*] Zharynov, "Pervye Voiny s Napoleonom i Russkoe Obshestvo."

In Vienna, as in St Petersburg, many initially refused to believe the magnitude of the defeat. Cobenzl described it to Metternich, then ambassador to Berlin, as "an engagement of little importance", and of the armistice concluded as "a suitable delay for burying the dead."* The truth struck home abruptly as Napoleon presented his terms.

With the Treaty of Pressburg, Austria's role as the dominant power in central Europe, eroded by the Prussia of Frederick the Great and challenged by the rise of Revolutionary France, had ended. Austria's Swabian territories and Tyrolia had been taken and used to expand Napoleon's south German allies. The Venetian territories, accepted from Napoleon in 1797 in a pragmatic but morally questionable compromise, were ceded to France. With its army decimated and its remaining influence in Italy and Germany destroyed, the Austrian Empire was left far weaker than it had been before the war. The leaders of the war party had been discredited by the disastrous outcome and Charles, the only high-ranking Austrian general who had emerged with his reputation intact, gained considerable influence in the aftermath of the war, both as a political and military figure. He secured the removal of the rivals who had opposed him prior to the war and initiated administrative reforms but Francis, who feared giving his brother too much power, thwarted many of these efforts, including a proposed purge of the officer corps. Mack and Auersperg were court-martialed with good cause, but few others were affected and the Austrian officers at Austerlitz, overall an entirely competent group, were unaffected. But under Charles's leadership, the Austrian Army would rebuild, safeguarded by his determination not to enter into a fresh conflict with France until the army was ready.

In Britain, still exultant over the great naval victory of Trafalgar, the news of Austerlitz was met by disbelief. Rumors of the great battle fought in Moravia on 2 December arrived in England on 18 December. Two days later, *The Times* published a description of an epic three-day battle resulting in an allied victory. The day after, *The Times* printed Napoleon's proclamation to his troops (from the *Moniteur*) and ridiculed its outrageous claims, stating that "We cannot bring ourselves to attach to it the smallest degree of credit whatsoever." Over the next several days, accounts in *The Times* reiterated that the allies had won at Austerlitz and enumerated reasons why contrary reports from the continent could be discounted, noting that "The bulletins from the Grande Armée have lost much of their credit on the Continent, and even begin to be suspected in Paris. They are fabricated nine times out of ten to suit the purpose of the moment . . ." It was not until as late as 30 December, that a detailed account describing the battle as an allied defeat was printed, but it

* Furse, p. 395.

was noted that "The falsehood and extravagance of this account are too manifest to require that we should direct the particular attention of the public to them." Reality set in the next day when an account from an irrefutable source was published along with the comment that "We are compelled to give it reluctant credit."*

As the allied expeditionary forces in Hanover and Naples withdrew from the continent, Britain settled in to endure another long conflict with France, secured from invasion by Nelson's great victory at Trafalgar. Pitt noted ominously that "The old map of Europe will not be needed for another ten years," and survived his coalition by less than a month, dying in January 1806. His death ushered in a new government, termed the Ministry of All the Talents, which included Charles James Fox, a long-time sympathizer of the French Republic. Fox opened peace negotiations with Napoleon, but found that Napoleon was only too aware of his dominant position and no longer saw a need to compromise, henceforth preferring to dictate terms to defeated enemies.

In northern Germany, Prussia fell briefly under the influence of a handful of influential Francophiles, while the court, led by Queen Louise, became more vehemently anti-French. The Treaty of Schönbrunn had placed Hanover in Prussian hands, though several outlying principalities had been ceded, but the agreement kept the Hanoverian ports closed to British commerce. Ironically, this had been the very issue that had prevented Prussia from accepting Hanover before the war. Now Prussia meekly accepted Hanover on Napoleon's terms. Prussia had hoped to profit by remaining neutral or, failing that, to intervene with decisive influence and thereby win the right to determine the distribution of the spoils of victory. In effect, however, Prussia's vacillation had placed it in a position of subservience to France, committed by treaty to further French economic policy against Britain to its own detriment. Although another war would be needed to force Prussia fully to accept the subservient role it had been backed into by its indecisiveness in 1805, the victory of Austerlitz had launched Napoleon into a position of domination over all of continental Europe to the frontiers of Russia.

In France, the news of Austerlitz was met with jubilation. The *Moniteur* gleefully reported the terse details that Lebrun brought to Paris:

> Forty thousand prisoners. Seventy pieces of artillery. The Guard of the Emperor of Russia routed and a part captured, including several officers and a colonel. The two emperors of Russia and Austria on the point of being taken and ran away in all haste to Olmütz. Many general officers captured, among others a Prince Galitzin. The rest of the Russian army

* *The Times*, London, 18–31 December 1805.

in the most complete rout. The battle called by the soldiers, the battle of the three emperors. The French army lost little.*

While Talleyrand grumbled about the folly of imposing severe terms on a defeated Austria, Paris celebrated the most glorious victory of the era.

For Napoleon, Austerlitz had accomplished everything he could have hoped for. At a blow he had shattered the fragile coalition, driving the Austrians to accept a peace that relinquished to France the dominant position in Germany and Italy and paved the way for the formation of Napoleon's Grand Empire. While a state of war remained with Britain and Russia, there was little to fear beyond small raids along the coast. In the north, Napoleon had ordered Augereau along with Dumonceau's Batavian division to Mayence by forced marches in preparation for an attack on the allied army on the Weser. Prussia's occupation of Hanover, however, sent the Swedes again scurrying back to Swedish Pomerania. Soon after, the British forces re-embarked for England and Alexander recalled the Russian contingent, which withdrew through Prussian territory. To the south, it took slightly longer for matters to be resolved. On 26 December, the day the Treaty of Pressburg was signed, Napoleon publicly announced his intention to wipe the Bourbon Kingdom of Naples from the map of Europe for reneging on its treaty with France and welcoming the Anglo-Russian expedition. "The dynasty of Naples has ceased to reign," he announced dramatically, and on 30 March it became fact. Lacy's Anglo-Russian force withdrew before the first French forces arrived on the Neapolitan border, leaving Naples to its fate. While one French army conquered Naples, another sent to take possession of Dalmatia encountered minor interference from a Russian expedition from the Ionians at Cattaro, but in the end the French secured the mainland, leaving only a handful of Dalmatian islands in Russian hands.

By removing the last vestiges of Austrian influence in central Europe, Napoleon was left free to redefine Germany. The Holy Roman Empire, dead in all but name, finally disappeared. In January 1806 Napoleon had proposed the formation of a Confederation of the Rhine under the protection of France, and that July sixteen members of the Holy Roman Empire declared themselves separated from the old empire and members of the new Confederation. In August, the old Imperial Diet declared the Holy Roman Empire formally dissolved. For the south German states, the shift from Austrian to French influence came with mixed feelings. Some, like Frederick I of Württemberg, expressed frustration at Napoleon's domination of the realignment. Feeling that he had simply traded one overlord for another rather than gaining any meaningful independence, he declared, "This is a fatal blow to my political

---

* *Le Moniteur*, 20 frimaire an 14 [11 December 1805], reprinted in Langeron, p. 155.

existence." Others were dismayed by the continued presence of a large French army on their territory, one Bavarian observer noting, "I was fond of the French who drove out our enemies and who returned our legitimate rulers, but I detest those who live like leeches at the expense of our poor country."[*] Overall, the south German states saw their countries expand in size, prestige and power, though in the end they were no more independent than before and were subject to a more efficient and demanding overlord.

Elsewhere the emasculation of Austria allowed Napoleon a free hand in strengthening French control over occupied and allied states. One by one, Napoleon established hereditary kingdoms for his relatives and most loyal marshals, coercing the Batavian Republic to accept brother Louis as king, awarding the crown of Naples to brother Joseph and distributing other principalities to brother-in-law Murat, loyal chief of staff and Minister of War Berthier, Foreign Minister Talleyrand and the Bonaparte sisters. Although hereditary and sovereign within their own realms, each was also a Grand Dignitary of the French Empire and as such subject to the authority of Napoleon himself. While the rest of Europe looked on in dismay, Napoleon secured his personal control over half of Europe, knowing that the other half was powerless to stop him.

No other single battle save Waterloo would match the broad impact of Austerlitz on the course of European history. So complete and lopsided was the victory that it left Napoleon with a free hand to do whatever he liked toward recreating Europe according to his own designs for the benefit of France, himself and his family. While the Treaty of Tilsit in July 1807 is often regarded as marking the height of the Napoleonic Empire, Tilsit merely represents the temporary suppression of the last opposition to the formation of the Grand Empire. The Grand Empire itself was the culmination of Napoleon's grand ambition, enabled by his resounding victory at Austerlitz.

[*] Lefebvre, pp. 244–5.

Appendix A

An Assessment of Allied Army Strength Estimates

When studying the Napoleonic period it is virtually impossible to calculate exact troop strengths at any battle with any degree of certainty. The Battle of Austerlitz is a classic example of the problems involved in attempting to produce an accurate figure for the strengths of the two armies. Nevertheless, Scott Bowden in *Napoleon and Austerlitz* provides the results of extensive research into archival materials in the French military archives at Vincennes (S.H.A.T.), presenting the details from French strength reports before and after the battle. From this, it appears that Napoleon had roughly 74,000 men under his command at Austerlitz (although unexplained discrepancies with other sources suggest French Army strength might have approximated 75,000). This figure is reported by Bowden, but also appears in Rüstow's 1853 account and is close enough to Colin's figure of 73,100 and the 75,000 calculated from itemized strength figures without Bowden's estimated deductions.[*]

Calculations of the strength of the allied army, however, are subject to very substantial variation. The figure most commonly offered for the combat strength of the allied army is 80,000 to 82,500 men. Mikhailovsky-Danilevsky's official Russian history of the campaign suggests 80,000; Stutterheim offers a total of 82,040 and Schönhals states 82,575.[†] Colin offers a slightly higher total of 85,700 and Langeron a slightly lower figure at 77,000.[‡] In opposition to this figure we have two extremes. On the one hand, we have contemporary French claims, which indicate a total strength of over 93,000 for the allied army, which are echoed by Duffy who gives a strength of 93,405.[§] On the other, we have the recent calculations of Bowden, which produce a figure of 72,789.[¶] This wide variation in stated strength totals demands closer examination, first of the available primary and contemporary source material and then of the varying calculations to determine their probable accuracy.

---

[*] Bowden, pp. 488–99; Rüstow, pp. 364–5; Alombert and Colin, V, pp. 143–5.

[†] Mikhailovski-Danilevski, p. 227; Stutterheim, pp. 42–5; Schönhals, pp. 177–8.

[‡] Alombert and Colin, V, 140–5; Langeron, pp. 37–42.

[§] See the notes by "a French officer" included with Kutuzov's "Relation de la bataille d'Austerlitz," in Langeron, p. 138. These notes are attributed to Napoleon himself. In his proclamation after the battle, Napoleon exaggerated the allied troop strength at 100,000 men. Duffy, *Austerlitz* pp. 182–5.

[¶] Bowden, pp. 500–5.

Computing the Strengths: The Available Allied Returns

Primary documents detailing the Russian regimental strengths at different points during the campaign are available in two large fold-out tables in *Kutuzov Sbornik Dokumentov*. These tables detail the strengths of each regiment in the Army of Podolia, starting from the "paper" strength of all men enrolled in the unit (*po spisku*), detailing deductions (in prison, left behind in Russia, etc.) to produce a total present and under arms (*na litso*). The first of these tables details the total present and under arms in each regiment at Radzivilov on 7 September (26 August on the Russian calendar).* A separate document reproduces the strengths shown in the 26 August table in what appears to be a working copy or summary that shows only the total available strength.† From this table, it is clear that on average 5 percent of total paper strength of the regiment was left in Russia. The second table provides a summation of losses over the entire course of the campaign. Dated 20 February (8 February on the Russian calendar), this table provides the paper (*po spisku*) strength of each unit in the armies of Podolia (as of 1/13 October at Braunau) and Volhynia (as of 13/25 October on leaving Russia) as well as Essen-1's corps.‡ For each, deductions are made for killed/missing, detached (on returning to Russia) and left in Austrian hospitals to produce a present-and-under-arms total effective as of February 1806.

The reports prepared for the Army of Podolia on 1/13 October and for the Army of Volhynia on 13/25 October provide a considerable amount of concrete data on which to base an assessment. Working backwards from the final totals, the losses reported for Austerlitz, dated 6 January (25 December on the Russian calendar), can be added back in to the final totals to arrive at an estimate of total forces available prior to Austerlitz.§ In performing these calculations, there are several assumptions made. First, the men left in Austrian hospitals must be assumed to be primarily ill and injured from Austerlitz. Wounded left behind during the retreat appear as prisoners in French reports and appear to be documented among the killed and missing in the Russian documents. This is supported by observing the numbers in hospital from regiments originally in Buxhöwden's corps, which are

---

* "1805 g. Avgusta 26—Iz Raporta o Sostoyanii Podol'skoi Armii," No. 9, in *Kutuzov Sbornik Dokumentov* [RGVIA (Moscow) F. VUA, D. 3108, ll. 60–1].

† "Sostav Armii Kutuzova," [RGVIA (Moscow], f. 26, op. 16, d. 3106, ch. 1].

‡ "1806 g. Febralya 8—Vedomost' o Proisshedshei Ubyli Liudyam vo Vremya Byvshikh c Frantsuzami Srazhenii . . ." No. 368, in *Kutuzov Sbornik Dokumentov* [RGVIA (Moscow), f. 26, op. 152, d. 307, ll. 196–9].

§ "1805 g. Dekabrya 25—Vedomost' ob Ubitykh I Bez Vesti Propavshikh v 20-e Chislo Noyabrya Voinskikh Chinakh i Stroevykh Loshadyakh," in *Kutuzov Sbornik Dokumentov*, pp. 235–6 [RGVIA, f. 26, p.152, sv.534, d.7, ll. 2–3].

proportional to those from Kutuzov's corps despite having spent a fraction of the time in Austria and having got no further than Wischau. Second, once hostilities ceased on the morning of 5 December, it can be assumed that the pace of march slowed and fewer men were left behind as the army made its way back to Russia. Therefore, the number of men falling out of the ranks after 5 December can be considered negligible. Finally, it must be considered that some wounded who are counted in the army totals after Austerlitz would later die of wounds or complications, even if they were not wounded seriously enough to leave them in Austrian hospitals. These would be offset by stragglers who, with the cessation of hostilities, were able to rejoin their units on the way back to Russia but who were still counted among the missing at the time losses at Austerlitz were computed. This last figure is likely to number in the hundreds, possibly in the thousands as reports indicate that stragglers continued to turn up in Russia into 1806 to rejoin their units. As a result, the method used to compute total strengths prior to Austerlitz will likely produce a figure that is somewhat higher than the actual total. Finally, totals for the Guard regiments are provided by Vasil'ev in his article on the Guard at Austerlitz in which he describes discrepancies in sources and presents the most probable figures.*

When we perform these calculations, we can derive the following figures for Russian Army strengths at Austerlitz:

Table 7:
Russian Army Strengths

	Strength	Notes
Army of Podolia		
Infantry and cavalry	31,195	Total marching from Russia less campaign losses plus reported losses at Austerlitz
Artillery and pioneers	1,390	Estimated
Total Army of Podolia	32,585	
Army of Volhynia		
Infantry and cavalry	24,442	Total marching from Russia less campaign losses plus reported losses at Austerlitz
Artillery	1,390	Estimated
Total Army of Volhynia	25,832	
Reserve Corps of Constantine		
Guard plus Life Grenadiers	9,591	Includes 7,457 from the Guard
Guard – attached artillery	1,017	Includes 767 from the Guard
Total Reserve Corps	10,608	
Total Russian Forces	69,025	

* Vasil'ev, "Gvardiya" <www.genstab.ru/voin/auster_01.htm>.

If we consider the men who had become separated from the army during the battle and later made their way back to Russia, it seems that some portion of these would have been counted in the February returns and would therefore be counted twice in these calculations. This suggests a range of perhaps 67,000–69,000 with something around 68,000 being the most likely total strength of the Russian forces at Austerlitz.

Computing Austrian strengths will remain somewhat more problematic until more archival research unearths concrete figures in regimental records. The figures detailed in Schönhals, taken from unspecified Austrian documents, have been used by many later writers but are plainly imprecise. The numbers are given in round figures, there appear to be some errors in transcribing them (resulting in totals that do not match the sum of the entries) and a number of them are suspiciously close to establishment for units that were reportedly very weak. Most dramatically, the figure given by Schönhals for the strength of the 6th Battalion of the Kerpen IR 49, Major Mahler's battalion, is 700.[*] This does not match the figure, 312, which is given by Mahler himself. Mahler notes that his unit lost many stragglers en route from Vienna to Olmütz and was hit by an epidemic, which put an additional 200 men in the hospital. Mahler goes on to note that his battalion was typical of the 6th battalions at Olmütz and that all were of comparable strength except Auersperg IR 24 which had twice as many.[†] In addition, French sources note about 700 Austrian prisoners taken between Vienna and Wischau, stragglers who fell into French hands.[‡] From the figures given in Schönhals, the Austrian contingent at Austerlitz numbered 15,500, which must be considered unlikely but can be used as an upper limit. Given the high numbers, it seems likely that Schönhals's source totaled unit strengths for forces at Vienna prior to the march to Olmütz, which may have been the last detailed accounting available.

Using Schönhals figures as the closest available to an official strength, we can calculate a reasonable reduction in strength based on other data available. Adjusting for the depletion of the 6th battalions between Vienna and Austerlitz, we can reduce their stated strength from 4,300 to 2,400 using the testimony of Mahler (most at half strength or less). Further, using a battalion strength of 500 instead of 650 for the Székler battalions (a figure that is noted in other accounts), we can reduce the total strength of these two regiments by 300 men each for a total probable reduction of 2,500 men from the stated total strength. This produces a total strength of not more than 13,000 men for the

[*] Schönhals, p. 177.
[†] Mahler, pp. 513–6.
[‡] "État sommaire des . . . prisonniers de guerre," in Alombert and Colin, III, pp. 860–1.

Austrian contingent, which matches contemporary estimates, assuming that cavalry strengths reported are reasonably accurate.

Therefore, based on the detailed figures for Russian armies that produce a probable total of around 69,000 men and using the estimated figure of 13,000 for the Austrian contingent, the total strength of allied forces at Austerlitz would appear to be around 82,000 men, validating Stutterheim's 82,040 figure. Given that Russian totals may be lower than 68,000 and Austrian totals may well be less than 13,000, the total strength of the Allied army could well have been several thousand fewer, even approaching Langeron's stated total of 77,000, but is unlikely to be much lower than that. Using Schönhals's 82,500 figure as an upper limit and Langeron's 77,000 as a lower limit appears reasonable based on the available data.

Resolving the Discrepancies: Analyzing the Conflicting Assessments

With analysis of the available strength returns and accounts by the individual commanders as evidence, why is there then such a broad deviation in other sources? Beginning with the lowest estimate, we can break down the strength estimates for the various components of the Allied army to determine where the substantial deviation occurs. Comparing Bowden's figures with those of the others, in particular the official Russian returns provided in *Kutuzov Sbornik Dokumentov*, there is very close correspondence in most respects. The accounts agree that the Austrian contingent was in the neighborhood of 14,000 (though it seems this should be somewhat lower), Buxhöwden's corps added about 26,000 to the combined armies and the Russian Guard provided roughly another 8,500—accounting for somewhere around 47,000 to 48,500 men. With no significant disagreements between the official Russian counts, the main secondary accounts, and Bowden's figures these can be taken as accepted figures. This means that the difference of roughly 10,000 men between Bowden's 72,789 and the figure derived from the primary source material results from a radical deviation in the calculated troop strengths given for the regiments in Kutuzov's original Army of Podolia.

For the Army of Podolia, we need to do a bit more digging to determine the source of the discrepancy. The figures Bowden uses can be traced back to a table of Russian regimental strengths between 25 August and 25 November.[*] This table demonstrates a dramatic total reduction in Russian strength of 19,313, a loss of over 40 percent of the Russian total, during the advance to Braunau between 25 August and 23 October. During this period, the Russian regiments were conducting a forced march over a considerable distance, but

---

[*] Bowden, p. 293.

had not yet fired a shot in action. This depletion is consistent with records describing substantial numbers of stragglers and matches other accounts of the total number of troops arriving at Braunau. However, Bowden shows these losses as permanent losses and does not appear to account for the recovery of detachments, stragglers and sick during the retreat over the same route, which would not seem to be a reasonable deduction considering the evidence.

Two pieces of evidence call into question Bowden's conclusions regarding the permanent reduction in strength of the Army of Podolia. First we can consider a parallel situation. Friant's division is typically shown with 3,200–3,500 men at Austerlitz, having lost a large number of stragglers during its epic forced march from the neighborhood of Vienna. Returns provided by Bowden show about 5,500 with Friant's division prior to the forced march, indicating roughly 40 percent loss en route, a proportional reduction that interestingly matches that occurring in the Army of Podolia. However, most of Friant's stragglers later rejoined the division and can hardly be considered permanent losses. Similarly, the reduction in strength that Bowden records between 25 August and 23 October cannot be considered a permanent loss though Bowden has treated it as such. Punin states that Kutuzov's army arrived at Braunau with 11,000 fewer troops than he had on leaving Radzivilov, but notes that this figure included 5,000 men detached along the line of communications and 6,000 ill, injured, exhausted or stragglers (or combinations thereof). Bagration reported recovering nearly all of the stragglers from his regiments and this appears to have been typical for the other Russian columns as well.

Going back to the Russian documents detailing the losses for the campaign, we can examine the substantial discrepancies with the figures given in Bowden by addressing individual regiments. As of 20 February 1806 (prior to any documented return of prisoners), the total number of effectives for the regiments originally in the Army of Podolia stood at 25,940 officers and men at the conclusion of the campaign, 4,000 more than Bowden credits them as having before Austerlitz.[*]

Examining the official report of Russian losses at Austerlitz we can also identify serious discrepancies with the figures presented by Bowden. The total of killed and missing at Austerlitz from the regiments of the Army of Podolia amount to 9,739, roughly half of the total losses reported. Examining the figures for individual regiments, there are two instances where the official account reports a substantially higher total number of killed and wounded

---

[*] Total losses from the regiments that had composed the Army of Podolia were shown as 19,971 for the campaign of which 4,444 were noted as being in Austrian hospitals. Those in hospitals were most likely wounded left behind after Austerlitz.

than Bowden shows as even being present with the regiments at Austerlitz. These specific instances are:

Table 8:
Conflicts in Regimental Strengths/Losses

	Reported Losses at Austerlitz	Total Strength at Austerlitz (Bowden)	Total Strength at Austerlitz (official)
Narva Musketeers	1,600	731	1,921
Butyrsk Musketeers	1,902	864	2,055

Further, Bowden's figures indicate all other regiments of the former Army of Podolia at 50 percent or less of the strength figures derived from Russian returns and the reports of losses at Austerlitz. While it is possible that strength returns and reports of losses could be deliberately adjusted, this could be expected to be for the purpose of minimizing losses. If Bowden's calculations are correct, then reports of Russian losses were inflated in official Russian reports. If this were the case, some explanation would need to be provided to explain why the Russians would deliberately exaggerate their own losses. This seems highly unlikely, particularly to the magnitude involved in this example.

Finally, the figure given by Bowden for Constantine's Guard columns is 8,500, a total that matches figures for the strength of the Guard at Austerlitz. Vasil'ev's excellent study of the Guard at Austerlitz, however, confirms a figure of 10,608 for Constantine's columns (10,358 plus approximately 250 artillerists of Merten's half battery and the artillery of the St Petersburg Militia that accompanied the column). This detailed analysis matches the figure of 10,500 given for this column in other sources. Therefore, while it is correct to state the strength of the Guard at Austerlitz as approximately 8,500, this figure does not include the Life Grenadier Regiment or the non-guard artillery attached to the Guard, making Bowden's figures for Constantine's column roughly 2,000 men too low.*

Having determined that the low-end figure given for the Allied army is certainly based on flawed interpretation of the surviving data, we can examine the other extreme. Napoleon's own estimate of the strength of the allied army was 93,000, a figure he stated with considerable certainty. While it would be easy to discount this figure as propaganda, Napoleon was extremely well-informed on the strength, composition and movements of the allied army

---

* Bowden mistakenly identifies the Life Grenadier Regiment as the detached first battalions of the three Guard regiments. In fact, only the 1st and 3rd Battalions of the Guard regiments were present at Austerlitz. The 2nd Battalions of all three regiments and the 4th Battalion of the Preobrazhensky, along with one Life Guard position battery, remained in St Petersburg under the command of GM Bashutsky. Aleksandr Konstantinovich Chicherin, S. Dolgov and A. Afanas'ev, *Istoriia Leib-Gvardii Preobrazhenskago Polka, 1683–1883* (St Petersburg: 1883–8), p. 20.

throughout the campaign due to an extremely effective network of spies. It seems likely, therefore, that Napoleon's figure derived from intelligence reports sent in by French spies and very probably referred to the total strength of the allied army at Olmütz. Napoleon's figure is reasonably close to the official Austrian figure of 89,110 for the forces assembled at Olmütz.* Ten Austrian 6th battalions plus the Moravian-Silesian Jäger Battalion (a newly raised volunteer unit) and a squadron of Erzherzog Johann Dragoons remained at Olmütz. In addition, a large body of Russian heavy artillery remained behind. In all, these forces, along with those left behind in hospitals in Olmütz, numbered about 10,000 men, neatly accounting for the discrepancy between the 93,000 figure appearing in French accounts and the more accurate 82,000 figure.

Considering the problems inherent in the high and low estimates of allied troop strengths and correcting for them, it seems that all sources approach agreement on the total strength of the allied army. From Bowden's base of 72,000 we must add an additional 2,000 for the non-guard units under Constantine's command (not accounted for by Bowden), 5,000 for the recovery of Kutuzov's detachments along his line of communications and the recovery of at least several thousand stragglers after Braunau, a total of 10,000 men or more. From the French estimates of total allied army strength at Olmütz, we must deduct the forces left at Olmütz, reducing the figure of 93,000 by something approaching 10,000 men. These calculations bring us to the same figure of roughly 82,000 given by Mikhailovsky-Danilevsky, Stutterheim and Schönhals for the total strength of the allied army at Austerlitz. While the totals of Russians and Austrians vary by a few thousand in the various accounts, their similarity indicates this number as the closest possible estimate. Obviously even this figure is open to debate.

The issue of allied army strength at Austerlitz can and should be the subject of additional archival research in Russian and Austrian records to improve the basis on which these numbers are derived. In the end, though, any figures relating to troop strengths must be regarded as being merely indicative of actual strengths, not precise figures. As Bowden notes, the situation of the forces changed daily, even hourly and with a dynamic and rapidly moving target it is impossible ever to derive a precise figure. However, by reducing the deviation between high and low estimates from 20,000 to something closer to 4,000 we can more closely approximate the actual strength of the forces engaged.

---

* This figure is given as 75,270 infantry and 13,840 cavalry. Josef Freiherr von Spiegelfeld, *Geschichte des Kaiserlichen und Königlichen Infanterie-Regimentes Freiherr von Mollinary Nr. 38* (Budapest, 1892), p. 162.

Biographical Notes

French Commanders

Emperor Napoleon I [Napoleon Bonaparte] (1769–1821) requires little introduction, but some description of his early career prior to assuming control of the government of France might be useful. Born in Corsica, Bonaparte attended military school in France, frequently returning to Corsica on leave. In 1792 he was present in Paris during some of the most turbulent days of the French Revolution and witnessed many of the excesses of the mob, which left a lasting impression on him. Bonaparte returned to Corsica later in 1792 and over the following year participated in a failed amphibious expedition and became embroiled in Corsican politics. Returning to France, Napoleon served first with the Army of Italy and then in the siege of Toulon, where his eye for placing artillery achieved dramatic results. Named général de brigade in 1794 for his performance during the siege of Toulon, Bonaparte refused his next assignment fighting royalist rebels in the Army of the West, and was therefore present in Paris when an uprising threatened the Directory. The Directory solicited his help in putting down the rising and with a small body of troops he dispersed the mob with his famous "whiff of grapeshot." A grateful Directory promoted him to général de division and gave him command of the Army of Italy in 1796. Assuming command of what was considered an army of secondary importance, Bonaparte launched a dramatic whirlwind campaign that quickly placed the whole of northern Italy under French control. After beating off several Austrian attempts to drive him out, in 1797 Bonaparte led his army deep into Austrian territory and negotiated a conclusion to the War of the First Coalition on his own initiative, presenting the results to a startled government in Paris. After briefly exploring possibilities for an invasion of England, Bonaparte offered a plan for an expedition to conquer Egypt. The Directory consented and authorized the formation of an Army of the Orient, which sailed to Egypt in 1798. The destruction of the French fleet at the hands of Nelson stranded Bonaparte in Egypt and operations soon stalled. Hearing news of repeated French defeats nearer home and being able to accomplish little in Egypt, in 1799 Bonaparte resolved to return to France to offer his assistance. On arriving in France, he learned that the crisis had passed, but he was approached by a party of conspirators seeking a "sword" to lead a new *coup d'état* to overthrow the

Directory. The success of the *coup* in November 1799 placed Bonaparte at the head of the French government as First Consul and his narrow but dramatic victory at Marengo the following June secured his position, allowing him to implement sweeping civil reforms and to make his position as head of state permanent, first as Consul for Life and then as Emperor in 1804. The remainder of his career is nothing less than the history of the period.

Jean Baptiste Jules Bernadotte (1763–1844) enlisted in the army in 1780, rising to the rank of sergeant-major by 1788. In 1792–4 he served in the Army of the Rhine and in 1794 he was transferred to the Army of the North and promoted to général de brigade. Later the same year he was promoted to général de division in the Army of the Sambre et Meuse. In January 1797 Bernadotte was transferred to General Bonaparte's Army of Italy where he commanded a division composed of regiments transferred from the Armies of the Rhin et Moselle and Sambre et Meuse, and participated in the invasion of Austrian territory that ended the War of the First Coalition. He was appointed French ambassador to Vienna in 1798, but his actions enraged the Austrians and he was quickly recalled. In 1799 Bernadotte served briefly as Minister of War. Bernadotte refused to participate on either side during Napoleon's November 1799 *coup d'état*, but in 1800 was named to command the Army of the West and successfully suppressed the royalist insurrection in the Vendée. In 1804 Napoleon appointed him to be the governor of French-occupied Hanover and commander of the Army of Hanover and he was named one of the original Marshals of the Empire in 1804. With the outbreak of war in 1805, Napoleon designated Bernadotte's Army of Hanover as the 1st Corps of the Grande Armée and he served in that capacity throughout the campaign. Bernadotte's relationship with Napoleon was never warm, but the open animosity that would mark their later dealings seems to have been absent during this campaign. Although Napoleon would criticize Bernadotte for being slow and allowing the Russian Guard to escape destruction, his performance appears to have been good enough to retain his position. Bernadotte commanded the 1st Corps through 1806, earning his emperor's wrath for failing to engage his corps at either Jena or Auerstadt, but again retained his post, commanding until wounded in June 1807. Bernadotte then served as Governor of the Hanseatic ports and commander of all French forces there. In the 1809 campaign against Austria, Bernadotte commanded the Saxon Army (the 9th Corps of the Grande Armée), but was removed from command following a dispute with Napoleon after the Battle of Wagram. In 1810 the Swedish government offered the position of Crown Prince to Bernadotte due to the absence of an heir to the throne and Napoleon consented to release

Bernadotte of all obligations to France to take the position. Bernadotte was instrumental in aligning Sweden with its traditional enemy, Russia, and joined the coalition against Napoleon, commanding the allied Army of the North in 1813–14.

Louis Alexandre Berthier (1753–1815) served as Napoleon's indispensable chief of staff for nearly the entire period from 1796 through 1814. He began his military career in 1766 as a topographical engineer, reaching the rank of captain by 1777. Berthier was a part of the French force sent to America and served on Rochambeau's staff. In 1789 he was promoted to lieutenant-colonel and in 1792 he was serving as chief of staff to Lafayette, then to a series of generals until relieved on suspicion of royalist sentiments in 1793. In 1795 he was reinstated at the rank of général de brigade and sent as chief of staff to Scherer's Army of Italy, receiving promotion to général de division soon after. He continued as chief of staff for the Army of Italy after Bonaparte assumed command of the army, briefly commanded the army after Bonaparte's departure, and then rejoined Bonaparte as his chief of staff for the campaign in Egypt in 1798. He returned to France with Napoleon in 1799 and after the *coup d'état* of Brumaire became Minister of War, serving in that capacity as well as being Bonaparte's chief of staff in 1800 (Marengo). Berthier was named one of the eighteen original Marshals of the Empire in 1804 and in 1805 he managed a mountain of logistics in transferring the Grande Armée from the Channel coast to the Rhine rapidly and with minimal confusion. Berthier's role placed him in the background throughout the campaign, effectively managing the largest single army ever assembled. After Austerlitz, Berthier continued in his dual role of Minister of War and Napoleon's chief of staff through the 1806–7 campaigns in Prussia and Poland. After Tilsit, Berthier relinquished his responsibilities as Minister of War but remained as Napoleon's chief of staff in every campaign until Napoleon's first abdication in 1814. With Napoleon's return from Elba in 1815, Berthier left France with Louis XVIII. He died in Bamberg in 1815 in a fall from a window, sparking a controversy—accident, suicide or murder?

Jean Baptiste Bessières (1768–1813) entered the Royal Army as a volunteer captain of the National Guard in 1789 and later served the royalist cause with the Constitutional Guard. After the overthrow of the monarchy, he served in the Pyrenees against Spain in 1792–5. He was transferred along with most of the troops from the Pyrenees to the Army of Italy after Spain withdrew from the war in 1795, and in the 1796–7 campaign in Italy he attracted the attention of Bonaparte. Bonaparte appointed Bessières to command his

Guides in the Army of the Orient in 1798, and Bessières returned to France with Napoleon in the autumn of 1799. After the *coup d'état* of Brumaire, he was named to command the cavalry of the Consular Guard, serving at Marengo. He became one of the original eighteen Marshals of the Empire and commander of the Imperial Guard in 1804, continuing in that capacity through 1808 with a brief interruption in November–December 1806 when he commanded the provisional 2nd Cavalry Reserve of the Grande Armée. At Austerlitz, Bessières played only a minor role, engaging the Russian Life Guard in a brief clash early in the afternoon. In 1808 he was named to command the 2nd Corps of the Army of Spain before returning to France and assuming command of the Cavalry Reserve of the Grande Armée against Austria in 1809. Serving in various capacities within France during 1810–11, Bessières again assumed command of the cavalry of the Imperial Guard for the 1812 Russian Campaign and the 1813 campaign in Germany until being killed in Saxony in May 1813.

Charles Joseph Boyé (1762–1832) served in the ranks of a hussar regiment of the royal army. Rising through the ranks, he served with the Army of the North through 1794. Transferring to the Army of the Sambre et Meuse in 1795, Boyé had earned promotion to the rank of général de brigade a few months later. Boyé served in Massena's Army of the Rhine and Switzerland in 1799, fighting at the Second Battle of Zurich. He then served in Moreau's Army of the Rhine in 1800 and led a brigade at the Battle of Hohenlinden. With the formation of the Grande Armée, Boyé received command of a brigade of dragoons in Beaumont's 3rd Dragoon Division and then assumed command of the division when Beaumont fell ill, commanding at Austerlitz. Boyé continued in command of a brigade in Beaumont's division through May 1807 when he was sent to Silesia. In 1808 he was employed on the staff of the Army of Spain and was appointed commandant of Vittoria in 1809. He retired from the service in 1812.

Marie François Auguste de Caffarelli du Falga (1766–1849) began his military career in the service of the King of Sardinia in 1785–92 before returning to France. He served in the Army of the Eastern Pyrenees from 1792–5, the Sambre et Meuse in 1795–7 and in Germany in 1799. Early in 1800 he joined the Consular Guard and served with the Army of Reserve at Marengo. In 1802 he was promoted to général de brigade and was sent on a mission to the Pope in 1804 to convince him to come to France to bless Napoleon's coronation. Promoted to général de division in 1805, Caffarelli served as an aide-de-camp to Napoleon and replaced Bisson in command of the 1st Division of Davout's 3rd Corps after Bisson was wounded. Caffarelli commanded the division for the remainder of the campaign. After Austerlitz, Caffarelli served in various positions in Italy and Spain, including Minister of War for the Kingdom of Italy, military governor of occupied Spanish provinces and commanding a division in Spain. In 1813 he was recalled to France, serving in Paris and accompanying the Empress Marie Louise and Napoleon's son to Vienna after Napoleon's abdication. In 1815 he rallied to Napoleon and again served as aide-de-camp during the Hundred Days.

Louis Nicolas Davout (1770–1823) entered the army as an officer after completing military school in 1788. With the outbreak of the revolution, Davout first served with the Army of the North, earning promotion to général de brigade in 1793 shortly before having to resign from the army as a suspected royalist. Reinstated the next year, he first served in the Army of the Moselle before being transferred to Moreau's Army of the Rhin et Moselle (1796–7). In 1798 he was assigned to the Army of the Orient and remained in Egypt after Bonaparte's departure, returning to France with Desaix in the spring of 1800. Selected to command the forces at Bruges on the Channel coast in 1803 (later the 3rd Corps of the Grande Armée), Davout became one of the eighteen original marshals. In 1805 Davout's 3rd Corps was one of the first across the Inn in pursuit of the Russians, and Davout's forces engaged the Austrian rearguard at Lambach and Steyr before inflicting a more serious defeat on them at Mariazell. At Austerlitz, Davout would conduct a savvy defense, launching well-timed counterattacks to keep the larger Russian forces he faced off guard. Davout continued to command the 3rd Corps through the 1806–7 campaigns in Prussia and Poland and remained with his corps in Germany when much of the Grande Armée was transferred to Spain. In 1809 he served against Austria and commanded the oversized 1st Corps in Russia in 1812. In 1813–14 Napoleon assigned Davout the independent command of defending Hamburg and the line of the lower Elbe and Davout's force at Hamburg was one of the last to surrender to the allies after Napoleon's abdication. Davout rallied to Napoleon in 1815, serving as Minister of War during the Hundred Days.

Jean Baptiste Drouet (1765–1844) entered the army in 1782. With the outbreak of the revolution, Drouet volunteered and served in the Army of the North and Army of the Moselle before joining the Army of the Sambre et Meuse (1794–7). In 1799 he served as chief of staff to General Lefebvre in Germany and was promoted to général de brigade. Later in 1799 he served under Massena in Switzerland and fought the Russians at the Second Battle of

Zurich. In 1800 he remained in Germany, serving in Moreau's Army of the Rhine at Hohenlinden. Drouet commanded the Advance Guard of Mortier's Army of Hanover and was promoted général de division in 1803, assuming command of the 1st Division (later the 1st Division of the 1st Corps of the Grande Armée). Drouet's division did not see much action during the campaign up the Danube and was only partially engaged with the Russian Guard at Austerlitz in the afternoon. After Austerlitz, Drouet continued to command Bernadotte's 1st Division through January 1807 when he became chief of staff to Marshal Lefebvre for the siege of Danzig. He then served as chief of staff to Marshal Lannes until being seriously wounded at Friedland. In 1809 he again served as Lefebvre's chief of staff in the war with Austria, assuming command of a Bavarian force in the suppression of the Tyrolean revolt. In 1810 he was sent to Spain to command a corps and served in Spain through 1814. He rallied to Napoleon and again commanded a corps during the Hundred Days.

Louis Friant (1758–1829) entered the army in 1781 and was a corporal at the outbreak of the revolution. Joining the Paris National Guard, he served first with the Army of the Moselle and then with the Sambre et Meuse, becoming général de brigade in 1795. In 1797 he was a part of the force sent to the Army of Italy under Bernadotte and participated in Bonaparte's invasion of Austria. In 1798 he served in Bonaparte's Army of the Orient in Egypt, remaining after the departure of Bonaparte and earning the rank of général de division. After the British captured Egypt, Friant was returned to France and at the Camp of Boulogne was named to command a division of Davout's force at Bruges, later the 2nd Division of the 3rd Corps of the Grande Armée. Friant's division crushed the Austrian forces at Mariazell and also conducted an epic forced march of 116 kilometers in twenty-four hours which placed the division within supporting range of the French forces at Austerlitz. In 1806–7 Friant continued to serve with the 3rd Corps and also served under Davout for the 1809 and 1812 campaigns. In Russia he was named to replace Dorsenne in command of the Old Guard and served with the Guard in 1813–14. In 1815 he rallied to Napoleon, serving with the Guard at Waterloo.

Jean Joseph Ange d'Hautpoul (1754–1807) entered the army as a volunteer in 1771, reaching the rank of lieutenant before the outbreak of the revolution. He served with the Army of the North (1792–4) and the Army of the Ardennes (1794) before joining Jourdan's Army of the Sambre et Meuse where he distinguished himself and earned promotion to général de brigade in 1795 and général de division the following year. He again served under Jourdan in the

Army of the Danube in 1799 and in 1800 served in Moreau's Army of the Rhine, participating in the victory of Hohenlinden. In 1805 he was appointed to command the 2nd Heavy Cavalry Division of the Cavalry Reserve of the Grande Armée. His aggressiveness and eye for opportunities allowed him to launch two significant charges on the French left at Austerlitz. In 1806–7, d'Hautpoul continued in command of the 2nd Heavy Cavalry Division in the campaign in Prussia and the winter campaign in Poland. D'Hautpoul was mortally wounded participating in Murat's epic cavalry charge against the Russians at Eylau.

François Etienne Kellermann (1770–1835) entered the army in 1785 as a Hussar officer and in 1791 was sent to America with the French embassy. He returned to France in 1793 and was placed under arrest along with his father under suspicion of royalist sentiments. Released in 1794, he served first under his father in the Army of the Alps and then was transferred to the Army of Italy under Bonaparte, earning promotion to général de brigade in 1797. In 1798–9 Kellermann remained in Italy, serving under General Macdonald. In 1800 Kellermann commanded a brigade of cavalry in the Army of Reserve, launching the pivotal charge that blunted the Austrian advance at Marengo and sparked the French counterattack that led to victory. This earned him promotion to général de division. In 1804 he was appointed to the command of the cavalry of the Army of Hanover, later to become the 1st Corps of the Grande Armée. At Austerlitz, Kellermann's cavalry division saw considerable action, participating in several notable charges during which Kellermann was wounded. In 1806–7, Kellermann remained in France in command of the cavalry of the Army of Reserve and in 1807 commanded the cavalry during Junot's invasion of Portugal. After the Convention of Cintra returned Junot's army to France, Kellermann participated in the 1808 invasion of Spain, remaining there until being recalled to France in 1811. In 1812, Kellermann was transferred to Italy and in 1813 to Germany. He served in the Cavalry Reserve of the Grande Armée until Napoleon's abdication in 1814. Kellermann rallied to Napoleon in 1815, commanding a cavalry corps at Waterloo.

Jean Lannes (1769–1809) is perhaps the most celebrated of Napoleon's marshals. He began his military career as a volunteer after the revolution had begun, serving first against Spain in the Army of the Eastern Pyrenees and then being transferred to Italy in 1795, serving first under Scherer and then under Bonaparte. His outstanding performance through the spectacular 1796–7 Italian campaign earned him promotion to général de brigade in 1797.

Lannes accompanied Bonaparte to Egypt with the Army of the Orient in 1798 and returned to France with him in 1799. In 1800 Lannes was promoted to général de division and commanded the advance guard of the Army of Reserve, distinguishing himself at Montebello and Marengo. After the end of the War of the Second Coalition, Lannes served briefly as Ambassador to Portugal, returning to Paris for Napoleon's coronation. Named one of the original eighteen marshals, Lannes was appointed to command the Advance Guard of the Army of the Ocean Coasts for the invasion of England, two elite divisions training near Boulogne (later the 5th Corps of the Grande Armée). In 1805 Lannes's corps spearheaded the French advance, engaging the Austrian forces east of Ulm. Lannes's subsequent advance on the left flank of the Grande Armée in its pursuit of the allied army brought his corps into direct contact with the Austro-Russian rearguard at Amstettin. His forces were among the first to enter Vienna and to cross the Tabor Bridge and were the main units engaged at Schöngrabern. At Austerlitz, Napoleon had intended Lannes's corps to lead the pivotal attack to turn the allied right flank and drive the entire army into the ponds to the south, but the allied positions and actions required a change in plans and left Lannes with a less important role to play. After Austerlitz, Lannes seems to have had a falling out with Napoleon, returning to France, but was ordered to resume command of the 5th Corps on the eve of war with Prussia in September 1806. He remained in command of the 5th Corps until wounded in December. After recovering, Lannes commanded the Reserve Corps in the spring 1807 campaign in Poland before being transferred to Spain in 1808. In 1809 he was recalled from Spain to command a corps in the war with Austria, but was mortally wounded when struck by an Austrian cannonball at Essling.

Claude Juste Alexandre Legrand (1762–1815) entered the army in 1777, reaching the rank of sergeant-major by 1786. He left the service briefly to be married, but with the outbreak of the revolution Legrand volunteered in the National Guard of Metz where he was rapidly promoted, reaching the rank of général de brigade by 1793. He served in the Army of the Moselle (1793–4) and the Sambre et Meuse (1794–7). Promoted to général de division in 1799, he served in Germany through the War of the Second Coalition (1799–1800), participating in the French victory at Hohenlinden. At the Camp of Boulogne, Legrand was selected to command Soult's 3rd Division in what would become the 4th Corps of the Grande Armée. At Austerlitz, Legrand did not play a major role, remaining at Kobelnitz until the main body of his division was committed to the action in mid-afternoon. Legrand remained in command of the 3rd Division of the 4th Corps through the 1806–7 campaign in Prussia and Poland, remained in Germany and commanded a division against Austria in 1809. In 1812 he commanded a division in the 2nd Corps, assuming command of the corps after first Oudinot and then St Cyr fell wounded. Legrand was severely wounded at the crossing of the Beresina and returned to France to recover, playing only a limited role in the 1814 defense of France. He died in 1815 from lingering complications from the wound.

Joachim Murat (1767–1815) joined the army in 1787, becoming an officer soon after the outbreak of the revolution. Commanding a squadron, Murat happened to be in Paris when the Directory asked the young General Bonaparte for assistance against the Paris mob. Murat's cavalry rode to retrieve some guns from an artillery park in advance of the mob sent to seize them, returning them to Paris in time for Bonaparte to crush the uprising. When Bonaparte was given command of the Army of Italy by a grateful Directory, Murat accompanied him on his staff. Promoted to général de brigade in the spring of 1796, Murat distinguished himself during the 1796–7 Italian campaign and then accompanied Bonaparte to Egypt with the Army of the Orient. Earning additional honors in Egypt, along with promotion to général de division, Murat was one of the inner circle that accompanied Bonaparte back to France, assisting in his *coup d'état*. Murat commanded the cavalry reserve of the Army of Reserve, fighting at Marengo. Named as one of the eighteen original marshals, Murat served as Governor-General of Paris and with the formation of the Grande Armée in September 1805 assumed command of the Cavalry Reserve. During the pursuit of the Russian Army down the Danube, Napoleon appointed Murat to command the semi-independent vanguard of the Grande Armée. After playing a leading role in the capture of the Tabor Bridge at Vienna, Murat was outfoxed by Bagration at Schöngrabern. At Austerlitz Murat's cavalry was positioned on the extreme left of the army to exploit the gap that would be opened when Lannes turned the allied flank. With the change in emphasis from the far left to the center, Murat played a significant but lesser role in the course of the battle. In the 1806–7 campaigns in Prussia and Poland, Murat also commanded the Cavalry Reserve. Sent to Spain in 1808, Murat had some hopes of being made King of Spain, but Joseph Bonaparte, who had been made King of Naples in 1806, was selected for the post and Murat was given the throne of Naples instead. In 1812, Murat was summoned from Naples to command the Cavalry Reserve for the invasion of Russia and after the disastrous retreat Napoleon left him in command of the remnants of the army. Murat quickly relinquished command to Prince Eugene and went back to Naples, but returned to Germany to command the Cavalry Reserve in 1813. In 1814 Murat made a separate peace with the allies, retaining Naples after Napoleon's abdication, but in 1815 he launched a premature attack on the Austrians and was defeated and forced to flee to France. Napoleon rebuffed Murat's offers to serve him during the Hundred Days and after Napoleon's second abdication Murat attempted to land in Naples to stage his own "Hundred Days." He was immediately captured and executed by firing squad.

Etienne Marie Antoine Champion Nansouty (1768–1815) entered the Royal Army as an officer in 1785 after completing military school, reaching the rank of captain before the outbreak of the revolution. He served in the Army of the Rhine and the Army of the Rhin et Moselle in 1792–1801, earning promotion to général de brigade in 1799. In 1803 he was promoted to général de division and appointed to command the cavalry of the Army of Hanover. The following year he was recalled to Paris to command the heavy cavalry of the Army of the Ocean Coasts. With the formation of the Grande Armée, Nansouty's division became the 1st Heavy Cavalry Division of the Cavalry Reserve of the Grande Armée. Nansouty's elite heavy cavalry played a significant role at Austerlitz in countering the Russian cavalry at the northern end of the battlefield. Nansouty remained in command of the 1st Heavy Cavalry Division through the 1806–7 campaigns in Prussia and Poland, and then accompanied Napoleon to Spain as a part of his household staff (first equerry). Nansouty again commanded a heavy cavalry division against Austria in 1809 and in Russia in 1812. In 1813 Nansouty was appointed to the command of the cavalry of the Imperial Guard, serving in that capacity until Napoleon's abdication in 1814. Nansouty died in Paris in February 1815 shortly before Napoleon's return to France.

Oliver Macoux Rivaud de la Raffinière (1766–1839) began service in the royal army and after the outbreak of the revolution served in the Army of the North (1792–3) and the Army of the West (1794) before being transferred to the Army of the Alps and then to the Army of Italy in 1796–7. Rivaud served in a number of staff positions, finally becoming chief of staff of the Army of Italy under General Berthier in 1798 after Bonaparte's departure. Promoted to général de brigade, Rivaud remained with the Army of Italy through 1799, then served with the Army of Reserve in 1800 and fought at Marengo. Rivaud was promoted to général de division in 1802 and was named to command a division of Mortier's Army of Hanover the next year (which later became the 2nd Division of the 1st Corps of the Grande Armée). Rivaud's division saw minimal fighting through the 1805 campaign and at Austerlitz appears to have only encountered the enemy briefly near Blaziowitz and later on to have sent out some skirmishers to harass the retreat of the Russian Guard. After Austerlitz, Rivaud continued in command of Bernadotte's 2nd Division until injured in January 1807. He then served in Germany and France with various corps of observation and administrative posts.

Louis Vincent Joseph le Blond, comte de Saint-Hilaire (1766–1809) entered the army as a cadet in 1777, reaching the rank of lieutenant by 1788. With the outbreak of war in 1792, St Hilaire served with the Army of the Alps, serving at the siege of Toulon and then with the Army of Italy. He was still serving in Italy as a provisional général de brigade when Bonaparte assumed command. Confirmed in the rank of général de brigade in 1796, he was left in command of the depots of Bonaparte's Army of the Orient in 1798. After Bonaparte's *coup d'état* in November 1799, St Hilaire was promoted to général de division and in 1800 he served under Suchet in Italy. At the camp of Boulogne St Hilaire was selected to command Soult's 1st Division in what would become the 4th Corps of the Grande Armée. One of many exceptional divisional commanders in the Grande Armée, St Hilaire performed extremely well in the most difficult position of the French forces advancing against the allies at Austerlitz. After the 1805 campaign, St Hilaire remained in command of the 1st Division of the 4th Corps, serving in the campaigns of 1806–7. After Tilsit, St Hilaire's division was left in Germany under Davout's command and with the outbreak of war with Austria in 1809 was one of the first to engage the Austrians. St Hilaire's exceptional performance in the 1809 campaign was noted by Napoleon and many consider him to have been almost certain to have received a marshal's baton, but he was mortally wounded at Essling.

Nicolas Jean de Dieu Soult (1769–1851) enlisted in the army in 1785 and rose quickly after the outbreak of the revolution, becoming général de brigade in 1794. Soult served with Jourdan's Army of the Sambre et Meuse in 1794–7 and again under Jourdan in the Army of the Danube in 1799, earning promotion to général de division. Later that year Soult commanded the reserve of Massena's army in Switzerland, participating in the victory over the Russians at Zurich and playing a key role in the attempts to cut off and destroy Suvorov's army marching north from Italy. In 1800 Soult accompanied Massena to Genoa. When the Austrians besieged the city, Soult was captured during a sortie. After returning to France, Soult was given command of the main French force assembled around Boulogne, four divisions that were later to form the 4th Corps and part of the 5th Corps of the Grande Armée. His exceptional administrative skills made the divisions under his command some of the finest in the French Army. With the outbreak of war in 1805, Soult's corps was involved in the encirclement of Ulm, capturing a sizeable Austrian force at Memmingen. Soult's forces occupied the Pratzen Heights in the week preceding the Battle of Austerlitz. Soult remained in command of the 4th Corps through the 1806–7 campaigns in Prussia and Poland. In 1808 he was sent to Spain where he commanded first a corps and later the Army of Andalusia. Soult remained in Spain through 1812 but was recalled to Germany for the first six months of 1813 before returning to Spain to oppose the army of the Duke of Wellington. After Napoleon's abdication in 1814, Soult served the Bourbons as Minister of War, but rallied to Napoleon on his return to France, serving as chief of staff for the Army of the North during the Hundred Days.

Louis Gabriel Suchet (1770–1826) entered the army in 1792 as a volunteer after the start of the revolution, serving at the siege of Toulon (1793) and then in the Army of Italy. Suchet participated in Bonaparte's successful 1796–7 campaign in Italy, achieving the rank of chef de brigade by 1797. In 1798 Suchet served as General Brune's chief of staff in the occupation of Switzerland. He was relieved briefly for political reasons, but was then requested by Massena to serve under him in Switzerland, becoming his chief of staff. By the summer of 1799, however, Joubert had been named commander of the Army of Italy and requested Suchet as chief of staff, resulting in his transfer. At the end of 1799, Suchet again served under Massena, who had been transferred back to Italy, and commanded a corps on the Var during the 1800 campaign. In 1804, Suchet was named to command Soult's 4th Division at the Camp of Boulogne (later to be detached to Lannes's 5th Corps of the Grande Armée). Suchet, having commanded an independent corps in 1800, was reportedly displeased at his appointment to a lesser position, but served capably through the 1805 campaign. His division saw heavy fighting in its position on the extreme left of the French Army at Austerlitz. Suchet continued to command a division in the 5th Corps through the 1806–7 campaign in Prussia and Poland and in 1809 was given command of a corps in Spain. His success in Spain in 1809–11 earned him a marshal's baton, and he held Catalonia for the French until forced to evacuate early in 1814 by the deteriorating military situation to the west. Suchet rallied to Napoleon in 1815, and led the Army of the Alps (VII Corps) during the Hundred Days.

Dominique Joseph René Vandamme (1770–1830) entered the army in 1788 and at the outbreak of the revolution he was a sergeant serving in Martinique.

Vandamme returned to France in 1791 and fought in Belgium in 1792–3 where he rose quickly, becoming général de brigade by 1793. After briefly serving with the Sambre et Meuse, Vandamme served under Moreau with the Rhin et Moselle in 1796–7. In 1799 he served in Jourdan's Army of the Danube until relieved for an over-zealous collection of "contributions" in Württemberg, but was sent to Holland to serve under Brune against the Anglo-Russian landing there. In 1800 he was again serving in Germany under Moreau. At the Camp of Boulogne he was selected to command the 2nd Division of Soult's forces (based at St Omer), later the 4th Corps of the Grande Armée. At Austerlitz, Vandamme's division would play two key roles, the first in seizing the Pratzen Heights and the second in the destruction of the allied 1st Column by the Satchan Pond. Always a difficult subordinate, Vandamme clashed with Soult throughout the 1805 campaign. In 1806–7 he commanded the Württemberg contingent employed in reducing Prussian fortresses in Silesia and again commanded the Württemberg contingent against Austria in 1809. In 1812 he led a division of Westphalians before being sent back to France for "brigandage." He was back in action in command of a corps in 1813, but was captured at Kulm. In 1815 he rallied to Napoleon and again commanded a corps.

Allied Commanders

Emperor Alexander (1777–1825), son of the abusive Tsar Paul, had been a favorite of Catherine the Great. His father had formed his own small model army and had uniformed and drilled it in an exaggeration of the Prussian style of Frederick the Great. However, Alexander received little military education and was too young to participate in the Turkish and Swedish wars. He did command a reserve corps in 1799, largely a titular post, but had no other practical command experience prior to assuming the throne following the assassination of his father in 1801. In 1805, Alexander resolved to join his army and assumed *de facto* command of the combined allied armies at Olmütz. Following Austerlitz, Alexander refrained from taking direct command of his armies, although he would accompany them periodically during the campaigns of 1812–14.

Prince Petr Ivanovich Bagration (1765–1812) came from an old Georgian family and entered the Russian Army in 1782. He served in the wars in the Caucasus (1783–6 and 1790) and against the Turks (1788) in the capture of Ochakov. In 1794 he served in a carabinier regiment in Poland, where he caught the attention of Suvorov. Promoted colonel in 1798 and general-major in the spring of 1799, Bagration served as commander of Suvorov's Advance

Guard and later earned high praise from Suvorov for his handling of the Russian rearguard in Switzerland. Named to command the 1st Column of Kutuzov's Army of Podolia in 1805, Bagration's performance throughout the campaign identified him as one of the most talented Russian generals and won him promotion to general-lieutenant in November of that year. Bagration served against the French again in Poland in 1806–7, played a major role in the conquest of Finland in the Swedish War of 1808 and was named general of infantry and commander-in-chief of the Army of Moldavia in the Turkish War in 1809. In 1812 he commanded the Second Army of the West against the French, and was mortally wounded at Borodino.

Fedor Fedorovich Count Buxhöwden (1750–1811) was a Livonian who entered the Russian engineer corps at the age of fourteen, taking part in Catherine the Great's first Turkish War. Buxhöwden was promoted to brigadir in 1789 and then general-major for his performance in the Swedish War. In 1794 he commanded a division under Suvorov in Poland, participated in the storming of Praga and was appointed commandant of Warsaw by Suvorov. Tsar Paul promoted him to general-lieutenant soon after ascending to the throne. In 1803 Buxhöwden was promoted yet again to general of infantry and assumed a dual position as Inspector of Livonia and Governor of Riga. In 1805 he was appointed to command the Army of Volhynia. His self-serving report earned him an undeserved decoration for the Battle of Austerlitz and in 1806 he was appointed to lead one of two armies initially committed to support the Prussians, but was outmaneuvered politically by Bennigsen and was removed from command in January 1807. Buxhöwden commanded the Russian army in Sweden in 1808 before retiring from service in December of that year.

Grand Duke Constantine Pavlovich (1779–1831), Tsar Alexander's younger brother, participated in his first campaign with Suvorov's Army of Italy in 1799, where Suvorov reportedly provided some instruction to him. During the course of the campaign, Constantine caused some political difficulties and was one of the most outspoken Russophiles, loudly criticizing Russia's Austrian allies, particularly during the disastrous Swiss operations. As Tsarevich, Constantine was the obvious choice to command the Life Guard in 1805, first as a part of GL Essen-1's Army of Lithuania and then under GoI Buxhöwden in the Army of Volhynia. In 1807, Constantine again commanded the Life Guard in Poland, serving at Heilsberg and Friedland. In 1812, Constantine led the Russian 5th Corps (Life Guard plus additional regiments) and continued to serve against the French through 1814.

Dmitri Sergeevich Dokhturov (1756–1816) entered the army in 1771 and was promoted to lieutenant in the Semenovsky Guard Regiment in 1781. He served in Finland against the Swedes (1789–90). He was promoted to general-major in 1797 and general-lieutenant in 1799. He received the Order of St George 3rd Class for his performance at Dürrenstein and commanded the allied 1st Column at Austerlitz. His conduct at Austerlitz won him the Order of St Vladimir 2nd Class. Dokhturov commanded a division in the 1806–7 war with France and commanded a corps in 1812–14.

Prince Petr Petrovich Dolgoruky-3 (also known as Dolgorukov, 1777–1806) was enlisted in a Guard regiment as an infant, becoming a captain at the age of 15. For the next six years he served with a number of garrison regiments, rising rapidly as a result of family patronage. He repeatedly requested field assignments, but was consistently refused, either due to family machinations or possibly because of his youth and inexperience. At age 21 he became a general-major and months later became an adjutant-general to Tsar Paul. Prince Petr was among the conspirators who assassinated Paul and, like many of the conspirators, he became a favorite of Alexander's, conducting several diplomatic missions to Prussia and Sweden in 1802–4. He accompanied Alexander during the 1805 campaign as one of his general-adjutants, receiving command of the infantry of Bagration's Advance Guard just before Wischau. In that capacity he was positioned to serve as the diplomatic link between Alexander and Napoleon. Young, confident and arrogant in his behavior, Dolgoruky irritated Napoleon. His performance on the battlefield appears to have been competent and he was awarded the Order of St George 4th Class and a gold epée for his conduct at Austerlitz, possibly due to his political connections and the resulting attention he received in Bagration's reports. In 1806 Dolgoruky was assigned to the Army of Moldavia but was transferred to Poland before he could join. In the course of his travels he became ill and died in December 1806.

Sergei Mikhailovich Kamensky-1 (1771–1834) entered the army as a cornet in a dragoon regiment. Distinguishing himself in the Turkish War (1790–1) and in the storming of Praga (1794), Kamensky had achieved the rank of general-major by 1798 but he was dismissed from the service by Tsar Paul for political reasons later that year. Reinstated in 1801 after the accession of Alexander, in 1805 Kamensky was *shef* of the Fanagoria Grenadiers and led a brigade in Langeron's 2nd Column at Austerlitz. His performance at Austerlitz won him promotion to general-lieutenant and he was given command of a division in the Army of Moldavia. Kamensky served against the Turks with distinction and for his performance in Moldavia he was promoted to general of infantry. In 1812, Kamensky served in Tormasov's army and he participated in the 1813–14 campaigns against France.

Michael Baron von Kienmayer (1755–1828) entered the Austrian service as a cadet in 1774 and participated in the 1778–9 campaigns against Prussia. During the 1788–91 Turkish War, Kienmayer particularly distinguished himself at Chotim and Fokshani. In 1793–4 Kienmayer served against the French in Belgium and earned the rank of Generalmajor. Kienmayer served against France in Germany in 1795–7 and in Germany and Switzerland in 1799–1800, earning the rank of Feldmarschalleutnant. In 1805 Kienmayer was appointed to command a corps to observe the French forces advancing from Hanover and as a result his corps escaped the encirclement of Ulm. With the union with Kutuzov's army, Kienmayer retained command of the heavy cavalry held in reserve and Merveldt took over command of most of the remainder of his corps operating on Kutuzov's left. During the advance from Olmütz, Kienmayer was given command of the Austrian Advance Guard. In 1809 Kienmayer commanded a corps against the French, but in 1813–14 he held regional commands, first in Galicia and then in Transylvania.

Johann Karl Count Kollowrath-Krakowsky (1748–1816) entered the Austrian service in 1766 as a lieutenant. He distinguished himself during the War of the Bavarian Succession (against Prussia) and also in the 1788–91 Turkish War. In 1792–7 Kollowrath served against France, winning the Commander's Cross of the Order of Maria Theresa. In 1800 Kollowrath was promoted to Feldzeugmeister, was named to the Hofkriegsrat the next year and in 1803 became Commandant-General of Bohemia. In this last capacity, in 1805 Kollowrath assisted Ferdinand in assembling a new army in Bohemia after the capitulation of Ulm and played a part in the repulse of French probes across the Bohemian frontier. Joining the main army at Olmütz, Kollowrath was given command of the main Austrian contingent. In 1809 Kollowrath commanded a corps in the war against France, his last campaign. In 1813–14 he assisted allied operations as Commandant of Bohemia, but did not exercise a field command.

Mikhail Ilarionovich Golenishev-Kutuzov (1745–1813) began his military career as a corporal of artillery before entering the corps of cadets of artillery and engineers. After completing his technical education, Kutuzov entered the new Jäger corps. He served in Poland in 1764–9 and in the Crimea in 1770–4 where he was severely wounded in the head and lost an eye leading the assault on the Turkish works at Touma. Kutuzov served under Suvorov during the annexation of the Crimea and later in the Turkish War, participating in the siege of Ochakov and the storming of the fortress of Ismail. At the conclusion of the Turkish War, Kutuzov was sent as Ambassador to Constantinople. On his return, Kutuzov was appointed Military Governor of Finland. In 1805 Kutuzov was named to command the Army of Podolia, one of four Russian armies that were originally intended to be under the overall command of General Michelson. Kutuzov's army formed the advance guard of the Russian forces marching west to support Austria, but he inherited the role of overall allied commander after Mack's capitulation at Ulm. With the arrival of Alexander, Kutuzov relinquished his authority to his Tsar, receiving blame for being "too much the courtier" and not exercising a more demonstrative role in the planning of the allied offensive at Austerlitz. Following Austerlitz, Kutuzov was left in command of the Russian forces withdrawing eastward and in February 1806 was named to command a new Army of Volhynia (the Russian forces that had fought at Austerlitz being divided between this army and the Army of Moldavia). In the fall of 1806 Kutuzov was passed over for a field command and was named Military Governor of Kiev. Kutuzov was made chief of staff to the elderly Prozorovsky commanding the Army of Moldavia against the Turks in 1808–9 until dismissed for political reasons. In 1811 Kutuzov was appointed to command the Army of Moldavia and within twelve months had brought the six-year war to a successful conclusion. In 1812 Kutuzov was appointed overall commander of the combined Russian armies, continuing the Russian withdrawal in the face of a larger French Army, as in 1805, before making a stand at Borodino, then observing and harassing the fringes of the French army during its withdrawal from Moscow. Exhausted by the rigors of the 1812 campaign, Kutuzov died in Silesia in 1813.

Alexandre Andrault comte de Langeron (1763–1831) was born in Paris. He served in the French Army and as a young ensign was part of the French force sent to America in 1777. With the upheavals of the French Revolution, in 1789 Langeron emigrated, entered the Russian service and distinguished himself in the war with Sweden in 1790. Later the same year, Langeron participated in Suvorov's assault on the Turkish stronghold of Ismail. After the Turkish War, Langeron volunteered in the war against France (though Russia had not entered the war) but remained in Russian service, reaching the rank of general-major in 1797 and general-lieutenant in 1798. After Russia's departure from the Second Coalition in 1800, Langeron returned to Russia and was appointed first as Inspector of Orenburg and then Inspector of Brest-Litovsk. He was named to command one column of Buxhöwden's Army of

Volhynia assembling around Brest-Litovsk and was selected to command the allied 2nd Column at Austerlitz. After the 1805 Campaign, Langeron served in the Turkish War (1806–12) and against the French in 1812–14.

Prince Johann Liechtenstein (1760–1836) entered the Austrian service in 1782 as a lieutenant. Liechtenstein was decorated for his service against the Turks during the 1788–91 Turkish War, and in 1792–7 served against France, earning the Commander's Cross of the Order of Maria Theresa for his performance during Archduke Charles's victorious 1796 campaign in Germany. Liechtenstein served in Italy under Suvorov in 1799, distinguishing himself at the battles of Trebbia and Novi, earning promotion to Feldmarschalleutnant. In 1800, Liechtenstein served in Germany and was present at the Austrian disaster at Hohenlinden. In 1805, Liechtenstein was given command of the Austrian forces retiring from Vienna after the disgrace of Auersperg, performed well in command of the Allied 5th Column at Austerlitz and undertook a diplomatic mission from Francis to Napoleon in the aftermath of the battle. In 1808 Liechtenstein was promoted to general of cavalry. Liechtenstein served through the 1809 campaign and in the aftermath of the Battle of Wagram took over command of the Austrian army from Archduke Charles.

Mikhail Andreevich Miloradovich (1771–1825) entered the Russian service as an ensign in the Ismailovsky Guard Regiment at the age of nine. He was sent to study abroad at Königsberg and distinguished himself as a young officer in the Swedish War (1790). His military qualities attracted attention and he rose quickly during the period when Tsar Paul was removing many of the older generals, becoming colonel in 1797 and general-major in 1798. He earned the praise of Suvorov for his actions in Italy in 1799 and was named to command a column in Kutuzov's Army of Podolia in 1805. Like Langeron, Miloradovich served in the Turkish War (1806–12), distinguishing himself and earning promotion to general of infantry in 1809. After leaving the Army of Moldavia, he served as Military Governor of Kiev before fighting against France in 1812–14.

Zakharii Dmitrievich Olsufiev-3 (1773–1835) was enrolled at the age of three in the Ismailovsky Guard Regiment, reaching the rank of lieutenant in 1788 and general-major in 1798. Olsufiev retired from the service for two years, presumably due to political conflicts during the reign of Paul, but received the position of *shef* of the Vyborg Musketeer Regiment after the accession of Alexander. He served in this capacity through the 1805 campaign, commanding a brigade in Langeron's 2nd Column at Austerlitz despite his lack of field experience. Olsufiev would serve with somewhat greater distinction in the 1806–7 war with France, first as *shef* of the Vyborg Musketeers and then as commander of the 14th Division at Heilsberg. Promoted to general-lieutenant after Tilsit, Olsufiev commanded a division and later a corps against France in 1812–14.

Ignatii Yakovlevich Prshibyshevsky (1755–?) began service in the Polish Army but entered Russian service after the Second Partition of Poland (1793) as a colonel. His Russian commanders were apparently impressed with his abilities and he was promoted to general-major in 1795. In 1799 he fought against France in the army of Rimsky-Korsakov, distinguishing himself in the Russian defeat at the Second Battle of Zurich. In 1805, he marched with the Army of Volhynia and was selected to replace Wimpfen in command of a column during the march from Olmütz to Austerlitz. Captured at Austerlitz, Prshibyshevsky did not return to Russia until well into 1806, only to face a court martial for his conduct at Austerlitz. Although he was found not guilty of surrendering to the French, he was found guilty of not adhering to the dispositions for the battle—despite Buxhöwden's accusations that his failure had been stubborn adherence to the letter of the dispositions and failure to react to events. He was stripped of his rank and discharged from the army in 1810, later dying in disgrace.

Fedor Petrovich Uvarov (1773–1824) was enrolled as a child in the Cavalier Guard Regiment before being transferred to the line and being named major in the Smolensk Dragoons. He distinguished himself in the suppression of the 1793 Polish insurrection that resulted in the Second Partition of Poland, being promoted to lieutenant-colonel in 1797 and colonel in 1798. He became a favorite of Tsar Paul, who honored him with command of the Life Guard Horse Regiment, and was promoted general-major and general-lieutenant in rapid succession. Following the accession of Alexander, Uvarov served as a general-adjutant and during the advance to Austerlitz was given command of a cavalry brigade in Liechtenstein's 5th Column. In spring 1807 he again served against France and served with the Army of Moldavia in 1810. Uvarov fought against France once more in 1812–14.

Prince Petr Mikhailovich Volkonsky (1776–1852) began service as an ensign in the Semenovsky Guard Regiment, reaching the rank of 2nd captain and becoming an aide-de camp to Tsarevich Alexander in 1797. On his accession to the throne, Alexander named Volkonsky a general-adjutant. A capable administrator, Volkonsky also served as assistant to the chief of the central army administration. In 1805, Volkonsky accompanied Buxhöwden's Army of Volhynia as "service general" and then passed into Kutuzov's service after the two armies united. His exceptional conduct at Austerlitz earned him the Order of St George 3rd Class. After Tilsit, Volkonsky was sent to France to study French Army organization and staff structure and was named Quartermaster-General of the Russian Army in 1810 and was instrumental in reforming the Russian general staff. Volkonsky remained close to the Emperor during 1812 and served as the chief of staff of the Russian Army in 1813–14.

Franz von Weyrother (1755–1806) entered the Austrian Army as a cadet at the technical academy in Vienna. He served against the Turks during the Turkish War of 1788–90, earning promotion for his courage. In 1794–5 he served on the staff of the Governor of Mainz (Mayence) and led several actions, earning promotion to major. In the spring of 1796 he served under Archduke Charles in Germany and then in the autumn of that year transferred to Italy on the staff of Feldzeugmeister Alvinczy, again earning promotion despite drafting the plan for the Austrian defeat at Bassano. In 1799, Weyrother served as chief of staff to Feldzeugmeister Kray in the opening phases of the campaign and with the departure of Suvorov's chief of staff, Chasteler, he joined Suvorov's staff. Weyrother was promoted to Generalmajor in 1805 and was selected as chief of staff to the combined armies assembled at Austerlitz. Although apparently a capable staff officer, Weyrother never seems to have shown any particular genius and his plans for Austerlitz fared little better than his plans for Bassano. The magnitude of the defeat and the blame placed on him personally weighed heavily on him and he died only a few months after the battle.

Ferdinand Fedorovich Baron Winzingerode (1770–1818) began his military career with the Hessian Army and passed into Austrian service in 1790, serving in the Netherlands during the wars of the revolution. Briefly returning to Hesse in 1797, Winzingerode entered Russian service as a major of cuirassiers and almost immediately was promoted to lieutenant-colonel in the Ismailovsky Guard Regiment. He served as aide-de-camp to Constantine in the 1799 campaign in Italy and was promoted to general aide-de-camp in 1802. Assigned to Kutuzov's Army of Podolia, Winzingerode undertook some diplomatic missions including the bogus armistice negotiations prior to Schöngrabern. Winzingerode joined the Austrians in 1809 before returning to Russian service in 1812–14.

Petr Kristianovich Wittgenstein (1768–1842) was the Russian descendent of a German who had entered the Russian service under the Empress Elizabeth. Enrolled in the Semenovsky Guard Regiment, he advanced quickly, reaching the rank of 1st major in 1793. He served as a volunteer in the Polish War (1795) and participated in the infamous storming of Praga. After Poland, Wittgenstein served in the Caucasus where he distinguished himself and was promoted to colonel of a hussar regiment in 1798. In 1799 he was promoted to general-major and named *shef* of the Mariupol Hussars only to leave the service briefly in January 1801 (probably due to political difficulties with Paul). After the accession of Alexander, Wittgenstein was almost immediately appointed as *shef* of the Elisabetgrad Hussars before being reinstated as *shef* of the Mariupol Hussars three months later in January 1802. He served with Kutuzov's Army of Podolia throughout the 1805 campaign and commanded the cavalry of Bagration's Advance Guard during the allied offensive. In 1806–7, Wittgenstein served in the Army of Moldavia against the Turks, earning promotion to general-lieutenant. In 1812, Wittgenstein commanded the Russian 1st Corps, successfully holding the Russian right flank against Oudinot and St Cyr and earning the rank of general of cavalry. After the death of Kutuzov in 1813, Wittgenstein was named commander of the combined Russian and Prussian armies opposing France and served in that capacity until the 1813 armistice. With the resumption of hostilities until the end of the war in 1814, Wittgenstein commanded an allied corps.

Appendix C

Order of Battle of the French Army at Austerlitz

The following order of battle has been compiled from a variety of sources, most notably the returns included in *Relations et Rapports*, Bowden's *Napoleon and Austerlitz*, Alombert & Colin, and unpublished orders of battle prepared by George Nafziger (citing Alombert & Colin and *Histoire des Campagnes de l'Empereur Napoleon en 1805–1806 et 1807–1809*, Vol. 1, Paris, 1845). In addition, I have adjusted the details to reflect various detachments and last-minute reassignments noted in the primary materials and regimental histories. Nafziger's figures mostly agree with Bowden's, suggesting a common source. Where the figures in the various sources have conflicted, I have used what I consider to be the most probable figures based on comparison of the documents, reported total (approximate) strengths for divisions, and information contained in reports and memoirs where available. All figures noted below should be considered approximations only, and most likely represent an upper limit for the actual strengths of units due to illness, straggling and detachments of parties for various purposes. The organization shown reflects the actual organization of forces and command structure in place on the morning of 2 December 1805, including the disposition of detachments as noted.

Commander-in-Chief	**Napoleon I, Emperor of the French**
Aides-de-Camp	*GdD Caffarelli* (assigned), *GdD Jean Andoche Junot,*
	GdD Anne Jean Marie René Savary, GdB Antoine Joseph Bertrand,
	GdB Charles Mathieu Gardane, GdB Jean Léonor François
	Lemarois, GdB Georges Mouton, GdB Jean Rapp
Chief of Staff	*Maréchal Louis Alexandre Berthier*
Maréchal des Logis	*GdD Mathieu Dumas*
Directeur du Service Topographie	*GdB Nicolas Antoine Sanson*
Inspector of Artillery	*GdD Nicolas Marie Songis des Courbons*
Inspector of Engineers	*GdD Armand Samuel Maréscot*

	Btn/Sqn/Guns	Men	Remarks
Escort Squadron – detachment	0.5	61	

1st Corps	**Maréchal Jean Baptiste Jules Bernadotte**		**11,281**
1st Division	*GdD Olivier Macoux Rivaud de la Raffinière*		5,266
1st Brigade	*GdB Charles Dumoulin*		
8th Line		3	1,858
Colonel Jean François Etienne Autie			
45th Line		3	1,603
Colonel Jean Leonard Barrie			

	Btn/Sqn/Guns	Men	Remarks

2nd Brigade   *GdB Michel Marie Pacthod*

54th Line	3	1,614	
Colonel Armand Philippon			

Artillery

1st Company, 8th Foot Artillery	6	} 191	Bowden notes only 5 guns
2nd Company, 3rd Horse Artillery	6		Bowden notes only 5 guns

2nd Division   *GdD Jean Baptiste Drouet*   **6,015**

1st Brigade   *GdB François Jean Werle*

27th Light	3	2,069	
Colonel Jean Baptiste Charnotet			

2nd Brigade   *GdB Bernard Georges François Frère*

94th Line	3	1,814	
Colonel Jean Nicolas Razout			
95th Line	3	1,903	
Colonel Marc Nicolas Louis Pechaux			

Artillery

2nd Company, 8th Foot Artillery	6	} 229	
3rd Company, 3rd Horse Artillery	6		

3rd Corps   ***Maréchal Louis Nicolas Davout***   **5,656**

2nd Division   *GdD Louis Friant*   **3,773**
Based on estimated total strength of 3,800

Advance Gd Brigade   *GdB Etienne Heudelet de Bierre*

108th Line	2	818	
Colonel Joseph Higonet			
15th Light		63	2 companies

1st Brigade   *GdB Georges Kister*

15th Light	2	317	10 companies (excluding detachment to
Major Jean Michel Geither			Advance Guard and 5th Gren. Regt)
33rd Line	2	607	
Colonel Jean Saint-Raymond			

2nd Brigade   *GdB Pierre Charles Lochet*

48th Line	2	633	
Colonel Joseph Barbanegre			
111th Line	2	720	
Colonel Jacques François Gay			

Artillery

2nd Company, 7th Foot Artillery	6	} 286	
1st Company, 5th Horse Artillery	3		

Cavalry

1st Dragoons	3	329	Detached from 1st Dragoon Division
Colonel Jean Thomas Arrighi de Casanova			

Appendix C

	Btn/Sqn/Guns	Men	Remarks

4th Dragoon Div   *GdD François Antoine Louis Bourcier*   1,883

1st Brigade   *GdB Jean Baptiste Antoine Laplanche*

15th Dragoons	3	338
Colonel Nicolas Martin Barthélémy		
17th Dragoons	3	364
Colonel Joseph Nicolas de St Dizier		
27th Dragoons	3	347
Colonel Denis Teyrere		

2nd Brigade   *GdB Louis Michel Sahuc*

18th Dragoons	3	334
Colonel Charles Lefebvre-Desnouettes		
19th Dragoons	3	412
Colonel Auguste Jean Gabriel Caulaincourt		

Artillery

3rd Company, 2nd Horse Artillery	3	88

4th Corps   **Maréchal Nicolas Jean de Dieu Soult**   **25,904**

1st Division   *GdD Louis Vincent Joseph Saint-Hilaire*   8,568

1st Brigade   *GdB Charles Antoine Louis Alexis Morand*

10th Light	2	1,488	
Colonel Pierre Charles Pouzet			

2nd Brigade   *GdB Paul Charles François Adrien Henri Dieudonné, Baron Thiébault*

14th Line	2	2,051	Bowden and Nafziger 1,551
Colonel Jacques François Marc Mazas			
36th Line	2	1,592	Bowden 1,643; Nafziger 1,486
Colonel Antoine Charles Houdard de Lamotte			

3rd Brigade   *GdB Louis Prix Varé*

43rd Line	2	1,593	
Colonel Guillaume Raymond Amant Viviès			
55th Line	2	1,614	Bowden 1,658; Nafziger 1,709
Colonel François Roch Ledru des Essarts			

Artillery

12th Company, 5th Foot Artillery	8	230	Including Train

2nd Division   *GdD Dominique Joseph René Vandamme*   8,346

1st Brigade   *GdB Joseph François Ignace Maximilien Schiner*

24th Light	2	1,310	Bowden and Nafziger 1,291
Colonel Bernard Pourailly			

2nd Brigade   *GdB Claude François Ferey*

46th Line	2	1,559	Bowden and Nafziger 1,350
Colonel Guillaume Latrille de Lorencez			
57th Line	2	1,771	Bowden and Nafziger 1,743
Colonel Jean Pierre Antoine Rey			

3rd Brigade   *GdB Jacques Lazare de Savetier de Candras*

4th Line	2	1,822	Bowden and Nafziger 1,658
Major Auguste Julien Bigarré			
28th Line	2	1,636	Bowden and Nafziger 1,599
Colonel Jean Georges Edighoffen			

	Btn/Sqn/Guns	Men	Remarks
Artillery			
13th Company 5th Foot Artillery	8	248	Including Train

3rd Division   *GdD Claude Juste Alexandre Legrand* 7,949

	Btn/Sqn/Guns	Men	Remarks
1st Brigade *GdB Pierre Hugues Victoire Merle*			
26th Light	2	1,587	Bowden and Nafziger 1,564
Colonel François René Pouget			
2nd Brigade *GdB Victor Levasseur*			
18th Line	2	1,507	Bowden and Nafziger 1,402
Colonel Jean Baptiste Ambroise Ravier			
75th Line	2	1,532	Bowden and Nafziger 1,688
Colonel François L'Huillier			
Tirailleurs Corse	1	635	Bowden and Nafziger 519
Colonel Philippe Antoine Ornano			
3rd Brigade *GdB Jean Baptiste Michel Féry*			
Tirailleurs du Po	1	587	Bowden 340 (excl. det. of 100 at Tellnitz)
Colonel Etienne Hulot			
3rd Line	3	1,888	At Tellnitz. Bowden 1,644
Colonel Laurent Schobert			
Artillery			
14th Company, 5th Foot Artillery	8	213	Including Train
Corps Light Cav Bde *GdB Pierre Margaron*			
11th Chasseurs	3	317	
Colonel Bertrand Bessières			
26th Chasseurs	3	331	
Colonel Alexandre Elisabeth Michel Digeon			
4th Coy, 5th Horse Artillery	5	143	Including Train
Corps Artillery			
17th and 18th Coys, 5th Foot Artillery	6	250	6 x 12-pdr
CdB Fontenoy			
Detachment			From 4th Corps Cavalry Brigade – Margaron
8th Hussars	3	276	Left at Auspitz, arrived P.M. 2 Dec. Not inc.
Colonel Jean Baptiste Francheschi-Delosne			in 4th Corps total, but inc. in army strength

5th Corps   *Maréchal Jean Lannes* 13,227

3rd Division   *GdD Louis Gabriel Suchet* 6,857

	Btn/Sqn/Guns	Men	Remarks
1st Brigade *GdB Michel Marie Claparède*			
17th Light	2	1,373	
Colonel Dominique Honoré Antoine Marie Vedel			
2nd Brigade *GdB Nicolas Léonard Bagert Beker*			
34th Line	2	1,615	
Colonel Jean Antoine Dejean			
40th Line	2	1,149	
Colonel François Marc Guillaume Legendre d'Harvesse			
3rd Brigade *GdB Jean Marie Mellon Roger Valhubert*			
64th Line	2	1,052	
Colonel Claude Nerin			
88th Line	2	1,428	
Colonel Philibert Jean Baptiste François Curial			

	Btn/Sqn/Guns	Men	Remarks

Artillery
15th Company, 5th Foot Artillery — 8 — — Colin notes 20 guns with this division
16th Company, 5th Foot Artillery — 2 — }191
5th Company, 1st Foot Artillery — 4 —

1st Division *GdD Louis Marie Joseph Maximilien de Caffarelli du Falga* 6,370
Detached from 3rd Corps

1st Brigade *GdB Joseph Laurent Demont*
17th Line — 2 — 1,561
  Colonel Nicolas François Conroux
30th Line — 2 — 1,011
  Colonel François Valterre

2nd Brigade *GdB Jean Louis De Billy*
51st Line — 2 — 1,214
  Colonel Joseph Alphonse Hyacinthe Alexandre Bonnet d'Honnières
61st Line — 2 — 1,175
  Colonel Jean Nicolas

3rd Brigade *GdB Georges Henri Eppler*
13th Light — 2 — 1,240
  Colonel Pierre Castex

Artillery
1st Company, 7th Foot Artillery — 6 — 169 — Colin notes 12 guns with this division

Cavalry Reserve *Maréchal Joachim Murat*   **7,543**
1st Heavy Cav Div *GdD Etienne Marie Antoine Champion, Comte de Nansouty* 1,479

1st Brigade *GdB Joseph Piston*
1st Carabiniers — 3 — 195
  Colonel Antoine Cristophe Cochois
2nd Carabiniers — 3 — 182
  Colonel Pierre Nicolas Morin

2nd Brigade *GdB Armand Lebrun Comte de La Houssaye*
2nd Cuirassiers — 3 — 249
  Colonel Jean Frédéric Yvendorf
9th Cuirassiers — 3 — 250
  Colonel Jean Pierre Doumerc

3rd Brigade *GdB Antoine Louis Decrest, Comte de Saint-Germain*
3rd Cuirassiers — 3 — 279
  Colonel Claude Antoine Preval
12th Cuirassiers — 3 — 232
  Colonel Jacques Roland Belfort

Artillery
4th Company, 2nd Horse Artillery — 3 — 92

2nd Heavy Cav Div *GdD Jean Joseph Ange d'Hautpoul*   1,128

1st Brigade *Adjutant-Commandant François Xavier Octavie Fontaine*
1st Cuirassiers — 3 — 298
  Colonel Marie Adrian François Guiton
5th Cuirassiers — 3 — 270
  Colonel Jean Baptiste Noirot

	Btn/Sqn/Guns	Men	Remarks

2nd Brigade *GdB Raymond Gaspard de Bonardi, Comte de Saint-Sulpice*

10th Cuirassiers   3   224
Colonel Pierre François Lataye
11th Cuirassiers   3   251
Colonel Albert Louis Emmanuel Fouler

Artillery
4th Company, 2nd Horse Artillery   3   85

2nd Dragoon Div   *GdD Frédéric Henri Walther*   **1,217**

1st Brigade   *GdB Horace François Bastien Sebastiani de la Porta*
3rd Dragoons   3   177
Colonel Edme Nicolas Fiteau
6th Dragoons   3   150
Colonel Jacques Lebaron

2nd Brigade   *GdB Mansuy Dominique Roget, Baron de Bellonguet*
10th Dragoons   3   207
Colonel Jacques Marie Cavaignac
11th Dragoons   3   196
Colonel Ferdinand Pierre Agathé Bourdon

3rd Brigade   *GdB André Joseph Boussart*
13th Dragoons   3   269
Colonel Armand Louis Broc
22nd Dragoons   3   134
Colonel Jean Auguste Carrié

Artillery
2nd Company, 2nd Horse Artillery   3   84

3rd Dragoon Div   *GdB Charles Joseph Boyé*   **1,723**
GdD Beaumont was ill and Boyé commanded on 2 Dec.

1st Brigade   *GdB Charles Joseph Boyé*
5th Dragoons   3   234
Colonel Jacques Nicolas Lacour
8th Dragoons   3   289
Colonel Louis Beckler
12th Dragoons   3   297
Colonel Joseph Pagès

2nd Brigade   *GdB Nicolas Joseph Scalfort*
9th Dragoons   3   291
Colonel Pierre Honoré Anne Maupetit
16th Dragoons   3   242
Colonel François Marie Clément
21st Dragoons   3   285
Colonel Jean Baptiste Charles Rene Joseph Mas de Polart

Artillery
3rd Company, 2nd Horse Artillery   3   85

	Btn/Sqn/Guns	Men	Remarks

Light Cavalry Div   *GdD François Etienne Kellermann*   1,267
Detached from 1st Corps

    1st Brigade   *GdB Joseph Denis Picard*   Bowden adds 3 guns from 1st Company,

2nd Hussars	3	328	3rd Horse Artillery

      Colonel Ignace Wilhelm Rith

5th Hussars	3	342	

      Colonel François Xavier Nicolas Schwartz

    2nd Brigade   *GdB Frédéric Christophe Henri Pierre Claude Marizy*

4th Hussars	3	280	

      Colonel André Burthe

5th Chasseurs	3	317	

      Colonel Claude Louis Constant Esprit Juvenal Corbineau

Light Cavalry Bde   *GdB Edouard Jean Baptiste Milhaud*   423

16th Chasseurs	3	205	Bowden 338

      Colonel Antoine Jean Auguste Henri Durosnel

22nd Chasseurs	3	218	Bowden 272

      Colonel Marie Victor Nicolas de Fay, Marquis de Latour-Maubourg

Light Cavalry Bde   *GdB Anne François Charles Trelliard*   306
Detached from 5th Corps

9th Hussars	3	145	Bowden 233

      Colonel Etienne Guyot

10th Hussars	3	161	Bowden 261

      Colonel Louis Chrétian Carrière Beaumont

Reserve   ***Emperor Napoléon I***   **10,668**

Imperial Guard   ***Maréchal Jean Baptiste Bessières***   **5,674**

Infantry of the Imperial Guard

    1st Brigade   *GdB Pierre Auguste Hulin*   Hulin was absent, commanding in Vienna

Grenadiers à Pied	2	1,519	

      Colonel-Major Jean Marie Pierre François Lepaige Dorsenne

    2nd Brigade   *GdB Jerome Soulès*

Chasseurs à Pied	2	1,613	

      Major Jean Louis Gros

    3rd Brigade   *GdB Teodoro Lecchi*   Italian Guard

Grenadiers à Pied	1	}753	
Chasseurs à Pied	1		

Cavalry of the Imperial Guard

    Gendarmerie d'Elite   Detached to Brünn

    1st Brigade   *GdB Michel Ordener*

Grenadiers à Cheval	4	706	

      Colonel-Major Louis Lepic

    2nd Brigade   *Colonel-en-Second François Louis de Morland*

Chasseurs à Cheval	4	375	

      Colonel-en-Second Nicolas Dahlmann

Mamelukes	0.5	48	

      Chef d'Escadron Antoine Charles Bernard Delaitre

	Btn/Sqn/Guns	Men	Remarks

Artillery
  1st Company Horse Artillery   8 ⎫
  2nd Company Horse Artillery   8 ⎬540
  Horse Arty of the Royal Italian Guard 8 ⎭
  Bataillon de Marins   1   120
    Commander François-Henri-Eugene Daugier

1st Division   *GdD Nicolas Charles Oudinot*
                         GdD Géraud Christophe Michel Duroc   **4,994**
Detached from 5th Corps, shared command

  1st Brigade   *GdB Claude Joseph de Laplanche-Morthières*
    1st Grenadier Regiment   2   762   13th & 58th Line
      Colonel Jacques Froment
    2nd Grenadier Regiment   2   1,025 9th & 81st Line
      Major Michel Sylvestre Brayer

  2nd Brigade   *GdB Pierre Louis Dupas*
    3rd Grenadier Regiment   2   941   2nd & 3rd Light
      Colonel Jean Adam Schramm
    4th Grenadier Regiment   2   857   28th & 31st Light
      Major Marc Cabannes de Puymisson

  3rd Brigade   *GdB François Amable Ruffin*
    5th Grenadier Regiment   2   1,070 12th & 15th Light
      Colonel Jean Charles Desailly

  Artillery
    1st Company, 1st Foot Artillery   6 ⎫
    4th Company, 5th Horse Artillery   2 ⎬339
  Grand Artillery Park   18   400

Total Army Strength (estimated)   **74,955**

Outlying commands

  Cavalry Brigade   *GdB Jean Louis François Fauconnet*
  Detached from 5th Corps north toward Zwittau, remained on far left
    13th Chasseurs   259
      Colonel Nicolas Pultière
    21st Chasseurs   256
      Colonel Jean Baptiste Berruyer

  Detachment
  Left on line of communications at Raigern
    25th Dragoons   3   479   Bowden 359 (detached from Bourcier)
      Colonel Antoine Rigau

  Detachment
  Left on Line of Communications at Brünn
    Légion de Gendarmerie d'Elite   2   180
      Colonel-Major Jean Baptiste Jacquin

	Btn/Sqn/Guns	Men	Remarks

En Route to Austerlitz (involved in subsequent pursuit)

3rd Division   *GdD Charles Etienne Gudin de la Sablonnière*   6,618
From 3rd Corps – reached Raigern by evening of 2 Dec.

1st Brigade   *GdB Claude Petit*

12th Line	2	1,301	
Colonel François Vergez			
21st Line	2	1,709	
Colonel François Bertrand Dufour			

2nd Brigade   *GdB Nicolas Hyacinthe Gautier*

25th Line	2	1,567	
Colonel Louis Victorin Cassagne			
85th Line	2	1,579	
Colonel Sebastien Viala			

Cavalry

12th Chasseurs	3	275	
Colonel Claude Raymond Guyon			

Artillery

3rd Company 7th Foot Artillery	6	187	Including train

Light Cavalry Bde   *GdB Jean Baptiste Théodore Viallanes*   895
3rd Corps Light cavalry brigade. Reached Raigern by evening of 2 December

1st Chasseurs	3	334	
Colonel Louis Pierre Montbrun			
2nd Chasseurs	3	186	
Colonel Ignace François Bousson			
7th Hussars	3	375	
Colonel Daniel Marx			

1st Dragoon Div   *GdD Dominique Louis Antoine Klein*   941
Reached Raigern by evening of 2 December

1st Brigade   *GdB Fenerols*

1st Dragoons			Detached to Friant's Division (3rd Corps)
2nd Dragoons	3	231	
Colonel Ythier Sylvain Privé			

2nd Brigade   *GdB Antoine Charles Louis Lasalle*

14th Dragoons	3	270	
Colonel Guillaume Joseph Nicolas Lafond Blaniac			
26th Dragoons	3	355	
Colonel Pierre Delorme			
Artillery	3	85	

Appendix D

Order of Battle of the Allied Army at Austerlitz

The following Order of Battle was compiled from a variety of sources, including the original dispositions in *Kutuzov Sbornik Dokumentov* and *Dokumenty Shtaba Kutuzova*, Mikhailovsky-Danilevsky, Langeron, and Schönhals. Strengths shown are approximate and are based on available data as described in Appendix A. The overall strengths should be regarded as an upper limit for Allied army strength.

Abbreviations:

GoI = General of Infantry
GKAV = General of Cavalry
FZM = Feldzeugmeister
GL = General-Lieutenant
G-Adj = General-Adjutant
FML = Feldmarschalleutnant
GM = General-Major
PK = Polkovnik (Colonel)
PPK = Podpolkovnik (Lieutenant-Colonel)
Kdr = Komandir (Commander)

d. p. = Dragoon Polk (Polk = Regiment)
eger p. = Jäger Polk
gr. p. = Grenadier Polk
gu. p. = Gusar Polk (Hussar Regiment)
k. p. = Cossack Polk
m. p. = Musketeer Polk
u. p. = Uhlan Polk (Lancer Regiment)

DR = Dragoner Regiment
GR = Grenz Regiment
HR = Husaren Regiment
IR = Infanterie Regiment
KR = Kürassier Regiment
UR = Uhlanen Regiment

Supreme Commander	*Aleksandr I, Emperor of Russia*		
Chief of Staff	*GM Franz von Weyrother*		
Quartermaster General	*GL Petr Kornilovich Sukhtelin*		
Inspector of Artillery	*GL Aleksei Andreevich Arakcheev*		
Adjutants	*GM P. Dolgoruky (assigned), GM Prince Grigori Ivanovich Gagarin, GM Kristofer Andreevich Lieven, GM F. Uvarov (assigned), GM Prince Dmitri Mikhailovich Volkonsky, GM Ferdinand Fedorovich Winzingerode*		

	Btn/Sqn/Guns	Men	Remarks
Escort			
Pavlograd gu. p.	0.5	40	Operated with 4th Column during the battle

Commander-in-Chief	*GOI Mikhail Ilarionovich Kutuzov*
General of the Day	*GM Ivan Nikitich Inzov*
Quartermaster-General	*GM Login Ivanovich Gerard*
Commander of Russian Artillery	*GL Petr Ivanovich Müller-Zakomelsky*
Commander of the Russian Horse Artillery	*GM Nikolai Ivanovich Bogdanov*
Commander of Russian Volunteer Artillery	*GM Andrei Andreevich Arakcheev*
Chief Engineer	*General Glukov*

Appendix D

	Btn/Sqn/Guns	Men	Remarks

Commander, Austrian Army   *FML Prince Johann Liechtenstein*

Observer   *Franz I, Emperor of Austria*

GL Prince Karl Schwarzenberg

Quartermaster-General   *GM Bubna*

Adjutant   *GL Lamberti*

Escort

Kaiser KR 1	2	140	Did not play any part in the battle

Left Wing   *GL Fedor Fedorovich Buxhöwden (Buksgevden)*

Commanding First Three Columns

Advance Guard (Left)   *FML Michael Baron von Kienmayer*   **4,665**

	Btn/Sqn/Guns	Men	Remarks
Cavalry Brigade *GM Johann Nepomuk Nostitz*			
Hessen-Homburg HR 4	6	225	
Oberst Johann Freiherr von Mohr			
Schwarzenberg UR 2	0.5	100	From the regimental depot
Merveldt UR 1	0.25	40	From the regimental depot
Cavalry Brigade *GM Moritz Fürst Liechtenstein*			
Székler HR 11	5	500	
Oberst Gabriel Geringer von Oedenburg			
Cavalry Brigade *GM Karl Freiherr von Stutterheim*			
O'Reilly Chevauxlegers-Regiment 3	8	900	
Oberst Friedrich Graf Degenfeld-Schonburg			
Supporting Artillery			
Horse Artillery Battery (Austrian)	4	125	
Oberst Degenfeldt			
Infantry Brigade *GM Carneville*			
2 Székler GR 15	2	1,100	
Oberst Johann Chevalier Grammont			
1 Székler GR 14	2	1,000	
Oberst Georg Ritter von Knesevich			Died from wounds 10 Jan 06
Broder GR 7	1	500	
Oberstleutnant Desullenovich			
Supporting Artillery	8 btn guns		
Detachment *Oberstleutnant Rakovsky*			Never rejoined column, covered retreat of
Hessen-Homburg HR 4	2	75	4th Column
Oberstleutnant Rakovsky			
Székler HR 11	1	100	

	Btn/Sqn/Guns	Men	Remarks

1st Column — *GL Dmitrii Sergeevich Dokhturov* — **11,745**

Advance Guard — *GM Ivan Ivanovich Miller-3*

7th eger p. — 1 — 413 — 3rd Battalion. Detached from 3rd Col 29 Nov
Shef *GM Ivan Ivanovich Miller-3** — Commanding brigade in 3rd Column
Kmdr *PK Pavel Petrovich Tolbukhin*

5th eger p. — 1 — 396 — 3rd Battalion. 1st and 2nd Btns det. to
Shef *PK Fedor Grigor'evich Gogel** — Bagration's Advance Gd 29 Nov. Gogel
Kmdr *Maior Fedor Ivanovich Pantenius* — commanding main body of regt, Advance Gd

Pioneer Company Kudzevich — 0.25 — 160

Brigade — *GM Fedor Fedorovich Leviz*

Novoingermanland m. p. — 3 — 1,787
Shef & Kmdr *GL Ivan Karlovich Baron Rozen**

Yaroslav m. p. — 3 — 1,337
Shef *GM Fedor Fedorovich Leviz (Löwis) of Menar** — Commanding brigade
Kmdr *PPK Osip Karlovich Sokolovsky*

Supporting Artillery — 12 btn guns

Brigade — *GM Nikolai Ivanovich Liders*

Vladimir m. p. — 3 — 1,543
Shef *GM Sergei Kornilovich Shevlyakov*
Kmdr *PPK Timofei Ivanovich Zbievsky*

Bryansk m. p. — 3 — 1,311
Shef *GM Nikolai Ivanovich Liders** — Commanding brigade
Kmdr *PPK Nikolai Kirillovich Rubanov-1*

Supporting Artillery — 12 btn guns

Brigade — *GM Nikolai Iur'evich prince Urusov-1*

Vyatka m. p. — 3 — 1,289
Shef *GM Nikolai Iur'evich prince Urusov-1** — Commanding brigade
Kmdr *PK Bibikov*

Moscow m. p. — 3 — 1,637
Shef *GL Dmitrii Sergeevich Dokhturov** — Commanding 1st Column
Kmdr *PK Nikolai Semenovich Sulima*

Kiev gr. p. — 3 — 1,172
Shef *GL Karl Fridrik prince Saksen-Veimarsky** — Honorary*
Kmdr *GM Ivan Nikitich Inzov** — General of the Day

Supporting Artillery — 16 btn guns

Supporting Cavalry
Don k. p. Denisov — 2 — 200

Heavy Artillery — *PK Count Yakov Karlovich Sivers*

3rd Artillery Regiment Position Battery — 12 — 250
PK Count Sivers

3rd Artillery Regiment Position Battery — 12 — 250
Maior Sigizmund

	Btn/Sqn/Guns	Men	Remarks

2nd Column **GL Alexander Andrault de Langeron**   **10,959**

Advance Guard *PK Vasily Danilovich Laptev*

	Btn/Sqn/Guns	Men	Remarks
8th eger p.	2	572	1st and 2nd Battalions. 3rd Battalion
Kmdr *PK Vasily Danilovich Laptev*			detached to 3rd Column 9:00 A.M. 2 Dec
Pioneer Company Berg	0.25	160	Russian

Main Body *GM Zakhar Dmitrievich Olsuf'ev-3*

	Btn/Sqn/Guns	Men	Remarks
Vyborg m. p.	3	2,052	
Shef *GM Zakhar Dmitrievich Olsuf'ev-3* *			Commanding brigade
Kmdr *PPK Egor Maksimovich Pillar*			
Perm m. p.	3	2,047	
Shef *GL Georg Fridrik Baron Wimpfen* *			Commanding brigade in 3rd Column
Kmdr *PK Andrei Andreevich Kuznetsov*			
Kursk m. p.	3	2,032	
Shef *GL Ignatii Yakovlevich Prshibyshevsky* *			Commanding 3rd Column
Kmdr *PK Aleksei Matveevich Seleverstov*			
Supporting Artillery	18 btn guns		

Reserve *GM Sergei Mikhailovich Kamensky-1*

	Btn/Sqn/Guns	Men	Remarks
Ryazhsk m. p.	3	2,054	
Shef *GL Aleksei Fedorovich Lanzheron* *			Or "Langeron." Commanding 2nd Column
Kmdr *PPK Bogdanov*			
Fanagoria m. p.	3	2,042	
Shef *GM Sergei Mikhailovich Kamensky-1* *			Commanding brigade
Kmdr *none*			
Supporting Artillery	12 btn guns		

Supporting Cavalry *PPK Mikhail Dmitriyevich Balk*
Attached from 5th Column, A.M. 2 Dec.

	Btn/Sqn/Guns	Men	Remarks
St Petersburg d. p.,	2		4th and 5th Squadrons. Included in 5th
Kmdr *PPK Balk*			Column totals
k. p. Isayev	1		Included in 5th Column totals

3rd Column **GL Ignatii Yakovlevich Prshibyshevsky**   **8,527**

Advance Guard *GM Ivan Ivanovich Miller-3*

	Btn/Sqn/Guns	Men	Remarks
7th eger p.	2	823	1st and 2nd Battalions. 3rd Battalion
Shef *GM Ivan Ivanovich Miller-3* *			detached to 1st Column 29 Nov
Kmdr *PK Pavel Petrovich Tolbukhin* *			Commanding detachment with 1st Column
8th eger p.	1	286	3rd Btn. Det. from 2nd Column, A.M. 2 Dec
Kmdr *PK Vasily Danilovich Laptev* *			Commanding main body of regt, 2nd Column
Pioneer Company Virubov	0.25	160	

	Btn/Sqn/Guns	Men	Remarks
Main Body	*GM Fedor Borisovich Strik*		
Galitz m. p.	3	1,487	
Shef *GM Ivan Antonovich Loshakov*			
Kmdr *PK Yakovlev Andreevich Voeikov*			
Butyrsk m. p.	3	2,055	
Shef *GM Fedor Borisovich Strik**			Commanding brigade
Kmdr *PPK Mikhail L'vovich Treskin*			
Narva m. p.	3	1,921	
Shef *GL Iosip Vasilievich Rotgof*			May not have been present
Kmdr *none*			
Supporting Artillery		18 btn guns	
Reserve	*GL Georg Fridrik Baron Wimpfen*		
Podolsk m. p.	3	799	
Shef *GM Mikhail Ivanovich Levitzkii*			
Kmdr *PPK Nechaev-2*			
Azov m. p.	3	996	
Shef *GM Aleksei Abramovich Selekhov*			
Kmdr *PPK Otto Vladimirovich Shtakel'berg*			
Supporting Artillery		12 btn guns	

	Btn/Sqn/Guns	Men	Remarks
Center	***General of Infantry Mikhail Ilarionovich Kutuzov***		
4th Column	***GL Miloradovich and FZM Kollowrath***		**13,035**
Advance Guard	*GM Wodniansky*		
Erzherzog Johann DR 1	2	125	
Oberst Ludwig Ritter von Hentzy			
Novgorod m. p.	2	825	2nd and 3rd Battalions
Kmdr *PPK Fedor Fedorovich Monakhtin*			
Apsheron m. p.	1	402	1st (Grenadier Battalion)
Kapitan Morozov			
Pioneer Company Dreier (Austrian)	0.25	160	
Division	*GL Mikhail Andreevich Miloradovich*		**4,311**
	Miloradovich promoted to GL 08 Nov 1805		
Brigade	*GM Sergei Yakovich Repninsky*		
Novgorod m. p.	1	412	1st (Grenadier) Battalion
Shef *GM Sergei Yakovlevich Repninsky**			Commanding brigade
Kmdr *PPK Fedor Fedorovich Monakhtin**			With 2nd and 3rd Btns, Adv. Gd. 4th Column
Apsheron m. p.	2	805	2nd and 3rd Battalions
Shef *GM Mikhail Andreevich Miloradovich**			Commanding division
Kmdr *PPK Aleksei Vasilievich Knyaz Sibirsky-1*			
Brigade	*GM Grigorii Maksimovich Berg*		
Malorossiisky gr. p.	3	1,446	"Little Russia" Regiment in main text
Shef *Gol Karl Ludwig Friedrich von Baden**			Honorary position
Kmdr *GM Grigorii Maksimovich Berg**			Commanding brigade
Smolensk m. p.	3	1,398	
Shef *GM Petr Mikhailovich Koliubakin*			
Kmdr *PK Leontii Kristoforovich Baron fon der Osten-Saken*			
Artillery			
3rd Artillery Regiment Position Battery	12	250	
PK Dmitri Ivanovich Kudriatsev			
Supporting Artillery		24 btn guns	

	Btn/Sqn/Guns	Men	Remarks
Division — *FZM Johann Karl Graf Kollowrath-Krakowsky*			7,212
Brigade — *Oberst Ferdinand Freiherr von Sterndahl* (acting brigadier)			
Salzburg IR 23	6	2,800	Part of Rottermund's brigade of march
Oberst Ferdinand Freiherr von Sterndahl			
Brigade *GM Graf Rottermund*			
Kaunitz IR 20	1	300	6th Btn. Part Rottermund's brigade of march
Major von Breslern			
Auersperg IR 24	1	600	6th Btn. Part Rottermund's brigade of march
Oberstleutnant Bach von Ulm			
Kaiser IR 1	1	700	6th Btn. Part Jurczik's brigade of march
Commandant not known			
Czartoryski IR 9	1	600	2nd Btn. Part Jurczik's brigade of march
Hauptmann Graf Orlandini			
Brigade *GM von Jurczik*			
Reuss-Greitz IR 55	1	300	6th Battalion
Oberstleutnant Scovaud			
Württemberg IR 38	1	500	3rd Battalion
Major Lompret			
Beaulieu IR 58	1	500	3rd Battalion
Commandant not known			
Kerpen IR 49	1	312	6th Battalion
Major Mahler			
Lindenau IR 29	1	400	6th Battalion
Commandant not known			
Supporting Artillery	8	200	Position guns
	28 btn guns		
Detachment *Oberstleutnant Rakovsky*			From Kienmayer's Advance Guard
Hessen-Homburg HR 4	2		Included in Advance Guard totals
Székler HR 11	1		Included in Advance Guard totals

Imperial Guard *Grand Duke Constantine*			**10,608**
1st Guard Column *Grand Duke Constantine*			7,163
Preobrazhensky	2	1,491	1st and 3rd Battalions
Shef *Emperor Aleksandr I**			Commanding Allied army
Kmdr *GL Petr Aleksandrovich Count Tolstoi**			Commanding Hanover force
Acting Kmdr *PK Mikhail Timofeovich Kozlovsky*			
Semenovsky	2	1,487	1st and 3rd Battalions
Shef *Emperor Aleksandr I**			Commanding Allied army
Kmdr *GM Leontii Ivanovich Depreradovich-1*			
Ismailovsky	2	1,461	1st and 3rd Battalions
Shef *Grand Duke Nikolai Pavlovich**			Remained in St Petersburg
Kmdr *GL Petr Fedorovich Maliutin**			Commanding 2nd Guard Column
Acting Kmdr *PK Matvei Evgrafovich Khrapovitsky*			
Life Guard Jäger	1	483	
Shef *GL Petr Ivanovich Bagration**			Commanding Advance Guard
Kmdr *PK Count Emmanuil Frantsevich Sen-Pri*			

	Btn/Sqn/Guns	Men	Remarks
Life Guard Horse	5	784	
Shef *Grand Duke Konstantin Pavlovich* *			Commanding Guard Column
Kmdr *GM Ivan Fedorovich Yankovich*			
Life Guard Hussars	5	690	
Shef *GKAV Duke Liudvig Viurtembergsky* *			
Kmdr *GL Andrei Semenovich Kologrivov*			
Life Guard Artillery Battalion			
GM Ivan Fedorovich Kaspersky			
Guard Horse Artillery Company	10	192	
PK Vasily Grigorevich Kostenetsky			
Guard Artillery Btn Position Company	12	280	
PK Fedor Fedorovich Rall			
Guard Artillery Btn Light Company	10	148	4 guns served as battalion guns for
Kapitan Aleksandr Khristoforovich Eiler			Preobrazhensky
Guard Artillery Btn Light Company	10	148	8 guns served as battalion guns for
PK Fedor Ivanovich Resleyna			Semenovsky and Ismailovsky
			Remaining 8 guns of 2 light coys formed
			a combined battery (not used as btn guns)

2nd Guard Column   *GL Petr Fedorovich Maliutin*   3,437

	Btn/Sqn/Guns	Men	Remarks
Leib gr. p.	3	2,134	"Life Grenadiers" in main text
Shef *Imp. Aleksandr I* *			Commanding Allied army
Kmdr *GL Vasily Mikhailovich Lobanov*			
Cavalier Guard	5	766	
Shef *GAd Fedor Petrovich Uvarov* *			Commanding brigade in 5th Column
Kmdr *GM Nikolai Ivanovich Depreradovich-2*			
Life Guard Cossacks	2	295	
Kmdr *PK Petr Abramovich Chernozubov-5*			
Supporting Artillery			
4th Artillery Regt Position Company	6	121	
PK Aleksei Mertens			
Imperial Militia Btn Light Company	6	121	Probably battalion guns for Life Grenadiers

5th Column   *FML Prince Johann Liechtenstein*   8,706

Austrian Cavalry Div *FML Hohenlohe*

		Btn/Sqn/Guns	Men
Brigade	*GM Caramelli*		
Nassau KR 5		8	300
Oberst Friedrich von Minutillo			
Lothringen KR 7		8	300
Oberst Clemens Freiherr von Thünefeld			
Brigade	*GM Weber*		
Kaiser KR 1		6	420
Oberst Wilhelm von Motzen			
Supporting Artillery			
Horse Artillery Battery		8	200
Kapitän Zocchi			

	Btn/Sqn/Guns	Men	Remarks

Russian Cavalry Div *GL Aleksei Alekseivich von Essen-2*   7,486

Brigade   *GM Vasily Fedorovich Shepelev*

	Btn/Sqn/Guns	Men	Remarks
Life-Kirasirskii EE Velichestva p.	5	761	"Empress Cuirassiers" in main text
Shef *GM Dmitri Maksimovich Esipov-1*			
Kmdr *PK Yakovlev Osipovich Count Witt*			
St Petersburg d. p.	2	200	4th and 5th Squadrons detached to
Shef *GL Vasily Fedorovich Shepelev*			2nd Column A.M. 2 Dec
Kmdr *none*			
Constantine u. p.	10	1,386	
Shef *Grand Duke. Konstantin Pavlovich*			Commanding Guard Column
Kmdr *GM Egor Ianovich Baron Müller-Zakomelsky*			
Don k. p. Gordeev	5	500	
Don k. p. Isayev	4	500	1 squadron det. to 2nd Column A.M. 2 Dec

Supporting Artillery

	Btn/Sqn/Guns	Men	Remarks
Light Battery	11	230	
PK Gabriel Alexandrovich Ignatiev			

Brigade   *GM (G-Adj) Fedor Petrovich Uvarov*

	Btn/Sqn/Guns	Men	Remarks
Chernigov d. p.	5	782	
Shef *GL von Essen-2**			Commanding division
Kmdr *PK Ivan Davydovich Panchulidzev-1*			
Kharkov d. p.	5	741	
Shef *GM Varfolomei Kaetonovich Gizhitzkii*			
Kmdr *PK Minitzkii*			
Elisabetgrad gu. p.	10	1,356	
Shef *GM Erofei Kus'mich baron fon der Osten-Saken-3*			
Kmdr *PK Grigorii Ivanovich Lisanevich*			
Don k. p. Denisov	3	300	
Don k. p. Melentev	5	500	May have been with Kienmayer

Supporting Artillery

	Btn/Sqn/Guns	Men	Remarks
1st Horse Artillery Btn Light Battery	12	230	
PK Aleksei Petrovich Ermolov			

Advance Guard   *GL Petr Ivanovich Bagration*   13,687

Left Flank

	Btn/Sqn/Guns	Men	Remarks
6th eger p.	3	922	
Shef *GM Karl Karlovich Ulanius*			
Kmdr *PK Ivan Petrovich Belokopytov*			
Mariupol gu. p.	10	1,234	
Shef *GM Petr Khristianovich Count Vitgenshtein*			Or "Wittgenstein"
Kmdr *PK Aleksei Andreevich Laskin*			
Don k. p. Kiselev	5	500	
Don k. p. Malakhov	5	500	

	Btn/Sqn/Guns	Men	Remarks
Right Flank			
5th eger p.	2	794	1st and 2nd Battalions
Shef *PK Fedor Grigor'evich Gogel*			3rd Battalion detached to 1st Column, 29 Nov
Kmdr *Maior Fedor Ivanovich Pantenius*			With Advance Guard of 1st Column
Pavlograd gu. p.	10	1,409	
Shef *GL Karl Fedorovich Bour Sr.**			Remained in Russia (sick)
Sr. Kmdr *GM Yefim Ignatievich Chaplits*			
Kmdr *PK Semen Davydovich Panchulidzev*			
Don k. p. Khaznekov	5	500	
Don k. p. Sisoyev	5	500	May have been with Kienmayer
Brigade	*GM (G-Adj) Prince Petr Petrovich Dolgoruky-3*		
Staroingermanland m. p.	3	2,023	
Shef *GM Grigorii Grigor'evich Engel'gardt-1*			Or "Engelhardt"
Kmdr *none*			
Pskov m. p.	3	2,050	
Shef *Gol Mikhail Ilarionovich Golenishev-Kutuzov*			Commanding army
Kmdr *GM Evginii Ivanovich Markov-1*			
Arkhangelgorod m. p.	3	1,931	
Shef *GM Nikolai Mikhailovich Kamensky-2*			
Kmdr *PK Mikhail Ivanovich Berlizeev*			
Supporting Artillery	18 btn guns		
Reserve Cavalry			
Tver d. p.	5	794	
Shef *GM Pius Savelovich Voropaisky*			
Kmdr *none*			
St Petersburg d. p.	3	300	1st, 2nd and 3rd Squadrons. Detached from
Shef *GL Vasily Fedorovich Shepelev*			5th Column after Wischau
Kmdr *none*			
Supporting Artillery			
1st Horse Artillery Btn Light Battery	12	230	
PK Yashvil			
Artillery Park			
Erzherzog Johann DR 1	5		
Oberst Ludwig Ritter von Hentzy			
Artillery			
1 Russian Position Company	12		Probably PK Boguslavsky's battery
2 Russian Light Companies	24		
Unspecified Austrian Artillery			Inc. Major Frierenberger's battery (12 guns)

Total Army Strength (estimated, inc sovereigns' escorts)	**81,112**
Russians (does not include artillery park)	**68,590**
Austrians	**13,522**

Notes

1. Regimental officers marked * were not present with their regiments during the battle

2. 3 or 4 Russian position batteries were ordered to join the baggage at Teschen and Troppau – these appear to have been the entire heavy artillery of 5th Artillery Regt. Two companies of Vienna Jäger (approx. 300 men) appear in either Kienmayer's Advance Guard or Kollowrath's division of the 4th Column. All sources agree that this unit did not play a part in the action and Wrede indicates that it did not fire a shot, suggesting it was left behind on the line of communications.

	Btn/Sqn/Guns	Men	Remarks

Olmütz Garrison   6,800

Many of the men in all of the battalions in Olmütz were ill. A large number also remained behind from the battalions that marched with the main army.

Brigade *GM von Augustinetz*			
Hoch und Deutschmeister IR 4	1	600	6th Battalion
Mitrowsky IR 40	1	600	6th Battalion

Brigade *GM Freiherr von Bolza*			
Klebek IR 14	1	600	6th Battalion
Stain IR 50	1	600	6th Battalion

Brigade *GM Graf Mercandin*			
Erzherzog Karl IR 3	1	600	6th Battalion
Erzherzog Ludwig IR 8	1	600	6th Battalion

Brigade *GM Graf Khevenhüller*			
Coburg IR 22	1	600	6th Battalion
Manfredini IR 12	1	600	6th Battalion

Brigade *GM von Bianchi*			
Schroeder IR 7	1	600	6th Battalion
Wenzel Colloredo IR 56	1	600	6th Battalion
Moravian-Silesian Jäger	1	700	
Erzherzog Johann DR 1	1	100	

Detached Corps   *FML Maximilian Graf von Merveldt*   5,000

Brigade *GM Roschovsky*			
Erzherzog Maximilien IR 35	1	170	Grenadier Battalion
Württemberg IR 38	1	199	Grenadier Battalion
Gyulai IR 60	1	200	Grenadier Battalion
Hoch und Deutschmeister IR 4	1	212	Grenadier Battalion
Riese IR 15	1	175	Grenadier Battalion
Gemmingen IR 21	1	269	Grenadier Battalion

Brigade *GM Schustek*			
Hoch und Deutschmeister IR 4	4	828	1st–4th Battalions
Colloredo IR 57	3	627	1st–3rd Battalions
Gyulai IR 60	2	600	1st and 2nd Battalions
Peterwardiner GR 11	2	385	
Kaiserin Maria Theresa Frei Korps	1	820	

Brigade *GM Mondet*			
Merveldt UR 1	6	378	
Kaiser HR 1	6	290	

Detachment – observing Pressburg and lower March

Gyulai IR 60	2	600	3rd and 4th Battalions
Unspecified btns from Army of Italy			Referenced in IR 60 regimental history

Sources

Primary Documents

Assorted documents from RGVIA, Fond 846, Opis' 16

Bulletins de la Grande Armée : Campagne d'Austerlitz, 1805. Paris: La Vouivre, 1999. English translations are contained in Markham, J. David, *Imperial Glory: The Bulletins of Napoleon's Grande Armée, 1805–1814;* London: Greenhill, 2003

Campagne de 1805 en Allemagne, 5 Vols in 7; Alombert, P. C. and J. Colin. Paris: Editions Historiques Teissèdre, 2002. Originally published as *Campagne de 1805 en Allemagne,* 4 Vols; Alombert, P. C. and J. Colin; Paris: Chapelot, 1902–8. The revised edition includes a new 5th volume containing the multi-part article by J. Colin, "La Campagne de 1805 en Allemagne" and other articles originally published in *Review d'Histoire,* 1905–8. Includes a thorough campaign study by Colin along with thousands of French documents.

Campagne de l'an 14 (1805) Le corps d'armée aux ordres du maréchal Mortier, Alombert, Paul Claude; Paris: Berger-Levrault, 1897. Essentially an annotated collection of documents relating to the French 8th Corps.

Correspondance du Maréchal Davout, Prince d'Eckmühl, ses Commandements, son Ministère, 1801–1815; Paris: Plon, Nourrit, 1885

Correspondance de Napoléon 1er. Online edition by Robert Ouvrard; <http://www.histoire-empire.org/correspondance_de_napoleon/correspondance_de_napoleon.htm>. Originally published as *Correspondance de Napoléon 1er,* 32 Vols; Paris: Plon, 1858–70

Dokumenty shtaba M. I. Kutuzova, 1805–1806 Sbornik; Vilnius: 1951. This collection of documents includes orders and reports for the entire 1805 campaign through the army's return to Russia early in 1806.

Lettres et Documents pour Servir à l'Histoire de Joachim Murat, 1767–1815, Murat, Joachim Napoléon, Prince; Paris: Plon-Nourrit, 1908–14

M. I. Kutuzov: Sbornik Dokumentov, edited by L. G. Beskrovnyi; Moscow: 1951. This collection of documents partially duplicates *Dokumenty shtaba M. I. Kutuzova, 1805–1806,* but includes a large number of unique documents drawn from Kutuzov's personal papers. This collection does not include all of the reports that are included in the other collection and some of the documents are slightly different in the two collections, either due to variations in the source documents or variations in transcription from the original documents.

Relations et Rapports Officiels de la Bataille d'Austerlitz, 1805; Paris: La Vouivre, 1998. This volume collects the reports from the French side, including those of Soult, Davout, Murat and Berthier, along with the official account of the battle prepared by Tranchant Laverne.

The Times (London), 24–30 December 1805

Memoirs and Secondary Sources

Anonymous, *Geschichte der k. und k. Infanterieregiments Markgraf von Baden No. 23;* Budapest: 1911; pp. 717–20

Adam, A., *Historique du 111e Régiment d'Infanterie;* Bastia: Ollagnier, 1890

Alombert, P. C. and J. Colin, *La Campagne de 1805 en Allemagne*, 5 Vols; Paris: Editions Historiques Teissèdre, 2002

Amon von Treuenfest, Gustav, *Geschichte des k. k. 11. Huszaren-Regimentes Herzog Alexander v. Württemberg 1762 bis 1850 Székler Grenz-Huszaren;* Vienna: 1878

_____ *Geschichte des K. und K. Bukowina'schen Dragoner-Regimentes General der Cavallerie Freiherr Piret de Bihain Nr. 9 von seiner Errichtung 1682 bis 1892;* Vienna: 1893

Andolenko, C. R. [Serge], *Aigles de Napoléon Contre Drapeaux du Tsar, 1799, 1805–1807, 1812–1814;* Paris: Eurimprim, 1969

Barrés, Maurice, *Souvenirs d'un Officier de la Grande Armée;* Paris: Plon-Nourrit, 1923. Also published as *Memoirs of a Napoleonic Officer*, translated by Bernard Miall; London: Allen & Unwin, 1925; reprinted London: Greenhill, 1988

Beamish, N. Ludlow, "The End of the Electorate of Hannover and the Formation of the King's German Legion 1803," in N. Ludlow Beamish, *History of the King's German Legion*, Vol. 1; London: Thomas and William Boone, 1832–7. Reprinted London: Buckland and Brown, 1993 and Dallington, East Sussex: Naval & Military Press, 1997. Electronic text available at: http://www.kgl.de/KingsGermanLegion/geschichte/1803errichtung_1806/1803errichtung_1806home.htm

[Beauvais de Preau, Charles Theodore], *Victoires, Conquêtes, Désastres, Revers et Guerres Civiles des Français, de 1792 a 1815.* Vol 15; Paris: C. L. F. Panckoucke, 1819

Belhomme, Lieutenant Colonel, *Histoire de l'Infanterie en France*, Vol IV; Paris: Henri-Charles Lavauzelle, 1893–1902

Bigarré, Auguste Julien, *Mémoires du Général Bigarré, 1775–1813*; Paris: Kolb, 1893; reprinted Paris: Grenadier, 2002

Bjorlin, Gustaf, *Sveriges Krig i Tyskland aren, 1805–7*; Stockholm: Militärlitteratúr-Föreningens förlag, 1882

Boguslavski, A. L., *Istoriia Apsheronskago Polka, 1700–1892*; St Petersburg: 1892

Borisevich, A. T., *Organizatsiya, Raskvartirovanie i peredvizhenie voisk. Vypusk I (Period 1801–1805 gg.)*; St Petersburg: 1902. Series Stoletie Voennago Ministerstva, 1802–1902.

Bourgue, Marius, *Historique du 3e Régiment d'Infanterie, ex-Piémont, 1569–1891*; Paris: Charles-Lavauzelle, 1894

Bowden, Scott, *Napoleon and Austerlitz*; Chicago: The Emperor's Press, 1997

Broughton, Tony, *French Cavalry Regiments and the Colonels Who Led Them 1792–1815; French Infantry Regiments and the Colonels Who Led Them 1792–1815; French Light Infantry Regiments and the Colonels Who Led Them 1792–1815*; <http://www.napoleon-series.org/military/c_organization.html>

Castle, Ian, *Austerlitz 1805: The Fate of Empires*; Oxford: Osprey, 2002

Chandler, David G., *Austerlitz*; Oxford: Osprey, 1990

———— *The Campaigns of Napoleon*; New York: Macmillan, 1966. Reprinted New York: Scribner, 1995

———— ed. *Napoleon's Marshals*; New York: Macmillan, 1987

Chaperon, Henri, *Historique du 46e regiment d'infanterie*; Paris: H. Charles-Lavauzelle, 1894

Chicherin, Aleksandr Konstantinovich, S. Dolgov and A. Afanas'ev, *Istoriia Leib-Gvardii Preobrazhenskago Polka, 1683–1883*; St Petersburg: 1883–8

Coignet, Captain Jean-Roch (translated by Martha Wand Carey), *The Note-Books of Captain Coignet*; London: Peter Davies, 1928; reprinted London: Greenhill Books, 1998. Original title *Les Cahiers du Capitaine Coignet*; Paris: Hachette, 1896

Comeau, Baron de, *Souvenirs des Guerres d'Allemagne pendant la Révolution et l'Empire*; Paris: Plon-Nourrit, 1900

Criste, Oskar, *Erzherzog Carl von Österreich*; Vienna: W. Braumuller, 1912

Curély, Général, *Itinéraire d'un Cavalier Léger de la Grande-Armée*; Paris: Berger-Levrault, 1887

Czartoryski, Adam, *Memoirs of Prince Adam Czartoryski and his correspondence with Alexander I*, edited by Adam Gielgud; London: Remington, 1898. Originally published as *Alexandre I et le prince Czartoryski*; Paris: Calmann-Levy, 1865

Drouet d'Erlon, Jean-Baptiste, *Le Maréchal Drouet, Comte d'Erlon : Vie Militaire*; Paris: G. Barba, 1844

Duffy, Christopher, *The Army of Frederick the Great*; New York: Hippocrene Books, 1974

———— *The Army of Maria Theresa*; New York: Hippocrene Books, 1977

———— *Austerlitz 1805*; London: Seeley Service, 1977

———— *Eagles Over the Alps: Suvorov in Italy and Switzerland, 1799*; Chicago: The Emperor's Press, 1999

———— *The Military Experience in the Age of Reason*; London: Routledge & Kegan Paul, 1987

———— *Russia's Military Way to the West: Origins and Nature of Russian Military Power, 1700–1800*; London: Routledge & Kegan Paul, 1981

Egger, Rainer, *Das Gefecht bei Dürnstein-Loiben 1805*; Vienna: Österreichischer Bundesverlag, 1965

———— *Das Gefecht bei Hollabrunn und Schöngrabern 1805*; Vienna: Österreichischer Bundesverlag, 1974

Elting, John, *Swords Around a Throne*; New York: The Free Press, 1988

Ermolov, A. P., *Zapiski A. P. Ermolova, 1798–1826*; Moscow: 1991

Esposito, Brigadier General Vincent J. and Colonel John R. Elting, *A Military History and Atlas of the Napoleonic Wars*; New York: Frederick A. Praeger, 1965; revised edition London: Greenhill, 1999.

Estrabaut, A., *Le Livre d'Or du 8e Régiment d'Infanterie*; Paris: Henri-Charles Lavauzelle, 1891

Flayhart, William H., *Counterpoint to Trafalgar: The Anglo-Russian Invasion of Naples, 1805–1806*; Columbia: University of South Carolina Press, 1992

Fortescue, J. W., *A History of the British Army, 1803–1807*, Vol 5; London: Macmillan, 1910

Frèche, Louis, *Mémoire de mes Campagnes (1803–1809)*, edited by Fernand Emile Beaucour; Paris: Centre d'études Napoléoniennes, 1994

Furse, George Armand, *A Hundred Years Ago: Battles by Land and Sea: Ulm, Trafalgar, Austerlitz*; London: Clowes, 1905; reprinted as *Campaigns of 1805: Ulm, Trafalgar, & Austerlitz*; Felling: Worley, 1995

Griffith, Paddy, *The Art of War of Revolutionary France, 1789–1802*; London: Greenhill, 1998

Guibert, Florent, *Souvenirs d'un Sous-Lieutenant d'Infanterie Légère (1805–1815)* and François-René Cailloux, dit Pouget. *Souvenire de Guerre (1790–1831)*; Paris: La Vouivre, 1997

Hollins, David, *Austrian Grenadiers and Infantry, 1788–1816*; Oxford: Osprey, 1998

Hourtoulle, F. G., *Austerlitz: The Empire at its Zenith*; Paris: Histoire & Collections, 2003

d'Ideville, Count Henri (translated by Charlotte Mary Yonge), *Memoirs of Colonel Bugeaud*; London: Hurst and Blackett, 1884; reprinted Tyne and Wear: Worley Publications, 1998. Originally published as *Le Maréchal Bugeaud: d'après sa correspondance intime et des documents inédits, 1784–1849*; Paris: Firmin-Didot, 1881

Janetschek, Clemens, *Die Schlacht bei Austerlitz : 2. December 1805*; Brünn: Päpstliche Benedictiner-Buchdruckerei, 1898

Journaux et Souvenirs sur la Campagne de 1805; Paris: Librairie Historique F. Teissèdre, 1997

Keep, John L. H., *Soldiers of the Tsar: Army and Society in Russia, 1462–1874*; Oxford: Clarendon Press, 1985

Keilmansegg, Oswald, *Schwarzenberg-Uhlanen*; Vienna: 1887.

Lachouque, Henry and Anne S. K. Brown, *The Anatomy of Glory: Napoleon and His Guard*; Providence: Brown University Press, 1961; reprinted London: Greenhill, 1997. Originally published as *Napoleon et la Garde Imperiale*; Paris: Bloud & Gay, 1957

Langeron, Alexandre Andrault de, *Journal Inédit de la Campagne de 1805: Austerlitz*, With Karl Freiherr von Stutterheim, Mikhail Hilairionovich Golénistchev-Kutusov, *Relations de la Bataille d'Austerlitz*; Paris: La Vouivre, 1998

Las Cases, Count, *Memoirs of the Life, Exile, and Conversations of the Emperor Napoleon*, 4 Vols; New York: A. C. Armstrong & Son, 1883. Originally published as *Le Memoriale de Sainte-Helene propos de l'Empereur*

Ledru des Essarts, François Roch (edited by Jean-Louis Bonnery), *Ledru des Essarts, un grand patriote sarthois méconnu, la vie de ce soldat courageux qui n'aimait que la paix*; Le Mans, J. L. Bonnery, 1988

Lefebvre, Georges (translated by Henry F. Stockhold), *Napoleon from 18 Brumaire to Tilsit, 1799–1807*; New York: Columbia University Press, 1969. Originally published as *Napoléon*, Peuples et Civilisation Vol XIV; Paris: F. Alcan, 1935

Lejeune, Louis François (translated by Mrs Arthur Bell [N. D'Anvers]), *Memoirs of Baron Lejeune*; London: Longmans Green, 1897

Lloyd, Peter A., *The French are Coming! The Invasion Scare, 1803–5*; Turnbridge Wells: Spellmount, 1991.

Mackesy, Piers, *The War in the Mediterranean, 1803–1810*; Cambridge: Harvard University Press, 1957

Mahler, Major, "Tagebücher ans dem Jahre 1805." *Mittheilungen des K. und K. Kriegs-Archivs.* 6 (1881), pp. 499–523

Markov, Polkovnik (Colonel), *Istoriia Leib-Gvardii Kirasirskago Eia Velichestva Polka*; St Petersburg: 1884

Mikaberidze, Alexander, *The Russian Officer Corps in the Revolutionary and Napoleonic Wars, 1792–1815*; New York: Savas Beatie, 2005

Mikhailovski-Danilevski, A. (translated by Lieutenant General Léon Narischkine), *Relation de la Campagne de 1805*; Paris: J. Dumaine, 1846

Morvan, Jean, *Le Soldat Impérial (1800–1814)*; Paris: Plon, 1904–7

Nafziger, George, *The French Army: Royal, Republican, Imperial, 1792–1815*, 5 Vols; Pisgah, Ohio: G. F. Nafziger, 1997

Nafziger, George F., and Warren Worley, *The Imperial Russian Army (1763–1815)*, 2 Vols; Pisgah, Ohio: George F. Nafziger, 1996

Nikolaev, N. G., *Istoriia 17-go Pekhotnago Arkhangelgorodskago Ego Imperatorskago Vysochestva Velikago Kniazia Vladimira Aleksandrovicha Polka, 1700–1900*; St Petersburg: 1900

Officers of the Regiment, *Istoriia Leib-Gvardii Egerskago Polka, 1796–1896 GG*; St Petersburg: 1896

Oyon, Maréchal des logis-chef, *Campagnes et Souvenirs Militaires (1805–1814)*; Paris: Librairie Historique F. Teissèdre, 1997

[Ozanne, Henriette], *Austerlitz: Raconté par les Témoins de la Bataille des Trois Empereurs*; Geneva: Éditions de Crémille, 1969

Park, S. J. and George Nafziger, *The British Military: Its System and Organization, 1803–1815*; Cambridge, Ontario: RAFM, 1983

Parkinson, Roger, *The Fox of the North: The Life of Kutuzov, General of War and Peace*; London: P. Davies, 1976

Phipps, Ramsay Weston, *The Armies of the First French Republic and the Rise of the Marshals of Napoleon I*, 5 Vols; London: Oxford University Press, 1926–39; reprinted Cambridge: Ken Trotman, 1999

Pion des Loches, *Mes Campagnes, 1792–1813*. Paris: Librairie de Firmin-Didot, 1889

Pirozhnikov, A. I., *Istoriia 10-go Pekhotnago Novoingermanlandskago Polka, 1790–1896*; Tula: 1913

Podmazo, Aleksandr, "Shefy I Komandiry Regularnykh Polkov Russkoi Armii, 1796–1815"; <http://www.museum.ru/museum/1812/Library/Podmazo/>

[Popaditchev, I. O.], *Vospominaniya Suvorovskago Soldata*; St Petersburg: 1895

Pravikov, R., *Kratkaia Istoriia 10-go Grenaderskago Malorossiiskago Polka*; Morshansk: 1889

Punin, L., *Feldmarshal Kutuzov: voenno-biograficheskii ocherk*; Moscow: Voennoe izdatelstvo Ministrstva Oboroni Souza SSR, 1957

Puzanov, Poruchik (Lieutenant), *Istoriia Leib-Gvardii Grenaderskago Polka, 1756–1845 GG*; St Petersburg: 1845

Rapp, Jean, *Memoirs of General Count Rapp*; London: H. Colburn, 1823; reprinted Cambridge: Ken Trotman, 1995. Originally published as *Mémoires du Général Rapp, aide-de-camp de Napoléon*; Paris: Bossange, 1823

Rothenberg, Gunther E., *Napoleon's Great Adversary: Archduke Charles and the Austrian Army, 1792–1814*; London: Batsford, 1982; reprinted Staplehurst: Spellmount, 1995

Rüstow, Wilhelm, *Der krieg von 1805 in Deutschland und Italien*; Frauenfeld: Verlags-Comptoir, 1853

Sandstedt, Fred, ed. *Between the Imperial Eagles: Sweden's Armed Forces during the Revolutionary and the Napoleonic Wars, 1780–1820*; Stockholm: Armémuseum, 2000

Saul, Norman E., *Russia and the Mediterranean, 1797–1807*; Chicago: University of Chicago Press, 1970

Savary, Anne Jean Marie René, Duke of Rovigo, *Memoirs of the Duke of Rovigo*; London: H. Colburn, 1828. Originally published as *Mémoires du Duc de Rovigo : pour servir à l'histoire de l'empereur Napoléon*; Paris: Bossange, 1828

Schönhals, Karl Freiherr von, *Der Krieg 1805 in Deutschland*; Vienna: Selbstverlag der Redaction der Österreichischen, 1873

Schneid, Frederick C., *Napoleon's Italian Campaigns, 1805–1815*; Westport, CT: Praeger, 2002

Schwertfeger, Bernhard Heinrich, *Geschichte der Königlich Deutschen Legion 1803–1816*, Vol 1; Hannover and Leipzig: Hahn'sche, 1907

Segur, Philippe-Paul (translated by H. A. Patchett-Martin), *An Aide-de-Camp of Napoleon: Memoirs of General Count Segur*; London: Hutchinson, 1895; reprinted Tyne & Wear: Worley Publications, 1995. Originally published as *Histoire et Mémoires*; Paris: Firmin-Didot, 1873

Séruzier, Théodore Jean Joseph, *Mémoires Militaires du Baron Séruzier*; Paris: L. Baudoin, 1894

Sherwig, John M., *Guineas and Gunpowder: British Foreign Aid in the Wars with France, 1793–1815*; Cambridge: Harvard University Press, 1969

Simond, Émile, *Le 28e du ligne : Historique du Régiment d'après les documents du Ministère de la guerre*; Rouen: Mégard, 1889

Six, Georges, *Dictionnaire Biographique des Généraux et Amiraux Français de la Révolution et de l'Empire (1792–1814)*, 2 Vols; Paris: Gaston Saffroy, 1934; facsimile reprint 1974

Smith, Digby, *The Greenhill Napoleonic Wars Data Book*; London: Greenhill Books, 1987

———— *Napoleon's Regiments*; London: Greenhill Books, 2000

Spiegelfeld, Josef Freiherr von, *Geschichte des kaiserlichen und königlichen Infanterie-Regimentes Freiherr von Mollináry Nr. 38*; Budapest: Verlag des Regiments, 1892

Spring, Laurence, *Russian Grenadiers and Infantry, 1799–1815*; Oxford: Osprey, 2002

Stein, F., *Geschichte des Russischen Heeres*; Hanover: Helwingsche Verlagsbuchhandlung, 1885

Stiegler, Gaston, *Le Maréchal Oudinot, Duc de Reggio : d'après les Souvenirs Inédits de la Maréchale*; Paris: Plon, Nourrit, 1894

Stutterheim, Major-General [Karl] (translated by Major John Pine-Coffin), *A Detailed Account of the Battle of Austerlitz*; London: T. Goddard, 1807; reprinted Cambridge: Ken Trotman, 1985. Originally published anonymously as *La Bataille d'Austerlitz*; Paris: Fain, 1806

Thiébault, Paul Charles François (translated by Arthur John Butler), *The Memoirs of Baron Thiébault*, 2 Vols; London: Smith Elder, 1896; reprinted Tyne & Wear: Worley, 1994. Originally published as *Mémoires du Général Baron Thiébault*, 5 vols; Paris: Plon, 1893–5

Torchalovski, Sokolovski, Mikhailov, Popov and Verbitski, *Ocherki iz 200-Letniago Proshlago Vyborgskago Polka, 1700–1900*; Novgorod: 1901

Turlan, Patrick, *L'Histoire du 57ème Régiment d'infanterie*; Bordeaux: L'Amicale des anciens du 57° R.I, 1990

Vanicek, Fr., *Specialgeschichte der Militärgrenze, aus Originalquellen und Quellenwerken geschöpft*; Vienna: Kaiserlich-Königlichen Hof- und Staatsdruck, 1875

Vasil'ev, A., "Russkaya Gvardiya v srazhenii Pri Austerlitse, 20 Noyabrya (2 Dekabrya) 1805 g." Voin Nos 3 & 4; <http://www.genstab.ru/voin/auster_01.htm>.

Viskovatov, *Istoricheskoe Obozrenie Leib-Gvardii Izmailovskago Polka, 1730–1850 GG*; St Petersburg: 1850.

Viskovatov, A. V. (translated by Mark Conrad), *Historical Description of the Clothing and Arms of the Russian Army: Volume 10a, Organization 1801–1825*; Hopewell, NJ: On Military Matters, 1993. See also the original Russian text at <http://www.museum.ru/museum/1812/Army/Viskowatov/index.html>. First published St Petersburg, 1851

———— *Historical Description of the Clothing and Arms of the Russian Army: The Organisation of Regiments during the Reign of Tsar Paul, 1796–1801*. (English translation extracted from Vol 7 of the Russian edition by Laurence Spring); Woking, Surrey, England: Spring Offensive, 1999

Wilson, Sir Robert, *Brief remarks on the character and composition of the Russian army, and a sketch of the campaigns in Poland in the years 1806 and 1807*; London: C. Roworth, 1810

Wrede, Alphons, *Geschichte der K. und K. Wehrmacht*, Vols 1–3; Vienna: L. W. Seidel & Sohn, 1898–1901

Zharynova, D.A., "Pervye Voiny s Napoleonom I Russkoe Obtshestvo," in Sytina, I.D., *Otechestvennaya Voina I Russkoe Obtschestvo*, Tom I; Moscow: 1911; <http://www.museum.ru/MUSEUM/1812/Library/Sitin/book1_14.html>

Zhmodikov, Alexander and Yuri Zhmodikov, *Tactics of the Russian Army in the Napoleonic Wars*, 2 Vols; West Chester, Ohio: The Nafziger Collection, 2003

Index